Iuif de la Terre sainte.

Ce Medecin a longue barbe   Qui d'une dose de Rhubarbe,
Est vn chymiste intelligent   Fait comme il veut l'or et l'argent.

chez Bonnart vis a vis les Mathurins au coq avec pri

INSIGHT GUIDES

The world's largest collection of illustrated travel guides

INCLUDING THE PALESTINIAN TERRITORIES

Edited by Simon Griver
Photography by Richard Nowitz and others
Editorial Director: Brian Bell

APA PUBLICATIONS

Part of the Langenscheidt Publishing Group

L

This is a new edition of one of the most successful books in the 190-strong Insight Guides series. Both text and photography have been radically overhauled because, such is the dynamic nature of the State of Israel that, even when peace reigns, nothing stays the same for long – except, of course, the amazing energy of the Israelis.

Such a country lends itself perfectly to the effective mix of hard-hitting journalism and stunning photography pioneered by Apa Publications more than 25 years ago. *Insight Guide: Israel* is much more than a guidebook, therefore: it delves behind the current headlines and daily crises to discuss the history and nature of this cradle of Christianity, Judaism and Islam.

This edition was edited by **Simon Griver**, a writer who was born in England but who never really felt he had found his true home until he settled in Israel. The experience is typical of many immigrants to Israel and enabled Griver to contribute valuable insights to this book. He wrote the history and people chapters dealing with contemporary Israel, plus essays on the army, kibbutz life, and the economic importance of high technology.

As well as introducing much new material into this edition, Griver built on the solid foundation provided by earlier editions. The original book assembled an expert team of writers and photographers under the leadership of a single project editor, **George Melrod**. A native New Yorker and (by definition, therefore) a born critic, Melrod majored in visual and environmental studies at Harvard University and studied communications at Hebrew University. His chapters include essays on the Southern, Central and Northern Coasts, and Jerusalem's New City.

Photography is central to any Insight Guide because it is designed not only to illustrate a destination but also to communicate visually and directly to readers life as it is lived by the locals. **Richard Nowitz**, a major contributor to the very first edition of the book, provided many fresh images for this edition. Nowitz, a regular contributor to Insight Guides, was based for many years in Jerusalem. He now lives in the United States but travels the world on assignments for *National Geographic* and tries to ensure that Israel is regularly on his itinerary.

The first three chapters of the history section are by **Geoffrey Wigoder**, editor-in-chief of the *Encyclopedia Judaica*. Educated at Trinity College, Dublin, and Oriel College, Oxford, he moved to Israel in 1949.

New York freelancer **Walter Jacob** contributed the chapters on the history of Zionism and the Yishuv. Jacob graduated *magna cum laude* from Yale University with a speciality in European intellectual history.

The modern history chapter was penned by **William M. Recant**, a political consultant who studied in both Jerusalem and Cairo, and received his PhD in political science from George Washington University.

Writing about Jews, Arabs and Christians alike, **Helen Davis** is the talent behind much of the People section. Born in New Zealand and now living in Israel, Davis has worked as a reporter and as foreign correspondent.

Daniel Gavron, a feature writer on the *Jerusalem Post*, contributed chapters to the Places section on the Negev Desert, Dead Sea and Central Crossroads regions, as well as shorter chapters on Druze and Bedouin in the People section. A native of London, he moved permanently to Israel in 1961.

Our Tel Aviv correspondent, **Michal**

Nowitz

Griver

Melrod

Davis

Gavron

Yudelman, was born in Beersheba, Israel, in 1950 and grew up on a kibbutz in Negev. A graduate of Hebrew University and the University of Chicago, she became a reporter for the *Jerusalem Post*.

The author of the Haifa chapter, **Muriel Moulton**, is a writer and teacher, and former lecturer at the University of Illinois at Chicago. She has lived in Haifa since 1978.

Leora Frucht, who wrote about the Galilee, was educated at Montreal's Concordia University. She later became assistant editor of *Israel Scene*.

Clark

Bill Clark spans the country with chapters on the Golan Heights and Eilat, and an essay on ecology. Born in New York and an Israeli resident since 1980, Clark joined the Society for the Protection of Nature in Israel.

Matthew Nesvisky, who wrote on the Old City of Jerusalem, was born in the US and made his pilgrimage to Jerusalem in 1971. He joined the staff of the *Jerusalem Post*.

Nesvisky

Amy Kaslow, an American, described the controversial territories of the West Bank and Gaza Strip. A graduate of Vassar College, she lived for two years in Tel Aviv, and became an editor for the *Mid-East Report*.

The task of delineating the country's various religious groups was assigned to **Mordechai Beck,** who attended art school, yeshiva and university in London, and made his *aliyah* to Israel in 1973.

Nancy Miller, who describes the archaeology scene in Israel, was assistant to the editor of the *Biblical Archaeology Review*.

London-born **Asher Weill** moved to Israel in 1958. He became editor of *Israel Scene* and *Ariel*. His contributions to this volume include essays on Culture and Language, and an introductory English-Hebrew vocabulary.

Barbara Gingold is a journalist, editor and photographer specialising in Jewish arts and crafts. A New Yorker, she has lived in Israel for many years.

In addition to Richard Nowitz's work, photographs were also provided by, among others, **Gary-John Norman**, an English photographer who shot much of our companion *Compact Guide: Israel*; **Werner Braun**, who was born in Germany and emigrated to Israel in the mid-1940s; **David Harris**, a graduate of the School of Modern Photography in New York and one of the best known names in Israeli photography; **Neil Folberg**, whose work is immensely graphic; **Bill Clark**, who is more fully represented in this volume as a writer; **Vivienne Silver**, who also contributed to the visual side of the book with historical material from her extensive SilverPrint collection; **Joel Fishmann**; and **Israel Hirshberg**.

Braun

Harris

Insight Guides, with close to 400 titles in print, spread across three distinct series, has become a truly international publishing operation, with offices in several continents, and its books now appear in as many as 11 languages. Even in English, however, language poses a problem: which version of English? Insight Guides' pragmatic answer is to publish titles to North and South American destinations (and associated areas) in American English and titles to European destinations in British English. Colors look just as good in colour!

Keeping up with a dynamic country such as Israel is difficult at the best of times, and Insight Guides welcomes new information from readers which can be used in future editions. This edition was finalised in Insight Guides' London editorial office, where the proof-reading and indexing was completed by **Pam Barrett**.

CONTENTS

Preceding pages: an 18th-century European image of a Jewish doctor; a Yeminite bride in traditional wedding costume.

TRAVEL TIPS

Israel is intense. Few locations offer as much per square mile to sustain the spirit, feed the intellect and stimulate the senses. It is a place where three continents – Africa, Asia and Europe – meet, and the landscape and the people are a fusion of these three continents, a sometimes infuriating mixture of conflict and harmony.

First and foremost, Israel is the Holy Land, generating the highest expectations for religious visitors, while such proximity to the sacred sites nurtures hopes of supernatural experiences even among the more cynical of secular tourists. After all, this was the Promised Land where, many believe, Abraham forged his covenant with God, Moses led the Children of Israel, Christ preached his sermons, and Mohammed ascended to heaven on a horse.

You don't have to be a believer to savour all this. The miracles may be a matter of personal faith but what can't be historically disputed is that this is the land of the Bible, the cradle of monotheism, a geography familiar from childhood religious instruction. The names resonate in our minds and stimulate our curiosity: Jerusalem, the Galilee, Bethlehem, Nazareth, Jaffa, Jericho and the River Jordan.

You can visit the site of the Temple and pray at the one remaining wall the Romans left intact. You can walk along the Via Dolorosa to the Church of the Holy Sepulchre. You can visit the Al Aksa Mosque on the Temple Mount where the Prophet Mohammed came to pray during his lifetime. Much history has been made around the River Jordan in the past two millennia, most recently the emergence of modern Israel, "the Jewish State", as a complex dynamic entity.

The empty stretches and open blue skies of the Arava and Negev deserts aside, this is one of the world's most densely packed pieces of real estate. Israel's population is approaching 6 million, while 2 million Palestinians live in the Gaza Strip and West Bank. For many visitors the enduring attraction of Israel is its people – the inheritors of the rich tapestry of invading cultures who have woven their history into the region.

The Return to Zion: Many devout Jews and Christians regard the return of the Jewish people to their ancestral homeland as part of a divine plan. But Muslims have a different perspective: they sense a European colonialist conspiracy to dispossess them of land that is rightfully theirs.

For most Israelis, however, the 20th-century exodus and return to Zion has been a practical rather than a mystical move. European Jewry, assimilationist and secular, plagued by anti-Semitism which culminated in the Holocaust, simply sought a refuge. The more traditional Jews of North Africa and Asia found that historic Islamic prejudice, though not as brutal as European anti-Semitism, reached

Preceding pages: a teenage Sephardic Israeli; praying at Jerusalem's Western Wall; a Passover dinner; harvesting at a kibbutz; a Bedouin shepherd near Bethlehem. **Left,** an Orthodox Jew plays the *shofar* (ram's horn) at the Western Wall.

crueller proportions with the establishment of the State of Israel, and they too emigrated. Onto this base have come more recent waves of immigrants from the former Soviet Union, Eastern Europe, Latin America and Ethiopia, as well as idealists from Western Europe and North America.

But the Zionists aren't simply refugees. The underlying motivation of establishing a Jewish State has been to preserve Jewish tradition and culture and adapt it to the modern age. Hebrew, the language of the Bible, has been successfully resurrected so that immigrants can communicate. Initial hostility towards Zionism from Orthodox and ultra-Orthodox Jewry in the Diaspora has given way to acceptance of Jewish nationhood, often with strident nationalistic overtones and a zealous desire to keep every inch of the Land of Israel regardless of the presence of Palestinians on much of it.

Never indifferent: Although Israelis are diverse and heterogeneous, they share common traits. They are informal, but get straight to the point. They are highly hospitable and generous, but often brusque to the point of rudeness. They usually speak English well and like to practise it, with unbridled enthusiasm.

The person sitting next to you on the bus or in a shared taxi may tell you his entire life story during the 45-minute ride between Tel Aviv and Jerusalem, and may draw intimate secrets from you. Alternatively, he may spend the entire journey shouting into his mobile phone, or he may fall asleep on your shoulder. The best advice is to take Israelis as they come. There's nothing more inspirational than talking with an old man or woman, concentration number tattooed on their arm, whose life is nevertheless built around love rather than bitterness.

That a democratic, affluent, high-tech and cultured society has been built in only half a century, despite the humble and heterogeneous origins of most Israelis in countries with authoritarian regimes, is impressive enough. Even more remarkable, is the fact that it has been accomplished against a recurring backdrop of war.

The Israel–Arab conflict has been a war between two nations with justice on their side. The Palestinians feel uprooted by European invaders, while the Jews point out that they were escaping annihilation in Europe. Arab hostility to Israel ironically helped it to consolidate. The essential Palestinian tragedy was not so much the arrival of the Zionists but the under-estimation of their strength.

Contrary to perceived stereotypes, most Israelis are neither right-wing religious zealots nor left-wing Peace Now activists. Most are middle of the road, looking for peace with security. Most Palestinians, too, realise that violence is counter-productive. They want a state of their own, however small, and a decent standard of living.

Ultimately peace seems likely to prevail, not because Israelis and Palestinians will ever fall in love with each other but because the alternative is too unpleasant to endure.

<u>Right</u>, the modern-minded Israeli, never far from a beach or a telephone.

Mons Arnon.   Arnon, Schia...

Carehar

Phi ladelphia
Rabba uch

Vallis
Her
mon.

Daria.

Hic hodie multa et
ruinosa habitacula
uisuntur sed deserta
et nominibus carentia.

Emathitæ

Nabathæi.

Mons Galaad.

ITVR AEA.

Seberh.   Elea

BASAN   Silebath.

Zoba

Baalag.

Theman

Bath enæi.   Geruy   Rama   Mahanaim

Manæi.

Argob.   REG
NVM.   Baalgad.

Echatana.
Asteroth.

Iaboc   Arab

Adai

Phiala fons.

Carnay.   Fons Car
naym.

Iabis.

TERRA   HVS.

Pinel.

Gamela
Cedar.

Sepulchrum
Iob.

Masphath.

Tubbin.

Masphа

Gaulana.

nitæ.

Aruma

TRACHO Zwetha.

GERASAEORVM
RE GIO.

Datheman.

Casphor.   Gadeu.

Cæsarea
Philip.

Seleuua.

NITIS
REGIO.

Astaroth.

Bara
za.

Pella
Pella.

Ephruim.

nunc
Bellena

Gau   Iordanis fluu.
la   lu:

Labis.

Galaad.

Ior fons   Pan
ias

Samchoni tis lacus.

Cæsarea
Philip.

Adа
ma.

Amma us topar
chia.

Enhazo.

Lekum

Gadara.

Bethfemes

Callas.   Iordanis flu.

Rama

lerron.   Ahon.

Magech.

Illustris vallis.

Hazeryth.   TRI

Meroth.

Capharna
um.

Debir.

Hippon.

MANA...

Asgdal.   BVS NEP

Mare Galileæ, uel
Tiberiadis.

Amnaus.

ACRABA...

Libanus
mons

Cha

Hamath   Edras
Racoth.

nan   æi.

Asnoth.   Tabur.   TALIM.

Hamon

Magdalum.

Arbel.

Itaburi
us mons

ON TO

Asor. uel Hgron.
nunc.   Antiopa.

Chartan.   Hinaslach.

Tibu
rias.

Genna
bar

Thebes

Enabris.

GALI

Hamon

GALI

Hary
arch.

Abel.

Nicopada Iuliaс.

Anchum

Genezaret

Berth:ran
Orthopolis.

Magnus

Cana.   Rebuk.

Horma   LEA SVP

ERI

Belina.

Jesruel Geri
num.

Ca

Berithus

Naz

Speloz

OR, SEV

GEN

Antalu.   Belsi

Sa

Italy.

Beta
fort.

Capharnes

Iotapata

tha

Naym

Adrem.

Canana   Rama

Ebrun   Arbelena

Elkosa.

Bethu
lia

Endor

Kison.

Qynum
Gelun

Antilibanus
mons

Asaph.

Arbula

Dothaim.

Tabok.

Naym.

SAMA

Sidon   Brega

Regum
ciluae

Hanathon

Abelina

Gadara.

Daraben

TRI

Sarrep
ta

Cideossa.

TRIBVS ASER

Naa
son.

ZA BVLON

LE   A.

Abez

Ammа
Mont. fort.

Ramа

Buria

Eiba

Scandula   Imead.

Masal.

Charta.

HEVAEI.

Aphec.

PHOE   Hosta.

Vallis Ieph
thael.

Roohim.

GALILEA   Nazareth. IN FERIOR

Phere laei

Estrlon

NI   Asor   Indo

GALILEA

Iakno
am.

Gabaa:
Hippon

Betleems

BV

SCandalium.

S.Georgy   Cana Ga
lilea:

Sephor.

Msturn.

Maron. uel
Lamperia.

Abdon.

Sihor.

Chison torrens

Narbathae toparchia.

Aron.

Ptolemais

SCIA.

Carmelus mons.

Cain.   Arethu

SA

MARE

Saron, uel
Lamperia.

Belus torrens

CHAR.

Montes

Cedar
Pagan torens

Csia
Cpi...

SYRIA CVM.

SEPTEMTRIO.

TERRA SANCTA.

A Petro Laiestain perlustrata, et ab eius ore et schedis a Christiano Schrot in tabulam redacta

MARE MORTVVM. *olim Salinarum vallis, prædicatæ fæcunditatis, et amœnitatis: quam Iordanis mediam irrigabat. adeo vt ob fœlicitatem paradiso Dei conferebatur. Post autem Sodoma euersa, et vicina opida, mutata est in illam sterilitatem, quæ hodie adhuc conspicitur. Diuinæ ultionis admirandæ vestigia.*

Terra Macces

Amor.

PERAEA.

rhæi.

Bamoth uallis.

TENAE rch

IVDAEA.

Desertum Adomin.

BENIAMIN.

Engadi mons.

Vallis benedictionis.

Desertum Maon

Carmelus mons

Sinæi.

Gophnæ toparchia.

TRIBVS

Iebusaei.

TRIBVS IVDA.

Enachim.

TRIBVS SIMEON.

RIA.

Sichem.

Thamnatica regio.

TRIBVS DAN.

Philis.

IDVMAEA.

Ioppe. Iaffa.

DENS.

DECISIVE DATES

10,000 BC–6000 BC: Some of the world's oldest human settlements are established in the Jordan Valley, Judean Desert and Mediterranean coast.
3,000 BC: Cannanite city kingdoms develop based on trade between Egypt and Mesopotamia.

The Biblical Period

c.2,000 BC: Abraham settles in Beer Sheva.
c.1,280 BC: Moses leads Israelites out of Egypt.
c.1225 BC: Joshua captures Jericho.
c.1000 BC: King David declares that Jerusalem

63 BC: The Romans conquer Judea.
37 BC: King Herod assumes the throne, founds Caesarea and rebuilds the Second Temple.

The Christian Era

AD 30: Crucifixion of Christ.
66: Jews revolt against Rome.
70: Romans recapture Jerusalem after a long siege and destroy the Temple.
73: Jewish zealots, hopelessly outnumbered in the remote stronghold of Masada, commit mass suicide rather than be taken by the Romans.
132: Bar Kochba revolt against the Romans fails and most Jews go into exile.
325: Constantine, the Byzantine emperor, converts

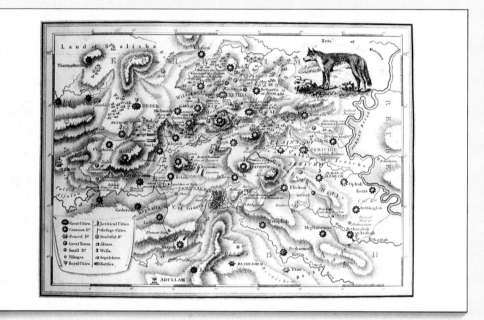

will be his capital.
c.950 BC: King Solomon builds the First Temple.
722 BC: Assyrians destroy the kingdom of Israel.
586 BC: The First Temple is destroyed after the Babylonians conquer Jerusalem and take the Jews into exile.
546 BC: The Jews return to Jerusalem after the Persians defeat the Babylonians.
520 BC: The Second Temple is built.
444 BC: Jerusalem's walls are re-built under Nehemia.
333 BC: Alexander the Great conquers Jerusalem but allows the Jews freedom of worship.
164 BC: Successful Jewish uprising led by the Maccabees after Seleucid Greeks defile the Temple.

to Christianity. Palestine is recognised as the Holy Land and Constantine's mother arrives a year later to identify the sacred sites.

The Muslim Conquest

638: Fired by the new religion of Islam, Muslim armies conquer Jerusalem.
691: Dome of the Rock built on the Temple Mount.
705: The Al-Aksa Mosque is built.
750: Abassid caliphs succeed the Umayyads.
969: Fatimid rule begins
1009: Fatimids destroy the Church of the Holy Sepulchre.

Crusaders, Mamelukes and Ottomans

1099: Crusaders establish Kingdom of Jerusalem.
1149: The current Church of the Holy Sepulchre is consecrated.
1187: Saladin defeats the Crusaders.
1260: Mamelukes take control of the Holy Land.
1267: Nahmanides re-establishes Jerusalem's Jewish community.
1291: Last Crusader stronghold in Acco falls to the Mamelukes.
1492: Many Jews return to the Holy Land after expulsion from Spain.
1516: Ottomans capture Palestine.
1541: Suleiman the Magnificent completes the construction of Jerusalem's walls.

1799: Napoleon occupies parts of the Holy Land.
1832: Egyptian Mohammed Ali captures Palestine for eight years.

The Birth of Zionism

1878: The first Zionist settlements in Rosh Pina, Rishon Le Zion and Petah Tikvah are established.
1881: Anti-Semitism in Russia forces millions of Jews to emigrate. Some come to Palestine.
1897: Theodore Herzl convenes the first-ever Zionist Congress in Switzerland.
1901: The Jewish National Fund is established to acquire land in Palestine.
1917–18: The British capture Palestine and publish the Balfour Declaration favouring "the establishment in Palestine of a national home for the Jewish people."
1920: Arab riots make the British re-think policy.
1923: The British cede the eastern part of Palestine to the Jordanian Hashemite dynasty.
1925: Large-scale Jewish immigration from Central and Eastern Europe.
1933: Hitler assumes power in Germany, increasing Jewish emigration.
1945: World War II ends and the full horrors of the Holocaust are known. Survivors emigrate to Palestine but are imprisoned by the British in Cyprus.
1947: The UN votes for partition of Palestine into Jewish and Arab states and the British prepare to withdraw.

The Establishment of Israel

1948: David Ben Gurion declares the State of Israel and becomes the first prime minister.
1949: An armistice agreement concluded after the War of Independence.
1950: The Jordanians formally annex East Jerusalem and the West Bank, and Egypt takes the Gaza Strip.
1956: Israel captures and returns the Sinai following the Suez campaign.
1964: The PLO is formed.
1967: Israel captures East Jerusalem, the West Bank, Gaza, Sinai and the Golan Heights during the Six Day War.
1973: The Yom Kippur War.
1977: Menachem Begin becomes Prime Minister for the Likud, ending 29 years of Labour government.
1978: Egyptian President Anwar Sadat visits Jerusalem and an Israel–Egypt peace treaty is signed the following year.
1982: Israel invades Lebanon and the PLO is expelled to Tunisia.
1987: The Intifada begins.
1991: Scuds fall on Israel during the Gulf War.
1992: Yitzhak Rabin elected prime minister.
1993: Secret deal concluded in Oslo between Israel and the PLO.
1994: Israel signs peace agreement with Jordan.
1995: Yitzhak Rabin is assassinated, and Shimon Peres takes over as prime minister.
1996: Benjamin Netanyahu becomes Israel's first directly elected prime minister.

Preceding pages: 1584 map of Israel, with Jonah and the whale at lower left. **Left, 1812 map of the tribe of Benjamin, with Jerusalem at lower centre. Above, mosaic of an ancient Chanukah Menorah.**

The dusty desert sign on the highway down from Jerusalem points northwards to "Jericho – The World's Oldest Known City". Nobody has yet added that it is in the world's newest state, but then strictly speaking Palestine is an autonomous zone rather than a sovereign nation. In any event visitors can enter Jericho without having to show any passports.

At the northern tip of the town is a rather unimpressive series of wooden fortifications. Remarkably, however, scientists estimate that these fortifications were built more than 9,000 years ago. Evidence suggests that mankind first established farming communities, and the other trappings of civilisation as we know it, several thousand years before that. Caves in the Mount Carmel range near Haifa on the Mediterranean Coast have yielded jewellery and agricultural implements from 12,000 years ago.

But as the remains at Jericho indicate, 6,000 BC seems to have been an important era in the evolution of Neolithic man. A decade ago Israeli archaeologists discovered a treasure trove of artifacts dating from this period in a cave in the Judean Desert 30 miles (50 km) south of Jerusalem. The find, which includes woven fabrics, agricultural tools, decorated human skulls, painted masks and carved figurines, is on display in the Israel Museum. From these objects anthropologists have concluded that late Stone Age man was far more advanced than had previously been considered.

According to Genesis: Such archaeological evidence is an anathema to ultra-Orthodox Jewry, which has always insisted that the creation took place nearly 6,000 years ago. By then, both ancient Egypt to the southwest and Mesopotamia to the northeast had been established as powerful and sophisticated civilisations. Canaanite tribes emerged about 5,000 years ago, founding city-kingdoms based on trade between the two surrounding super-powers.

About 4,000 years ago, the book of Genesis relates, Abraham, the son of a wealthy

Mesopotamian merchant family in the city of Ur (today in Iraq) became the first man to recognise a single deity. Rejecting the idolatry of his father, he travelled westwards and pitched his tent near Beersheba.

Abraham is today revered as the father of monotheism. Believing in one God, he did not embrace the concept of one wife, though the world might have become a less complicated place had he done so. The Arab and Islamic heritage traces its roots to Abraham through his eldest son Ishmael, born to his

second wife Hagar, while the Judeo-Christian lineage can be traced back to Isaac, Abraham's second son born to him by his first wife, Sarah.

Sibling rivalry, Genesis tells us, compelled Abraham to cast out Hagar and Ishmael whose descendants would forever bear enmity to the offspring of Sarah and Isaac. On that score even the most devout atheist would have to admit that the Bible got it right. The precise location of Abraham's tent near Beersheba is not known, and this is probably just as well, for the site of Abraham's burial, the Tomb of the Patriarchs in Hebron, has seen more corpses than Abraham bargained

Left, Moses receives the tablets from God. **Right,** early shekels celebrate the fruit of the earth.

for when he acquired the plot as a family mausoleum. Jews and Arabs have massacred each other in Hebron throughout history.

Sibling rivalry, beginning with Cain and Abel, is an ever present theme in Genesis. Isaac's own two children quarrelled when Jacob, egged on by his mother Rebecca, cheated Esau out of his birthright by tricking his blind father. And Jacob saw the pattern recur as his own sons ganged up on Joseph, his favourite child, whom they sold into slavery in Egypt.

The Children of Israel: Jacob was also known as Israel (Hebrew for "he struggles"). The name was given to him after a dream in which he fought with an angel descending

Children of Israel's 40 years wandering in the wilderness Moses picked up the Torah, including the Ten Commandments, on Mount Sinai. His successor, Joshua, took the Children of Israel back to the promised land, scoring his first success in the battle of Jericho in 1225 BC.

This was the era in which the tenets of Judaism were established. The festival of Passover (Pesach) recalls the Exodus from Egypt, while Pentecost (Shavuot) marks the giving of the Torah on Mount Sinai. Tabernacles (Succot) recollects the 40 years spent in the wilderness.

Though the Israelites defeated the indigenous Canaanites and settled on the inland

from a ladder leading up to heaven. All told Jacob had 12 sons and one daughter who are known to us as the Children of Israel.

Joseph, the Book of Genesis concludes, prospered in Egypt where he became a senior advisor to the Pharaoh. He was reunited with his family after a drought compelled them to look for food and shelter in the Land of the Nile. The book of Exodus relates how successive generations of Pharaohs enslaved the Children of Israel.

In probably the most enduring of all biblical narratives Moses, the young Israelite, led his people out of bondage, across the Red Sea and through the wilderness. During the

hills, making Hebron their capital, the Children of Israel were unable to conquer the coastal plain where the Philistines in the south and the Phoenicians in the north reigned supreme. The historical importance of both these peoples, especially the Phoenicians, who had migrated to the region from Greece, is often overlooked.

The Phoenicians, who settled in the cities of Acco and Tyre in Northern Israel and Southern Lebanon, are believed to have devised the first alphabet and invented glassmaking. And the Philistines in Ashdod and Ashkelon in the south were not so much great warriors as skilful metalworkers who were able to manufacture effective, sophisticated weaponry.

The Israelites coexisted with their coastal neighbours, sometimes trading, sometimes fighting. Led at first by warrior-judges such as Gideon and Samuel, the Israelites felt the need for a king, who could strengthen the people by uniting the tribes. Saul was selected and he set the scene for the golden age that his successor David was to bring about.

The establishment of Jerusalem: David ascended the throne a little more than 3,000 years ago. A scholar, poet and notorious womaniser, he secured his place in history through military prowess and leadership, extending the borders of the Israelites to the

lent new capital. So he moved his court and administration there from Hebron and called his new city Jerusalem. The new city also helped unite the 12 tribes because it was located on neutral territory.

David's son Solomon became renowned for his wisdom. He consolidated his father's achievements and extended the Israelite empire down to the Arabian peninsula and northeastwards to the Euphrates. He inherited his father's taste for beautiful women, and sealed strategic alliances by marrying princesses. His exact relationship to the Queen of Sheba remains unclear.

Most significantly Solomon constructed the resplendent Temple to house the Ark of

Red Sea in the south and Syria in the north. However, despite David's anecdotal childhood victory with a slingshot over the mighty Goliath, he was unable to vanquish the Philistines, though he did win access to the Mediterranean.

Most importantly, in historical retrospect, David conquered a Jebusite hilltop enclave. He decided that the fortress settlement, perched near commanding mountain peaks, and with a plentiful supply of fresh underground spring water, would make an excel-

Left, Joshua's men hang five enemy kings. **Above,** a medieval view of Solomon and Sheba.

the Covenant, the focus of Jewish faith that was believed to have contained the actual tablets of the Ten Commandments that were given to Moses on Mount Sinai. A stroll around the Temple Mount in Jerusalem today palpably conveys what must have been a vast building.

Despite his reputed wisdom Solomon left no strong successor. Soon after his death tribal jealousies resulted in civil war and the secession of the northern 10 tribes who set up their own state in Samaria, known as Israel. The southern state of Judah, based on the tribes of Judah and Benjamin, remained faithful to Solomon's descendants. For two centuries an uneasy coexistence prevailed between Israel and Judah.

This was the age of the prophets. Men like Isaiah, who attacked corruption, and Elijah who attacked the idolatrous cult of Baal introduced by Israel's King Ahab and his notorious Phoenician wife Jezebel. Shortly afterwards, in 722 BC, Israel fell to the Assyrians and the people were dispersed. The fate of the "Ten Lost Tribes" is still unknown and peoples from the Andes to the Celtic fringes, through to East Africa and India and every corner of the globe occasionally claim descent from the Israelites of old.

The southern state of Judah survived by accepting Assyrian hegemony. This status

quo endured for 150 years. Its end was foretold by the prophet Jeremiah who preached gloom and doom and the destruction of Jerusalem from 650 BC onwards.

By the waters of Babylon: Jeremiah's prophecies came true in 586 BC. The Babylonians led by Nebuchadnezzar superseded the Assyrians. After entering a foolish alliance with the Egyptians, and expecting help from the Nile that never came, the Babylonians sacked Jerusalem and destroyed the Temple. The elite of Judah were transported to Babylon. Yearning for Jerusalem while in exile, a poet wrote in the Book of Lamentations: "By the waters of Babylon we sat down and wept when we remembered Zion."

In fact the Babylonian exile only lasted 40 years. Then the Babylonians were defeated by the Persians whose leader Cyrus the Great allowed all exiled peoples to return home. The Temple was rebuilt but the glorious age of Solomon was not recaptured. Judah remained an obscure Persian province for the following two centuries.

Now the balance of world power was moving westwards to Europe and away from the traditional regional super-powers in Egypt, Assyria and Persia. In 333 BC Alexander the Great conquered the region and Greek rule began. For several centuries the Jews were allowed freedom of worship. But policies of Hellenisation became more obtrusive, culminating in the second century BC with the sacrificing of a pig in the Temple and the prohibition of Jewish rituals such as circumcision and the observation of the Sabbath.

Armed resistance led by the Hasmonean family, known as the Maccabees, saw the Greeks defeated and Jewish control over Jerusalem restored. In 164 BC the Temple was rededicated and the victory is celebrated to this day by Jews during the festival of Hanukkah.

The Roman Empire: The following century of Jewish sovereignty saw prosperity, as past glories and lands were recaptured. But this was a taste of freedom that was subsequently lost for 2,000 long years.

In 63 BC the Romans conquered Judah. The Roman state of Judea was subject to the decree of the Roman governor of Syria but remained an autonomous province with its own kings. But these kings were corrupt and ruthless. The best known was Herod the Great, who reigned from 37 to 4 BC. Appreciated by Rome, he was given extra territory and expanded his kingdom to include all of Israel and much of today's Jordan. He rebuilt the Temple and constructed grand new cities such as Caesarea on the coast, which he dedicated to Rome. But Herod and his successors were ruthless despots who even killed their own children in their paranoia over potential conspiracies.

Oppressed by Rome and its vassal kings, the Judeans were ripe to be influenced by messianic preachers.

Left, Noah's Ark. **Right**, a Marc Chagall painting at the Knesset shows David playing his harp.

The son of a Galilee carpenter, Christ had a limited impact in his own lifetime, at least in Jerusalem. Few historical accounts of the time even mention him and the best-known contemporary historian, Josephus, only devotes several sentences to an obscure Galilee preacher. The Romans felt threatened enough to execute him, though in these times of state-sponsored massacres and constant bloodshed that was no great distinction either.

However, a devoted band of Christ's followers were convinced that their leader was

the messianic saviour that the Jews had craved. In the following decades the determined dissemination of these disciples was to change history. Christianity spread north and east to Armenia and Byzantium, and southwards, taking root in Africa, especially in Egypt and Ethiopia, and subsequently it took hold in Rome and all of Europe.

But the Jews themselves remained unimpressed. For the Jewish people Christ remains just one of a string of historical false messiahs, distinguished only by the fact that so many Gentiles accepted his teachings and interpreted them as good reason to persecute the Jews themselves, who were branded as

Christ killers. Yet there is no historical evidence that the Jews conspired in the crucifixion of Christ. When Rome subsequently embraced Christianity, a convenient scapegoat was needed to draw attention away from the fact that Rome itself had killed Christ. And so the claim that the Jews were Christ killers became the basis for anti-Judaism and anti-Semitism down the centuries.

Not that the Jewish establishment of the time would have shed a tear at Christ's execution. The aristocratic Saducees, who controlled the priesthood, and the scholarly Pharisees, who interpreted the law, would have regarded Christ – though it is not certain they were even aware of his existence – as an undesirable subversive element.

The Essenes might have been more impressed. This ascetic cult, which uniquely for Judaism included monastic communities that stressed celibacy, was in all likelihood a major influence on Christ's philosophy. As a result, the Essenes' culture and writings in the Dead Sea Scrolls (which are displayed in the Israel Museum and include the oldest known version of the Old Testament) have been of major interest to Western society.

Zealotry and defeat: The Zealots would have been too wrapped up in the nationalist struggle against Roman occupation to pay much attention to a Galilee preacher. Increased Roman oppression strengthened the popularity of the Zealots and other extremist groups, most notably the decision by the Roman emperor Caligula to have his image installed in the Temple.

In AD 66 the Jews rebelled. After initial Jewish successes, the Romans imported major reinforcements under the command of the future emperor Vespesian, and the revolt was slowly but surely crushed. By AD 69 only Jerusalem and several fortress outposts held out. After a year-long siege, Jerusalem was captured. The Romans mercilessly sacked the city, burning the Temple and carrying its sacred contents back to Rome. Jerusalem was renamed Aeolina Capitolina and all vestiges of Jewish culture were destroyed, except one wall of the Temple – the Western Wall – which was left standing to remind the Jews of Roman sovereignty.

Suicide at Masada: Several fortresses, the most famous being Masada by the Dead Sea, held out for even longer. But resistance was futile and the 15,000 soldiers of the Roman Tenth Legion finally conquered the hilltop stronghold in AD 73. But Rome was denied the satisfaction of capturing its inhabitants: the Zealots – nearly 1,000 of them – committed mass suicide.

Another failed Jewish uprising against the Romans in AD 132, led by Simon Bar Kochba, saw most Jews executed, sold into slavery or

Great and the Eastern Roman Empire early in the 4th century, the Jewish presence in the Holy Land dwindled into insignificance. From that point until modern times, the glory of Jewish culture was to be accomplished in what became known as the Diaspora.

From Christianity to Islam: It is one of the great ironies of Christianity that in the very Holy Land where Christ himself was born, preached and died, Christians have remained a small minority for most of history.

Constantine's mother, Queen Helena, is

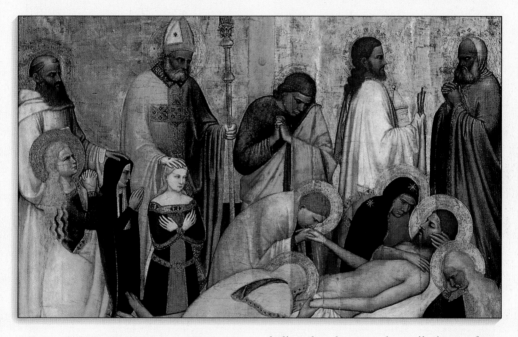

exiled, and this date is often considered as the start of two millennia of exile.

Nevertheless, Jewish culture continued to flourish in the region, especially in the Galilee. The Mishnah, the Talmudic commentary on the Old Testament, was written by sages in Tiberias in the 2nd and 3rd centuries, while rabbinical scholars in the Mount Meron region near Safed penned the Jewish mystical texts that comprise the Kabbalah.

But as Christianity took root in the region after being embraced by Constantine the

Illuminated manuscripts depict the birth of Jesus (left) and his death (above).

believed to have made a pilgrimage from Byzantium and personally identified the principal sites of Christendom, which include the Church of the Nativity in Bethlehem, the Church of the Holy Sepulchre in Jerusalem and the Church of the Anunciation in Nazareth, which are to this day revered by the Orthodox and Catholic churches. She initiated the construction of shrines on these sites. By the 5th century Christians were a majority in the Holy Land.

However, the Roman Empire was crumbling. The Persians temporarily conquered the region in the 7th century before the Byzantines reasserted their control. But in

640 the Arab followers of Mohammed swept through the region converting much of the Byzantine Christian population to Islam. Mohammed's emphasis on the Oneness of God and the need to revive Jewish rituals such as circumcision and dietary laws struck a popular chord in the region.

Islam and the Arab world has coveted the Holy Land ever since. Abraham, the father of the Arab people, is buried in Hebron, while Mohammed is believed to have made a miraculous journey on horseback after his death to the Temple Mount in Jerusalem from where he ascended to heaven. In 691 the Caliph Abd Al-Malik, horrified by the neglected state of the Temple Mount, built the the entire Holy Land by the end of the century. The Dome of the Rock became the headquarters of the Templars, while the Al Aksa Mosque was transformed into a church. The Kingdom of Jerusalem, ruled by King Baldwin I, who was installed in 1100, held sway over several subservient principalities.

But if the ostensible aim of the Crusades was to fight the infidel – and indeed both Muslims and Jews were massacred in their thousands by the ruthless, righteous invaders – the Crusaders slaughtered far more Christians than non-believers. En route, especially in the Balkans, the Crusaders laid waste entire Orthodox Christian communities. In the Holy Land itself, Christian villag-

Dome of the Rock over the supposed site of Mohammed's ascension. Several decades afterwards the Al Aksa Mosque was built on the southern section of the Temple Mount.

Jerusalem was now sacred to three major religions – Judaism, Christianity and Islam – attracting pilgrims from all three religions. But if individuals were often content simply to visit, others wanted not only to come and see but also to conquer.

Crusaders and infidels: Islamic control of the Holy Land especially irked the Christians of Europe. During the 11th century the Pope inaugurated a series of crusades which saw Christianity in possession of virtually ers greeted their supposed liberators only to be put to the sword. For, although the Crusaders were sponsored by Rome and religion, this was the first imperialistic awakening of English, French and German forces.

The Crusaders built a network of hilltop fortresses. From Nimrod in the north to Jerusalem in the south, the remains of these fortresses can be visited today. The Crusaders ruled until 1187, when the Egyptian leader Saladin won a great victory at the Horns of Hittim in the Galilee. Slowly but surely, the Europeans lost their foothold in the Holy Land. Even the fabled Richard the Lionheart, who led the Third Crusade in 1188, could not turn the tide. Four more Crusades kept the inevitable at bay, but in 1291 the Crusaders lost St Jean d'Acre (Acco), their last stronghold in the region, to the Mamelukes, who in their turn had defeated Saladin.

Mamelukes and Ottomans: The Mamelukes are the least remembered of the Holy Land's conquerors. For nearly 250 years these slave warriors to the sultans of Egypt, who had been brought over from Asia to be trained as elite soldiers, ruled over the region from Egypt to Syria. Even though they created some ornate architecture, this was an era of decline for the Middle East from which it has never fully recovered. As Europe flourished and America was discovered, the balance of

came a semi-desert and Jerusalem degenerated into a crumbling mountain village. The Ottomans, like the Mamelukes before them, ruled Palestine as a province of Syria, further belittling the status of the region in general and Jerusalem in particular. Voltaire, in his philosophical dictionary compiled in the mid-18th century, described Jerusalem as a barren wilderness of rocks and dust.

Napoleon's brief conquest of parts of Palestine in 1799 spelled a revival of interest in the Holy Land by the European powers. As the Ottomans weakened, the British and the French vied for hegemony. Offended by the fact that the Christian sites in the Holy Land were dominated by Greeks, Armenians and

world power slipped further away from the Eastern Mediterranean.

The rise of the Ottoman Turks stopped the rot, at least for a while. The Holy Land, too, regained some lustre after the Ottoman conquest in 1517. Suleiman the Magnificent, who ruled from 1520 to 1566, revived the economy of the region and built the impressive walls around the Old City of Jerusalem.

But from the 17th century onwards the Ottoman Empire went into a decline that lasted three centuries. The Holy Land be-

Above, Jerusalem from the Mount of Olives, painted by Luigi Meyer in the late 18th century.

Ethiopians, the Catholic, Protestant and Russian Orthodox churches, built institutions wherever and whenever possible, and were encouraged to do so by their governments.

In the event, it was the British who wrested control of Palestine from the Ottomans in 1917 during World War I. However, the League of Nations mandate stipulated that the British were to be temporary custodians. Even though significant numbers of Jews had begun returning to their ancestral homeland from the late 19th century onwards, nobody could have predicted that in just three more decades possession of much of Palestine would return to its ancient owners.

In nearly 2,000 years of exile the Jewish people never forgot Israel. They faced Jerusalem when they prayed and took to heart the sentence from Isaiah: "If I forget thee O Jerusalem then let my right hand wither."

Although the Jews never forgot Jerusalem, they showed no great inclination to return for most of their exile. Many individuals made pilgrimages to the Holy Land but there was no significant mass movement to return to Zion. Over time, the conventional orthodox belief took root that the return

would occur only with the coming of the messiah. Eventually it was a combination of European enlightenment, nationalism and anti-Semitism that would shake this conviction and promote the belief that a return to Zion was necessary both for the physical survival of the Jewish people threatened by extermination, and for the perpetuation of Jewish culture corroded by assimilation.

For the most part, the first millennium of exile was unremarkable. Most Jews lived in the Middle East and Mediterranean basin where they suffered what was to become a familiar mixture of intolerance and persecution, while being patronised for their skills,

crafts and merchant abilities. But if Islam and Orthodox Christianity, centred in Constantinople, had occasional outbursts of anti-Jewish sentiment, this paled into insignificance compared to the experiences the Jews were to have in Europe in their second millennium of exile.

Inquisitions and pogroms: By the 11th century large Jewish communities had established themselves in France and Germany. They arrived just in time for the Crusades, and a familiar pattern of massacres was begun which was to haunt the Jews all the way to Auschwitz. The Church institutionalised the belief that the Jews were satanic Christ killers who craved money above all else.

Nevertheless, in the 11th, 12th and 13th centuries the Jews entered a golden age, especially in Spain, where Jewish aristocrats formed a bridge between the Christian north and Moorish Arab Muslim south. Communal life and autonomous religious institutions flourished both in Spain and Germany and the Jews even developed their own languages – Ladino and Yiddish – medieval Spanish and German respectively, mixed with Hebrew and written with Hebrew characters.

Despite their accomplishments Jews pined to be elsewhere. In the early 12th century the Spanish Jewish poet Yehuda HaLevi wrote such poems as "My Heart Is In The East", "Jerusalem" and "Longing for Zion".

But HaLevi was in the West where ultimately Christianity's obsession with witchcraft and evil spirits was always bound to work against the Jews. The belief that Jews killed Christian children so that they could use their blood for Passover rituals persisted through to the 20th century. The Jews were blamed for the Black Death in 1348 and it was widely believed that they had poisoned wells to spread the epidemic. And as Spain drove the Moorish infidels back into Africa, it turned its attentions to the non-Spanish, non-Christian infidels in its midst.

For a century Jews were either massacred or forced at sword point to convert. The Inquisition was ruthless and cruel, and finally, in the 1490s – coincidentally as Columbus was discovering America where the Jews would enjoy a new golden age – the

Jews were expelled from Spain. Many stayed and lived secretly as Jews, others returned to North Africa or settled in the newly emerging Ottoman Empire. Several thousands returned to the Holy Land, settling in Jerusalem and especially in the Galilee town of Safed, which became a major centre of Jewish scholarship. Some Jews found their way to Holland and subsequently to England, when Oliver Cromwell readmitted the community that Richard the Lionheart had expelled.

The Jews of Germany fared no better.

Jews could live, excluding them from Russia itself, while pogroms, government-inspired massacres, kept the Jews in fear of their lives. Ironically, the Pale of Settlement became a kind of homogenous Jewish State. Located in Eastern Poland, Western Ukraine, Lithuania, Bylorus and Eastern Romania, the Yiddish-speaking Jews evolved their own distinct ethnic culture.

Emancipation and nationalism: The industrial revolution and the forces of emancipation and enlightenment transforming Europe

Hounded by the Catholic Church, huge communities moved east to Poland and Russia, establishing the *shtetls*, small self-sufficient village communities portrayed romantically in the Hollywood musical *Fiddler on the Roof*, based on the Yiddish story of Sholom Aleichem. The rabbi's blessing in *Fiddler on the Roof* – God bless the Tsar and keep him far away from us – reflected the antagonism that Russian rulers developed for the Jews.

The Pale of Settlement defined where the

also affected Jews. Some turned to messianic cults such as Hasidism but many became more secular. Nationalism was now sweeping across Central and Eastern Europe. Many Jews became secularised. But their language was still Yiddish and their culture was not Russian or Polish or Ukrainian.

At the same time Europeans started investigating Jewish culture. Academics, especially in Germany, discovered that Hebrew was completely outside Indo-European linguistic evolution and was instead a Semitic language related to Arabic. This led to the rise of anti-Semitism. If previously the Jews suffered religious persecution but were at

Left, an idyllic view of 18th-century Jerusalem.
Above, delegates to the Sixth Zionist Conference at Basle, Switzerland, in 1903.

least accepted into the Church, albeit often through forced conversions, now they were set apart racially. The ovens of Auschwitz were being prepared.

Jews assimilated into middle-class European society. In England Benjamin Disraeli's father had the country's future prime minister baptised rather than bar mitzvahed when he was 13. But baptism did not make tens of thousands of Jews of mainland Europe seem European enough. Ultimately they were still hunted down as Semites.

Indeed the Enlightenment, with its anti-religious liberal emphasis, often worked against the Jews too, who were viewed as reactionary, religious fundamentalists. Vol-

new agricultural villages like Rishon Le Zion, Zichron Yaakov and Rosh Pina.

Meanwhile, the assassination of Tsar Alexander II in Russia in 1881 was blamed on the Jews and unleashed awesome pogroms. Jews emigrated in their millions to Western Europe and especially to the United States, which from the outset had guaranteed religious freedom in its constitution. But some Jews, eager to return to Palestine, were persuaded by the philanthropists to settle in the Holy Land.

The birth of Zionism: But it was in France that modern political Zionism was conceived. In the 1890s a young Viennese Jewish journalist, Theodor Herzl, was despatched by his

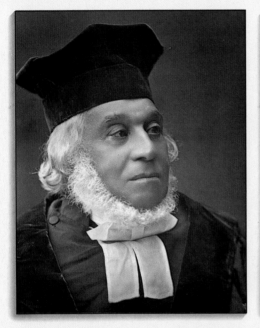

taire railed against the Jews and his anti-religious rationalist and atheistic writings were developed in the 19th century, ironically, by a young German Jew named Karl Marx, who rejected his heritage and spoke of a war against capitalists and clerics.

In this era of great change some Jews remembered Jerusalem. Though the Jewish masses of Eastern Europe would eventually provide the manpower for Zionism, it was the smaller more affluent communities of Central and Western Europe that got the Zionist ball rolling. British philanthropists like Moses Montefiore and the Rothschilds set up Jewish communities in Jerusalem and

newspaper to Paris to cover the trial of Captain Albert Dreyfus, the French Jewish officer who was framed as a spy and blamed for his country's defeat in the Franco–Prussian war of 1870. As the trial unravelled, in the land where Jews had been granted full equality following the French Revolution in 1789, Herzl despaired of the fate of European Jewry.

Though an assimilated Jew, who knew virtually nothing of his cultural roots, Herzl wrote a book, *Alteneuland* ("Old-new Land"), in which he described the re-establishment of a Jewish commonwealth in ancient Israel. He was written off as a dreamer, to which he responded, "If you will it, then it will be" –

the ambitious motto that has since motivated the Israeli people.

Herzl was a man of action as well as words. In 1897 he convened the first Zionist Congress in Basle, Switzerland, establishing the World Zionist Organisation, the institutional forerunner of what was to become the Israeli government. He effectively lobbied political leaders and successfully courted European royalty, making his only ever trip to Palestine in 1898 to meet with Kaiser Wilhelm II of Prussia when he visited Jerusalem.

After Herzl's premature death in 1904, the unofficial leadership of the Zionist movement eventually fell to Chaim Weizmann, a Russian-born professor of chemistry at Man-

needed diplomatic access, the foot soldiers in the field were the Jews of Eastern Europe. As Tsarist Russia hurtled towards the revolution, increasing numbers of ideologically motivated Zionist socialists found their way to Palestine. Between 1904 and 1917, some 100,000 came, though less than half of them remained.

Among them was a young lawyer's son named David Ben-Gurion who was to assume the leadership of the *yishuv*, the pre-state Jewish entity. These men, products of pre-revolutionary Russia, were essentially Bolsheviks with a more liberal, humane streak. They set up trade unions, rejected the capitalist villages of the Rothschilds and

chester University. Weizmann won the confidence of London's ruling elite and, after the British conquest of Palestine in 1917, that meant everything. Most importantly, he persuaded the British Foreign Secretary, Lord Balfour, to issue a declaration promising British support for a Jewish homeland. This lent the Zionist movement the international legitimacy it desperately needed.

However, if the likes of Herzl and Weizmann gave the Zionist movement much

established their own agricultural collectives called kibbutzim.

Unfortunately, there was an oversight in the Zionist slogan "A land for a people for a people without a land". At first the indigenous Palestinian population welcomed the Jewish settlers. Their numbers were small, they brought with them wealth and development and, while most Palestinians lived on the inland hills, the Jews were prepared to buy relatively worthless land and settle the humid, sparsely populated coastal plain. But the Balfour Declaration took the Arabs by surprise and indicated that they had greatly underestimated the Zionist potential.

Left, Nathan Adler, a 19th-century chief rabbi in England, and Zionist visionary Theodor Herzl. **Above**, Turkish cavalry officers in Palestine, 1917.

PERFIDIOUS ALBION

Even today the question is often asked in the Middle East: did the British favour the Arabs or the Jews during the Mandatory period? The answer is probably neither and that, as elsewhere in the British Empire, they pursued their own interests favouring whoever it was convenient to favour.

In the aftermath of World War I, the likes of Lord Balfour and David Lloyd George were strong supporters of the Zionist cause because they perceived a Jewish homeland as a potentially friendly outpost of Empire. The notion also appealed to the religious sentiment of the British protestants. But Balfour had underestimated the strength of Arab nationalism that would emerge from the ashes of the Ottoman Empire, as well as the emerging economic and strategic importance of Middle East oil.

The British government's most hostile opponent of the Balfour Declaration was Edwin Montagu, secretary of state for India, and the only Jew in the cabinet. Like a large section of secular world Jewry, he fiercely opposed Zionism because it called into question his national loyalties. He insisted that Judaism was a religion, not a nationality.

Thirty years later, Emanuel Shinwell, a Jewish member of Clement Attlee's post-war Labour cabinet, was proud to identify with the Zionist cause and the establishment of the state. However, he pointed out that, as secretary for energy in His Majesty's government, he was duty-bound to protect British interests and that involved sympathising with Arab states.

Other British politicians were less candid. Of course, the making and breaking of promises is an essential part of politics. But the problem with the British U-turn in Palestine was the plight of the Jewish people after the rise of Nazism. In effect, the British found themselves assisting Adolf Hitler in his policy of exterminating European Jewry, by refusing entry visas to Palestine for Jewish refugees trying to escape Nazi persecution. And, even after the full horrors of the concentra-

tion camps were known, the British did not relent, imprisoning some 73,000 refugees, many of them concentration camp survivors, in detention camps in Cyprus.

Arab riots: The British miscalculation in making the Balfour Declaration soon became apparent. In March 1920 a bloody riot in Jerusalem left more than 200 Jews dead. Widespread Arab violence soon made the British regret the Declaration and by 1921 Winston Churchill, the Colonial Secretary, previously a fervent Zionist sympathiser,

told Chaim Weizmann that 90 percent of the British government was opposed to a Jewish homeland in Palestine.

But the Zionists were better organised than the Arabs and more determined than the British. The Histadrut trade union organisation was founded in 1920, while the Haganah, an underground paramilitary organisation, effectively defended Jewish settlements and became the forerunner of the Israel Defence Forces. Tel Aviv developed as the flourishing economic capital of the emerging Jewish entity, and kibbutz agricultural settlements made the local Jewish population self-sufficient in food.

Left, a Henschel portrait of a Palestinian Arab. **Above**, Zionist Dov Ber Borochov and friends in Plonsk, Poland, *circa* 1920.

Most vitally, large numbers of Jews began emigrating to Palestine. In the 1920s the Jewish population of Palestine doubled from 85,000 to 170,000. The Arab population numbered about 850,000. These Jewish newcomers included socialists disillusioned by the results of the Russian revolution as well as many middle-class merchants and professionals from Poland. While David Ben-Gurion and his socialist followers became the establishment through the Jewish Agency, a kind of government in waiting, the right-wing nationalist revisionist movement of Vladimir Jabotinsky also enjoyed strong support.

In particular, Jabotinsky and his supporters vehemently opposed Churchill's unilateral decision in 1923 to cede all of Palestine east of the River Jordan, nearly two-thirds of the land mass of Palestine, to Britain's Arabian Hashemite ally the Emir Abdullah.

were bourgeois boulevards lined with fashionable large houses, shops and banks, schools, universities and hospitals. An immigrant with means could live well here, while a poorer man could earn a reasonable working wage.

In any event, by 1939, on the eve of World War II, the Jewish population of Palestine had doubled again to 350,000. Bitter hostility to Zionism was led by Haj Amin Husseini, the Mufti of Jerusalem, who had consolidated his position as the local Arab leader and formed an anti-Jewish understanding with Hitler. The region may have subsequently been more peaceful had the more moderate King Abdullah of Jordan been able

The rise of Nazism: Hitler's 1933 assumption of power in Germany, together with the rapid economic development of Palestine, attracted even larger numbers of Jewish immigrants. While the majority of Jews went to Palestine as a safe haven from anti-Semitism, many were now being drawn to the budding Jewish state for other reasons.

Palestine's coastal plain where most Jewish towns were established was no longer dominated by sand dunes and swamps. There

to gain the upper hand.

In an attempt to win Arab support for the impending war with Germany, the British passed a White Paper limiting Jewish immigration to 20,000 a year. So, as the Nazi stranglehold tightened around Europe, there was nowhere for Jewish refugees to flee.

All the same, Ben Gurion and the Jewish Agency insisted that there was no alternative but for the Jews to support the British war effort. The revisionists were not so certain. The Irgun Zvi Leumi led by Menachem Begin agreed to a ceasefire with the British for the duration of the war, but an extremist fringe, Lehi, led by Yitzhak Shamir, continued attacks against British targets throughout World War II. Many Jews, however, enlisted in the British army, which even formed a Jewish brigade to fight the Axis forces, and this provided invaluable experience for subsequent battles.

The revelation of Nazi atrocities made the Jews of Palestine all the more determined to achieve independence. The horrors of the Holocaust were no surprise to the Zionists, who had always feared something of the sort but had expected it to be Russian rather than German-inspired. The prevailing belief was that had Israel existed at the time, then 6 million Jews could have been saved.

Stalin to the rescue: Ben Gurion, grasping post-war realities, switched the focus of his lobbying from London to Washington. An intense diplomatic offensive was launched at the newly formed United Nations in New York and quiet channels were opened to the Soviet Union. The support of Josef Stalin in the establishment of Israel was to prove crucial. The United States, which voted against the UN sponsored partition of Palestine into Jewish and Arab states in 1946, supported the same resolution just a year later. Britain abstained from voting both times. But Stalin, though undoubtedly anti-Semitic and paranoid about his own Jewish population, saw a potentially socialist Israel as a Marxist bulwark against the puppet Arab administrations in the Middle East being set up by Britain and France. Consequently he threw his full diplomatic weight, as well as that of his European satellites, behind the Zionists. He voted for the UN partition plan in November 1948 and even sent arms to help Israel during the War of Independence.

The right-wing Irgun and Lehi denounced Ben Gurion's diplomacy as futile. Their strategy was simple – to bomb the British out of Palestine. British soldiers were killed, Irgun and Lehi members were hanged, and more British soldiers were killed in retaliation. Following the bombing in 1947 of the British administrative HQ at the King David Hotel in Jerusalem, which killed 91 people, British public opinion clamoured for a withdrawal. After much government deliberation, the pullout was fixed for 15 May 1948.

Although the socialists and revisionists

had a violent hatred for each other and their methods, in truth it was probably their joint efforts that brought about the establishment of Israel. Ben Gurion's diplomatic success at the United Nations and in gaining the support of both Stalin and the American president, Harry Truman, gave the Jewish state solid international legitimacy. The revisionists' all-out war against the British forced their withdrawal.

And so modern Israel arose out of the ashes of the Holocaust. Yet it is one of the myths of our time that Israel came into existence *because* of the Holocaust. This is a romantic idea that appeals to a sense of justice and poetry. The Jewish people suf-

fered and were at least compensated with their own state.

This is not the way Israelis see it. They argue that Israel came into being despite the Holocaust and that had just 1 million of the 6 million Jews who perished reached Israel, then the birth of the state would have been much easier. They recall that while Israel enjoyed much international sympathy after the Holocaust, little was actually done to help them. Israel had to work hard diplomatically to swing the UN vote and when the British withdrew Israel was left completely alone to face the combined armies of the Arab world.

Left, British soldiers in Jerusalem, 1917. Right, a young David Ben-Gurion, in Turkish fez.

As Israelis danced in the streets following the Declaration of Independence in May 1948, they knew that there would be little to celebrate in the ensuing months. Though vastly outnumbered by the surrounding Arab armies, better organisation saw the Israel Defence Forces not only defend Jewish territory but also conquer large areas of the Negev and Western Galilee that had been allocated to Palestine under the United Nations partition plan.

However, if subsequent Israeli military victories were relatively swift, this first war ground on for nearly a year, costing the new country 6,000 lives, about 1 percent of the Jewish population. Jerusalem saw especially fierce fighting. Under the UN plan, the city was meant to enjoy international status. But Jordanian Legionnaires overran the Old City, including the Jewish quarter, while the western Jewish half of the city was besieged for months, relieved only when a new road was built through the hills. Eventually the city was divided into two, with the Israelis controlling the western half and the Jordanians annexing the eastern section, including the holy sites, as well as the entire West Bank. Egypt helped itself to the Gaza Strip and so Arab Palestine never came into existence.

The fate of the Palestinians: The Israelis have always officially claimed that the Palestinians ran away from their homes in 1948 to escape the fighting, expecting to return after an Arab victory. The Palestinians claim that they were forcibly expelled. Research has shown that both versions are probably right. About a third of the 500,000 Palestinians living in the region that was to become Israel were coerced into leaving, becoming refugees in surrounding countries; about a third voluntarily fled, and the final third stayed put and eventually became citizens of Israel, which today has an Arab minority of some 20 percent.

Meanwhile, David Ben-Gurion set about building his new nation. The architect of such powerful institutions as the Histadrut

trade union movement and the Haganah, now renamed the Israel Defence Forces, Ben Gurion was easily able to outflank world Jewish leader Chaim Weizmann, who also aspired to lead the new nation. He offered Weizmann the post of president, the titular head of state.

At the same time Ben-Gurion, while allowing the revisionists led by Menachem Begin to participate in Knesset elections, acted tough with their pre-state paramilitary organisations, outlawing them and even

blowing up a ship, the *Atalena*, bringing arms for the Irgun in June 1948. Menachem Begin and his Herut Party, which won 14 seats out of 120 in the 1948 elections, were to remain in the political wilderness until the 1960s. Only in the post-Ben-Gurion era in the 1960s was the rift healed, and in the run-up to the Six Day War in 1967 Begin was invited by prime minister Levi Eshkol to join a national unity government. In elections a decade later, he won outright power.

Although authoritative and unforgiving of his opponents, Ben-Gurion knew how to delegate responsibility. After his socialist Mapai Party won 46 seats in the 1949 Knesset elections, he formed a coalition with the Stalinist Mapam Party to the left and religious and liberal groups to the right. Ben-Gurion became prime minister and defence minister. Moshe Sharett, as foreign minister, became Ben-Gurion's heir apparent and eventually the second prime minister.

Ben-Gurion had a good eye for young talent, both inside and outside the army. In particular, he spotted the creative organisational abilities of a young Polish immigrant called Shimon Peres and charged him with the task of developing a defence manufacturing infrastructure. Peres' accomplishments were remarkable, giving Israel a nuclear capability and enabling the country

The Law of Return: The most significant new legislation introduced by the Knesset was the Law of Return in 1950, guaranteeing free immigration of World Jewry to Israel. The religious parties wanted to restrict immigration only to candidates whose mothers were Jewish. However, in the wake of the Holocaust and Hitler's Nuremburg Laws which had defined anybody with one Jewish grandparent as Jewish, this yardstick was also adopted by the Law of Return.

In the years following the establishment of Israel waves of immigrants flooded in. Nearly 700,000 arrived between 1948 and 1951, doubling the population. By 1964 another 500,000 immigrants arrived and the popula-

to produce its own tanks and fighter aircraft. Many Israeli weapons, such as the versatile Uzi sub-machine gun, became sought after export items.

Within the army itself, Ben-Gurion advanced the promotion of the daring Moshe Dayan, a notorious one-eyed womaniser who had sustained his trademark injury while fighting for the British against the Vichy French in Syria. Another man who caught Ben-Gurion's attention was the dashing young Yitzhak Rabin, the debonair commander of the Harel brigade, who was given a leading role in the armistice agreements negotiated after the War of Independence.

tion of Israel passed 2 million. But Israel's European-born founding fathers were surprised to find that large numbers of immigrants were arriving not only from Poland, Germany, Romania, Hungary, Yugoslavia and Czechoslovakia but also from Morocco, Egypt, Yemen, Iraq and other Arab countries from where entire Jewish communities were expelled following an anti-Zionist backlash.

By the 1960s Israel's Jewish population was split 50–50 between Ashkenazi European Jews and Sephardi Oriental Jews. This cultural divide, accentuated by socio-economic gaps, was to generate major communal tensions in the 1970s.

International orientation: Ben-Gurion had initially planned to pursue a neutral policy in the emerging Cold War confrontation. During the War of Independence the Soviet Union had been the only country to send Israel arms, though the US had turned a blind eye to the military aid given to Israel by American Jewry. But, even though a Stalinist party shared power in Israel's first government, the country was after all a parliamentary democracy with more in common with the West.

Moreover, Israel desperately needed financial aid and only the US could supply that in the post-World War II world. So in 1949, when Israel took a loan of $100,000 from the US, a pattern of economic dependence on Uncle Sam was begun. In parallel, Israel's relations with the Soviet Union were strained as Stalin refused to allow free emigration of Soviet Jewry.

However, Israel, in partnership with Britain and France, antagonised both the US and the Soviet Union in 1956 when it launched the Suez campaign. Following the nationalisation of the Suez Canal by Egypt's charismatic young president, Gamal Abdel Nasser, British and French paratroopers seized the canal, and within less than a week Israeli troops had occupied all of Sinai. But the Americans sided with the Egyptians, forcing the British and French to relinquish control of the canal and compelling the Israelis to withdraw from Sinai. Instead of being humiliated, Nasser became a hero, and survived to fight another war.

Economic development: Despite taking in so many impoverished immigrants and illiterate newcomers, and despite the cost of remaining on a constant war footing, Israel's economy developed steadily during the 1950s and '60s. Major national projects were undertaken, including the draining of the Hula Swamp in the Upper Galilee and the building of the national carrier bringing water from the north to the Negev. The desert literally turned green. Forests were planted on the barren hillsides and the arid land was transformed into green fields and groves.

Even with its burgeoning population, the

country was self-sufficient in food, and a major export industry, especially in citrus fruit, developed. Highways were built, and a health, education and energy infrastructure was put in place. In this formative stage, the Arab boycott and unwillingness of overseas investors to put money into a country that might soon be driven into the sea turned out to be an asset, for Israel developed a home-owned industrial infrastructure. The economy was heavily centralised and socialist, but there was scope for entrepreneurs with the patience to unravel bureaucratic red tape.

In this stage of the country's development, donations from overseas Jewry, especially from North America, were a vital source of

capital. In addition, a reparations agreement with the West German government was concluded which compensated hundreds of thousands of survivors, or their relatives, for the loss of life, the suffering and the property lost during the Holocaust. Menachem Begin bitterly opposed this agreement, insisting that no amount of money could atone for the devastation caused by the Nazis.

In 1963, when Levi Eshkol became the country's third prime minister, Israel was not a wealthy country, nor a full member of the developed world. But it did not suffer the food shortages, disease and illiteracy which characterised the developing world.

Left, crowds of illegal immigrants gaze out from a British troop ship. **Right**, a waxwork commemorates Chaim Weizmann's swearing-in as the nation's first president.

The Arabs have always maintained that Israel instigated the Six Day War in 1967 in order to seize more Palestinian territory. This interpretation of history overlooks the blockade of the Straits of Tiran by the Egyptian president Gamal Abdel Nasser, which cut of the shipping route to Israel's Red Sea port of Eilat, as well as Nasser's boast that he would drive the Jews into the sea.

In hindsight, Nasser's threat was probably bluff, but Israel was not to know. As the Yom Kippur War revealed seven years later, Israeli intelligence was poor at the time and a first strike was crucial for such a tiny country with no strategic depth. So Israel took Nasser's threats at face value and attacked, and the Egyptian air force was destroyed on the ground minutes after the war started. The Golan Heights, from which Syria had been bombarding northern Israel, were captured. Israel also won the Sinai peninsula and Gaza Strip from Egypt and the West Bank from Jordan. Jerusalem was reunited. Defence Minister Moshe Dayan and Chief of the Army Yitzhak Rabin were hailed as heroes.

Permanently on the map: Israel was never the same after the Six Day War. It wasn't only that the borders had changed and more than a million Palestinians had fallen under Israeli occupation. Perceived worldwide as the underdog in the Middle East conflict, Israel was now viewed as the oppressor. But the countries of the West, especially the United States, now looked on Israel as a potentially strong and reliable ally in the Cold War confrontation with the Soviet Union. Military collaboration strengthened between Israel and America while Britain and France maintained the arms embargo imposed at the start of the Six Day War.

Israel itself was intoxicated by its own success. Prime Minister Levi Eshkol died and was replaced by Golda Meir, who had grown up in the United States and was able to consolidate the US–Israel romance. The country's new euphoria was not even tempered by a war of attrition between 1967 and

1970 in which Egypt constantly shelled Israeli forces across the Suez Canal; nor the emergence of the Palestine Liberation Organization (PLO), which carried out bloody terrorist attacks against Israeli targets worldwide, including the kidnapping and killing of 11 Israeli athletes during the Munich Olympic Games in 1972.

When Jordan and Egypt annexed the West Bank and Gaza Strip, the PLO had been suppressed and its leader from 1965 onwards, Yasser Arafat, was imprisoned. But

after 1967 the PLO was encouraged to spearhead the Arab nation's campaign to regain "the Zionist entity". By 1970 the PLO was so strong that Arafat attempted, with Syrian backing, to take over Jordan. In a 10-day bloody war in "Black September", King Hussein quelled the attempted Palestinian coup. The Syrian troops massed on the border turned back when Israel indicated it would intervene to support the Hashemite Kingdom. Arafat and his fighters were expelled to Lebanon.

War and peace: The PLO was popularly viewed as a terrorist organisation that would eventually go away, and Israel considered

Left, students celebrate Independence Day at Jerusalem's Western Wall. **Right,** Israeli soldiers reach the Wall in 1967's Six Day War.

itself invincible. In 1973 the Yom Kippur War stunned the nation. With a surprise assault the Egyptians under President Anwar Sadat conquered much of the Sinai while the Syrians nearly broke through to the Galilee. Israel recovered, counter-attacked, retook the Golan Heights and even managed to cross the Suez Canal before the Americans, who had for the first time become committed allies of Israel by airlifting emergency military supplies to the Middle East, forced a stop to the fighting.

Nevertheless, the war restored Egyptian pride and was portrayed by Sadat as a great victory. He then felt confident enough to sign a peace treaty with Israel in 1979 in

Oriental Jews alienated by the Ashkenazi socialist establishment, and Orthodox Jewry, attached to the biblical sites in the West Bank, which now became known as Judea and Samaria.

Yitzhak Rabin had first allowed right-wing Jews to settle Hebron and other West Bank towns in 1975, and in so doing opened a pandora's box. Under Begin and his successor, Yitzhak Shamir, tens of thousands of Jews settled the West Bank and even the Gaza Strip, and the Palestinians saw the little that was left of their homeland slipping away from them.

All the same, the right-wing Likud, though nationalist in character and reluctant to relin-

exchange for the return of the Sinai peninsula. Remarkably, Sadat did not shake hands with Golda Meir, or her successor Yitzhak Rabin, but with Menachem Begin, the right-wing nationalist who won the election of 1977 and vowed that he would retire to the Sinai village of Yamit.

The birth of two-party politics: Begin's success changed the face of Israeli politics which from here on would be a two-party affair, characterised by bitter divisions over the future direction of Israeli society. After 29 years of power, Labour lost office because of its failures in the Yom Kippur War. Moreover, Begin's populism appealed to young

quish land, has tended to make pragmatic concessions when pressured by the US. Menachem Begin gave up the Sinai after American arm twisting and received the Nobel Peace Prize for his pains.

By the late 1970s, the US viewed Israel as a significant player in its Cold War global strategy. Israel was seen as a vital support to NATO's vulnerable southeastern flank, comprising the two bitter enemies, Greece and Turkey. The policy meant that large sums of money – about $1.5 billion a year – was ploughed into Israel to pay for arms and to improve the country's military capabilities. Another $1.5 billion was given annually to help repay loans taken for previous acquisitions and the expensive redeployment after the Sinai withdrawal in 1982.

Anti-Zionism: Israel's close identification with the US made it a target for the enmity of the Soviet Union. The communist bloc, Arab and Muslim nations, and the developing world combined effectively to isolate Israel as a pariah nation. The country was depicted as a racist, Nazi state and Zionism was denounced by a United Nations resolution as an intrinsically fascist ideology.

The tactic was extremely effective and even many of Israel's friends in the liberal west distanced themselves from Zionism. And this was before the Likud had ever come to power and there was barely a settler in the West Bank. For Israelis anti-Zionism was the flip side of anti-Semitism. Persecuted in Europe as Semites, they were now being denounced by the Semitic Arabs as European colonialists.

Ironically, while the Soviet Union was hounding Israel diplomatically and arming Syria, it eased restrictions on Jewish emigration. More than 180,000 Jews reached Israel from the USSR in the 1970s and an even greater number emigrated to the US.

Begin won a second election victory in 1981 and the following year turned his attentions on Lebanon. Israel's northern neighbour had been a model of democracy and affluence despite its divisions between Maronite Christians, Druze, Sunni and Shi'ite Muslims and Palestinian refugees. But the arrival of the PLO and its fighters in 1970 had disturbed the delicate balance and the country plunged into civil war in 1975. The PLO used Lebanon as a base for attacks on Israel from sea and land.

Ariel Sharon, the Minister of Defence, convinced Begin that a military incursion into Southern Lebanon was required to clear out PLO bases, similar to the Litani Operation, carried out in 1978. The invasion was launched in June 1982. Begin, like the rest of the nation, was surprised to learn a short while later that Israeli tanks were rolling through the streets of Beirut. The Americans intervened to prevent the IDF from finishing

off Arafat, who together with his fighters was given safe passage to Tunisia.

In the aftermath of the Lebanese war, Begin lost his previous vigour. The once great orator fell silent and resigned the following year. He felt betrayed, not only by Sharon but also by his Finance Minister, Yoram Aridor, whose economic policies led to three-digit annual inflation.

The years of power sharing: The 1984 election result was inconclusive and a unique rotation pact was agreed, with Labour's Shimon Peres serving as prime minister until 1986, followed by Likud's Yitzhak Shamir for the subsequent two years. Peres withdrew Israeli troops from Lebanon with the

exception of a security belt closest to the Israeli border, and stabilised the Israeli economy, reducing the annual rate of inflation from 425 percent to 16 percent.

During the two decades that Israel had occupied the West Bank and Gaza, relations between the Israelis and Palestinians had gradually deteriorated. Immediately after 1967, the Palestinians were infatuated by Israeli liberalism and the economic opportunities that occupation brought. A free press flourished, municipal elections were held and employment in Israel, mainly in menial jobs, saw improvements in the Palestinians' standard of living.

<u>Left</u>, Egyptian president Anwar Sadat is greeted by Menachem Begin as he lands in Israel in 1977. <u>Right</u>, an Israeli soldier checks work permits of Palestinians at a Gaza checkpoint.

But the marriage turned sour, especially after the Likud triumph in the 1970s, as it became clear that Israel was integrating the Palestinian territories into a Greater Israel. The Palestinians wanted a divorce, but with right-wing settlers becoming more powerful, the Israeli government was talking of annexation of the biblical Land of Israel.

Palestinian frustration exploded in 1987 with the outbreak of the Intifada, which was characterised by the throwing of rocks and molotov cocktails at Israeli troops, and by strikes preventing Arab workers from coming to Israel. World opinion strongly sympathised with the Palestinians, and Israelis were reminded of the "green line" dividing Israeli

proper from the territories. No more would Israelis pop into Gaza to buy cheap groceries, or dine in their favourite restaurant in the West Bank town of Ramallah. More significantly, the demographic debate was renewed in Israeli politics, with Labour speaking of territorial concessions.

The elections of 1988 saw the Likud win the upper hand in a closely fought contest. Shamir continued to lead a national unity government which broke down in 1990, when Shamir formed a right-wing coalition.

The collapse of the Soviet Union: The unexpected disintegration of the USSR was like a dream come true for Israel. From 1990 onwards Russian-speaking Jewry flooded into Israel. Over 700,000 immigrants had arrived by 1997. Moreover, the demise of the Soviet Union saw Israel renew diplomatic relations with the former communist countries of Central and Eastern Europe and all the former republics of the USSR. In addition, the supply of Russian-made arms to Syria and the PLO dried up.

Before the post-Cold War situation could be digested, Iraq invaded Kuwait and the Gulf War ensued in 1991. Scud missiles fell on Israel but, under American pressure, the right-wing government did not retaliate so as not to disrupt the allied coalition, which included Syria.

By November 1991 Israel was sitting round the table with the Palestinians and Syrians at the Madrid peace conference. In the wake of these preliminary peace talks, China, India and much of Asia established full diplomatic relations with Israel for the first time. African countries such as Nigeria renewed ties and the UN resolution equating Zionism with racism was repealed. But Shamir stalled on progess in the peace talks, continuing to expand settlements in the West Bank. A confrontation with the United States was averted by Yitzhak Rabin's election victory in 1992.

Peace agreements and assassination: Though Rabin had been elected on a dovish platform, both Israelis and the world were taken by surprise by the secret agreements concluded with the PLO in Oslo. In September 1993 Prime Minister Rabin and PLO Chairman Yasser Arafat shook hands on the White House lawn and by 1994 Israel had withdrawn from most of the Gaza Strip and all the towns on the West Bank save for Hebron. A peace agreement was signed with Jordan, and some Arab countries such as Morocco and Tunisia opened low-level diplomatic offices in Tel Aviv.

The peace process combined with the end of the Arab economic boycott, ongoing immigration and an Israeli penchant for developing innovative high-tech products, saw the economy boom. Average annual growth of 6 percent in the 1990s enabled the standard of living to rise rapidly and reach Western European levels.

But Rabin's right-wing religious and nationalist opponents were unimpressed by the economic benefits of peace. The opposition to territorial compromise strengthened following a terrorist bombing campaign by the extremist Palestinian Hamas movement. Vociferous anti-government demonstrations took place as the right took to the streets.

A young law student, Yigal Amir, decided to take matters into his own hands. He stalked Rabin for several months, pistol in pocket. His opportunity came following a peace rally in Tel Aviv in November 1995, when he took advantage of a lapse in security to pump three bullets into Rabin's back from point-blank range.

The premiership was assumed by Foreign Minister Shimon Peres who, as architect of the Oslo accords, had won the Nobel Peace

Netanyahu puts on the brakes: Benjamin Netanyahu became the first prime minister to be chosen directly by the electorate. He would have won more handsomely under the old system by which the Knesset faction with the best chance of forming a government received a mandate from the president.

Netanyahu won because of a late move to the centre. In contravention of traditional Likud policy, he agreed to abide by the Oslo Agreements and even to meet with PLO chairman Yasser Arafat. This pragmatic step enabled him to pull back the 20 points by which he trailed Peres.

Ideally, Netanyahu wanted to see the status quo of the first stage of Israel's with-

Prize along with Rabin and Arafat. Peres pushed ahead vigorously with the peace process, but Syria's president Hafez El-Assad refused to meet with him, even though Peres had agreed in principle to return the Golan Heights. With a large lead in the polls, Peres brought forward elections by six months to May 1996. But a lacklustre campaign combined with Hamas terrorist attacks and Hizbullah missiles raining down on the Galilee saw Peres defeated by the narrowest of margins.

Left, Yitzhak Rabin, assassinated in 1995. Above, Benjamin Netanyahu meets Yasser Arafat.

drawal from the population centres of the West Bank and Gaza as a permanent settlement. For their part, the Palestinians demanded the full status of statehood in most of the West Bank and Gaza, including some kind of arrangement on East Jerusalem, a sticking point even for liberal Israelis.

According to the Oslo Agreements, the final status settlement should be concluded by 1999. American pressure aside, Netanyahu is bound to seek tough conditions – probably too tough for the Palestinians to accept. In all probability, the Israeli electorate will once again have a fateful choice to make in the elections in 2000.

Israel confounds expectations. It is a nation rooted in religion, yet the majority of the people are brazenly secular, turning to religion for births, barmitzvahs, weddings and funerals. There are picturesque bastions of orthodoxy in Jerusalem, in Bnai Brak near Tel Aviv, and elsewhere a quaint mixture of medieval Poland and the Middle East, but for the most part long rabbinical beards are rare, many restaurants serve forbidden un-kosher foods, the Sabbath is barely observed, and women dress anything but modestly.

Women, like their counterparts in the West, have cut the umbilical cord tying them to their homes but have not escaped from their traditional roles. Expected to pursue a career and raise a family, they have lost ground in some aspects of Israeli life. On the kibbutz, women once undertook all the same jobs as men. Today they tend to be found in the kitchen and the kindergarten. In the army, many women fought as front-line troops for Israel's independence. Today women rarely occupy combat positions.

A people's army: It is the army generals rather than the rabbis who have forged the nation's values. Modern Israel is a nation whose military has a peerless reputation for executing the swift, the precise and the dramatically unexpected. "Visit Israel before Israel visits you," goes the joke.

Yet the ubiquitous Israeli soldier, rifle slung casually over his shoulder, seems so slovenly and unregimented. Israel's famous informality extends even to the Israel Defence Forces (IDF) with long-haired paratroopers, unshaven officers and pot-bellied reservists. The soldier at the roadside hitch-hiking post might be gay and may have refused an order to serve in Lebanon or the West Bank because of his political conscience. These are the unstereotypical heroes who undertook the Entebbe rescue, bombed the Iraqi nuclear reactor and triumphed in the Six Day War.

Vigorous democracy: Israel's greatest achievements, however, have not been on the battlefield. A nation has been created out of immi-

grants from more than 80 countries, who shared a religious heritage and a desire to return to their ancestral homeland, but little else – not even a language. In the street you will hear an astonishing Babel of languages: Russian, English, Arabic, Amharic, Hungarian, French, Persian, Spanish, Yiddish. But Hebrew, the language of the Bible, has been resurrected and adapted to everyday life.

Even more astonishingly, parliamentary democracy has flourished – despite the fact that most Israelis originate in countries with

no experience of such democracy, despite the frictions between religious and secular, right and left, Arab and Jew, and despite the centrality and power of the army. Even when Prime Minister Yitzhak Rabin was gunned down in 1995, there was no danger of the Knesset's sovereignty being overthrown.

If a general seeks political power, he does not plan a *coup d'état* but resigns his commission and enters the political fray. The late Yitzhak Rabin was a former chief of staff of the IDF and half a dozen other former generals served in Benjamin Netanyahu's first government, including Defence Minister Yitzhak Mordechai, Agriculture Minister Rafael Eitan,

Preceding pages: soldiers on the Mount of Olives. **Left,** line-up on a kibbutz. **Right,** shoppers on Ben Yehuda Street, Jerusalem.

Infrastructure Minister Ariel Sharon and former Foreign Minister Ehud Barak. Another political safety-valve is the system of proportional representation that allows all interest groups to be represented in parliament. This enables small parties to hold the balance of power between the major blocs, often granting them unreasonable powers. Civil rights, freedom of the press and an independent judiciary further reinforce democratic values in a country that takes an exuberant pride in flouting authority and disobeying regulations.

Organised chaos: The eye may initially see Levantine chaos and Mediterranean madness, but beneath the surface is a society that functions effectively. The wars have been won, the

residents of Jerusalem, Judea and Samaria (West Bank).

The heat of the summer leaves the country looking parched and brown except for the ripening grape vines, cotton fields and well watered lawns. But, come November, the rains begin, driving forcefully down throughout the winter, and occasional snowfalls can cover the inland hills. Flash floods in the desert destroy all in their path, uprooting trees and shifting boulders. By spring, the countryside is ablaze with flowers and fields are as emerald as Ireland. But then the rains cease and gradually the land becomes thirsty and faded. The land, like its people, is in a state of constant flux and renewal.

desert has bloomed, high-tech industries compete on world markets. From a socialist base, a dynamic capitalist economy has been built with sustained economic growth, enabling Israel, with considerable military aid from the United States, to enjoy living standards comparable to those of Spain or Italy.

Moreover, the diverse landscape and climate complement the heterogeneous nature of the people. The verdant, rolling Galilee hills in the north lead down to the stark and stunning canyons of the Dead Sea and Negev desert. The secular sun worshippers along Israel's heavily populated Mediterranean coast lead up to the more religious and conservative

Ingathering of the exiles: The essence of this ongoing change is *aliyah*, Hebrew for immigration. Since 1989, more than 700,000 immigrants have poured into Israel, principally from the former Soviet Union, though some 25,000 were from Ethiopia. This figure represents 15 percent of Israel's population, and is the equivalent of Britain taking in 8 million immigrants or the US 40 million newcomers.

The process has been tackled with relish, though inevitably problems abound. Housing shortages, for example, resulted in the setting up of caravan sites, especially for the more acquiescent Ethiopians, which many fear will become ghettoes for the weaker sectors of society. And unemployment plagues the newcomers, most of them highly educated professionals who, even if they find work, must often accept a drop in status. Many fall a long distance. Physicians sweep the streets with clinical meticulousness and former members of prestigious orchestras in Moscow and Minsk serenade passers-by in pedestrian malls with the best quality busking in the world.

Angry with the attempts of both the right-wing Likud administration and the subsequent Labour government to absorb them, these new immigrants set up their own party for the 1996 elections: they won seven out of 120 Knesset seats.

But Israel is good at blending waves of

There has also always been a steady flow of immigrants from North America, Britain, France, Benelux and Scandinavia, South Africa and Australasia – immigrants prepared to forgo a comfortable life to rebuild Zion. Golda Meir, prime minister from 1969 to 1974, grew up in America, while former President Chaim Herzog was born in Belfast. There are prejudices against newcomers, but immigrants can eventually reach the top despite their heavily accented and awkward Hebrew.

Nurtured by determined government attempts towards social integration, the cultural mosaic becomes a melting pot over several generations. Contemporary Israeli music attests to the fusion between east and west.

newcomers into its society. Jews have come from Russia before the revolution, from Germany and Austria fleeing the Nazis, from Poland, Hungary and Romania out of the ashes of the Holocaust, from Iraq, Syria, the Yemen and North Africa escaping Arab anti-Zionism, from Latin America and Turkey fleeing cruel military juntas, from Iran escaping the ayatollahs, and most recently from the Soviet Union and Ethiopia.

Left, an official in Jerusalem Post Office's dead letter department, which receives hundreds of sacks of mail addressed to God, Jesus, etc. **Above**, a Franciscan waters a garden in Galilee.

Food, too, produces interesting combinations: felafel and chips, goulash and couscous, chicken soup and kubbe.

A stable economy: Ben-Gurion built Israel's economy around the all powerful Histadrut trade union movement. Onto this socialist base – which encompasses agricultural production through the kibbutz collectives and moshav cooperatives, much of the health service and industrial conglomerates that include the country's largest bank – a dynamic capitalist system has been grafted. In the 1980s, when three-digit inflation raged, Israelis spoke of their "muddled" economy as opposed to the "mixed" economies of Western Europe.

But since 1986 economic order has been restored, with manageable inflation and impressive economic growth averaging 6 percent annually since 1990.

Meanwhile, the Histadrut is in decline. Many of its unprofitable assets have been sold off. Even so, union membership today is remarkably universal, including not only the blue-collar industrial workforce but also senior management up to the highest echelons as well as white-collar professionals. Visitors may be surprised to find suddenly that all the banks are on strike, or that doctors are receiving only emergency cases. The high-status composition of its membership has seen the Histadrut retain much of its power and influ-

mated and computerised mining techniques, the Dead Sea Works exports $500 million worth of goods a year. Elsewhere, Israel must rely on know-how rather than nature. Nowhere epitomises Israel's prosperity more tangibly than the glistening, glass high-rises of the Diamond Exchange in Ramat Gan, adjacent to Tel Aviv. This is the nerve-centre of a $5 billion-a-year export industry in polished diamonds, precious stones and jewellery.

Other exports include high-tech machinery, computer software and electronics goods, agricultural produce and petrochemicals, with some 40 percent of goods sold to Western Europe, a further 30 percent purchased in North America and 20 percent sold to the Far

ence when union movements elsewhere in the world have lost their significance. All the same, although the Histadrut is still capable of calling a general strike, its power has been diluted by a combination of Likud rule and the kind of competitive-edged capitalism needed to sell commodities overseas.

For the fact is that Israel must export to survive. The early 1990s saw the country selling overseas about $12 billion worth of goods a year. By 1996 the figure exceeded $20 billion. This has been accomplished with almost no natural resources save for the potash, bromine and other minerals extracted from the Dead Sea. Through efficient auto-

East. From developments as diverse as new strains of fruit, metal coils to remove the hair on women's legs, colour imaging systems for publishing and Uzi machine guns, Israeli manufacturers are best at improvising according to market needs. As an associate member of the European Union and with a free trade pact with the US, Israel has tariff-free access to the world's two largest markets.

Israel also enjoys an income approaching $3 billion a year from tourism, and a similar sum from donations by supporters of the country. These donations are channelled through organisations such as the Jewish Agency, responsible for bringing immigrants to Israel, and the Jewish National Fund, which takes care of aforestation. World Jewry also gives generous support.

In addition, aid from the United States, amounts to over $3 billion a year. This aid was initiated in the 1970s when Israel was perceived as an important military ally of America against the Soviet Union. In the post-Cold War era, such help cannot be taken for granted. US aid is viewed ambivalently by Israelis. It has allowed them to build an affluent society, but the money also makes them more dependent on the diplomatic desires of the US.

The quest for peace: The main anxiety caused by dependence on the US concerns peace and territorial compromise. Many Israelis fear Yasser Arafat, begun in 1993. The difficulties of setting up a Palestine council to administer and legislate for all the territories occupied by Israel since 1967 (except for East Jerusalem) were a daunting test of diplomatic skills. On the right, the West Bank settlers – one of whose maverick sympathisers killed Rabin – do not wish to yield an inch of land. On the left, the doves of Peace Now have sought to cede the territories unilaterally.

But what of the silent majority in Israel, whose opinions are seldom heard in the international press? It was a large block of these Israelis who switched their allegiance at the last minute from Shimon Peres to Benjamin Netanyahu in the 1996 election. They feared

that American pressure to hand back more land to the Arabs will leave Israel vulnerable to a future Arab attack. The return of the Golan, for example, which the US has pressed for, is strongly opposed and not just by Jewish settlers in the area.

Giving up the Sinai for peace with Egypt was one thing. The Sinai is now a vast, demilitarised desert providing an effective trip-wire should Egypt ever want to attack Israel. Much more fraught with difficulties were the negotiations between Yitzhak Rabin and

Left, a female army instructor teaches a new recruit. **Above**, children at the festival of Purim.

that Peres was giving away too much too quickly, and that the Hamas terrorists were exploiting the vacuum. These centrist voters want Prime Minister Netanyahu to continue the peace process but at a slower pace.

However, Netanyahu comes from an ideological camp bitterly opposed to territorial compromise. The question is whether he is a pragmatist or an ideologue. Time will tell whether his shift to the centre was a cynical ploy to assume power and impose his right-wing agenda, or a genuine reading of Middle East realities. If he stalls, then domestic public opinion, American pressure and Arab sanctions will be brought to bear.

PEOPLE

The only valid generalisation to make about Israelis is that there is no such thing as a typical Israeli. The ingathering of the exiles has brought Jews to Israel from 80 countries and, beneath their often surly surface, Israelis can behave with Latin American panache, European civility or overwhelming Middle Eastern hospitality.

Israeli society itself has distinctly different sectors. These include black hatted ultra-Orthodox Jews and more modern Orthodox Jewry as well as secular European Jews and more traditional Oriental Jews. New immigrants from the former Soviet Union comprise 15 percent of Israeli society, while Ethiopian Jews add African colour to the social landscape. Slick Tel Aviv yuppies are becoming more prevalent, but the pioneering spirit still lives on and rugged kibbutznikim, bronzed and bearded, can still be found.

Kibbutzim aside, Israelis are predominantly urban and suburban creatures. More than half the population lives in the country's three largest cities. Jerusalem has a population of 600,000 and over 2 million people live in the Greater Tel Aviv area and an additional 500,000 in the Haifa Bay conurbation.

The Arabs are more rural. About one-fifth of Israel's population of nearly 6 million belong to the Arab minority, which is mainly Muslim but also includes Christians and Druze. Many Arabs are still loyal to their nomadic Bedouin tribes even though they have moved to permanent accommodation. Israeli Arabs don't include the 2 million Palestinians of the West Bank and Gaza.

Israel's other minorities include several thousand Circassians, Turkic Muslims from the Southern Russian Caucasian mountains brought to the region in the 1800s to protect Ottoman interests. The Samaritans are an ancient Samarian sect, and the Baha'i religion has its world headquarters in Haifa. The Negev town of Dimona is home to several hundred Black Hebrews and in the 1970s the country took in over 100 Vietnamese boat people. Israel also has an estimated 200,000 guest workers.

Educational institutions and the army have been powerful influences for social assimilation. The Hebrew language enhances social cohesion and, although communities often jealously guard their distinct Jewish traditions, inter-marriage between European and Oriental Jewry is common. Some figures put it as high as 25 percent.

The native-born Israeli is often known as a *sabra* after the prickly pear, a cactus fruit which has a spiky outside but a sweet and succulent heart. This is an appropriate description of young Israelis who are brash, self-confident and always in a rush. Yet they can also be surprisingly considerate, and their openness and curiosity delights the gregarious as much as it intimidates the reticent.

Preceding pages: Georgian Jews in traditional dress at Ashdod; and Orthodox Jews in Mea She'arim. **Left**, the rugged charm of the Sabra.

For many non-Jews the term secular Jewry would seem to be a contradiction in terms. Many Jews, too, argue that Judaism is a religion and not a nationality and, therefore, Jews can be Orthodox or not Orthodox but never secular. Such semantic discussions overlook the realities of everyday Israeli life. The fact is that most Israeli Jews define themselves as both secular and Jewish.

It is difficult to ascertain who is a secular Jew. By and large European Jews clearly identify themselves as either secular, Orthodox or ultra-Orthodox and tend to be more extreme in their allegiances. It was Ashkenazi secular Jews from Europe who were the architects of the state in the early 1900s. Oriental Jews, who in the main came later in the 1940s and '50s are more traditional. Many non-religious Oriental Jews have assimilated European Jewish contempt for Orthodoxy but most remain more respectful and even deferential.

Indeed the divide between Ashkenazi and Oriental Jewry remains today. But intermarriage is common and most Oriental Jews have made it out of the poor apartment buildings constructed for them when they arrived. In the most senior positions in the current government Foreign Minister David Levy was born in Morocco, while Defence Minister Yitzhak Mordechai comes originally from Iraq and Deputy Prime Minister Moshe Katzav hails from Iran.

But virtually all of the most impoverished Jewish Israelis are Oriental Jews, and it is this sector that is antagonistic to Ashkenazi Jewry. This deprived sector of society also tends to have strong religious leanings and is hostile to the secularism of Ashkenazi Jewry.

Politics and religion: Israel's secular Jews share the liberal, universalist views of their North American and Western European counterparts. Democracy, freedom of expression and minority rights are the sacred values. They would not mind if their daughter wanted to marry a non-Jew and would quite likely be more bothered if she brought home a black-hatted ultra-Orthodox Jew. Though secular Jews firmly hold the reins of political power, there is an almost paranoid belief that they are slipping out of their hands.

Secular Jewry, especially in Jerusalem, feels it is a besieged community, threatened demographically by both the Arab minority and ultra-Orthodox Jewry, both of whom have much higher birth rates.

Secular Jewry often complains about the existence of Orthodox religious parties, but the fact is that it is impossible in Israel to separate politics from religion. The left-wing Meretz faction, which together with allies on the left of the Labour Party probably commands the support of a third of Israelis,

spearheads the political fight against orthodox attempts to legislate over the definition of a Jew, social issues like abortion or the import of un-kosher meat and pig rearing, or practical matters such as the closing of roads on the Sabbath.

But it would be a mistake to assume by reading the political map from left to right that secular Jewry only commands minority support. There is often as much support on the right for secular causes. Prime Minister Benjamin Netanyahu himself, like most of the Likud leaders, is a staunchly secular figure. His personal lifestyle has never endeared him to his religious bedfellows in his coalition government. He is currently married to his third wife, and his second wife was not Jewish.

Indeed the Tzomet bloc within the Likud, led by Rafael Eitan, is known for its anti-clerical leanings. But political expediency has led to an alliance between the essentially anti-religious Likud and religious elements. The Likud is reluctant to relinquish the West Bank and Gaza for security and nationalistic reasons, while the religious cherish the biblical concept of the Land of Israel. Moreover,

the Likud has traditionally relied on support from the Oriental Jewish communities, who incline towards tradition.

Sentimental attachment to Judaism: If non-Jews and sometimes Diaspora Jews are surprised by the extent to which Israel's secular majority disregards religious practice, it can be misleading to think that Israelis have no regard for religion. It is difficult for outsiders to know where lines are drawn between the acceptable and unacceptable. Take dietary laws, for example. McDonald's, the multi-

Left and **above**, Ashkenazi faces exude a sun-washed, healthy diversity.

national hamburger chain, undertook detailed market research before moving into Israel. The result: bacon Macmuffins were non-starters, but cheeseburgers were introduced successfully even though kosher laws prohibit the mixing of meat and milk. But bread is not permissible during Passover, so McDonald's serves cheeseburgers in potato flour buns.

On more substantive issues such as marriage and burial, opinion polls consistently show that the majority of Israelis support the Orthodox monopoly of these rites. This has greatly anguished the Reform and Conservative movements, imported to Israel from America, which attempt to adapt Judaism to the modern age, and in particular to integrate women into the synagogue service.

The fact is that secular Israelis have Zionism, which remains an ideology capable of drawing a high level of commitment to the building of the state and is closely linked to conservative family values. And even the most outwardly secular of Jews still tends to have an inner belief in the essential Jewish values – belief in God and a divine plan. This fills the spiritual vacuum. In the wake of Yitzhak Rabin's assassination young Israelis were able to cope with their grief over the death of a loved leader.

Family values: Like the post-Christian West so post-Jewish Israel suffers from rising crime, violence, drug addiction and inner-city poverty. But despite a growing divorce rate family ties remain strong and there is a deep respect for symbols of state as well as a high motivation to serve in the army.

Deceptively, secular Israel is at once both radical and conservative. The long-haired teenager with an earring through his nose, for example, is happy to have a short back and sides and submit to army discipline at the age of 18. The divisions in Israeli society, though real, are misleading. The assassination of Yitzhak Rabin, a left of centre, secular Ashkenazi, by Yigal Amir, a right-wing religious Jew from a Yemen-born family, seems to epitomise enmities. But this violent deed was an astounding, exceptional event. When the chips are down Israelis have a surprising capacity to join ranks.

ORTHODOX AND ULTRA-ORTHODOX JEWRY

To the non-Orthodox Jew these two groups have much in common. Both strictly observe the all-encompassing world of *halacha* – Jewish Orthodox practice. This means that the men keep their heads covered and pray at least three times a day. Kosher dietary laws are strictly followed and the Sabbath is a day for absolute abstention from work, including "lighting a spark", thus making travelling, cooking, switching on a light and even smoking prohibited activities.

The diverse head coverings of the men often indicate degrees of Orthodoxy. Generally, the larger the *kippa* (skull cap) the more Orthodox the wearer. The *kippot* range from the small knitted variety, worn by the modern Orthodox, to the large knitted and black *kippot* of the mainstream Orthodox and the large black skull caps beneath even larger black hats of the ultra-Orthodox.

It is usually the clothes of the woman rather than the size of the man's *kippa* which hints at the Orthodox Jew's lifestyle. A man with a small knitted *kippa* is likely to be accompanied by a woman with "immodest" jeans or other tight clothing. Women in the large knitted *kippa* community will wear long dresses and keep their arms covered but may not be wearing wigs or head scarves.

Women in the ultra-Orthodox communities are literally kept under wraps. Not a square inch of flesh is seen other than the face and hands, and female visitors to the ultra-Orthodox quarters of Mea Shearim in Jerusalem and Bnei Brak near Tel Aviv should heed warnings not to wear immodest dress. Those in violation of this edict may be sworn and spat at and even stoned.

The ultra-Orthodox woman cannot be in an enclosed room with men other than her immediate relatives. At weddings and parties women will sit in a separate area.

Ultra-Orthodox Jewish society comprises a collection of sects as much medieval Eastern European as biblical in their origins. On Saturdays and festivals the men wear fur hats more suitable for a Russian winter than a Middle Eastern summer.

From anti-Zionism to Ultra-Zionism: Historically Jews were by definition Orthodox and three or four centuries ago all of Eastern European Jewry would have followed a moral code similar to that of Mea Shearim today. Growing secularism in 19th-century Christian Europe compelled Jews to find other outlets of cultural expression, and Zionism emerged as a secular movement. Therefore, at first all Orthodox Jews were anti-Zionist, opposed to the use of Hebrew, the holy tongue, for everyday use and the notion that a Jewish state could contemplate any degree of separation between synagogue and state.

However, in the 1990s a strong national

religious movement emerged, combining the nationalistic values of Zionism with the tenets of Orthodoxy. With its own kibbutzim and workers' movements, it was bolstered by the mass immigration of Oriental Jewry which had deeper ties with Jewish tradition.

Commanding the political support of about 10 percent of the population, the national religious movement, which historically contained strong elements of liberalism, veered sharply to the right after 1967. Holding the Land of Israel to be sacred, the Gush Emunim settlers' movement sprung up from the national religious movement. It has come to be perceived as the fiercest opponent of territorial compromise. The national religious movement has its own religious schools distinct from their secular counterparts.

Ultra-Orthodox Jewry, known in Hebrew as Haredim, also has its own education system. These black-clad communities are at best critical of Zionism and at worst still opposed to the Jewish State. Each sect has its own rabbinical leaders and most of them sit in New York rather than Jerusalem.

The largest and best known Haredi sect is the Lubatvitchers. Under the late Rabbi

Schneerson, who was revered by his followers as a messianic figure, the Lubatvitchers took a pro-Israel hawkish stand supporting continuation of Jewish control of the West Bank. The Satmar, on the other hand, also a New York headquartered sect, refuses to recognise the government of Israel as legitimate representatives of the Jewish people.

An extreme Jerusalem based sect called Netorei Karta even supported the PLO when its charter called for the destruction of the Jewish state. Netorei Karta believes that the

Left, at the Western Wall in Jerusalem. **Above**, an Orthodox Jew at prayer.

Zionists are worse than the Nazis, for while the Nazis sought to destroy the Jews physically, the Zionists are spiritually destroying the Jewish people.

Prayer power: All these sects, even those with pro-Zionist leanings, tend to have contempt for the institutions of modern Israel – the flag, the army, the Supreme Court, etc. Few ultra-Orthodox Jews serve in the army and those who do will often end up in the Rabbinical corps checking that kitchens are kosher. Even the right wing Lubavitchers will argue that praying for the strength of Israel is as important as fighting for it.

As a result secular Jewry detests ultra-Orthodox Jewry for its lack of patriotism, while ultra-Orthodox Jewry holds secular Jewry in contempt for its non-religious lifestyle. Orthodox Jewry is often caught in the middle justifying and condemning both sides.

Individual prejudice aside, secular Israel is tolerant towards Orthodoxy. This is mainly because the ultra-Orthodox parties hold the balance of power between left and right. Moreover, many Jews believe that to harass the ultra-Orthodox communities could leave them open to charges of anti-Semitism.

Oriental Jewry: Religious Jews from Asian and African countries have never fitted comfortably into the European pattern of sects, though Israel's European religious establishment did succeed in imposing black hats and suits on large numbers of Jews from the Yemen and North Africa.

But ultimately religious leaders like the charismatic former Sephardi Chief Rabbi Ovadia Yosef, who wears oriental robes rather than a black hat, have prevailed. His Shas political party today controls nearly 10 percent of Knesset seats. Much of Shas's support comes from traditional rather than Orthodox Oriental Jews indicating that the divide between observant and non-observant Oriental Jews is narrower than between their European counterparts.

Overall, an estimated 20 percent of Israeli Jews are Orthodox. This number has remained constant over the past decade for, though Orthodox Jewry has a much higher birth rate, the overwhelming majority of new Jewish immigrants from Russia are secular.

"Let My People Go" was the slogan coined by campaign activists pushing for the right of Soviet Jewry to emigrate freely. Nobody believed it would ever actually happen even in the era of détente in the 1970s when nearly 400,000 Soviet Jews were allowed out of the Soviet Union, about half of them reaching Israel while the rest headed for the US.

But as glasnost gained momentum in the late 1980s the right to emigrate was suddenly granted to Soviet Jewry during the final months of the decade. For Israel the event

keeping their options open with an anxious eye on political developments.

Transforming Israel: During the 1990s, Russian-speaking Jewry surpassed Moroccans as Israel's largest immigrant group. By 1996 more than 700,000 had arrived in the latest wave of immigration, making more than a million Soviet-born Israelis, when combined with the émigrés from the 1970s and Soviet veterans from earlier in the century.

As a result, Israel's urban landscape has a decidedly Slavic feel. Cyrillic shop signs

was as momentous as the breaching of the Berlin Wall. It was like a dam bursting. During the course of 1990 more than 200,000 Jews reached Israel, while in 1991 more than 170,000 arrived. After the break up of the Soviet Union the pace slackened with some 60,000 Jews emigrating to Israel each year from the former Soviet republics.

Not every Russian-speaking Jew has wanted to come to Israel. The US has allowed in about 40,000 every year, while Germany, Canada and other Western countries have taken in tens of thousands more. Moreover, more than a million Jews remain by choice in the former Soviet Union,

abound, vying for space with Hebrew, English and Arabic lettering. News-stands are bursting with Russian-language publications, and in some suburbs of Tel Aviv and Haifa, Russian is the lingua franca.

The full political and economic potential of Russian-speaking Jewry is yet to be realised. True, it was these new immigrants who, despite their hawkish tendencies, voted in the more dovish Labour Party in 1992 as a protest against Likud neglect of their economic needs. Then, disillusioned by both Labour and Likud, the renowned refusnik Natan Scharansky, who had spent years in Soviet prisons fighting for the right to emigrate, set up his own immigrant party, Yisrael Ve'Aliyah, and gained an impressive seven seats (6 percent of the vote) in the 1996 Knesset elections. Scharansky joined Prime Minister Benjamin Netanyahu's right-wing government haggling over the negotiations in Russian with Yvette Liberman, the Russian-born director of Netanyahu's office.

The newcomers may also cause crowding in the professions. Generally speaking, the latest wave of Russian immigrants has a high educational profile. They are academically trained scientists and engineers, musicians and teachers. Even before this immigration started, Israel had the world's highest proportion of doctors per capita. With 15,000 more doctors among the newcomers, many have not been able to qualify for medical licences or get jobs in their professions.

But it takes time to master Hebrew and adjust to the more assertive behaviour of a Western society. Too often, Russian-speaking newcomers expect to be given jobs, housing and other benefits, and it takes them time to realise they must get these for themselves. It usually takes a year of sweeping streets or washing dishes before an immigrant finds a job in his or her profession.

Such immigrants have changed the demographic balance of Israel. Before their arrival, Israel had a small Oriental Jewish majority. Russian Jewry has tipped the scales back in favour of Ashkenazi Jewry, although some 10 percent of these newcomers are Oriental Jews from the ancient Persian-speaking communities in Georgia, Azerbaijan and the Russian Caucasus as well as Uzbekistan.

Kosher and un-kosher: In the main Russian-speaking newcomers are Ashkenazi and secular, if they are Jewish at all. Between 20 and 40 percent of newcomers are not halachically Jewish. They qualify for Jewish citizenship by virtue of having one Jewish grandparent but do not meet the Orthodox Jewish requirement of having a Jewish mother.

Even those Jews who are rabbinically kosher know little about their Jewish heritage after growing up under the Soviet regime. Israel was already a highly secular society before the newcomers arrived. Once acculturated, these immigrants are bound to push for more secular legislation, disturbing the delicate religious–secular status quo. At present a large number of Russian-speaking newcomers cannot be buried in Jewish cemeteries or have a Jewish marriage ceremony.

Nor are these newcomers Zionists. The immigrants of the 1970s risked imprisonment in order to leave for Israel. The major-

ity of those who reached Israel in 1990 and 1991 had a profound sense of Jewish identity; they simply put out their wings and migrated with the flock at the first opportunity. But recent arrivals have a less clear agenda. They seek a more secure economic life amid the greater opportunities of Israel.

The latest wave of immigrants represents over 20 percent of the Jewish population. Undoubtedly they and their children will assimilate Zionist norms of allegiance to the state, service in the army, and fluency in Hebrew. In parallel, influenced by the secularism of these immigrants, Israel is likely to move further away from traditional Judaism.

Left, Russian immigrants arrive at Lod Airport in the early 1960s. **Right**, Russian-language newspapers are now available in Israel.

The dramatic airlifts of Ethiopian Jews from the heart of Africa to the Promised Land in 1984 and 1991 captured the world's imagination. For centuries, Ethiopian Jews cherished the dream of one day returning to Jerusalem. The dream came true, but the reality has been somewhat different from their expectations.

Before arriving in Israel, most Ethiopian Jews had been semi-literate subsistence farmers living in simple villages, usually without electricity. Being thrust into a fast-moving,

of the Ethiopians. Thus Ethiopian Jews are required to undergo symbolic conversion to Judaism by being immersed in a ritual bath. In addition the *kessim* are not permitted to officiate at marriages.

The younger generation (half the community is younger than 18) has been adept at assimilating Israeli values. The vigour with which they have protested their grievances through demonstrations, the media and political lobbying bodes well for the future. For their part, the Israeli establishment has allo-

high-tech society has been traumatic, especially for those people who were over 30 when they arrived.

Some of Israel's 50,000-strong Ethiopian Jewish community have done well. Adisu Massala, for example, was elected to the Knesset in 1996 as a Labour Party delegate, and Belaynesh Zevadiah became Israel's vice-consul in Chicago. These success stories are both children of the *kessim*, the community's religious leaders.

Alienation: The sense of alienation felt by many Ethiopians has been exacerbated by the reluctance of Israel's rabbinical authorities to recognise the unequivocal Jewishness

cated major resources for the education of the young generation and has introduced positive discrimination measures, such as more generous mortgages than those available to other new immigrants.

While racism against the Ethiopians is rare (the most anti-Ethiopian racist sector in Israeli society is probably found among the new immigrants from Russia), the community sometimes suffers as a result of excessive political correctness. For example, the Health Ministry decided that Ethiopians were not suitable blood donors because of a higher incidence of Aids, tuberculosis and other diseases. Instead of the decision being announced publicly, a secret memo was sent to blood donation staff asking them to accept Ethiopian blood and then throw it away. The discovery of the policy provoked a storm of protest. An enquiry found that the policy was justified but that its underhand method of implementation was inappropriate.

The Ethiopians began reaching Israel via Sudan in the early 1980s and Operation Moses in 1984 saw 7,000 airlifted to Israel. Most had trekked hundreds of miles across the desert to the Sudanese border and many

tribes. The Ethiopians themselves claim to be the descendants of King Solomon and the Queen of Sheba.

Cut off from world Jewry for two millennia, the community has sustained traditions remarkably similar to mainstream Judaism. There are distinctions, though; for example, the Ethiopians took with them into exile the Five Books of Moses and the stories of the Prophets, but have no knowledge of the Oral Law, which was codified only after the fall of the Second Temple in AD 70.

had died en route. Even more dramatically, 14,000 Ethiopians were flown to Israel in Operation Solomon in a 24-hour period in 1991. These Jews had gathered in Addis Ababa over the course of a year but had been prevented from leaving by the Marxist regime. The Israeli Air Force rescued them just as the regime was toppled by rebels.

The origins of Ethiopian Jews are shrouded in mystery. Known in Ethiopia as *falashas* (invaders), they are believed by some scholars to be remnants of Dan, one of the 10 lost

In modern times Ethiopian Jewry was located in two regions of Africa. Those Jews who reached Israel in the early 1980s came primarily from Tigre, while the subsequent wave originated principally from Gondar. The two groups use the same Amharic alphabet but speak different Ethiopic languages.

All but several hundred Ethiopian Jews have now left Africa. Israel has rejected the claims of the Falash Mura, Ethiopian Christians who claim they converted from Judaism in the 19th century, who wanted to emigrate to Israel. But immediate relatives of Falash Mura mistakenly brought out of Africa and granted citizenship are entitled to settle.

Left, an Ethiopian Jewish soldier guards a tomb at Hebron. **Above**, Ethiopian crafts.

ISRAELI ARABS

Not all the Arab inhabitants of Palestine heeded the call of the surrounding states (and "promptings" from the nascent Israeli army) to flee their homes when Israel was established, with the promise that they would return within weeks once the Jewish state had been snuffed out by the invading armies.

About 150,000 remained and numbers have since grown to their present 950,000. Half of Israel's Arab population is urbanised in the towns and villages of the Galilee. There are large Arab communities in Nazareth, Haifa, Ramle, Jaffa and Jerusalem.

Israeli Arabs – 77 percent are Muslim, 13 percent Christian and 10 percent are Druze and Bedouin – present the real paradox of being at once Arab, with linguistic, historic, cultural, religious and familial ties to the Arab world, and also citizens of a state which, for 38 years, has been in conflict with that world. And yet, Israel's Arabs have managed to walk the tightrope.

The only legal discrimination against Israeli Arabs is that they are not liable to military conscription – although they may volunteer – because it is thought to be unreasonable to ask them to fight against their co-religionists and kinsmen (only the small Druze community is subject to the draft – and that at their own request).

But exemption from military service is a double-edged sword. The army is, after all, the great equaliser, the shared national experience, the common thread that unites Israelis from wildly different backgrounds. Exclusion from it inevitably involves social handicaps. In a more tangible form, it renders Israeli Arabs ineligible for certain jobs and state benefits.

In spite of this and other disabilities, the Arabs of Israel have flourished, making great strides in health, education and generally improved living standards.

One indicator of the process of change is education. Arab illiteracy has plunged from 95 percent in 1948 to just 5 percent today. While in 1948, only 32.5 percent attended grade school, by 1982, 92 percent had five to eight years of education, and more than 30 percent nine to 12 years, reflecting the growing numbers of Arabs enrolling in Israeli institutes of higher learning.

Most Israeli Arab parents choose to send their children to Arabic-language schools, which combine instruction in Arab history and culture with that of the Jews.

Today around 6,000 Arabs are studying at Israeli universities. Others travel abroad to study, but not, like the Arabs from the West Bank and Gaza, to the Arab world because they carry Israeli passports.

The impact of education and involvement with Israel's vigorously open and democratic society has been profound. These days most young Arabs live with their own Western-style nuclear families and are economically independent of their elders. There is still, to be sure, strong attachment to traditional values and customs, but these are tinged with a clear preference for the comforts of the affluent West.

Israeli laws granting women equal rights have helped to liberalise attitudes towards women in Arab society. The changing aspirations of women (and their husbands) is reflected in the birthrate – down from an astonishing average of 8.5 children per family in 1968 to 5.5 in 1982 and expected to continue falling during the 1990s to the Jewish average of 3.2 children per family.

For all that, there is a strong trend towards polarisation of Jewish and Arab Israelis, though programmes to foster understanding between youngsters are arranged by Israel's Education Ministry.

A spiral of radicalism is not inevitable. A new breed of young Arab mayors and leaders – educated in Israel and at ease with the Israeli system – is emerging at a grass-roots level. They are demanding that facilities in their areas be brought up to the standard of their Jewish neighbours, and their style demonstrates a self-confidence that is at once proudly Arab and unequivocally Israeli.

The increasing Arab clout in the political arena is another significant development. At present, there are seven Arab members of the Knesset out of a total of 120, representing a broad spectrum of opinion.

Left, an Arab Jerusalemite presents a handsome profile to the city.

DRUZE

Although some of the first clashes between the Jewish pioneers in the 1880s and the local residents were with Druze villagers in Metulla and other parts of Galilee, Israel's Druze community has traditionally been loyal to the Israeli state. Young Druze are conscripted into the Israel Defence Forces, and many serve in the regular army in the paratroops, armoured corps and reconnaisance units and border police. Traditionally a warlike people, always ready to defend their interests, they have proved to be first-class soldiers and large numbers of Druze have been decorated for bravery.

In the Lebanon war of 1982–84, Israel's Druze found themselves in a delicate position, when the IDF was aligned with Christian forces in Lebanon fighting the Lebanese Druze. It is a tribute to the strength of the friendship between the Jewish and Druze that their alliance survived this period.

The Druze have been a persecuted minority in the Middle East since they broke off from mainstream Islam in the 11th century, accepting the claims to divinity of the Egyptian Caliph El-Hakim Abu Ali el-Mansur. For this reason they tend to inhabit inaccessible mountain ranges, where they can defend themselves against their enemies. Most Druze live today in the Mount Lebanon region of Lebanon, in Jebel Druze in Syria, and some 70,000 of them in the hills of Galilee and on the Carmel range in Israel, with a further 15,000 in the Golan Heights.

There are records of Druze communities in Galilee as early as the 13th century, but the first Mount Carmel settlement was established in 1590 when Syrian Druze fled their homes after an abortive revolt against the Turkish sultan.

Their villages are not very different from Arab villages in Galilee and the coastal plain, although the elders do not wear a black headband with their *keffiye* head-dresses, as the Arabs do. The older Druze tend to cultivate impressive moustaches. The women dress in modern style, the younger ones in jeans and short-sleeved blouses. The young men are indistinguishable from Israeli Jews, and indeed many of them affect Hebrew names, such as Rafi or Ilan.

There are tendencies both to assimilate into the Jewish society, and to convert to Islam and assimilate into the local Arab society; but these are definitely minority movements, and most Druze are proud of their identity and culture and do not intermarry with other communities.

Some Israeli Druze live in mixed villages, notably Pekiin in Galilee, where they coexist alongside their Christian Arab neighbours and some Jewish families, who have lived there since Second Temple times.

The Druze were recognised as a separate religious community with their own courts in 1957. Their religion is said to be similar to that of the Isma'ili Muslims. The sheikhs, the religious leaders of the community, guard its secrets, and the ordinary Druze are simply required to observe the basic moral laws prohibiting murder, adultery, and theft.

They have their interpretations of Jewish, Muslim and Christian prophets, believing their missions were revealed to a select group, first of whom was Jethro, the father-in-law of Moses. One of their religious festivals is an annual pilgrimage to the putative grave of Jethro, near the Horns of Hittim in Galilee.

Traditionally the Druze were successful hill farmers; but with the development of modern agriculture this declined. However, their traditional weaving, carpet-making, basketwork and other crafts are flourishing. Daliyat el-Carmel, south of Haifa, has the biggest market offering Druze wares, and is a popular spot for tourists. Most young Druze work in industry and the service sector.

Serving alongside the Druze in the minorities unit of the IDF are the Circassians, which in Israel number nearly 3,000. The Circassians are a Caucasian mountain people, originating in Russia; most of them are blond, and have blue or green eyes. Although many of the Russian Circassians are professing Christians, the Middle East branch of the people are Muslims. Almost all the Israeli Circassians live in the village of Kfar Kama, overlooking Lake Kinneret in Galilee, and Rechaniya.

Left, a Druze village elder in Pekiin looks dapper in his traditional clothing.

BEDOUIN

The Bedouin is the quintessential Arab, the nomad herdsman, dressed in flowing robes, riding his camel across the sands, pitching his tent under the palms before riding on to his next camping site. Like many romantic images, this one is false – or at least rather out of date.

Some 20 percent of Israel's 70,000 Bedouin live in Galilee and the coastal plain in settled villages, virtually indistinguishable from other Arab villages.

In the Negev traditions are stronger, and you can still be invited for coffee, reclining on cushions under the black goat's hair, but few Bedouin still live in the traditional manner. Some still live in tents; more possess camels and herd sheep and goats; but increasing numbers are moving into permanent housing, and work in construction, industry, services and transportation.

They farm the loess soil extensively, growing mostly barley and wheat, but also cucumbers, tomatoes, peppers, watermelons, and almonds, figs and vines. For irrigation, they use both dams, which they have built themselves, and former Nabatean structures, which they have restored. They also use ancient water cisterns which they have excavated and, of course, old wells.

While the Bedouin are not conscripted into the Israel Defence Forces, many serve in the army as scouts and trackers, and several have reached senior rank.

Scores of Bedouin fled from the Negev from 1947 to 1949, around the time of Israel's War of Independence, but later returned. The situation was stabilised in 1953, when a census was conducted, all those present at the time being accepted as citizens of Israel.

Formerly wandering freely between Transjordan, the Judean Desert, the Negev and Sinai, the Bedouin were forced to recognise the new international realities in the early 1950s. Israel's Bedouin are now confined to an area east of Beersheba going north as far as the former border with Jordan, and south as far as Dimona. This is only some 10

percent of the area over which they once wandered, but includes some excellent farming land. Today, there is no tribe that does not farm as well as herd.

The traditional life of the Bedouin shepherd, which involved moving their herds from pasture to pasture, is a thing of the past and their camps have long been permanent in the Negev; but their nomadic tradition, and their tendency to live with their dwellings spread out all over the desert, have made it difficult to plan modern villages for them.

Today, most of the major tribal centres have their own elementary schools and there is now a modern high school at Kuseifa near Arad. Bedouin take education seriously, walking more than 10 miles to school where necessary. It is a common sight, when driving from Beersheba to Arad or Dimona, to see a Bedouin boy, walking through the desert, his nose buried in the pages of a book, or sitting on a rock, writing in a notebook.

Bedouin arts and crafts still exist, with a flourishing home industry, based on weaving, sewing and embroidery. These wares are on sale, notably in the Beersheba market every Thursday, a popular tourist attraction.

Left, tending the fire in a Bedouin guest tent. **Right**, displaying touristic wares at Beersheba Bedouin market.

CHRISTIANS

Nowhere in the world is the observant traveller more aware of the rich and fascinating diversity of Christianity than in the Holy Land. On a morning's stroll through the Old City of Jerusalem, you might encounter Greek Orthodox or Syrian Orthodox monks, Ethiopian and Coptic clergymen, Armenian priests, Catholic priests and, without knowing it, clerics and scholars from virtually every Protestant church in Christendom.

There is no mystery to the extraordinary variety of Christian congregations in the Holy Land. From the time of the Byzantines (AD 324–636) through the era of the Crusader kingdoms (l099–1291) and 400 years of Ottoman rule (1517–1917) until today, churches sought to establish – then struggled to retain – a presence in the land where their faith was born.

The result is a plethora of denominations served by 2,500 clergy from almost every nation on earth. The Greek Orthodox, Russian Orthodox, Roman Catholics, Syrian Catholics, Maronites, Greek Catholics, Armenian Catholics, Chaldean Catholics, Armenian Orthodox, Syrian Orthodox (Jacobites), Copts, Ethiopian Orthodox – all have secured claims, sometimes competing claims, to revered holy sites.

The "younger" churches – the Anglicans, the Church of Scotland, the Seventh Day Adventists, the Pentecostals, the Church of Christ, the Baptists, the Brethren, the Menonnites and the Jehovah's Witnesses – also maintain institutions and congregations.

The founding of Israel provoked unease among the Christians, who were uncertain what to expect from the new Jewish state and were deeply suspicious of Jewish intentions (the Vatican still does not recognise Israel). Nevertheless, Israel's Declaration of Independence spelt out the state's attitude to the diverse faiths within its borders, pledging to "guarantee the freedom of religion, conscience, education and culture (and) safeguard the holy places of all religions."

The Six Day War of 1967, which left Israeli forces in control of the old city of Jerusalem, revived religious misgivings. Yet, the Israeli government has been scrupulous in its attitude towards the rights and preroga-

tives of the churches, adhering to the intricate balance created by the Ottoman rulers and British Mandatory authority in apportioning responsibility for the holy places.

As a result, relations have been good – or at least correct – between the Jewish state and the churches. Indeed at times, the Israeli government has found itself a reluctant referee of intra-Christian rivalries.

A recent phenomenon that is having an impact on the face of the Holy Land and Christian–Jewish relations is the world-wide

growth of Christian Zionism, which regards the birth of the State of Israel as a fulfilment of biblical prophecy. Over the past decades, theological and ecumenical institutions have mushroomed to cater to this movement and enable young Christians to study in Israel.

The "Christian Embassy" in Jerusalem – the focus of much Christian–Zionist activity – has delighted and intrigued many Israelis. But it has dismayed others who fear that the real intention of their proclamations of friendship is the conversion of Jews.

This deeply held suspicion was given expression in vociferous opposition to a Mormon project on 4 acres (1.6 hectares) of prime land overlooking the Old City – a likely precursor of other Christian groups which are seeking a toehold in the Holy Land. Among them, the Apostolic Church of Switzerland, Nigeria's Celestial Church of Christ, the Korean Evangelical Church and the Hope of Israel Church in California.

The work of Christian-Jewish reconciliation is, however, not the sole preserve of the "new" churches. The Roman Catholic order of the Sisters of Zion, established in Jerusalem in 1855 by French Jewish converts to

Christianity, has been working towards such understanding for many years.

Every year, some 250,000 pilgrims visit the order's Ecce Homo Convent next to the Second Station of the Cross on the Via Dolorosa and many stay to hear the sisters speak of Jesus the Jew and of Judaism as the wellspring of their faith. The sisters study Jewish history and the Talmud and sometimes celebrate Mass in Hebrew. They hold classes for Jews and Arabs wanting to learn each other's

Above, Greek Orthodox Christians celebrate Christmas amid the rich surroundings of their church in Bethlehem.

languages, and have set up a department of adult education at the Hebrew University with a convent sister as its administrator.

The Hebrew University boasts yet another Catholic of note: Father Marcel Dubois, a Dominican monk, is chairman of the university's philosophy department.

The grassroots language of Christianity in Israel is Arabic. The great majority of Israel's 100,000 Christians (including the 13,700 Christians of East Jerusalem) are Arabs and the parish clergy who serve them are either Arabs or Arabic-speaking.

The allegiances of Christian Arabs in Israel clearly favour the established Patriarchates: there are 35,000 Greek Catholics; 32,000 Greek Orthodox; and 20,000 Catholics. There are small communities of Anglicans and Lutherans (both churches are stronger on the West Bank than in Israel proper), and despite more than 100 years of missionary work by more than 50 organisations, there are no more than 1,000 local Arab adherents of evangelical churches. There are also about 2,000 Messianic Jews, mostly immigrants from Eastern Europe.

The Roman Catholic Church has established indigenous orders, such as the Rosary Sisters and the Sisters of St Joseph, and at its seminary in Jerusalem trains Arab priests from both Israel and Jordan.

Arab Christians, while growing in numbers and flourishing economically – particularly those living in areas that attract Christian tourism – have been hesitant about asserting themselves politically to press issues of specific Christian concern. As a group, the Christian community displays many of the characteristics of a marginal minority trying to maintain a balance between its Christian identity, Arab nationalism and its delicate relations with its Muslim neighbours – all within the context of a Jewish society.

Nonetheless, an Anglican Arab clergyman is prominent in the Arab–Jewish Progressive List for Peace, a political party which supports the establishment of a Palestinian state on the West Bank. Israel's Greek Orthodox community, on the other hand, traditionally supports the oddest political bedfellow: the Communist Party.

PALESTINIANS

The birth of the Palestinian national movement was a reaction to Zionism. As Jews began buying up Arab land at the turn of the century so the indigenous Arab population was compelled to question its own identity. Historically that identity had revolved around the extended family, the village, the Arab people and Islam. But in the modern world of emerging nations such an identity was either too parochial or too broad.

Just as many Jews and non-Jews originally opposed the notion that the Jews constituted

Jews were unable to counter the militant rejectionism of Syria and Egypt and of local leaders such as Sheikh Haj Amin Husseini.

The tragedy of the Palestinian people was the stubborn inability of its leadership to accept the *fait accompli* of a Jewish state. Arab anger may be understandable, as European anti-Semitism drove Jews back to the Middle East and resulted in the loss of Palestinian land. But attempts to "drive the Jews into the sea" in 1948 and 1967 and the expulsion of over a million Jews from Arab

a nation, so the Palestinians found their legitimacy under fire from both friends and foes. Arabs within Palestine and without spoke of pan-Arabism and of one Arab nation encompassing North Africa and Asia Minor. Often such talk cloaked the expansionist ambitions of Syria, Jordan and Egypt.

Irreconcilable aims: For the Jews, of course, the Palestinian national movement which denied the right of a Jewish State to exist could never be reconciled with Zionist aspirations. Moderate Palestinian leaders as well as the Hashemite kings (King Abdullah and his grandson, King Hussein) who were amenable to national coexistence with the

countries simply saw Israel strengthened territorially and demographically.

The founding of the PLO in 1964 proved to be a crucial stage in the evolution of the Palestinian national entity. Even so, its leader from 1965, Yasser Arafat, found himself in prison in Damascus. The fact is that since the Muslim conquest Palestine had been ruled from Damascus and the region had become known as Lower Syria. Thus the modern Syrians saw Palestine – and for that matter Lebanon and Jordan – as an integral part of the modern Syrian nation.

The Six Day War of 1967, and the further expansion of Israel, saw the PLO come into its own. It was now in Syria's interest to encourage Arafat to regain Arab lands. Before 1967, the West Bank was in Jordanian hands, while Gaza was under Egyptian rule. But if the PLO and its many factions, each owing allegiance to a different Arab leader, were puppets designed to restore Arab sovereignty over as much of Israel as possible, Arafat – and most especially the Palestinians of the West Bank and Gaza – proved to be more independently minded than either Israel or the Arab world had anticipated.

Israel presumed that the Arabs of the West Bank and Gaza would prove as malleable as the Palestinian Arabs who had stayed behind in 1948 and taken up Israeli citizenship. But Israeli Arabs were mainly village people, while the Arabs of Gaza and the West Bank had a large urban intelligentsia who identified strongly with the Palestinian nationalism espoused by Arafat and the PLO. Many of them were Christians.

When given the right to assume Israeli citizenship, the 150,000 Arabs of East Jeru-

Occupation and acrimony: Israel, after its occupation of the West Bank and Gaza in 1967, enjoyed good relations with its newly conquered Palestinian subjects. The Arabs of the West Bank and Gaza, for their part, were beguiled by Israeli liberalism and other Western ways. A free press was set up, universities were established, elections were held for the local municipalities, and the economy flourished. (One reason it flourished, of course, was thanks to the menial work done cheaply by Palestinians in Israel.)

Left, group portrait in an Old City café. **Above**, a Palestinian policeman on duty.

salem refused the offer to a man. It took Israelis, even on the left, many years to appreciate that Palestinian nationalism was not going to go away, just as many progressive Palestinians thought that Zionism was a passing phenomenon.

But while rejecting Israeli hegemony, the Palestinian notables in the West Bank and Gaza also felt alienated from the PLO leadership. Arafat, who built his own organisational hierarchy, first in Jordan, then in Lebanon and finally in Tunis, was often viewed as a wealthy Diaspora leader who represented the millions of Palestinians living in Jordan, Syria, Lebanon, Egypt, the Gulf and elsewhere in the world, but was out of touch with the Palestinians on the front line of Israeli occupation.

The effects of the Intifada: PLO tactics in the 1970s and '80s were a mixture of terrorism and diplomacy. Brutal terrorism against civilians both in Israel and around the world, forced the Palestinian question onto the international agenda. Moreover, Arafat forged powerful alliances with the Soviet bloc and Third World which unswervingly supported the Palestinian cause. But while the PLO was able to cause Israel untold political and economic damage and create a climate of national insecurity, it was unable

to achieve its ultimate goal of an independent Palestinian state.

The momentum for change came from within the West Bank and Gaza. The Intifada began in December 1987 in the Gaza Strip as a spontaneous uprising spawned by resentment against Israeli occupation. Within days, it became an orchestrated campaign against Israeli troops characterised by the throwing of rocks and occasional Molotov cocktails. The rebellion spread to the West Bank.

From the start, the Intifada was designed to make Israeli liberals and the country's Western allies uncomfortable. The objective was to get the international media to show Palestinian women and children defenceless against the might of the Israeli army. True, the defenceless Palestinians were throwing rocks, which can kill and maim, but this only heightened the biblical comparison with David and Goliath. The Palestinians had hit on a winning formula and it was only a matter of time before the Israeli Goliath would be felled.

Moreover, a new, young Palestinian leadership was emerging in the West Bank and Gaza. While it didn't discourage the throwing of stones at the Zionist enemy, it was also prepared to enter into dialogue with Israel. Faisal Husseini, nephew of the arch anti-Zionist Sheikh Haj Amin Husseini, learned fluent Hebrew as a gesture of goodwill towards Israel.

Arafat jumped on the Intifada bandwagon. But it was the local Palestinian leadership that was calling the tune, while Arafat and his entourage in Tunis were looking more and more remote from the Palestinians in the front line. Arafat put out diplomatic feelers, letting it be known that he was prepared to recognise Israel and discontinue terrorist tactics. But a brief flirtation with American diplomats in the late 1980s ended after Arafat was unable to prevent his own people from launching terrorist attacks against Israel. Nor was the right-wing government in Israel prepared even to contemplate an indirect dialogue with Arafat.

Arafat's stock fell even further after he threw his support behind Iraq's Saddam Hussein after the invasion of Kuwait in 1990. This decision isolated Arafat from many of his Arab allies and caused the mass expulsion of the affluent Palestinian communities of the Gulf. The collapse of the Soviet Union, the traditional superpower patron of the PLO, saw Arafat down and, many assumed, out.

Gaza via Madrid and Oslo: Arafat proved more resilient and compromising than many gave him credit for. He was allowed to attend the Madrid peace conference in 1991 as part of the Jordanian delegation. Furthermore, no Palestinian leader of any stature in the occupied territories had emerged to challenge Arafat's primacy during the Intifada.

After the election of the Labour government in Israel in 1992, Arafat seized the olive branch held out by Rabin's dovish advisors, and in less than a year he was shaking hands with the Israeli prime minister on the White

House lawn. In 1994 Arafat came in triumph to Gaza as Israeli troops withdrew from most of the Gaza Strip.

By 1995 the Palestinian Authority's jurisdiction comprised the major West Bank towns, excluding Hebron, and Arafat's rule over more than 2 million Palestinians living in the West Bank and Gaza was confirmed through democratically held elections.

The assumption of power may have brought Arafat international legitimacy, but it also brought problems in its wake. The Hamas, Islamic fundamentalists, stepped into the rejectionist vacuum left by the PLO's acceptance of Israel and carried out a viciously

unacceptable. Nevertheless, a period of consolidation in which the Palestinians focus on economic and social development while putting Israel under diplomatic pressure is likely to ensue. Major terrorist acts, even if committed by Hamas, are likely to push the peace process backwards rather than ahead.

Such a period of consolidation will enable the Palestinian Authority to establish a stable regime, and most importantly to develop a viable economic infrastructure. Until the start of the Intifada, the Palestinian economy was largely dependent on workers travelling each day to employment in Israeli factories, and the Palestinians have been pressuring Israel

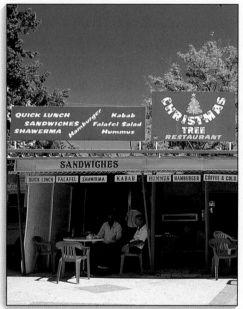

successful bombing campaign inside Israel that came close to derailing the peace process. Under Israeli pressure, Arafat was compelled to crack down on Hamas to save the Oslo accords.

A ragged economy: The principal problems confronting the Palestinians are political and economic. Arafat realised it would be hard to wring more territorial concessions out of the Netanyahu administration, but the status quo giving the Palestinians control of only the major cities of the West Bank was clearly

into re-starting this economic relationship. But good relations with Israel are a prerequisite for this economic symbiosis.

Palestine is in effect a state in the making. It has a flag, its own stamps and currency, it competes in the Olympics and World Cup, and it is a full member of the United Nations. But it has no control over its borders. The Israelis decide who comes in and who doesn't, thus denying entry to millions of Palestinians worldwide – although the Palestinians are not able to absorb so many refugees.

But the breakthrough has been made. Palestine exists. Progress is fraught with obstacles but the peace process is irreversible.

Left, making a point in Jerusalem. **Above**, Arafat-blessed souvenirs; a café in Bethlehem.

GUEST WORKERS

Israel attracts several million tourists each year. But above and beyond short-term visitors, whether they be pilgrims drawn by the holy sites, or sun-worshippers attracted to the country's beaches, Israel also has a large number of longer-term guests.

These include youngsters from around the world wishing to experience Israel in a more profound way on a longer stay, either as a kibbutz volunteer or on an archaeological dig, or perhaps studying in a religious institution. Back-packers travelling around the world often stay longer than planned, attracted by the informality of Israel and the fact that casual work is easy to find and there is plenty of cheap, youth hostel-type accommodation.

In fact, the availability of menial employment in Israel has attracted workers from around the world. There are an estimated 200,000 foreign workers in the country, about half of whom are here on legal contracts. This category includes Romanian construction workers, Thai agricultural labourers and Filipino domestic servants. In addition there are some 100,000 illegal workers, mainly from Nigeria and Ghana, living principally in Tel Aviv where they work as house cleaners and factory hands.

These overseas workers have taken the place of the many Palestinians who worked in Israel until the outbreak of the Intifada. Frequent strikes by the Palestinians and Israeli army closures due to terrorist attacks meant that Israeli employers could no longer rely on their Palestinian workforce and had to seek alternative sources of labour from overseas.

Corrupting the Zionist dream: The abundance of foreign workers in Israel contradicts the Zionist tenet of a Jewish state based on Jewish labour. Israelis decry the situation but, like most middle-class parents in the Western world, would rather their children became managers and professionals than blue-collar or manual workers.

While the legal Romanian and Thai workers tend to be males on contract, sending

money back home to their families, the West Africans are often in Israel en famille, creating a Western Europe guest worker-style situation. The area surrounding the old bus station in Tel Aviv is sometimes dubbed Little Lagos. These workers tend to remain low-profile, fearing expulsion, but their children are usually less passive. Some local authorities accept the children into schools, others don't.

Israel's newspapers regularly carry reports urging mass expulsions or the granting of

legal residency status to those who apply. Some denounce the dilution of the state's Jewish character, others applaud an enriching cosmopolitan element. While the foreign workers remain an important cog in the Israeli economic wheel, the status quo is likely to prevail.

Ultimately, politics as well as economics will dictate the outcome. If Arab terrorism is quelled, then the Israeli government will give preference to Palestinians seeking employment in Israel. In such an instance Israel's guest workers, whether legal or illegal, may suddenly find themselves out of a job and unwelcome.

Left, a worker from Cochin, India, at Nevatim.
Right, the building industry needs guest workers.

The declared policy of successive Chiefs of Staff of the Israel Defence Forces over the past decade has been to make the army smarter. Of course, the generals are talking about technological ability, for a quick glance at the unkempt array of soldiers that seem ever present, in every nook and cranny of the country, suggests that the policy has failed in sartorial terms.

The Israeli army is like no other army in the world. During basic training soldiers learn to salute their superiors, accept orders

without question and stick to clearly defined dress codes. Thereafter rules are made to be broken. Officers are never saluted, orders can be negotiated, and that pink T-shirt worn as a vest keeps the soldier warm in winter.

A people's army: The fact is that even as the peace process gains momentum, Israel is still a nation at war. The ubiquitousness of soldiers in Israel clearly shows this. They and their sub-machine-guns are everywhere: travelling on buses, hitchiking at roadside stations, sitting at streetside cafés and strolling through city streeets.

Israeli male soldiers fall into several categories. There are young conscripts aged 18

to 21 doing their three years' national service and a small number of professional soldiers, usually officers, who carry on afterwards. Then there are the reservists.

Miluim, Hebrew for reserve duty, is one of Israel's unique institutions. Grown men are plucked away from their families for a month or six weeks a year (even more during times of military tension) to serve on the Lebanese border or in the West Bank with the friends they have had since they were 21. There are, of course, rugged types who enjoy the macho lifestyle but for the most part Israelis see *miluim* as a burden that some will do anything to evade. While conscripts must have a short back and sides, reservists are allowed, apart from clothes, to maintain their civilian appearance including long hair and earrings.

Miluim also has a dovish effect. Even hawkish Israelis do not relish going to war, or serving in the West Bank or Gaza. Just suppose British men had to go and serve in Northern Ireland for a month each year. It would create much more pressure on the government to find a solution to the problem.

However, with bigger drafts of 18-year-olds each year, reliance on reservists is being scaled down. Where once soldiers served well into their fifties, now combat soldiers are released at 45, or in some corps even at 42. This policy is also aimed at minimising the disruption that *miluim* causes the economy.

Nor is military service as universal as even Israelis sometimes believe. About a third of Israeli Jewish men do not enrol for the army when they are 18. They are either ultra-Orthodox Jews requesting a deferment to study, or youngsters deemed unsuitable because of delinquent behaviour. An additional third of Israeli teenagers do not make it to the more prestigious combat units, and end up serving as storekeepers or kitchen staff.

Indeed an 18-year-old simply has to insist that he does not want to serve and he will not be drafted. For although the motivation of Israeli teenagers has supposedly dropped as the country has become more affluent, the number of teenage applicants for combat units is still higher than the places available. So regiments can pick and choose. National service is officially compulsory for Jews but Muslims and Christians are exempt, though some, especially Bedouin who are renowned for their abilities as trackers, serve as volunteers. The Druze and Circassian communities are, at their own request, conscripted.

A woman's place: While Jewish women often fought as front line soldiers before the struggle for independence, the IDF has confined them to non-combat roles since 1948 even though women are conscripted for two years. Too often female soldiers end

gence was refused promotion in 1982 on the grounds that his sexuality supposedly compromised his security rating. Yitzhak Rabin, when serving as Defence Minister some years later, apologised to the officer over the affair.

Despite the military informality, the IDF is a highly effective fighting force. Maybe the right of soldiers to question officers' orders is a strength rather than a weakness. Besides, in the heat of battle orders are usually obeyed and dramatic victories have been won.

Though still scruffy in appearance, the

up as office hands or, at best, instructors, albeit tank or artillery instructors. Recently women's rights groups have challenged convention. The Supreme Court ruled in 1995 that the army must accept female candidates for pilots' courses, and the women's organisations are now requesting that the paratroopers take women soldiers.

Sexism aside, the Israeli army is not, as in most countries, a bastion of conservatism. Homosexuals have always been accepted. A gay Lieutenant Colonel serving in Intelli-

Left, a female tank instructor. **Above**, a playful tug-of-war provides training for the real thing.

Israeli army places great value on smart technology. It is the Israeli Air Force more than any other branch of the services that has ensured Israel's military edge over its Arab neighbours. In an era of satellite surveillance there can be no more Yom Kippur-style surprise attacks, and anti-missile systems being developed, like the Arrow, will reduce the threat of long-range attacks.

As the Israeli army prepares itself for the 21st century the principal threats are seen as terrorism, and enemies further afield such as Iran and Iraq. But even in an era of peace Israel is likely to be a nation in uniform for some time to come.

There's more than an even chance that day or night, someone, somewhere in Israel will be praying. Whether under a prayer shawl in a synagogue, beneath a cross in a church or on a mat facing Mecca, the faithful will be lauding the Creator of the Universe.

The sheer intensity of the religious ardour in this small country is overwhelming: in Jerusalem's Old City, Jews at the Western Wall, Muslims at the Dome of the Rock and Christians at the Church of the Holy Sepulchre may well be saying their prayers simultaneously, to say nothing of the myriad other synagogues, churches and mosques in the Old City alone. Likewise, the diversity of religious experience here is of a category all its own. Hassidim in 18th-century *kapotas* and *shteimels* (coats and hats) rub shoulders with robed monks and nuns from every Christian denomination East and West, while Muslim *imams* in *tarboosh* and *galabiyah* walk unnoticed among secular Israelis and pilgrims to the Holy Land. Many of the holiest sites from the Bible have alternately hosted synagogues, churches and mosques over the centuries, and even today visitors of one faith may well find themselves paying respects to a chapter of their own history in the house of worship of another.

The Jewish presence: Jewish spiritual life revolves around the home, house of study (*cheder* for youngsters, *yeshiva* for adolescents and adults) and synagogue – of which the latter is the most accessible to the visitor. Jerusalem's 500 synagogues range from the humblest *shtible* and Sefardi community synagogue to the gargantuan Belzer Center (seats 3,500) and the "Great" along downtown King George Street. The Great's massive edifice gives people the idea that it might be the third Temple. Other large synagogues in Jerusalem include the Central, Yeshrun and Italian.

The Orthodox pray three times a day, but it is at weekends and festivals that the liturgy is at its most elaborate. This is a good time to

catch the Hassidic services whose more modest premises are compensated for by the fervour of the prayers. Such groups exist in Safed, Bnei Brak and in Jerusalem's Mea Shearim and Geula districts.

Among the warmest and most approachable of the Hassidic groups is the Bratslav, whose Mea Shearim premises contain the renovated chair of their first and only rebbe Rabbi Nahman. He was famous for his delightful tales; one of his sayings, "the world is a narrow bridge; the main thing is not to be afraid at all," has endeared him to all Israelis.

At the other end of Mea Shearim is Karlin, whose devotees screech their prayers – unlike their Geula neighours, Ger, whose tightly-knit organisation is reflected in their operatic music and self-discipline: "A true Ger Hassid," says one, "never looks at his wife." A similar outlook is espoused by Toledot Aharon, opposite Bratslav, whose purity of purpose is matched by their animosity towards political Zionism, which they view as usurping the divine process of redemption. In this they follow the line of Neturei Karta (Guardians of the City), which boasts its own government-in-exile in its campaign for political autonomy. Both, too, campaign against the Conservative and Reform Movements, which have their own centres and desegregated houses of prayer in Jerusalem (on Agron and King David streets, respectively).

The cycle of the Jewish year: The framework of Jewish piety is determined by the lunar cycle beginning around September and October with Rosh Hashona (the New Year) and Yom Kippur, the Day of Atonement – a rigorous fast of 25 hours duration. Synagogues are packed; services are long but moving. If you're Jewish and you hail from Minsk, Marrakesh or Manhattan, you're sure to find at least one service meeting your liturgical needs. An unusual and controversial custom precedes Yom Kippur: Kaparot, which entails swinging a white chicken above the head of the penitent, after which the slaughtered fowl is sold or given to charity. The gruesome ceremony can be witnessed in most open market-places.

Succot, the Festival of Rejoicing, combines harvest gathering and prayers for win-

Preceding pages, a summer concert at Jerusalem's Sultan's Pool, with the Citadel beyond; Dome of the Rock, Jerusalem. Left, a Torah scroll and its keeper.

ter rains and is celebrated on secular kibbutzim as well as by the Orthodox. The celebrants live in a temporary hut for seven days. During the evenings, the pious let down their sidelocks to dance, somersault and juggle to live, intoxicating music. Some Hassidic sects cap off the ceremonies with a candlelight procession by their children.

More lights burn during Channukah, usually in December, when eight-branched candelabra shine in most homes. This celebration of the Maccabean victory over the Greeks some 2,300 years ago was preceded by a couple of centuries by one over the upstart Haman, whose sad fate is recorded in the Scroll of Esther and read on Purim (usually

the Temples, culminating in the day-long fast on Tisha B'Av.

New Jews and Messiahs: Orthodoxy is fashionable, no less so among the Jews, and in the past 15 years a whole wave of "returnees" have passed through special *yeshivot* for the uninitiated, eventually to weave themselves into the fabric of the local religious life. Their devotion takes expression in a variety of ways, from those Jews who integrate their Western careers or professions with a pious daily routine, to such phenomena as the Selah Torah Rock Band, now located at the Israel Center on Jerusalem's Strauss Street, which blends Jewish and Western styles with consummate ease.

in March). Children and adults dress in costumes, shout, get drunk, and give each other presents of food or drink. In April, everyone spring-cleans for Passover, the annual feast celebrating the Exodus from Egypt. Seven weeks later is Shavuot, the Feast of Weeks, when thousands congregate at the Western Wall for dawn prayers, having spent the night studying Israel's national book, the Torah. Between Passover and Shavuot, the Orthodox invest Independence Day and Jerusalem Unity Day with spiritual significance, creating new festivals. The yearly cycle reaches full circle in high summer, with the three-week period of mourning for

The Christian presence: These messianic messengers are not always Jewish, but include long, blond-haired types with pre-Raphaelite faces. They may be part of the growing Evangelical presence in Israel whose belief in the redemption has made them enthusiastic supporters of Zionism. The Christian Embassy on Jerusalem's Brenner Street recently attracted over 5,000 people from 40 countries to participate in their Christian version of the Feast of the Tabernacles. Another sort of backing comes from Nes Ammim, a semi-collective village near Acco where Christians of various denominations work the land – in co-founder Christine

Pillon's words – "in returning to our sources and being subjected to a new kind of Reformation. Our principles include the rejection of proselytising and the call for respect for Judaism as a living, ongoing tradition."

Most of the traditional Christian communities in Israel – numbering in total roughly 120,000 souls – are more concerned with their own internal affairs. Many devote themselves to lives of prayer and meditation, and preserving the presence of their church in the Holy Land. Often the priests, monks or nuns watch over and maintain traditional shrines associated with figures in the New Testament: a cave where the Holy Family found refuge, or the site of one of Jesus's miracles. With the West Bank in its control, Israel holds practically all of what is commonly known as the "Holy Land", and the devoted visitor can follow in the footsteps of Jesus from Virgin Birth in Bethlehem to early life at Nazareth, to Crucifixion at Golgotha, in Jerusalem.

Complicated by their variety, the Christian groups celebrate some 240 feasts and holy days in any year, using two separate calendars, the Julian and the Gregorian. This provides three dates for Christmas: 25 December for Western Christians, 7 January for Greek Orthodox, Syrians and Copts, and 19 January for the Armenians – as well as two sets of Holy Weeks. Only genuine pilgrims are allowed into Bethlehem for Christmas, where the main events take place at the Church of the Nativity; just as, in Easter Week, there is a reenactment of Jesus's last days with readings and processions on the sites historically associated with the original events. These include walks from the Mount of Olives, complete with palm branches, and along the Via Dolorosa to the Church of the Holy Sepulchre. Here, two unique ceremonies take place: the Washing of the Feet (John 13; 1-18) on Maundy Thursday, and the Kindling of the Holy Fire (symbolising the coming world redemption), by the Orthodox and Eastern Churches on Holy Saturday. The climactic carrying of the cross on Good Friday between the Praetorium and Calvary (Golgotha), along the Via Dolorosa, is repeated weekly by the oldest resident group of priests, the Franciscans. One of the most

Left, a priest at Bethlehem's Milk Grotto. Right, a latter-day prophet spreads his word.

revered Christian sites is the place of Jesus's baptism on the Jordan River. For a long time neglected, the site has been newly marked and is now commemorated in word and deed by more and more devotees.

Interfaith, the dialogue of hope: The existence of modern Israel has brought together Christian, Muslim and Jew in a once-in-a-thousand-years opportunity for inter-faith dialogue. When they do occur, such encounters provide a means of transcending the most intransigent problems with new understanding. As Dr Abu Ghosh of Israel's Sharya Muslim Court says: "Islam is extraneous to the present political strife. Islam, Christianity and Judaism can live peacefully side by

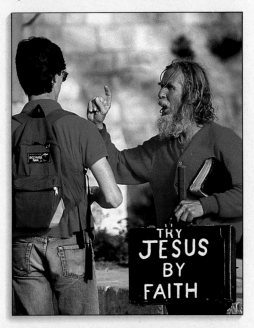

side, as is the case in Israel." Mary Carse, a Carmelite from Vermont, winters every year in Israel where she studies "at the feet of the rabbis." In Israel, she found that "everything began to fall into place." French Dominican priest Marcel Dubois also believes that "we are witnessing a Christian rediscovery of the continuity in the design of God." Sent to East Jerusalem in 1962, he became an Israeli citizen on Christmas Day, 1974. Appointed head of Hebrew University's Philosophy Department, he is fully aware of the tensions that exist around him, but speaks of more than just himself when he observes that "Jerusalem is the capital of contradictions."

Had one to name the single most fundamental contribution made by Israel and the Jewish people to mankind, obviously the immediate answer is the Bible. The Book of Books is the underlying philosophical and moral web which unites most of civilisation as the core of human values. And that book, for all its five millennia or so, remains the most important source and inspiration for much of Israel's cultural creativity.

It is, of course, only one of the strands, but it is the most pervasive. Other distinct strands are the great literary creations of the Jewish exile – the Mishna and the Talmud – the accumulated wisdom of 2,000 years of Jewish thought. No less important is the cumulative experience of a mere blink in the history of the Jewish people: the 38 years of modern statehood, and the reflection of the pressures of a society whose population has multiplied more than sixfold in those years and, through force of circumstances, had no alternative but to develop a siege mentality which has often produced a siege culture.

Israel, like the United States before it, has often been described as a "melting pot" as it has struggled with the absorption of one-and-a-half million immigrants from 100 nations speaking 70 tongues. But a melting pot – in which the id melts into a normative unity – is the wrong image. The cliché does not hold true. A better image, for all its disregard of *kashrut* (Jewish dietary laws), would be a *bouillabaisse*, the classic Mediterranean fish stew in which all the elements come together into a homogeneous whole, each retaining its own character, distinct identity and flavour.

Literature: If the heartbeat of a nation's culture lies in its written word, then here, already, is Israel's single most basic problem: its language. Hebrew, the language of the Prophets and of the Old Testament, ceased to exist as a vehicle for everyday speech during the exile and was replaced by the tongues of the nations among whom the Jews found refuge in their dispersion, and by a handful of composite Jewish languages such as Judeo-German (Yiddish), Judeo-Spanish (Ladino), and others.

The revival of modern Hebrew was the work of one man, Eliezer Ben-Yehuda. He determined, when he came to Palestine in 1881, that he and his family would utter no word in anything but Hebrew. His efforts and those of his followers created a whole new vocabulary, and in a scant decade or two helped one of the most ancient of tongues to become, at the same time, one of the newest.

Nevertheless, for all its revival, there are no more than 4 or 5 million people worldwide who can speak and understand Hebrew. If one is talking about those who can comfortably *read* Hebrew, the figure is certainly no more than 3 million. Hebrew can be considered an arcane, rather exotic language, one where those who choose to write in it must inevitably be faced with the frustrations of writing for a minuscule audience. But a lively, articulate and robust body of literature has evolved. While the giants of modern Hebrew – Bialik, Tchernikhovsky, Brenner, Agnon (who won the Nobel Prize for Literature in 1966) – and others, are still required reading in schools, they are supplemented by indigenous, increasingly Israeli-born writers whose work can stand comparison with the best of the world's contemporary authors.

One of Israel's best writers (and certainly best-known abroad) is Amos Oz. A former member of Kibbutz Hulda who now lives in Arad, Oz is heavily influenced by the Return to the Soil labour-Zionist *mores* espoused by the founding fathers of the kibbutz movement. Many writers who maintain a prolific literary output belong to the "Palmach Generation" (the Palmach was the pre-state élite fighting force drawn from the kibbutzim). Among them are Haim Guri, Moshe Shamir, S. Yizhar, Benjamin Tammuz and Hanoch Bar Tov. An important phenomenon of the last 15 years or so has been the maturation of a group of writers of Sephardic origin for whom Arabic, rather than Yiddish, was a formative influence. Such writers include A.B.Yehoshua, Samy Michael and Amnon Shamosh, whose *Esra Safra and Sons* became a popular television series.

Left, a Hebrew University student improves his mind in the shade of a sculpture by Menashe Kadishman, at Mount Scopus campus.

A one-man literary phenomenon is Ephraim Kishon. Israel's best-known humorist and a prophet somewhat without honour in his own country, his books have sold literally millions of copies overseas, especially in Scandinavia and Germany.

Literature, too, has been deeply influenced by the deaths of millions of Jews in the Holocaust. It is that theme which is the all-pervasive *leitmotif* in the writings of Aharon Appelfeld, whose books have been widely translated; Abba Kovner, "Ka-Tsetnik" (the pseudonym of Benzion Dinur) and others, all of whom experienced that period themselves. A younger generation of writers is exploring more universal literary themes. The Lebanon war, increased political polarisation, the appearance of anti-democratic trends in Israeli society, the threat of racism, are rightly the concern of these intellectuals.

The centre ground in Israeli writing is held today by those who came to literary maturity after the Palmach days and whose literary vision was tempered through the fires of austerity, of absorption of immigrants and four wars of survival. Such writers include Yitzhak Ben Ner, Shulamit Hareven, the late Ya'akov Shabtai, Yoram Kaniuk and others.

Poetry holds a special place in Israel's literary life. According to a calculation based on books and the literary magazines, 10,000 new poems are published in Israel every year. New works by Yehuda Amichai, Dan Pagis, Natan Zach, or T. Carmi are as avidly awaited as any by Michener or Le Carré.

Music: The musical life of Israel is a quintessential example of bipolarity. There is a constant inflow of immigrant musicians and an outflow of performers who have reached the highest international peaks. Yitzhak Perlman, Pinhas Zuckerman, Shlomo Mintz, Daniel Barenboim, all received their training in Israel and went on to glittering careers on the world's concert platforms. Israel's orchestras, including the Israel Philharmonic, the Jerusalem Symphony, the Beersheba Sinfonietta and many chamber groups, have provided a home for hundreds of players. Rehearsals are a Babel of Russian, German, Romanian, French and English – united by a lot of music and a little Hebrew.

Israelis are a concert-going people: subscription series to the major orchestras are sold out and a subscription to the IPO is jealously handed down from parents to chil-

dren. Music-loving tourists would have many opportunities to hear their best loved pieces being played by some of the world's greatest talents. Placido Domingo, incidentally, got his first job at the (late-lamented) Israel Opera, with whom he spent a year. Opera lovers, however, should leave their opera going for other climes. Choral singing, too, is on a very high level, especially with the United Kibbutz Choir, the Rinat National Choir and the Camaran Singers.

Israel hosts a series of international musical events including the Artur Rubinstein piano competition, the Pablo Casals cello competition, a triennial international harp contest, the Zimriya choirs festival, and an-

nual music festivals in Jerusalem, Kibbutz Ein Hashofet and, notably, at Kibbutz Ein Gev on the shores of the Sea of Galilee.

For all this wealth of musical life, it is not only the highbrow that is catered to. In Tel Aviv (Jerusalem from this point of view hardly counts!), there is a great deal of popular music around. While jazz aficionados will do better elsewhere, rockers, popsters and balladiers are out in force. Moshe Wilensky, Yoram Taharlev, Nurit Hirsch, Sasha Argov and, above all, Naomi Shemer, write music that is played on radio, television, in kindergartens and sunshine-home singsongs from Metulla to Eilat. Locals still remember Israel's two consecutive Euro-vision Song Contest victories with *Abani-bi* sung by Yizhar Cohen and *Halleluia* sung by Gali Atari. Pop superstars in Israel include Ofra Haza, Ilanit, Yehoram Gaon, Arik Einstein, Shalom Hanoch, and many more. A new generation of ethnic singers such as Boaz Shar'abi, Chaim Moshe, Moshe Giat and the Breira Hativ'it group have given a new sense of ethnic pride to young Israelis of Sephardic background.

Dance: Israel owes its place in the world of dance to three women. The first was a Russian-trained ballerina, Rina Nikova, who came to Palestine in the 1920s and determined to create a local art form incorporating

themes from the Bible, (remember Salome?), Middle East dance tradition, folk dance and Russian classical ballet. The second, Sarah Levi-Tanai harnessed the Yemenite dance tradition, one of the richest and most exotic dance cultures of the Middle East, into a modern framework and created the Inbal Dance Theater, the forerunner of several other successful ethnic dance groups. The third, Baroness Bethsabée de Rothschild founded the Batsheva and Bat Dor dance companies. Both remain leading exponents

Left, Israeli novelist Amos Oz burns elbow grease.
Above, conductor Zubin Mehta takes a bow.

of modern dance in Israel, and the latter also has three thriving ballet schools. The formative influence on modern dance in Israel was undoubtedly that of Martha Graham, but the companies have since grown and expanded their horizons with a series of overseas tours. In recent years, the two companies have been joined by the Kibbutz Dance Company and the Israel Ballet, the country's only classical ballet company.

Another company unique in concept and achievement is Kol Demama ("Voice of Silence"). This group is composed of deaf and hearing-impaired dancers, and their performances are electrifying, it being impossible to distinguish which dancers are deaf and which are not. The training method developed by director Moshe Efrati is based on vibrations through the floor transmitted by the dancer's feet.

Folk-dance groups abound throughout the country and there is not a kibbutz or town that does not have its own troupe. Outstanding among them is Hora Yerushalayim, a Jerusalem-based group, whose four companies, divided by age, perform to a very high standard at home and overseas.

Israelis take to dance happily and with easy élan, and any occasion is likely to end up with an exuberant and exhausting round of *horas*, *krakoviaks*, *debkas*, Hassidic dances and other European and Arabic dance forms, now part of the Israeli dance heritage.

Theatre: Israeli theatre owes its origins to the histrionic, melodramatic tradition exemplified in the first Hebrew theatre in the world, Habimah, founded in Moscow in 1917 (which moved to Palestine in 1931). Since then, theatre has come a long way in style, presentation method, and especially in content. Of all the arts in Israel, theatre is perhaps the most socially involved, with a new generation of playwrights breaking taboos, tackling controversial topics, and attempting to act as the mirror and conscience of society.

Concerns of the past, the Jewish experience in pre-war Europe, the Holocaust, all these still manifest themselves on the Israeli stage but, increasingly, dramatists are addressing themselves to contemporary issues, problems of daily life in Israel, the Arab-Jewish conflict, alienation between ethnic, religious and other social groups. A new play by Hanoch Levin, Yehoshua Sobol or Hillel Mittlepunkt is a major event which will be dissected, analysed and discussed as energetically as the Camp David Accords. Hanoch Levine, especially, is a defiant, iconoclastic writer whose works inevitably cause controversy and sometimes even attempted censorship. But his irreverent, nihilistic, often obscene satire makes him Israel's most interesting and original theatrical talent.

The major repertory theatres, most of whom enjoy substantial official support, such as the Habimah, Cameri, Ohel, Haifa Municipal Theater, Beersheba Municipal Theater and the Jerusalem Khan have subscription series which are usually heavily attended. Naturally, the language barrier prevents the visitor from sharing in the rich offerings. Efforts

outlying areas which do not generally get the chance to see live performances. For thousands of new immigrants and youngsters, Omanut La'am performances are their first introduction to the world of theatre.

Cinema: Film as an art form in Israel still has a long way to go. Most of its productions are strictly for local consumption and are based on stale ethnic sitcoms, sexcoms, and in-joke situations such as teenage affairs, marital conflicts and army life. Such products are loosely known as "Burekas" films (named after a kind of flaky pastry pie popular in Israel).

Serious filmmaking in Israel began in the early 1920s and 1930s, mainly with docu-

are being made, however, to bridge the gap. Several theatres have experimented in translations through earphones and others have attempted to mount versions of their works in English.

Great popular success has attended a recent annual theatrical innovation: the festival of Alternative Theater in Acre. It has become a hoopla occasion of theatrical dynamics, innovative performances and indoor and open-air attractions.

A programme enjoying substantial support is Omanut La'am ("Arts for the People"). This state-run enterprise brings theatre to settlements and development towns in

mentaries, as a fundraising device aimed at demonstrating the Zionist pioneering effort to audiences abroad. These films, with their images of muscle-rippling pioneers making the desert bloom and bringing water to the arid wastes, against a background of stirring music and an exhortatory sound track, became known as "Keren Kayemet films" after the Hebrew name of the Jewish National Fund which sponsored most of them.

Some Israeli films made in the 1960s managed to rise above mediocrity and brought actors like Haim Topol, Uri Zohar, Gila Almagor, Oded Kotler and Arik Einstein to the fore. Kotler's *Three Days and a Child* won the best actor's prize at the Cannes Film Festival in 1967. A film which made a lasting impression was *Sallah Shabtai*, written by Ephraim Kishon and starring a young Topol, which in a whimsical and ironic manner told the story of the recent North African immigration to Israel and their culture clash with the hidebound kibbutzim.

Israeli cinema-goers have been ill served in the past by cinema owners. This situation has recently changed in a radical way. Tel Aviv boasts a sybaritic cinema complex, the Rav Chen, which incorporates five halls, while Jerusalem has the Cinemathèque, which not only shows the best films in town, but is also the place where the capital's

beautiful people go to see and be seen. The one international superstar in Israel's cinematographic life is mogul Menahem Golan, who became one of the movers and shakers in Hollywood, together with his cousin, Yoram Globus. They were originally two small-town boys from Tiberias.

The plastic arts: Israeli art owes its fundamental quality to a combination of two factors. In the first place, a classical European tradition brought here by the country's early painters and art teachers, and second, the

Mordechai Ardon's stained-glass windows at Givat Ram are the artist's best-known work.

influences of the special quality of the light, and the natural attributes of the country.

In the space of about 80 years (since the establishment of the Bezalel School of Art in Jerusalem in 1906), an Israeli visual art has been created, possessing its own individual character. Israeli artists have experimented with all the movements and trends of the contemporary art world from expressionism to cubism, from Russian social realism to environment and performance art. However, not many Israeli artists have managed to make the quantum leap from local to universal recognition. Among contemporary artists who have are Ya'akov Agam (his kinetic room at the Pompidou Centre in Paris is a seminal work), Menashe Kadishman, Avigdor Arikha, Mordechai Ardon, Joseph Zaritsky and Avigdor Stematsky.

Two sculptors, Dany Karavan and Ygael Tumarkin, are well-known abroad, and their work can be seen all over Israel. Marcel Janco, (1895–1984) founder of the Dadaist Movement, Reuven Rubin (1893–1974) with his lyrical large-scale canvases, and Anna Ticho (1894–1980) with her exquisite line drawings of her beloved Jerusalem hills have also gained a considerable following.

At the end of the 1970s, Israeli art made its entry into the post-modernist era, following in the footsteps of the US and Europe. This art is energetic and forceful, often containing violent images which are, perhaps, part of the post-Lebanon War reality in Israeli life.

Museums and galleries all over the country cater to the art lover. The main galleries are concentrated in two areas, Gordon Street in central Tel Aviv, and in Old Jaffa. Others are in Jerusalem, Haifa, Ein Hod (an artists' village south of Haifa), Safed and elsewhere.

Tel Aviv Museum has a large and representative collection of Israeli modern art on permanent display along with temporary exhibitions. The Israel Museum, which has impressive collections of classic, impressionist and foreign modern art (as well as its vast collection of archaeology, Judaica and Jewish art, ethnography, *et al*), has, until recently, not been noted for its diligence in acquiring and showing Israeli art. This has now changed with the opening in 1985 of the new Ayala Zacks-Abramov Pavilion of Modern Art, which should eventually become the nation's main repository of contemporary Israeli painting and sculpture.

HEBREW: A LANGUAGE REBORN

One of the most remarkable facets of the rebirth of the Hebrew nation was the revival of the Hebrew language. Not that the language had been forgotten, but through the 2,000 years of dispersion it had become almost solely a language of worship and expression of the yearnings for Zion.

Some small communities of Sephardic Jews in Jerusalem used Hebrew for everyday speech but the lingua franca of the Jews in exile had become either the language of the country in which they found refuge, or special Jewish dialects that developed as an amalgam of the local language with an admixture of Hebrew. In such a way there evolved Yiddish as a combination of Hebrew with medieval German, Ladino – Hebrew with Spanish, Mughrabi – a North African blend of Hebrew, Arabic and French, and others. The first pioneers who arrived in 19th-century Palestine brought with them their own languages, usually Yiddish or Russian, but they insisted on using Hebrew in conversation in the early agricultural communities and the recreation of Hebrew became a cornerstone of Zionist ideology.

In fact, the rebirth of Hebrew was virtually the work of one man, the Zionist thinker and leader, Eliezer Ben-Yehuda. Born in Lithuania in 1858, he immigrated to Palestine in 1881. He saw the revival of the language as an indispensable aspect of the political and cultural rebirth of the Jewish people and with single-minded, almost fanatic, determination embarked upon a lone campaign to restore the Hebrew tongue as a vibrant, living vehicle for everyday expression, not just in the synagogue but in the street, in the market-place and in the home. When he and his new wife Dvora arrived in Jaffa he informed her that henceforth they would converse only in Hebrew and their son Itamar became the first modern child with Hebrew as his mother tongue. His efforts horrified the Orthodox population of Jerusalem who, when they realised that Ben-Yehuda proposed using the Holy Tongue to further secular, nationalist and political causes, pronounced a *herem* (religious excommunication) against him. To this day, the Ashkenazi ultra-Orthodox Jewish community condemns the secular use of Hebrew and the defilement of the "holy" language, and confine themselves to Yiddish for everyday speech.

Yet the introduction of Hebrew for secular communication was not greeted with universal acclamation even by the non-Orthodox, or the supporting Zionist bodies and organisations abroad. Bitter battles were fought over the language of instruction to be used at, for example, the Bezalel School of Art in Jerusalem (founded in 1906), and the Technion (founded in 1913). The latter was

opened with German as its official language and it took a strike by both faculty and students to compel the supporting institution, the *Hilfsverein*, to give way on the issue. Only a few years after that, the language of teaching in all Jewish schools in the country (except for those of the ultra-Orthodox, of course) was established as Hebrew.

The crowning achievement of Ben-Yehuda's life was the publication of his *Dictionary of Ancient and Modern Hebrew*, which was completed after his death by his son Ehud and his second wife, Hemda (Dvora's younger sister). This dictionary, and the Academy of the Hebrew Language, which Ben-Yehuda established in 1890, were the main vehicles through which a new and modern vocabulary was disseminated. He wrote in the introduction to his dictionary: "In those days it was as if the heavens had suddenly opened, and a clear, incandescent light flashed before my eyes, and a mighty inner voice sounded in my ears: the renascence of Israel on its ancestral soil." Through his dictionary, the Academy, and several periodicals that he founded and edited, Ben-Yehuda coined literally thousands of new

makushit ("something that is tapped upon") take the place of "piano".

No one has yet successfully coined Hebrew words to replace the ubiquitous "automati", "mekhani", "democratia," etc., although the existence of such words in the language seriously disturbs Hebrew purists, just as *le weekend*, *le piquenique* and *le football* disturb Francophone purists. Some post-Ben-Yehuda slang neologisms would undoubtedly make him turn in his grave as they have become soundly embedded in the

words and terms relating to every field of life and every discipline.

Not all of Ben-Yehuda's neologisms took root. Modern Hebrew, which is today the all-purpose language of the country from mathematics, physics, medicine, agriculture to the most arcane fields of scientific learning, still borrows a great number of words from other languages which sound familiar to the non-Hebrew-speaking ear. Ben-Yehuda's *sah rahok* ("long-distance speech"), for instance, never displaced "telephone", nor did

Left, a Torah scribe preserves the sacred script. Above, the secular script.

language. "Tremp" (clearly from "to tramp") is the Hebrew for "hitchhiking", a sweatshirt is a "svetcher", over which you might pull a "sveder" if it gets cold. When your "breks" fail, the garage might find something wrong with your "beck-ex," or even, God forbid, with your "front-beck-ex". Most of these words do have Hebrew equivalents, but they have often been pushed aside in common usage.

Despite these contemporary dilutions, there's no denying that Hebrew is once more a thriving, and still-evolving, vehicle of daily discourse employed in great works of literature and the backs of postcards alike.

108

From the artists' quarter in old Safed to the seaside boutiques in Eilat, on every major city avenue and in the oriental markets, there's a choice of an almost endless array of local handicrafts. Simple straw baskets and sleek stone sculptures, ceramic and textile arts, glassware and jewellery, mass produced religious mementos and one-of-a-kind ritual items are available everywhere. Not surprisingly, Israel has become the international centre of Judaica production, and tourists – whether they're looking for something "just like grandma had" or something just a bit more sophisticated – find what is undoubtedly the world's best selection of Jewish ritual arts concentrated in the shops and studios of Jerusalem.

Jewish art and craft, like almost everything else in 20th-century Israel, has its roots in the Bible Bezalel Ben-Uri Ben-Hur, specially blessed "with the spirit of God, in wisdom, in understanding, and in knowledge..." appears in the Book of Exodus to produce a divinely commissioned work of art, the Tabernacle, for the wandering Children of Israel. The order came down loud and clear: "To work in gold, and silver, and in brass, and in cutting of stones for setting, and in carving of wood, to work in all manner of skilful workmanship." Bezalel proved worthy of the task; under his direction, the desert Tabernacle was successfully completed, and from it emerged the Menorah, the seven-branched candlestick which became an eternal Jewish symbol.

When the wanderings in the desert were over and ancient Jerusalem established, the tourist industry was born. Three times a year – at the festivals of *Succot* (autumn), *Pesach* (spring), and *Shavuot* (early summer) – pilgrims came from outlying areas to worship at the Temple. On the slopes beyond the Temple Mount, they found Jerusalem's earliest art centres – special quarters for weavers, dyers, leather workers, glassmakers, potters and goldsmiths, all turning out functional and artistic wares for visitors to use during their Jerusalem sojourn and to take home as keepsakes.

The destruction of the Second Temple in AD 70 and consequent dispersion of the Jewish people left few opportunities for the artistic Jewish soul to express itself visually in the Holy Land for almost two millennia. But with the birth of the Zionist movement in the 20th century came a revival of interest in "Jewish art". Alongside the pioneers who set out to rebuild the land physically came a tiny group of artists, intellectuals and craftspeople dedicated to creating a new Jewish culture. Bezalel reappeared in the name of a fledging art academy, and its founder, a Lithuanian Jew named Boris Schatz, came from Bulgaria to prove that arts and crafts could become the touchstone of economic well-being and national pride in the Zionist settlements.

Today Jerusalem is again the centre of Israel's tourism and, not coincidentally, of its arts industry. As in ancient times, many of the city's craftspeople are to be found in their own centrally located artists' quarters. A unique feature of Jerusalem's art scene, in fact, is the immediate accessibility of its artists. Collectors can buy directly from the studio shops.

Ritual and tradition: Jewish ritual art, which forms the bulk of Judaica, is divided into two categories: holy vessels, directly associated with the Torah itself, and ritual utensils, used for fulfilling ritual tasks in the home and synagogue. While not considered holy themselves, these objects acquire a certain sanctity by virtue of their presence or use in the performance of religious duties (*mitzvot*). When a ritual object adds an aesthetic dimension to a ritual, its users have the benefit of fulfilling an additional commandment, *hiddur mitzvah* – glorification of the commandment. Thus, special value is attributed to lighting a beautiful pair of candlesticks for the Sabbath rather than two simple oil wicks, though the latter would fulfil the requirement.

Halacha, Jewish law, guides the craftsperson with only a few rules for creating specific ritual objects. The Hanukkah lamp is perhaps the most clearly defined. It must have eight separate lights of the same height, and a distinguishable ninth light for kindling the others; and they must burn, in a publicly visible spot, for at least 30 minutes past sundown. The rest is left to the artist.

Wine cups, candlesticks, and spice boxes

Left, a gouache-on-paper *mizrach* (wall-hanging) by Yoram and Jane Korman depicts one of the most traditional Jewish themes: Jerusalem.

used for Sabbath and holiday blessings; cases for *mezuzot* (tiny parchment scrolls hung on every Jewish doorpost); charity boxes, festive plates, decanters, hangings – these and many other objects long ago became associated with the Jewish ritual and are accepted today as Judaica. For most of them, there are no design restrictions, or even descriptions, in the *halacha*. Individual artisans throughout the centuries picked an artistic style and material of their choice to suit the religious need of the moment, and tradition was established.

In most cases, form and decoration closely followed the fashions of the time and place in which they were produced. We have Hanukkah lamps, dating from the 12th century onwards, seven-branched Menorah. Representations of the human figure and face were generally avoided in deference to the Second Commandment ("Thou shalt have no graven images..."), but they do appear from time to time.

Materials were usually the best the community or individual patron could afford: lavish textiles, parchment and gold leaf, semi-precious and precious stones and metals were the ideal. When these were not available, almost any other material would do: charming examples of Jewish folk art in wood, tin, paper, and other modest media have been preserved. (A magnificent collection of these is displayed in the Judaica/Heritage Galleries of the Israel Museum, where replicas are also on sale.)

with French Gothic windows, Moorish arches, or Italian garlands; wine cups and candlesticks reminiscent of the Renaissance and baroque periods. A single Hebrew letter can be the only sign that they were used by Jews.

Symbols of the artists' surrounding cultures – architectural details, national, and even political motifs – were given new significance in Judaica when combined with classic Jewish symbols. Long-standing favourites included (Torah) crowns and double columns invoking the Temple; biblical scenes and signs of the Zodiac; lions of Judah, grape vines and pomegranates, griffins and fish and a wealth of other flora and fauna; and, of course, the

Contemporary artists: Israel's contemporary Judaica artists, like their ancestors, favour semi-precious and precious metals for their work, but some items can be found in almost every other material, from rare woods to Lucite. Two distinct schools in Judaica have recently emerged. One is highly traditional, basing its shapes and decorations on patterns from the baroque period or earlier. Many of these works are uncamouflaged imitations or "adaptions" of well-known museum pieces; others are brought up to date by ingeniously incorporating the lines of modern Jerusalem or devices such as whimsical moving parts. The second school is strictly – sometimes aggressively –

contemporary. Here form prevails over function: the artist strives to create art works which may be used in Jewish ritual.

Proponents of both styles are usually highly proficient in their techniques, and many are world leaders in their field.

There are four or five major areas in the capital of note for Jewish art and craft hunters, all located at relatively short distances from each other. They are, according to general geographic proximity: the Old City's Jewish Quarter; Khutzot HaYotzer/Art & Crafts Lane (beneath Jaffa Gate); the House of Quality (12 Hebron Road, near the railway station); Yohanan MiGush Halav and Shivtei Israel streets (which both meet Jaffa Road at Zahal Square, facing the Old City); and the neighbourhoods of Geula/Mea Shearim.

An informal arts and crafts tour should begin at one of the two non-profit galleries which offer an instant overview of Israel's craft scene. Neither "gallery" sells anything but refers visitors directly to its selected artists. At the House of Quality, this means just going upstairs to the studios where several Judaica silversmiths, including famous veterans Arie Ofir and Menachem Berman, work full-time. At the Alix de Rothschild Crafts Center (4 Or HaHaim Street), recently set up in a renovated Jewish Quarter home, the director may be on hand for tea and a chat about his latest crafts discoveries.

Nearby, the Courtyard Gallery (16 Tiferet Israel Street) is the place for fibre-art fans seeking chic handmade baskets, fabrics and wall hangings. Those who prefer a strictly ethnic look can go across town to Kuzari (10 David Street, in the Bukharan Quarter), where local women embroider everything from tea cosies to Torah covers, based on traditional Near Eastern patterns.

Khutzot HaYotzer/Art & Crafts Lane boasts top craftspeople like Uri Ramot (ancient glass and beads in modern settings); the Alsbergs (ancient coins in custom-made jewellery); and Georges Goldstein (hand-woven tapestries and *tallitot* – prayer shawls). But the Lane's greatest distinction is its concentration of outstanding silversmiths. Yaakov Greenvurcel, Zelig Segal and Emil Shenfeld rank among the world's top designers of contemporary Judaica, and Michael Ende is one of

the founders and chief purveyors of the "nouveau antique" school.

Fans of the latter must also stop in at Yossi's Masters' Workshop (10 King David Street) and The Brothers Reichman (3 Ezer Yoldot Street, off Shabbat Square in Geula). Both offer extraordinary workmanship and classic designs in fine metal. Similiar style and quality characterise the ceremonial pieces by Catriel (17 Yohanan MiGush Halav), a carver of rare woods. Catriel's neighbours are worth visiting: silversmiths Davidson and Amiel, calligraphic artist Korman, and jeweller Sarah Einstein, who transforms antique Middle Eastern beads into high-fashion baubles.

Around the corner and down the block at 18

Shivtei Israel Street is a brand new co-op featuring ceramic *hanukkiot* by Shulamit Noy and the works of seven other Jerusalem potters. From here, it is a short walk either to the centre of town or the Old City, where for under $10, inveterate *chachka*-hunters can find happiness with "ivory" amulets, mother-of-pearl miniatures, carved stone mezuzot and crocheted *kepot* (skullcaps), olivewood camels or jangling goats' bells.

For the traveller who wants a trip in time as well as space, just $30 or so can buy a genuine ceramic lamp made when the Second Temple was still standing – and the earliest tourists came in search of Israeli arts and crafts.

Left, a silversmith crafts Menorahs and ceremonial objects. Right, temptations for tourists.

Entered, according to Act of Congress, in the year 1871, by D. Appleton & Co., in the Office of the Librarian of Congress at Washington.

No. 99.—Vol. V.]   SATURDAY, FEBRUARY 18, 1871.   { PRICE TEN CENTS. } { WITH SUPPLEMENT. }

THE RECOVERY OF JERUSALEM.*

THIS is the somewhat pretentious title of the narrative of recent English explorations of Jerusalem, by means of excavations conducted by Captain Wilson, of the Royal Engineers, under the auspices and at the expense of the Committee of the Palestine Exploration Fund. Without, perhaps, fulfilling the meaning of the old crusading war-cry, exact knowledge of the scenes and localities in which their religion first appeared on earth. The explorations have solved many difficult problems, and settled many fierce and protracted controversies. Shafts have been sunk and tunnels made in the most secluded and mysterious parts of the sacred city, and structures brought to light that have not

WILSON'S ARCH, DISCOVERED AT JERUSALEM IN 1867.

the "Recovery of Jerusalem," it is undoubtedly a record of researches and discoveries of the highest value, and of the greatest interest to scholars, antiquarians, and, above all, to Christians who desire an

been seen by mortal eyes since the days of Titus, or perhaps of Solomon.

The beginning of this great work was the Ordnance Survey of Jerusalem, made by Captain Wilson, of the English Royal Engineers, in 1864–'65. Early in the year 1864 the sanitary state of Jerusalem attracted considerable attention; that city, which the Psalmist has described as "beautiful for situation, the joy of the whole earth," has

* The Recovery of Jerusalem. A Narrative of Exploration and Discovery in the City and the Holy Land. By Captain Wilson, R. E., and Captain Warren, R. E. With an Introduction by Arthur Penrhyn Stanley, D. D., Dean of Westminster. D. Appleton & Co.

Archaeology is Israel's national hobby – from school child to senior citizen, from the curious to the serious scholar, tourists and natives alike are all encouraged to "dig in" to the land of the Bible.

With 3,500 sites in an area about the size of the state of Maryland and finds dating as far back as 150,000 BC, Israel boasts 22 archaeological museums in addition to numerous private collections. Yet only a small proportion of Israel's potential sites have been thoroughly explored: time, money, manpower – these have all placed limits on the scope but not the devotion to the exploration of Israel's past.

A gentlemanly hobby: Adherents past and present to what one scholar called the "study of durable rubbish" have been drawn to biblical archaeology for a range of reasons: greed, adventure, religion and scholarship. During the Victorian period it was something of a gentlemanly hobby.

The first known "archaeologist" to work in Israel was religiously inspired. In AD 325 Queen Helena, mother of Constantine, the emperor who declared Christianity the official religion of his empire, ordered the removal of a Hadrianic temple to Venus on a site she had determined was the hill of Golgotha. Constantine erected the Church of the Holy Sepulchre to commemorate the alleged site of the crucifixion and entombment of Jesus.

Over the next 16 centuries the territory, sometimes referred to as Palestine, the Levant, Syro-Lebanon, the Holy Land or Israel, exchanged hands numerous times. Explorers of all religions crossed its borders, armed with little more than a compass, pick, shovel and curiosity. Stories of bribery, untimely deaths and mystical reunions with sages and prophets from time past pepper their accounts. Medieval adventurers report that those who dared to enter the burial cavern of the patriarchs and their wives at Hebron were struck blind or senseless or worse. Such tales did not always deter others.

For Western explorers, interest in the Holy Land intensified after the Napoleonic conquest of Egypt in 1798 and the subsequent discovery of the Rosetta Stone. Scholars, amateurs and snake-oil salesmen descended on Palestine, then a sparsely populated backwater country. Some of these adventurers became the victims of this archaeological fever. For example, when the British Museum rejected as fake certain "ancient" parchments that Moses Wilhelm Shapira had bought from a Bedouin, the amateur archaeologist simply disappeared.

In 1911, Captain Montague Parker and his crew of treasure hunters barely escaped with their lives when they were discovered conducting an excavation under the Mosque of Omar on the Temple Mount. The British mission had been following the hunch of a Swedish clairvoyant who insisted that this was where they would find a cache of golden objects from King Solomon's temple. Offended Jerusalemites rioted in the streets.

Method in the madness: The foundations of modern archaeology as we know it were not laid until the late 19th century, and were marked by the establishment of major academic institutions sponsoring field trips and

Left, an 1871 journal recounts the discovery of Wilson's Arch. **Right**, Theo Seibenberg examines a newly found artifact.

publication societies. The Palestine Exploration Fund, founded in London in 1865, is the grandfather of these groups, which include such venerable institutions as the American Schools of Oriental Research and the Ecôle Biblique et Archaeologique Française. The work during this period of Edward Robinson, Claude R. Conder, Sir Flinders Petrie and other giants continues to cast a long shadow on modern archaeology.

It was Petrie who first recognised the importance of stratigraphy, that is, the examination layer by layer of a tel, the artificial mound formed by successive settlements. He was also among the first to recognise the importance of using pottery to date each of these layers or strata. He realised that in different periods, particular types of pottery would be associated with particular strata.

After World War I, Mortimer Wheeler and Dame Kathleen Kenyon refined the debris analysis method of pottery dating. At about the same time a separate methodology arose, emphasising the importance of uncovering large areas to expose the architecture of a settlement. Devotees of the so-called architectural method accused the debris analysis subscribers of overlooking the "big picture." The latter in turn accused their colleagues of ignoring the importance of stratigraphy.

Today an eclectic approach to excavating a tel prevails. Technological advances have altered archaeology to the degree that surveyors can provide archaeologists with considerable information before a single shovelful of earth has been removed. Carbon-14 dating has further improved the archaeologist's ability to fix an artifact in time. Archaeologists can now dig underwater, cross-reference finds on computers and learn more quickly what their colleagues have discovered. They can call on a host of specialists, including paleo-botanists, osteologists, ethnologists, philologists and biblical exegetes, whose talents can help interpret their finds.

Most important, archaeologists have come to emphasise that once a locus, that is, a three-dimensional area designated for excavation, is dug and artifacts removed, the site will have been ineluctably altered. By the very nature of their work, archaeologists destroy irreplaceable evidence in their search for remnants of the past.

Politics and pioneers: But, for many, archaeology is a field whose study bolsters or

threatens religious and political beliefs – as well as pet scholarly theories. In the late 1970s, for example, a small but vocal ultra-religious minority tried to stop a dig at the City of David, saying the archaeologists were desecrating ancient graves. But, the archaeologists countered, no evidence pointed to the existence of any graves at the original site of King David's Jerusalem.

For political reasons, Jordan has filed formal complaints with UNESCO against Israeli digs in East Jerusalem – even though the Israeli government has done much to preserve important archaeological sites there.

And among secular, apolitical scholars the real value of the Bible in their archaeological

work is hotly debated. Many have reason to doubt its utility as a historical document and a source of verifiable reference. Others cling firmly to the Bible's documentary importance and infallibility.

The careers of Israel's greatest archaeologists were hewn from this complex web of scholarly debate, political instability, plus a national passion to unearth the Jewish past. Eliezer Sukenik, his son Yigael Yadin, Moshe Dayan, Benjamin Mazar – who can think of these archaeologists except in conjunction with Israel's struggle for independence?

In an interview, Mazar, director of the excavations next to the Western Wall in

Jerusalem, remembers his 1936 dig at Beth She'arim in northern Israel: "Everyone had a keen interest in the excavation, because finding Jewish antiquities reinforced the meaning of Zionism and strengthened the reason for creating a Jewish state. We were interested in building a homeland, and Jewish antiquities were part of its foundation."

Of Sukenik's discovery in 1947 of the Dead Sea Scrolls, Yadin writes: "(My father) found something symbolic in the thought that this was happening at the very moment when Jewish sovereignty in Palestine was about to be restored after almost 2,000 years – the very age of the parchment he had seen." That parchment is now part of the collection

television mini-series in which millions learned about the heroic, suicidal stand of a handful of Jews against the Romans.

Today, digs at Tel Dan on the Israeli border with Lebanon, Tel Dor, south of Haifa, and nearby Caesarea, where digs are conducted on land and under water, attract a stream of volunteers from across the globe.

Despite difficulties, Israelis and scholars who come to dig in Israel from all over the world have produced an impressive amount of literature further illuminating the pages of the Bible. And, perhaps, in many ways archaeology is the perfect pastime for the inhabitants of the Middle East, who have a penchant for argument and disputation.

at the Shrine of the Book, the Israel Museum's home for the Dead Sea Scrolls.

Yadin's own digs and subsequent books on Masada, Hazor and the Dead Sea Scrolls have dramatised the history of the "people of the book." In addition, much of his work has been popularised by others. Hazor, a site in northern Israel with an impressive underground water system, is the subject of James Michener's novel *The Source*. Yadin's dig at Masada – where he discovered a ritual bath and synagogue – became the focus of a

Left, the underground city at Amatzia, a new attraction. **Above**, archaeologists in action.

Whether wandering the Arab markets of Jerusalem, visiting a kibbutz school house, or sipping coffee on Dizengoff Street in Tel Aviv, one of your neighbours will doubtless have an opinion on just who is buried in David's Tomb. Or you may stumble on to the multi-million dollar excavation of Theo and Miriam Siebenberg, amateur archaeologists who determined that their home in Jerusalem's Jewish Quarter was planted on top of important remains.

Indeed, for the average Israeli, the tumbling walls of Jericho are as vivid as the Gulf War. And in Israel everyone is welcome to rebuild its ancient past.

Wine, the Good Book says, "maketh glad the heart of man," (Psalms: 104, 15). In Israel, where that book was written, winemaking keeps the birds happy too. That's because Israeli wine is kosher, and ancient Jewish dietary laws require all fields – including vineyards – to lie fallow every seventh year – a practice that may be one of mankind's first displays of environmental awareness.

Each year, one-seventh of Israel's viticulture production hangs unharvested: a glorious banquet for the birds. As a bonus, these grapes usually ripen just in time for fall migrations, and songbirds flying from Eurasia to warm wintering grounds in Africa can enjoy a sweet and nutritious stopover on the way in Israel.

The birds' bonanza is but one of the many unique advantages nature enjoys in the Land of Milk and Honey. The creation of the modern State of Israel has proved an extraordinary benefit to nature. Special programmes have devoted energy and talent towards the revival of the land and the restoration of its ecological integrity. As a result, Israel today is a cornucopia of nature, abundant and diverse with many species of fauna and flora.

Redeeming the land: Early in the 20th century, when the Zionist ideal was little more than a philosophical debate, the region was a desolate backwater of the crumbling Ottoman Empire. Its ecological dynamics had suffered catastrophically. Nature had been ravished. The hand of havoc had reached into the Garden of Eden.

The introduction of modern firearms was an enormous tragedy for wildlife. Within a few decades, large numbers of the gazelles and ibex which had graced the landscape since the days of the prophets, were ruthlessly killed. A monstrous hunting binge shot several species into extinction.

The local race of ostrich, which so perplexed Job, was blasted to nothingness. Israel's native race of Asiatic wild ass, a creature which some religious scholars identify as the animal Jesus rode on Palm Sunday, was mercilessly annihilated. The spectacular

Left, kids do their bit for conservation. **Right**, ibex have been in Israel since biblical times.

white oryx antelope, the *re'em* of the Hebrew Bible, translated in the King James Version as "unicorn", suffered a similar fate. Fortunately for this species, however, a few specimens were captured for breeding before the last of the wild population was exterminated.

Flora was also destroyed. As far back as the Crusades, Christian pilgrims were scouring the countryside for biblical wildflowers. These were picked, pressed and sent back to Europe to serve as bookmarks in family

Bibles. Generations of Europeans could "consider the lilies" of the Holy Land – but these lilies were lifeless, dried, and incapable of reproduction. Today, Israel's native Madonna lily is a very rare plant.

The big disaster came a century ago, when the Ottoman Turks built a railway into the Arabian Desert, and the region's forests were levelled. The heavy timbers were used to bridge ravines, middle-sized logs became rail ties, and the smaller pieces were burned as fuel. By the time T. E. Lawrence (Lawrence of Arabia) was attacking the Ottoman trains, Israel had less than 3 percent tree cover.

With the loss of vegetation, the soil dried

out, turned to dust, and was swept out to the desert by the wind. The scant winter rains had no absorbent material to hold them, and water ran quickly to the sea. Wells dried out.

Early Jewish settlers determined to recreate the biblical Land of Israel were confronted by severe problems. The land was exhausted, and literally could not support either a human population or its own natural processes. The ecological integrity of the land had to be restored.

Plant a tree: The 15th day of the Jewish month of Shevat, Tu B'Shevat, is an Israeli Arbor Day; it is celebrated by planting trees in any of the scores of special planting zones in the nation's forests. Israelis plant trees on

ally. With the return of the trees, winter rains could be captured and channelled to the aquifer. Wells again became productive.

With the return of the trees – and particularly the fast-growing Jerusalem pine (*Pinus halepensis*) – soil was regenerated. In many places, once the soil was adequate, the pine trees were cut away and immediately replaced with apricot, almond and other fruit and nut trees.

With the return of trees, soil and water, Israeli agriculture prospered. Israel is one of the very few arid lands which grows enough food to feed itself, and which also has enough to spare to count agricultural exports as its major foreign exchange product.

other days, too – to mark birthdays and weddings, for example. Children honour their parents by planting trees – and parents honour their children the same way. In one forest about 20km (12 miles) west of Jerusalem 6 million trees have been planted as a memorial to the Jews who perished in the Holocaust. Entire classes of Israeli youngsters go each year to the forest to plant saplings, and to visit the ones they planted in former years.

Since the founding of the State of Israel in 1948, planted forests have grown to cover 2,000 sq. km (770 sq. miles) – 10 percent of the total land area of the country – hundreds of millions of trees, each planted individu-

With the return of the trees, nature also flourished, and the land began to recover. Life processes dependent upon a good vegetative cover were regenerated. Some are hardly noticed – for example, the sprouting of orenit mushrooms in the Jerusalem forest after the first winter rains, or the growth of colourful mosaics of lichen upon fallen logs. Others are so dramatic they are impossible to miss. The majestic golden eagles have returned to Israeli skies, and one pair even builds its nest each year in the branches of a planted pine forest just south of Jerusalem.

Much of this has been achieved by the Jewish National Fund (JNF), Israel's afforestation agency, which has also planted the northern hemisphere's most southerly non-equatorial forest, the Yatir Forest, in the northern Negev. It is particularly concerned with combating desert encroachment. However, some environmental organisations in Israel accuse the JNF of overkill, claiming that it is trying to create European-style forests in places where a semi-arid desert environment should exist.

Nature reserves: There are 280 established nature reserves in Israel, which together cover more than 4,000 sq. km (1,540 sq. miles) – more than than one-fifth of the country's total land area.

By international conservation standards,

remains of an ancient Greek temple dedicated to the god of the forests. Other archaeological treasures found in the area include the remains of the ancient Nimrod Fortress and the Crusader town of Belinas.

The reserve's colourful wild oleander and thick groves of myrtle, plane and willow trees appeal to the naturalist's eye. It is a haven for a great variety of birds and mammals. The rare stone marten and wild cat live here, and playful otters splash with carefree abandon in the waters flowing from the slopes of Mount Hermon.

These waters give a human dimension to this nature reserve, for they are the headwaters of the Jordan River. Much of this

the reserves are strictly run. They are maintained in as pristine a state as possible, and visitors are forbidden to pick flowers, camp or picnic. Administered by the Nature Reserves Authority, they serve a variety of functions. Generally, they reflect the need for humanity and nature to coexist. An example can be seen at Banias, a beautiful nature reserve at the foot of Mount Hermon, on Israel's northern border.

The name Banias is a corruption of the Greek "Panaeus", and here one finds the

Above, spring flowers bloom among the cacti at Yitzrael Valley in Galilee.

water eventually enters Israel's national water carrier system, and flows from taps in Tel Aviv and Haifa. It helps irrigate the fields of the Galilee, and fills the fish ponds of the Bet Shean Valley.

Not every nature reserve has a practical purpose. Many are established solely for the preservation of particular natural features: a seasonal pond, a secluded valley where rare flowers blossom, a sunny cliff with good nesting ledges. Some of these reserves are off-limits to human visitors because of their importance to nature and the ecological equilibrium of the region.

One of the most interesting projects to

restore natural ecological processes is the Hai-Bar programme. Hai-Bar is a Hebrew term which simply means "wildlife". But to Israeli conservationists, it also identifies an international effort to "return the animals of the Bible to the land of the Bible." Under the auspices of this project, conservationists have searched the world to find remnants of those species which once inhabited Israel. Some of the discoveries were prosaic: addax antelope were found in a Chicago zoo, and a few Asiatic wild ass were acquired from the Copenhagen zoo.

A few of the discoveries have involved some spectacular rescue work. Mesopotamian fallow dear, for example, were spirited

rehabilitate them to life in Israel's wild areas. One Hai-Bar reserve is deep in the Negev, about 40 km (25 miles) north of Eilat; it specialises in desert animals. Another is on top of Mount Carmel, on the Mediterranean coast near Haifa; it specialises in wildlife of the Mediterranean oak-forest region. A third Hai-Bar reserve is in the process of being set up on the Golan, to handle animals indigenous to the Galilean plains and Golan Heights.

The restoration process is comprehensive and involves years of painstaking work. Indeed, 14 years passed between the acquisition of those Asiatic wild ass from the Copenhagen Zoo, and the day when their offspring were judged tough and experienced

out of revolutionary Iran during a howling storm and on false export papers. White oryx – those "unicorns" of the King James version – reached their ancestral home in the Negev desert after a globe-trotting journey of tens of thousands of kilometres. Their source: a few hundred kilometres southeast of the Negev – in the personal zoo of the late Saudi King Faisal. And a flock of ostrich chicks was air-lifted out of Ethiopia's Danakil desert when the Israeli Air Force was sent on a special mission to fetch a few new immigrants to Israel.

All the animals, regardless of their origin, are first brought to special reserves set up to

enough to live freely in the wild. Those offspring were released, and today they are repopulating remote areas of the Negev and giving birth to wild foals.

The Hula Nature Reserve in the Upper Galilee is perhaps an example of over-zealous attempts by Israel to "improve" on the existing environment. In the 1950s the Hula Swamp was drained to make way for agriculture. Of the 10,000 acres drained, 1,000 of them were left as a nature reserve with water buffalo and diverse wildlife. But the farm land beneath the swamp, rich in peat, is becoming less and less fertile, and recently 1,000 acres was re-swamped. There are plans to restore the Hula Swamp in the long term.

Ecological diversity: Despite its small size, Israel is one of the most ecologically diverse countries in the world. Two factors contribute to this: geography and topography.

Geographically, Israel is located at the confluence of the great Eurasian and African land masses. Any land traffic between these land masses must pass through Israel. Many life forms have migrated through this channel; the evolutionary spread of the equines from Asia into Africa, and the migration of humanity itself from African origins through the rest of the world, filtered through what is now Israel.

Migration is still an extremely important

phenomenon in Israel, and, twice yearly, millions of migratory birds pass through on their way to and from northern nesting grounds and southern wintering areas. More than 150 species of migratory birds are seen in the town of Eilat alone.

Topography in Israel is a matter of spectacular contrasts. Mount Hermon, on the northern border, towers to a snowcapped 2,814 metres (9,223 ft); the Dead Sea, at 400 metres (1,300 ft) below sea level, is the

Left, a pair of scimitar-horned oryx at Hai Bar. **Above**, the impressive Pillars of Solomon at Timna National Park.

lowest point on the face of the earth. Broad plains stretch across parts of the Galilee, and fringe the northern Negev with expanses of steppe grasslands. Makhtesh Ramon, a natural crater 40 km (25 miles) across, is carved from the central Negev highlands. The north-south range of the Judean Mountains forms a continuous ridge nearly 1,000 metres (3,280 ft) high, an hour's drive east of the Mediterranean coast.

The great geographical and topographical diversity is responsible for tremendous biological diversity. One finds sub-alpine meadows on the slopes of Mount Hermon, and a mere 25km (16 miles) south, at the Hula Nature Reserve, there is a lush tropical jungle: the world's nothernmost papyrus swamp. Israel is a land of Eurasian oaks and African acacias, Eurasian foxes and wolves and African dorcas gazelles and rock hyrax. It is a land of blending continents, flora, fauna and geology.

Encroaching urbanisation: Though Zionism has always cherished the nature of the Land of Israel, the greatest threat to the Israeli environment is the success of the Zionist venture. A rapidly expanding population, which is increasingly affluent, means that more highways and cities are planned, often in some of Israel's most beautiful countryside. The Trans-Israel highway alone threatens to eat up a large swathe of the country between the Negev and the Galilee and the urging of environmentalists to build railways rather than highways seem to fall on deaf ears. The attractive valley by the western entrance to Jerusalem is slated to become an industrial zone.

Still, the environmentalists have won some major victories in recent years, most notably in stopping a Voice of America radio relay station planned for the Negev. Its complex mass of antennae would have been smack in the path of millions of migrating birds. Despite American pressure and the lucrative lure of a $2 billion project, Israel declined the installation and it was built in Kuwait instead. In general, though, "green" issues are rarely on the political agenda. This is not because Israelis are indifferent to environmental matters, but that issues of war and peace tend to dominate debate. Only when these questions are resolved will greater numbers of Israelis take to the streets to protest against environmental desecrations.

The kibbutz, the Israeli version of socialist collective communes, is proof that Marxist economic theories can be put into practice. Or is it? The latest challenge to the functioning of the kibbutz is economic success. This crisis stems from both the wealth of individual kibbutzim (plural of kibbutz) and the general affluence of Israeli society. Yet it is the inherent liberalism, social tolerance and pragmatic compromise of Marxist orthodoxy that enables the kibbutz to survive.

For beneath the ostensibly egalitarian eco-

put and 6.3 percent of manufactured goods.

Kibbutz lifestyles have changed since 1909 when the first Russian born pioneers established the original kibbutz at Deganya, where the River Jordan flows out of the Sea of Galilee. Within a decade there were 40 more kibbutzim. Moreover, these settlements enjoyed greater prosperity and social cohesion than the capitalist farms founded by the Rothschilds and other philanthropists in places like Rishon Le Zion, Petah Tikvah and Zichron Yaakov.

nomic surface of contemporary kibbutz society, there are vast differences in the amount of money each member may have. Today's kibbutznik is likely to have his own private bank accounts and credit cards, dabble on the Stock Exchange and even own property outside of the kibbutz.

Disproportionate economic output: Yet the kibbutz movement is flourishing despite, or perhaps because of, the gradual breakdown of traditional socialist ideology. There are about 130,000 people living on 270 kibbutzim in Israel, representing 2.5 percent of the country's population. The kibbutzim produce 33 percent of Israel's agricultural out-

By the time the state was established in 1948 the kibbutz formed the backbone of Israeli society. Kibbutz members, while always a small percentage of Israeli society, were looked up to as the social and moral ideal of what a person should be, not least because the kibbutzim had transformed large tracts of arid land into fertile fields. But even more importantly the kibbutzim, which had been strategically located as pioneering outposts, were created in order to define the borders of the Jewish state.

Most of the Palmach, the elite fighting force of pre-state Israel, were kibbutz members because by definition the kibbutz attracted members who were eager to defend the country's borders from the battlefront. But the fighting traditions of the kibbutz have been maintained today, and most young members are still eager to volunteer for elite combat units.

From austerity to affluence: The kibbutz initially succeeded because members were motivated to work together, pool very limited resources and prevail against the odds, overcoming a hostile environment and the Arab enemy.

onto crops or trees thus penetrating deeply into the soil and utilising minimal amounts of water. Drip irrigation works on a time clock and can be very simple, but in recent times sophisticated options have been added, such as computer control and the addition of fertilisers to the pipes.

The kibbutzim also diversified into industrial and tourist enterprises. In the 1960s and '70s austerity was gradually replaced by a more middle-class lifestyle. But a kibbutz member's home remained a modest place,

It was in a climate of austerity that the kibbutzim laid the foundations for future prosperity. By harnessing agriculture and technology, the finest fruit and vegetables were grown, bringing premium prices on European markets. Cows were bred to produce high milk yields and chickens that laid large numbers of eggs.

But perhaps the greatest kibbutz invention was drip irrigation, developed by members of Kibbutz Netafim in the 1960s. This system uses networks of pipes that drip water

and money was channelled into communal projects such as dining halls, swimming pools, sports and educational facilities and cultural amenities.

Thousands of members left the kibbutz, lured by the more individualistic lifestyle of the city. Many kibbutz children would not return home after serving in the army. But there was always an equal number of veteran Israelis or new immigrants eager to take their place as the new pioneers.

Tarnished image: It is difficult to know when the kibbutz stopped being universally admired as a place for selfless pioneers. One important date was 1977 when the Labour

Preceding pages: Kibbutz Brenner in spring. **Left,** family ploughing. **Right,** harvesting tomatoes.

Party lost the reins of power. The right-wing Prime Minister Menachem Begin poured scorn on the kibbutzim, which had traditionally supported Labour governments.

Begin described kibbutz members as "millionaires who sit around their swimming pools all day." It was an unfair label but it stuck. In particular Begin was politically exploiting the fact that kibbutzim were almost exclusively Ashkenazi, and their austere lifestyle was, nevertheless, considerably more desirable than the poverty suffered by the Oriental Jews in the nearby development towns of the Negev and the Galilee. The kibbutz members, who were

bailing out succeeded only in further tarnishing the kibbutz image.

The 1990s have seen the kibbutzim go from economic strength to strength, though some communal settlements still totter on the brink of bankruptcy. In particular kibbutzim near urban centres have profited by selling off land for the construction of housing or industry. These settlements have also provided profitable services to nearby towns by opening up enterprises that were already functioning for kibbutz members – catering, laundering, kindergartens and garages. And these days you don't even have to be a kibbutz member to live on one. Some kibbut-

generally opposed to the war in Lebanon in 1982 and espoused territorial compromise over the West Bank and Gaza were now portrayed as traitors rather than patriots.

It was also during this period that the kibbutzim got themselves into an economic mess. They borrowed large sums of money from Israeli banks in the early 1980s when annual inflation was triple digit and the banks charged high interest rates. The economy stabilised in 1986 but the interest rates remained locked at exorbitantly high percentages. Many kibbutzim staved off bankruptcy through loan repayment arrangements with bank and government help. However, this

zim will rent out spare houses to tenants.

The kibbutz founding fathers wouldn't approve of today's developments. Sixty years ago a kibbutz member who received a gift of money from wealthy relatives overseas had to hand it over to the communal kitty. Today the typical kibbutz member would certainly not contemplate handing over an inheritance or a win on the national lottery, let alone a gift, to the commune.

Nevertheless, egalitarianism remains the essence of the kibbutz. All houses are the same size even though the amount of electronic gadgetry inside may vary enormously, and no kibbutz member is allowed his or her own car. Income is distributed evenly, though more progressive kibbutzim may offer bonus incentives for working overtime.

The nuclear family has replaced the Marxist belief in alternative social structures. If kibbutz children were once brought up in baby houses by educational professionals to be part of the community first and foremost, a child's place in the modern kibbutz is once more with his or her parents.

From the point of view of socialist ideology the kibbutz may not be what it used to be, but it is still a very attractive place to live for other reasons. The kibbutz offers a rural lifestyle, guaranteed work in a variety of profes-

Meuhad members denounced Stalin as an anti-Semitic dictator, while Artzi remained faithful to the USSR. The Artzi movement realised that the Soviet experiment was going wrong long before the USSR's collapse in 1991 but still leans more towards socialist orthodoxy than the Meuhad movement.

For Israelis wanting a less socialistic form of communal living, the moshav offers a more individualistic alternative. Nahalal in the Galilee, the first moshav, was set up in 1921 by a breakaway group disillusioned by the socialist constraints of Deganya, the first kibbutz. The breakaways included Shmuel Dayan, the father of Moshe Dayan.

sions, and comfortable living standards including a house and garden. So if a well-established kibbutz advertises for new members the number of applicants usually far exceeds the number of places available.

Alternative lifestyles: There are three kibbutz movements in Israel today: the national religious kibbutz movement combines a communal way of life with Jewish Orthodoxy, while the other two movements – Meuhad and Artzi – are secular. The two movements split from each other back in 1951 when

In the moshav each family runs its own household and farms its plot but machinery is shared and marketing is done jointly. There are about 400 moshavim in Israel but most members now work in regular jobs, renting out their land to private farmers. The moshav shitufi, on the other hand, is closer to a kibbutz in that farming and industry is performed jointly. Income is shared equally and households spend their money as they wish.

Visitors wishing to enjoy a kibbutz or moshav experience can either stay at one of the many kibbutz and moshav guest houses around the country, or volunteer to work for a period of not less than a month.

Left, peach picking at Sde Boker. **Above**, swimming pool at the Ein Gedi kibbutz.

A HIGH-TECH ECONOMY

In recent years the Israeli economy has enjoyed impressive rates of economic growth, averaging about 6 percent annually since 1990. This has made Israel one of the world's fastest expanding developed economies, comparable to the famous "tigers" of Southeast Asia. The austerity of Israel's formative years has been swept away by a tide of affluence as Israel's standard of living approaches that of Britain and Italy. If the stereotypical Israeli hero was once a kibbutz pioneer, or daring paratrooper, today it is the high-tech business executive whose company provides innovative software solutions to many of the world's major computer and semiconductor corporations.

The arrival of some 700,000 new immigrants from the former Soviet Union, a high percentage of them well-educated scientists, has helped to fuel Israel's impressive economic development since 1990. Even before this wave of immigration Israel had, for example, the highest number of physicians per capita in the world. Between 1990 and 1996, the country's 13,000 doctors were joined by an additional 13,000 new immigrant doctors. Some 4 percent of the newcomers possess PhDs.

But this pattern of immigration alone is not enough to explain the country's economic success. Indeed many newcomers need time to adjust to the Western capitalist ethos. Two other factors, the peace process and the high-tech requirements of the modern world, have boosted Israel's economic performance and potential.

The end of the Arab boycott: The Middle East peace process has been of crucial importance to the Israeli economy. Trade between Israel and the Arab world remains negligible and is unlikely to increase significantly in the coming years. But, more importantly, the peace process has meant the end of the tertiary Arab boycott, which made business corporations and governments in other countries unwilling to do business with Israel because it jeopardised sales in the Arab world. Until the Madrid conference in 1991, dozens of

Left, part of an experimental solar power station at Sde Boker.

major multinational corporations like Pepsi-Cola, and Asia-based companies, including those in Japan, South Korea and China – highly dependent on Arab oil – virtually refused to do business with Israel.

The importance of this change can be gauged by the fact that 20 percent of Israel's $20 billion worth of exports in 1996 went to Asia, and nearly 10 percent to the countries of the former Soviet Union and Eastern Europe, who also only established diplomatic ties with Israel in the late 1980s.

Perhaps even more important than these diplomatic developments has been the changing emphases of the world's Western econ-

few countries worldwide capable of launching its own satellites.

But it is in the field of computer software that Israel has really come into its own. The country is said to be the largest producer of CD-Roms and multimedia products after the US and in such areas as data base, CAD/CAM, internet security and education, Israeli software houses have a worldwide reputation. The country has also found substantial worldwide markets in telecommunications, data communications, biotechnology and pharmaceuticals.

Developing natural resources: Opponents of Zionism always pointed out that Israel had

omy. It is estimated that 60 percent of Israel's exports (excluding diamonds) have some high-tech input. These range from microchips manufactured by Israeli subsidiaries of major world corporations like Intel, Motorola and National Semiconductor, through to the computerised imaging systems of Scitex, which pioneered automated page layout for the world's press and the CAT (computer assisted tomography) scanners of the Haifa-based Elscint.

The Arrow anti-missile, the first of its kind, will also be used by the US army when completed, while the Amos series of spacecraft has meant that Israel is now one of the

no natural resources and would, therefore, fail to develop economically. Proponents always claimed that the country's brain power would see it prosper. But even the latter group could never have envisaged how important ingenuity would become.

Indeed, even Israel's limited natural resources have become significant through technological developments. Israel exports more than $600 million worth of minerals from the Dead Sea, largely because scientists found more efficient ways of extracting potash from the water, and developed uses for the bromine found there. More recently an innovative method of producing magnesium metal from the liquid deposits in the Dead Sea promises to open up lucrative export markets. A new plant has been built by Israel Chemicals in partnership with Volkswagen.

Even Israel's traditional exports, such as diamonds and fruit and vegetables have major high-tech inputs. Israel is the world's largest centre for cutting and polishing diamonds, exporting $4 billion worth of the stones a year. Computers have greatly enhanced Israel's position by enabling cutters to calculate the optimum way to carve up large stones. An aggressive marketing campaign, especially in the Far East, has opened up the

can go onto the market when produce is scarce and prices are high.

Such ingenuity and endeavour has enabled the Israeli economy to succeed despite, rather than because of, government policies. Until the mid-1980s the country suffered from three digit annual inflation and constant devaluation of the shekel. More sober policies since 1986 have stabilised the currency, though average annual inflation of 10 percent and sometimes more is still a worrying factor, as is the growing trade deficit. And unemployment of only 6 percent has been a major achievement considering the massive wave of immigration.

Japanese market, where there was no tradition of acquiring diamonds.

The same combination of high-tech and marketing has also helped Israel's export sales in fruit, vegetables and flowers. In selling to Western European consumers the country has had to stay one step ahead of Mediterranean competitors, and this has been accomplished by developing new types of fruit and vegetables such as the avocado, the persimmon and cherry tomatoes, and new strains of existing fruits and vegetables that

In addition, successive Israeli governments have dragged their feet on economic reform. The government and the Histadrut trade union movement still own much of the economy and there is a tendency to wait until companies get into financial difficulties before change is brought about.

While Israel is reluctant to relinquish the socialist economics of its founding fathers, because the economy is export oriented, market forces must inevitably be obeyed. But ultimately this is not likely to prove a problem as there seems to be an increasing demand for Israeli goods and especially Israeli know-how.

Left, solar energy research at the Weizmann Institute. **Above**, making the desert bloom.

Disembarking at Ben-Gurion International Airport, visitors are likely to choose one of two directions: eastwards up through the Judaean Hills to Jerusalem, with its history and religion, or westwards past the fragrant citrus groves to Tel Aviv, Israel's bustling, economic capital. Calling itself the "city that never stops", Tel Aviv is a brash place with golden beaches and a pulsating nightlife. It is a city looking to its future rather than its past – a city of the flesh rather than the spirit. Though Tel Aviv has a vibrant cultural life, tourists here are more likely to indulge in midnight revelry than receive divine revelation.

From east to west, Israel (including the Palestinian autnomous zones) is less than 100 km (60 miles) at its broadest points. Tel Aviv is at the heart of the coastal plain – a densely populated, narrow piece of land stretching from the Gaza Strip in the south to Lebanon in the north. With mild, wet, yet sunny winters and hot, humid summers, this is the least remarkable region of Israel, geographically speaking, in spite of its beaches and Mediterranean vistas.

The inland hills to the east offer cooler, drier climes. Jerusalem is perched at one peak 830 metres (2,700 ft) high, as are other ancient cities such as the West Bank towns of Bethlehem, Hebron and Nablus. Here the hot, dry summers are tempered by delicious late afternoon breezes and in the winter there can even be a dusting of snow. In the spring, the best time to visit, the hillsides are ablaze with flowers. The terraced hillsides of olive groves and grape vines have a biblical charm, but otherwise the landscape has a Mediterranean familiarity.

From forest to desert: Not so the terrain east of Jerusalem, which has an alien, exotic charm to those used to the greenery of Europe. For, in addition to its social divisions, the Holy City is also a continental divide. The western slopes lead down through forest and field to the Mediterranean but the east dips down dramatically through rugged desert to the Dead Sea basin, the lowest point on earth, and the northern stretch of the Great Africa-Syria rift valley.

The craggy canyons and enchanting billowing beige hills of this desolate rock desert have historically attracted religious hermits and contain concealed monasteries. The Dead Sea itself is really a lake, with becalmed waters that nestle amidst a unique landscape of shimmering mountains. Eerily, the sea's high salt content enables bathers to float – a highlight of any trip to Israel. With ideal winter temperatures of 20°C (68°F), the region can be blisteringly hot in the summer: more than 40°C (104°F).

The 500 km (300 miles) from north to south takes the traveller from the majestic snow covered peaks of Mount Hermon and the

Preceding pages: evening at the Dead Sea; Mount Hermon; Monastery of St George at Wadi Kelt. **Left,** tour bus in Timna Valley, Negev.

rolling green hills of the Galilee down to the tropical waters of the Red Sea resort of Eilat. En route are the Sea of Galilee, the Jordan Valley and Dead Sea, and the Arava desert. In theory, it is possible in the winter to ski on the slopes of Mount Hermon in the morning and go scuba diving in the Red Sea in the afternoon, where remarkable coral formations and exotically coloured fish of all shapes and sizes are a feast for the eye.

Using the Places section of this guide: Our first Places chapter focuses on Jerusalem. This city of cities is the capital of modern Israel. Sacred to three religions, its sites include the Western Wall, the Dome of the Rock and the church of the Holy Sepulchre.

Then we tour the country from north to south. The Golan Heights, wrested from Syria in 1967, are a looming natural fortress crowned by snowcapped Mount Hermon.

The Galilee is Israel's lush reclaimed bread-basket, and its green valleys hold communities of Arabs, Druze and Jews alike. The land of Jesus's youth, it cradles the biblical town of Nazareth as well as the ancient Jewish holy cities of Tiberias and Safed. The Sea of Galilee, Israel's placid northern lake, channels the twisting Jordan River southward from its mountainous headwaters.

The fertile coastal plain is Israel's summer playground; the site of some of the country's first settlements and the centre of its thriving citrus and diamond industries. The modern city of Haifa, rich in technology and spirit, sits atop Mount Carmel further north, sharing the coastline with ancient Crusader forts.

Tel Aviv is Israel's Mediterranean metropolis. A cosmopolitan city of beachfronts, boulevards, cafés and modern architecture, it serves as the hub of the nation's cultural life, and holds close to a quarter of Israel's population.

The Inland Plains (*shfela*) serve as the historic corridor between the coast and Jerusalem, while Jerusalem itself glitters, golden at the centre of the country.

The Dead Sea and Judean Desert, along Israel's southeastern rim, once the realm of ancient ascetics, include the site of the famed citadel of Masada, oases, mineral spas and spectacular geology.

The Negev desert, the vast and rugged southern badlands, is receiving new life with a variety of agriculture and its boom-town capital, Beersheba. Eilat is Israel's strategic Red Sea playground.

The West Bank, including the hills of Samaria in the north and Judea in the south, remains a political hot potato: captured by Israel in 1967, the main Arab cities (except Hebron) have now been transferred to the Palestinian Authority following the Oslo Peace Accords signed in 1993. The ancient cities of Bethlehem, Jericho (both under Palestinian control) and Hebron (still under Israeli control) lie within this volatile area. The Gaza Strip, along the coast, is now also under the Palestinian Authority.

They all await you in the pages that follow.

Right, a street in the Muslim quarter of Jerusalem.

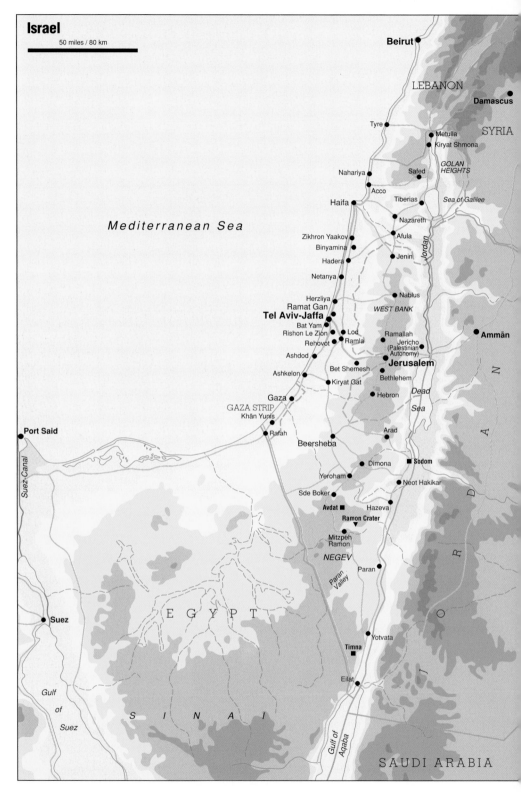

Israel

50 miles / 80 km

Beirut

LEBANON

Damascus

Tyre

Metulla
Kiryat Shmona

SYRIA

GOLAN
HEIGHTS

Nahariya

Safed

Acco

Tiberias

Sea of Galilee

Haifa

Nazareth

Mediterranean Sea

Zikhron Yaakov

Afula

Binyamina

Hadera

Jenin

Jordan

Netanya

Herzliya

Nablus

Ramat Gan

WEST BANK

Tel Aviv-Jaffa

Bat Yam

Rishon Le Zion

Lod

Ramallah

Rehovot

Ramla

Jericho
(Palestinian
Autonomy)

Amman

Ashdod

Jerusalem

Ashkelon

Bet Shemesh

Bethlehem

Kiryat Gat

Hebron

Dead

Gaza

Sea

GAZA STRIP

Khān Yunis

Arad

Port Said

Rafah

Beersheba

Dimona

Sodom

Yeroham

Neot Hakikar

Sde Boker

Hazeva

Avdat

Ramon Crater

Mitzpeh
Ramon

NEGEV

Paran

Paran
Valley

Suez

Suez Canal

EGYPT

Yotvata

Timna

S I N A I

Eilat

Gulf
of
Suez

Gulf of
Aqaba

SAUDI ARABIA

142

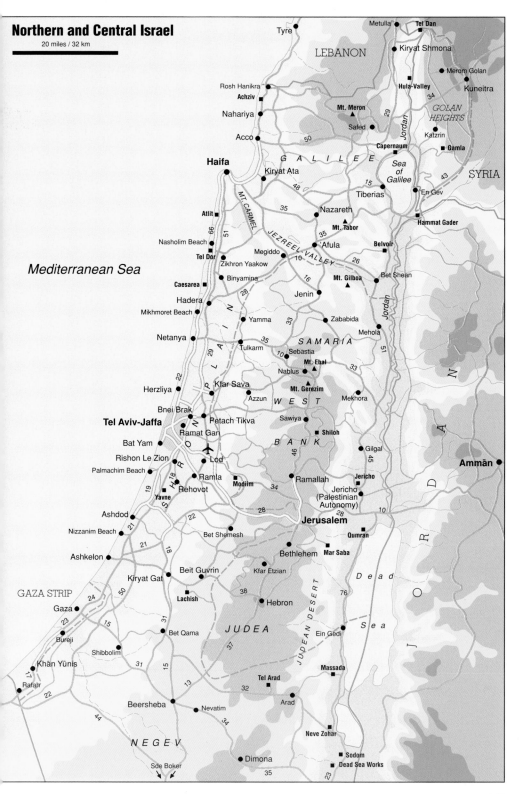

Northern and Central Israel

20 miles / 32 km

LEBANON

Tyre

Metulla • ■ Tel Dan
■ Kiryat Shmona

● Merom Golan

Rosh Hanikra ●
Achziv

Hula-Valley ■
*GOLAN
HEIGHTS*
● Kuneitra

Nahariya

Mt. Meron ▲

29
34

Acco ●

Safed ●

Katzrin ■

Capernaum ●

■ Gamla

50

G A L I L E E

*Sea
of
Galilee*

SYRIA

Haifa ●

Kiryat Ata ●

15
43

● En Gev

48

Tiberias ●

MT. CARMEL

35

Nazareth ●

Atlit ■

66
51

35

Mt. Tabor ▲

Hammat Gader ■

Mediterranean Sea

Nasholim Beach ●

JEZREEL VALLEY

'Afula ●

Belvoir ■

Tel Dor ■

Megiddo ●

10

26

Zikhron Yaakow ●

16

Bet Shean ●

Binyamina ●

Mt. Gilboa ▲

Caesarea ■

Jenin ●

Hadera ●

Jordan

28

Mikhmoret Beach ●

Yamma ●

33

Zababida ●

Netanya ●

S A M A R I A

Mehola ●

51

29

Tulkarm ●

35

22

10

Sebastia ●

Herzliya ●

Kfar Sava ●

Nablus ●

Mt. Ebal ▲

33

Azzun ●

W E S T

Mt. Gerezim ▲

Mekhora ●

Bnei Brak ●

Sawiya ●

Tel Aviv-Jaffa ●

Petach Tikva ●

B A N K

■ **Shiloh**

Bat Yam ●

Ramat Gan ●

46

Gilgal ●

Rishon Le Zion ●

✈ Lod ●

45

Palmachim Beach ●

Ramallah ●

Jericho ●

■ Ramla

Modiim ■

Ammān ●

Yavne ■

Rehovot ●

34

Jericho
(Palestinian
Autonomy)

10

Ashdod ●

22

28

28

Nizzanim Beach ●

21

Bet Shemesh ●

Jerusalem

Qumran ■

21

18

Ashkelon ●

Bethlehem ●

Mar Saba ■

Beit Guvrin ●

Kfar Etzian ●

D e a d

Kiryat Gat ●

GAZA STRIP

24

50

31

38

76

Lachish ■

Hebron ●

S e a

Gaza ●

23

15

Bet Qama ●

J U D E A

JUDEAN DESERT

Ein Gedi ●

Bureji ●

Shibbolim ●

31

15

Massada ■

Khān Yūnis ●

13

Tel Arad ■

17

Rafah ●

32

22

Arad ●

Beersheba ●

Nevatim ●

44

34

Neve Zohar ●

N E G E V

■ Sodom

Dimona ●

■ Dead Sea Works

Sde Boker ●

35

JERUSALEM: GETTING YOUR BEARINGS

Jerusalem has been called many things: the Golden City, the Eternal City, the City of David, the City of Peace. Sadly, it is also a city of strife.

To Jews, it is their national and spiritual epicentre; the incarnation of ancient Israel; where Abraham went to sacrifice Isaac; the site of David's glory and Solomon's Temple; the eternal capital of the Jewish people. To Christians, it is the city where Jesus spent his last days on earth; the site of the Last Supper; the Crucifixion and Resurrection. To Muslims, it is Al Quds ("The Holy"), the place where Mohammed is said to have ascended to Heaven on his steed; indeed, it is Islam's third holiest city after Mecca and Medina.

From its enduring power as a spiritual symbol to the quality of daylight, Jerusalem is unique. And today, some 3,000 years after David made the city his capital, Jerusalem still has the ability to stir emotion and fire imagination like no other city on earth.

Visiting Jerusalem: Still the centrepiece of many a journey to Israel, as it has been throughout the centuries, Jerusalem continues to reward the traveller with her riches. The market-places, shrines, ruins, hotels, temples, churches and mosques are all readily accessible and the city's tourist board is more than willing to provide directions. Yet the soul of the city is more elusive. The rhythm of daily life here is governed by prayer, usually channelled through tightly knit religious communities, and the visitor who merely barters for *chachkas* in the Old City between hops to famous churches or museums is missing the source and substance of the city's daily being.

Similarly, as the seat of government for the state and an important academic centre, Jerusalem also has an important secular profile, which shouldn't be overlooked.

Physically, Jerusalem is actually three cities in one, totalling over 500,000 residents. The modern part of the city spreading out to the west, northwest and south is West Jerusalem, a Jewish enclave since its inception in the late 1800s, and since 1950 the capital of the State of Israel. East Jerusalem describes the new part of the city east of the old "green line" that divided it from 1948 to 1967, during which time it was Jordanian. This section is still largely Arab in population and culture. In the centre of it all is the Old City, wrapped in its ancient golden walls, containing so much of historic Jerusalem and its shrines. It, too, was in Jordanian hands up to the Six Day War of 1967.

The Israeli victory that week in June 1967 not only rolled away the barbed wire and roadblocks, but fulfilled the two thousand year dream of the Jewish people returning to the Western Wall and the Old City. Jerusalem is once more a united city with an open flow of traffic. Israel officially annexed the Old City and East Jerusalem in 1967. The Arab states still look upon these as occupied territory and their return is the ultimate goal of the PLO in the peace

Preceding pages: the Western Wall. **Left,** sunset from the Mount of Olives. **Right,** an Orthodox Jew protests about the building of a new road.

process. But it seems unlikely that Israel will ever voluntarily part with the Old City with its thriving Jewish Quarter and the Western Wall.

David's capital: In ancient times it was said that the world has 10 measures of beauty, of which nine belong to Jerusalem. If the city's acclaim (or immodesty) made it that much more attractive to conquerors, so be it: since its greatest hour of glory as the capital of the Israelite kingdom, the city has been the object of repeated siege and conquest. In part this was due to its strategic situation on a vital trade route, at the crossroads between East and West. Ironically, however, it was later the very holiness of the city that inspired its would-be champions' relentless ferocity.

Jerusalem first crops up in biblical narrative during Abraham's migrations from Ur to Canaan. Here, he was greeted warmly by Melchizedek, King of Salem, "priest of the most high God." The Israelites were already well-ensconced in the hills of Judea when David captured the city from the Jebusites in 1000 BC.

Building an altar for the Ark of the Covenant on the crown of Mount Moriah, he made the city his capital, rechristening it Jerusalem – "Dwelling of Peace".

The 35 years under David's rule, and the ensuing 40 under Solomon brought splendour to the once modest fortress town. The site of David's altar saw the rise of Solomon's magnificent Temple, incorporating the much sought-after cedarwood from Lebanon, copper from the mines at Timna, and a wide variety of rich metals and carved figures. The city was embellished with the wealth of an expansive empire, its walls reaching in an oblong shape to include David's city on the slopes of the Ophel to the pool of Silwan below.

Around 926 BC King Solomon died, and in the absence of his authority the kingdom was split in two by his successors. Jerusalem remained the capital of the southern Kingdom of Judah, as the following centuries saw the city and its kingdom succumb to the expanding control of the Assyrians. In 586 BC

The classic panorama of the walled city.

Nebuchadnezzar of Babylonia plundered the city, sending its inhabitants into exile. They returned in 539 BC under the policy of the new king, Cyrus the Great of Persia, and set once more to the task of building a Second Temple.

Alexander the Great's conquest of Jerusalem in 332 BC initiated a brief Hellenisation of Jewish culture in the city. But, in 198 BC the Seleucids took control. Deprived of religious rights, the Maccabees spearheaded a Jewish uprising, leading to the reconsecration of the destroyed Temple in 165 BC.

The Hasmonean rule gave way in 63 BC to Rome, with the conquering armies of the Roman general Pompey. In 40 BC the Roman Senate conferred rule on Herod the Great (Jewish on his father's side) and sent him to Judea; during his reign up to 4 BC his horrific, psychopathic acts towards his family and others were matched only by his extensive architectural endeavours, most notably the Second Temple which, according to the historian Josephus, was built by 10,000 workmen and 1,000 priests. It took eight years to complete the courtyard and another couple of years for the Temple itself.

When it was finished, it was widely regarded as one of the wonders of the world. Jerusalem was still a Jewish city under Roman rule when Jesus was ordered crucified by the procurator Pontius Pilate around AD 30.

The increasingly insensitive Roman administration was challenged by the Jewish Revolt of AD 66, which was crushed four years later by Titus, who in the process razed Jerusalem and plundered the second Temple. A second rebellion was instigated by the Emperor Hadrian's decree to lay the city out anew on a Roman plan and call it Aelia Capitolina; but the Bar Kochba revolt of AD 132 was stamped out and in AD 135 Hadrian initiated the reconstruction of the city, making it illegal for any Jew to enter its boundaries.

The great Christianisation of Jerusalem was inaugurated in the 4th century by the Byzantine Emperor Constantine; in the 7th century it fell to Muslim rule,

and in 1099 to the bloody grip of the Crusaders for some 80 years. The city once more came into its own under the Ottoman Emperor Suleiman, who rebuilt its walls from 1537 to 1541. From his death until modern times it fell into ignominious decline.

To this day, Suleiman's walls remain the most impressive monument to the city's multi-layered history. From stone stairways at various points in its span you can mount the restored Ramparts Walk, which follows every circuit but that by the Temple Mount. A "green belt" of lawns now surrounds much of the circumference, adding to the aesthetics of the view.

The seven gates of the city are often a source of fascination in themselves. Clockwise from the Western Wall, they are: the Dung Gate; the Zion Gate, pockmarked by gunfire from 1948; the Jaffa Gate; the New Gate; the Damascus Gate, the grandest of all the entrances, opening to East Jerusalem; Herod's Gate; and St Stephen's (or Lion's) Gate, at the Via Dolorosa. The Golden Gate, facing the Mount of Olives from Mount Moriah, has been sealed since 1530, and is said to be the one through which the Messiah will one day enter Jerusalem.

Just inside the Jaffa Gate, which serves as the main entrance to the Old City from West Jerusalem, is the famous Citadel, or Tower of David. In reality, the structure doesn't have all that much to do with David; it was built by Herod who named its three towers after his wife Mariamne, his brother Phaesal and his friend Hippicus, and was so impressive that Titus let it stand after burning the city. The Mamelukes and later Suleiman reinforced it, adding its familiar minaret.

David's capital was the centre of massive celebrations throughout 1996 for its 3,000th anniversary, called Jerusalem 3000. At a cost of $6.5 million, this educational, artistic and cultural feast of events included a project to light up some 150 historical sights, and the building of an ampitheatre and a children's park.

For practical purposes, we have divided the rest of the city into two chapters. The Old City (*pages 153–71*) describes not only the sites within the city walls but also those religious shrines of age-old devotion just outside its bounds. Both East and West Jerusalem are discussed in the chapter on the New City (*pages 173–87*).

You shouldn't hesitate to follow your own instincts in exploring this city or to examine the possibilities of taking day-trips or detours to the less obvious sites. For us to attempt to describe all of Jerusalem in a few chapters is like asking a rabbi to describe the entire Talmud while standing on one foot.

Probably this is just as well, for no amount of historical recitation can hope to capture the spirit of this complex place: the tired patina of gold on the Mount of Olives at sunset, the shifting moods of its houses and hills, the combination of thoughtfulness and pride in the eyes of its citizens and, of course, the bizarre but beautiful echo of interwoven prayers – of all religions – that envelop the city walls, blowing in the wind, night and day.

Left, a wall plaque in the Garden of Gethsemane. **Right**, at the Church of the Holy Sepulchre.

JERUSALEM: THE OLD CITY

It's a museum, a bazaar, a collection of sacred shrines. It also happens to be home for 40,000 residents crammed within the 4-km (2½-mile) circumference of its old battlements. And its gates never close, night or day, for the 1 million visitors who are drawn to the Old City of Jerusalem each year.

The Jewish, Christian, Armenian and Muslim quarters of the Old City each have their own special significance. We'll look at each of these, as well as the shrines and monuments immediately outside the walls of the city.

The Jewish Quarter: Inhabited by Jews as far back as the First Temple Period 3,000 years ago, the **Jewish Quarter** today is a modern neighbourhood housing nearly 700 families, with numerous synagogues and *yeshivas* (academies for Jewish studies).

This thriving little community was literally rebuilt out of the rubble follow-

Left, Dome of the Rock.

ing the reunification of Jerusalem in the 1967 Six Day War. Families who had lived in the quarter prior to their expulsion by the Jordanians in 1948 were the first to move back in. Religious Jews revived many of the old study houses and congregations. Artists, attracted by the picturesque lanes, soon took up residence. Today the Jewish Quarter is one of the city's most desirable (and expensive) areas.

Nowhere is the old-new character of the quarter more evident than in the **Cardo**. With its modern lamps and smart shop fronts, this submerged pedestrian byway at first looks like a trendy shopping mall incongruously set next to the old bazaar.

The Cardo was the north–south axis of the garrison town that the Romans built after they destroyed Jerusalem in AD 70. Called Aelia Capitolina, the town was laid out geometrically like an army camp, with the Cardo (from Latin: cardinal, or principal) as its main thoroughfare. In the Byzantine period this colonnaded avenue ran for 180 metres (600 ft) to a looming church called the Nea, built by the Emperor Justinian in AD 543 and destroyed in an earthquake in the 8th century. Later the Crusaders used the Cardo as a main market street. After they were expelled by the Muslims, Jerusalem reverted to a backwater and the Cardo was eventually buried beneath 4 metres (13 ft) of rubble, to be excavated and brought to life again only in the 1980s.

Signs and diagrams along either side of the "new" Cardo show the remains of the various civilisations that conducted their daily commerce here. A large excavation reveals the outer wall of the city of the Judean King Hezekiah. At another point, Byzantine Corinthian-style columns have been restored, along with roofing beams, to illustrate how shops lined the thoroughfare.

The southern end of the Cardo is open to the sky. Here the big paving stones lie bright in the sunlight, the columns exposed in all their classic beauty. It's also from this point outdoors that visitors can best appreciate the reconciliation of demands for museum and neighbour-

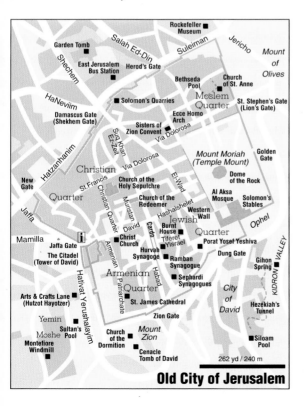

Old City of Jerusalem

262 yd / 240 m

hood. City planners had wanted apartments along the route, while archaeologists insisted that the historical heart of the city be exposed. The compromise: apartments standing on stilts above the ancient avenue.

Running parallel to the Cardo is Jewish Quarter Road, site of the **Jewish Quarter Museum**, which offers a 15-minute multi-media presentation on the history of the area from the Israelite Period to the present. The emphasis is on how the Jewish Quarter was lost to the Arab Legion in Israel's War of Independence in 1948; how it was subsequently regained in the Six Day War of 1967; and how it has since been reconstructed. The museum also has an unusual collection of pictures taken by *Life* magazine photographer John Phillips during the battle in 1948, and again in 1975 when Phillips returned to find and photograph the survivors.

A few steps away from the museum is a **memorial** to the fighters who fell defending the quarter. An electronic map recreates the battle, house by house.

Between the museum and the memorial is the **Ashkenazi Court**, a synagogue and residential complex established in 1400 by European Jews. The great **Hurvah Synagogue** was burned by angry creditors in 1720 (hence its name, which means ruin). In 1856 it was rebuilt, but in May of 1948 it was blown up by the Arab legion; today only the dynamic span of its front archway rises over the site.

Beneath the Hurvah is the **Ramban Synagogue**, built shortly after the noted Bible commentator Rabbi Moses Ben Nahman emigrated from Spain in 1267, and possibly the oldest of the many houses of worship in the Jewish Quarter. Now it is used every day.

The most enchanting of the quarter's venerable houses of worship are on Hakehuna Street in the complex known as the **Four Sephardi Synagogues**. Destroyed during the 1948 battle and used as stables during the 19-year Jordanian rule of the Old City, these synagogues have been lovingly restored to serve both as houses of worship and as Late-afternoon daylight bathes the Jewish Quarter.

a museum documenting their destruction and rebirth. Of particular interest are the Italian hand-carved **Arks of the Law** in the **Stambouli** and **Prophet Elijah Synagogues**, and the early 17th-century **Yochanan Ben-Zakkai Synagogue** with its cheery folk characters.

A short walk up Or Ha-Haim Street, the **Old Yishuv Court Museum** (Sun–Thurs, 9am–4pm) illustrates the lifestyles of the Jewish community of the Old City in bygone days when immigrants from a particular village in, say, Poland or Hungary would cluster communally around one court, sharing many facilities. The grounds incorporate two courts and two synagogues.

At the end of Tiferet Israel Street is the most remarkable archaeological site in the Jewish Quarter: the **Burnt House**. This, apparently, was the residence of the priestly Bar-Kathros clan at the time of the Jewish revolt against Rome.

Among other clues, ashes from a great conflagration indicate that the house was destroyed when Titus razed the city. The numerous finds displayed within the house include a measuring weight bearing the name Kathros, and the skeletal arm of a woman in the kitchen who was apparently struggling to escape the fire.

The Western Wall: The wide stone steps at the end of Tiferet Israel lead down to the most important site – not only within the quarter, but in all of Jewish civilisation. This, of course, is the **Kotel Ha-Ma'aravi**, or the **Western Wall**.

Clambering up and down these steps at all hours of the day and night – like so many angels ascending and descending Jacob's ladder – is a stream of worshippers, pilgrims and tourists. The hum from the right comes from the students of the rebuilt **Porat Yosef Yeshiva**, the largest in the quarter and the work of noted Israeli architect Moshe Safdie.

Midway down the steps is an observation platform, a good place to take in the famous postcard panorama. Below and to the left is the Western Wall plaza and the Wall itself.

Above the Wall: The **Temple Mount**, the biblical Mount Moriah where

Praying at the Western Wall.

Abraham nearly sacrificed Isaac, where the First and Second Temples once loomed, and where the golden Dome of the Rock and the silvery Al-Aksa Mosque now stand. To the right of the Temple Mount is a vast maze of archaeological excavations which lead to the Old City wall and to Dung Gate.

The Jewish Quarter area was known in Temple times as the Upper City. The plaza below occupies the lower end of what was called the Tyropoeon Valley, the rift that cuts through the entire length of the Old City. Because this was the lowest point in the Old City, rubble and trash have been dumped here over the centuries, filling in much of the space between the upper level and the Temple Mount (and giving Dung Gate its inglorious name).

Rising to a height of 15 metres (50 ft), the Western Wall consists chiefly of massive carved stone blocks from the Herodian era, topped by masonry from the Mameluke and Turkish periods. Contrary to popular belief, it was not a part of the Temple itself, but merely the retaining wall for the western side of the Temple Mount. Nevertheless, because it was the only remnant of the Temple complex to survive the Romans' sack of the city, it has inspired the reverence of Jews for 1,900 years. Because Jews also gathered here to bemoan the loss of the Temple, the place earned the sobriquet "Wailing Wall".

The tunnel-like enclosure at the northern end of the Wall is the site of continuing excavations. The main arch, named for the 19th-century British explorer Captain Charles Wilson, may have supported a huge pedestrian bridge between the Temple Mount and the Upper City. Below the arch is the deep shaft dug by Wilson's contemporary, Sir Charles Warren. Archaeologists have determined that the Wall extends another 15 metres (50 ft) below ground level.

In front of the Wall is the entrance to the controversial **Hasmonean Tunnel**. Here archaeologists have dug out a 2,000-year-old street leading along the rim of the Temple Mount several hundred metres northwards to the Via

Left, celebrating a Bar Mitzvah at the Wall. Below, men and women pray in different sections at the Wall.

Dolorosa as it passes through the Muslim Quarter. The Arabs have always feared that the tunnelling was a Zionist plot to enter under the Temple Mount and blow up the mosques, even though excavations are not under the Haram El Sharif at all. In fact the tunnel has been open to visitors as a cul-de-sac for nine years, but the opening of the northern entrance at the Via Dolorosa in 1996 sparked serious Palestinian rioting.

The southern excavations at the opposite end of the Wall contain a broad stairway where prophets harangued the crowds on their way to the Temple, the abutment called Robinson's Arch (after its 19th-century American discoverer Dr Edward Robinson), and the remains of palatial buildings and purification baths from Temple times. From the walkway above the excavations, the site is a jigsaw puzzle of incomprehensible stone. A licensed guide with Bible in hand makes the area come alive. New excavations, uncovered in 1996, enable the public to see the actual shop-lined street that bordered the surroundings of the Second Temple before it was destroyed in AD 70. At the southwestern edge of the Temple Mount, adjacent to the Western Wall plaza, these new findings are preserved in an archaeological park, open daily to visitors.

Above the Kidron Valley: More major sites of Jewish interest remain just outside the Old City walls. These include the City of David, the Kidron Valley and Mount Zion.

The **City of David** excavations are on the steep hillside outside the Dung Gate. This hill is called the Ophel, and the archaeological dig here, which is still going on, has been the scene of violent protests by religious zealots claiming that ancient Jewish graves have been violated. The diggers dispute this, and say that in any case the site is too important to leave buried. That's because the Ophel is where the earliest incarnation of Jerusalem stood: the Jebusite city of more than 3,000 years ago.

Around 1,000 BC, King David captured the city and made it his capital. Although his son Solomon was to build

City of David excavations at the Ophel.

the Temple above it on the high ground, the main residential portion of the city itself remained clinging to this slope above the Kidron Valley. It did so because at the foot of the slope is the **Gihon Spring**, at the time the only water supply for Jerusalem.

Since the spring was located in a cave on the floor of the Kidron, Jerusalemites were in danger of being cut off from their water when the city was attacked. But the stunning engineering project known as **Hezekiah's Tunnel**, carried out by King Hezekiah about 300 years after King David's time, managed to connect the Gihon Spring to the Silwan Pool inside the city some 533 metres (more than a quarter of a mile) farther down the valley. The intrepid 19th-century archaeologist Charles Warren not only explored the tunnel, but also discovered a shaft reaching up through the Ophel to an underground passage from where city residents could come to draw water in buckets.

In 1867 Warren had to crawl on his belly through the stream bed to explore the water system. Today visitors can study the schematics in comfort in the City of David archaeological park, and then stroll through the illuminated passageway to the top of Warren's shaft to peek at the water rushing below. In the Kidron Valley itself, visitors with candles can tramp along the knee-deep stream in Hezekiah's Tunnel from the Gihon Spring and through the Ophel until it emerges at the Silwan Pool.

The upper end of the Kidron Valley, the portion also known as the **Vale of Jehosaphat**, contains several Jerusalem landmarks. The slope off to the northeast is the **Mount of Olives**, containing a Jewish cemetery dating back thousands of years.

In the valley itself are the **Pillar of Absalom** and the **Tomb of Zachariah**. Despite their traditional names, these stately tombs are not thought to be the resting places of David's rebellious son or of the angry prophet. Rather, archaeologists believe these tombs were part of the vast 1st-century necropolis that encircles Jerusalem, and probably served

Left, Jewish cemetery, Mount of Olives. Below, the Tomb of Zachariah.

wealthy citizens or notables of the Herodian court. Take special note of the graceful pillars and elaborately carved friezes. The handsome Tomb of Hezir nearby bears an inscription identifying it as the burial cave of a noted priestly family. Isolated, silent and still, the tombs at this end of the hot and dusty Kidron Valley evoke something of the mood of Egypt's Valley of the Kings.

Occupying the promontory outside the Old City's Zion Gate, where bullet marks testify to the fierce fighting that took place here during the War of Independence, is **Mount Zion**. For ages symbolic of Jewish aspirations for a homeland, it bestowed its name on the national liberation movement. Suleiman is said to have executed the architects of his great wall for neglecting to include Mount Zion within the circumference of the Old City.

The Dormition Abbey on Mount Zion. After 1948, the Old City fell to Jordan but Israel retained Mount Zion and from 1948 to 1967 the historic ridge was a vital lookout point for the young country, as well as its closest approach to the shrines of the Old City and Western Wall. Today's Mount Zion is less controversial, if no less beloved. Churches and *yeshivas* huddle side by side amid the landmark's gardens and wind-bent pipes.

Within the **Diaspora Yeshiva** complex is the site of **King David's Tomb**. Archaeologists maintain that this is another example of a site not corresponding to historical truth, but that hasn't prevented the tomb from being venerated. The adjacent **Chamber of the Holocaust** is a memorial to the destroyed Jewish communities of Europe.

From here, the new stone pedestrian walk between Zion Gate and the church complex leads to a fine vista of the new Jerusalem.

The road to Calvary: Rome likes to think of itself as the centre of the Christian world, and St Peter's Basilica is certainly grander than anything Jerusalem has to offer. Yet within the worn walls of Jerusalem are two places that stir the most casual Christian: the Via Dolorosa and Calvary. Indeed, these names reside in the consciousness and

reverberate in the vocabulary of all Western civilisation.

Archaeologists, as they are wont to do, maintain that neither the Way of Sorrows nor any of the other major sites that we identify today with the Crucifixion correspond to historical reality. But if the Via Dolorosa that we traverse was not walked upon 2,000 years ago, some ancient road at least is indeed buried underneath the present ground level.

In the same vein, pilgrims should not be unduly distressed that today's Via Dolorosa is a commercial street, complete with a Jesus Prison Souvenir shop and a Ninth Station Boutique. They should bear in mind that the lane was a bustling city steet at the time of Jesus.

The **Via Dolorosa** begins at St Stephen's Gate (also called Lion's Gate) which, despite the surrounding churches, is actually in the Muslim Quarter.

The municipality's East Jerusalem Development Corporation recently opened a **Pilgrim's Reception Plaza** here, about 30 metres (100 ft) inside St Stephen's Gate. This plaza was the finishing touch to an elaborate and delicate project of repairing the Via Dolorosa that included restoration of collapsing buildings and overhead arches, replacement of the 400-year-old sewage system, and proper demarcation of the Stations of the Cross. When the plaza was cleared of rubble, huge paving stones dating from the Roman period were exposed. These stones, which have been revealed at a few points elsewhere along the route, may very well have been walked on by Jesus and his followers.

Guided tours generally begin at the reception plaza, and are recommended, especially as some of the Stations of the Cross are difficult to locate in the hustle and maze of the Old City.

Directly opposite the plaza is the **Church of St Anne**, considered to be the best-preserved Crusader church in the entire Holy Land. In addition to a crypt designated as Mary's Birthplace, the church compound contains the **Bethesda Pool** where Jesus performed a miraculous cure.

The **First Station of the Cross**, where

A doorway (left) on Via Dolorosa (below).

Jesus was sentenced, is tucked away inside the courtyard of the Umariyah school, a Muslim boys' institution. The **Second Station**, where Jesus received the Cross, is opposite on the street outside the **Chapel of Condemnation** and the **Church of the Flagellation**. It was here that Jesus was scourged and had the crown of thorns placed on his head. The latter church also has a graceful courtyard and quiet garden.

The events associated with the first two stations are believed to have taken place in Herod's **Antonia Fortress**, remains of which are found today beneath the churches along both sides of the Via Dolorosa. In the nearby **Church of the Sisters of Zion**, for example, is a huge underground chamber called the **Lithostrotos**, often said to be the place where Pilate judged Jesus; on the paving stones are signs of board games played by Roman soldiers.

Outside is the **Ecce Homo Arch**, which some maintain was constructed by the Emperor Hadrian in the 2nd century and which takes its name from Pilate's jeer "Behold the man!". At the end of 1985, the Sisters of Zion dedicated a Roman arch inside the church which they contend is the Ecce Homo.

Almost all of the ensuing stations on the Via Dolorosa are marked by plaques bearing the appropriate quotations from the Bible, and many are accompanied by a fan-like design in cobblestone on the street.

The **Third Station**, where Jesus fell with the Cross, is commemorated by a column in a wall on El-Wad Street, which the Via Dolorosa traverses. Just beyond is the **Fourth Station**, where Jesus encountered Mary. On this site is the **Armenian Catholic Church of Our Lady of the Spasm**, which has a notable Byzantine mosaic within its crypt.

The Via Dolorosa at this point becomes a fairly steep and crowded commercial lane ascending to the right from El-Wad. The **Fifth Station**, just at the juncture of El-Wad and the Via Dolorosa, is where Simon the Cyrenian helped Jesus carry the Cross. A bit farther on is the **Sixth Station**, at the **House**

Below, Ecce Homo Arch. Right, olivewood images of Mary and Jesus in a Via Dolorosa gift shop.

of **St Veronica**, where Veronica cleansed the face of Jesus with her veil.

At the point where the Via Dolorosa bisects the Souk Kahn ez-Zeit bazaar is the **Seventh Station**, where Jesus fell again. This is also believed to be the site of the **Gate of Judgement** from which Jesus was led out of the city to the place of crucifixion, and where his death sentence was publicly posted.

The Via Dolorosa at this point disappears; buildings cover the rest of the route to the Church of the Holy Sepulchre. But the church and the last Stations of the Cross are very close by.

The **Eighth Station** is outside the Greek Orthodox **Chapel of St Charalampos**, built on the site where Jesus addressed the women with the words, "Weep not for me, but weep for Jerusalem." At the Ethiopian Coptic Church compound off the Khan ez-Zeit bazaar, a pillar marks the **Ninth Station**, where Jesus stumbled for the third time. The final Stations of the Cross are all encompassed within the vast Church of the Holy Sepulchre.

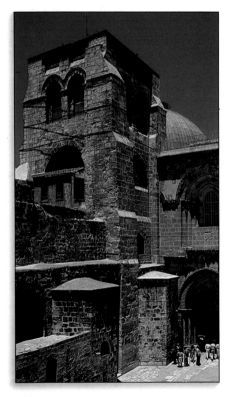

The Holy Sepulchre: Experienced travellers are probably aware that the more venerated the shrine in the mind of the pilgrim, the more disconcerting the reality upon arriving at the site.

In this case the church is rather bewildering in its size and complexity. Here, at the highest point in the Old City, the Romans had a temple dedicated to Venus. Constantine erected a church here in the 4th century, after his mother Helena identified the tomb of Jesus. Constantine's church was later destroyed, and the present church was built by the Crusaders in the 12th century. Much more has been added since the Crusaders left.

Several Christian communities currently share the church, each maintaining its own chapels and altars and conducting services according to its own schedule. Each is responsible for the sanctity and maintenance of a scrupulously specified area. Church fathers have battled in the past over such issues as who cleans which steps.

With its gloomy light, its bustle of construction work, its competing chants and multiple aromas of incense, the **Church of the Holy Sepulchre** can seem intimidating. Freelance "guides" cluster about the doorway, offering to show visitors around for an unspecified fee. While some are competent and sincere, many have a routine in English limited to: "Here chapel, very holy. There picture, famous, famous."

Despite all this, the church maintains its unique magnificence. The focal points, of course, are the section built over the hillock where the Crucifixion took place (called Golgotha, from the Hebrew, or Calvary, from the Latin), and the tomb where Jesus was laid. These sites encompass the continuation of the Via Dolorosa and the final Stations of the Cross.

Stairs to the right just inside the door to the church lead up to **Calvary**. The **Tenth Station** where Jesus was stripped of his garments, is marked by a floor mosaic. The **next three stations** are located at Latin and Greek altars on this same level and within a few paces of each other. They mark the nailing of

The Church of the Holy Sepulchre.

Jesus to the Cross, the setting of the Cross in place, and the removal of Christ's body. The **Fourteenth Station** is below, the Holy Sepulchre itself.

The **tomb** is located downstairs under the church's main rotunda. Within the Holy Sepulchre are the Angel's Chapel, the rock that was miraculously rolled away from the tomb entrance, the chapel containing the burial site, and the adjacent tomb of Joseph of Arimathea.

Other notable sites within the church complex include the **Catholicon**, the Greek cathedral close to the main rotunda, with its stone chalice on the floor marking the centre of the world; **chapels** dedicated to St Helena, to Adam, and to the Raising of the Cross, and **tombs** of the Crusader Kings of Jerusalem.

It is these side chapels and cavern-like tombs that offer contemplative visitors respite from the troops of tour groups that pour through the church. In a chapel beneath the main floor of the church one can sit in relative silence, listening to an Eastern Orthodox mass being chanted in a distant nave, or perhaps watching a solitary monk polishing a candlestick.

Outside the church of the Holy Sepulchre are churches of almost every denomination. Immediately to the left of the Holy Sepulchre plaza is the **Lutheran Church of the Redeemer**, a tall, graceful edifice whose tower – open to the public – offers a magnificent view of the Old City. One of the more unusual churches is the **Ethiopian Coptic Compound** mentioned above, at the Ninth Station of the Cross. The monastery is a replica of an African mud-hut village, and the nearby Coptic chapel is located on the roof of the Holy Sepulchre.

The main entrance to the Christian Quarter is **New Gate** – so named because it was punched through the Old City walls in 1887. It remains the newest of the city's entrances. Winding into the city from the gate are Greek Orthodox Patriarchate Road, Greek Catholic Patriarchate Road and Latin Patriarchate Road. All of these, logically enough, lead to their respective compounds, with churches that often contain interesting libraries and museums.

Priest lights candles over the Holy Sepulchre.

Armenian Orthodox Patriarchate Road is the street leading around the Citadel up from the David Street bazaar. Along this road, just between the Christian Information Center and the post office, stand **Christ Church** and the **Anglican Hospice**, home base in the 19th century to many of the British diplomats and clergymen who encouraged the exploration and modernisation of slumbering Ottoman Jerusalem.

The road next passes through a brief tunnel and then into the **Armenian Quarter**. A modest doorway leads to the Armenians' **St James' Cathedral**, one of the most impressive churches in the Old City after the Church of the Holy Sepulchre. A little further on is the **Armenian Museum**, a graceful cloister housing a fascinating collection of manuscripts and artifacts.

Jerusalem's 2,000 or so Armenians live in a tightly-knit community behind the cathedral-museum complex. As one of the city's smallest ethnic groups, the Armenians have a reputation for keeping to themselves. But in fact they are generally quite outgoing, proud of being descendants of the first nation to adopt Christianity, usually fluent in English and most hospitable to visitors.

This openness applies to the Armenian clergy (identifiable by their tall, pointed headgear), who train at the modern seminary on the other side of the road from the museum. Just around the bend from here, Armenian Orthodox Patriarchate Road leads past Zion Gate, with Mount Zion outside.

Primary among the Christian sites here is the **Cenacle**, believed to be the Room of the Last Supper (although the Syrian Orthodox Church's St Mark's House on Ararat Street in the Armenian Quarter makes the same claim). Today, the Cenacle is basically an elegant but bare room, empty but for the flow of daylight, and it requires considerable imagination to fill it as Leonardo did in his classic fresco.

The Cenacle is located on the second floor of the large, rambling complex that contains David's Tomb.

Adjacent to this building is **Dormition**

Left, the ornate interior of St James' Cathedral. **Below,** an Armenian choirboy at Easter.

Abbey, a handsome Benedictine edifice commemorating the place where Mary fell into eternal sleep. The abbey has a noteworthy mosaic floor and crypt, and its basilica is frequently the site for concerts of liturgical and classical music. The Armenians, meanwhile, are constructing a church nearby that promises to be equally splendid.

Also on Mount Zion is the **Old Protestant Cemetery**, the resting place of the British subjects who figured in the religious, cultural, archaeological and diplomatic life of 19th and early 20th-century Jerusalem. They were instrumental in the initial expansion of Jerusalem outside the walls of the Old City, especially by establishing Anglican Church institutions (and not, incidentally, by promoting a site to rival the Holy Sepulchre – the Garden Tomb).

The **Garden Tomb** is on Nablus Road, leading from Damascus Gate into East Jerusalem. Within a landscape reminiscent of a sumptuous English garden, is a dual-chambered cave that Anglicans and other Protestants claim could have been the tomb of Jesus. The Garden Tomb is situated on a hill that, viewed from the East Jerusalem bus station, suggests to many the shape of a skull, which is the meaning of Golgotha.

Mount of Olives: Wherever the historical Golgotha is located, it's agreed that Jesus made his triumphal entry into Jerusalem from the **Mount of Olives**. This hill, with its breathtaking view of the Old City, is mainly a Jewish cemetery dating back to the biblical period and still in use today. Round about the cemetery, the Mount of Olives has numerous sites of significance to Christians for, in a meeting of faiths, many Jews and Christians believe that the Messiah will lead the resurrected from here into Jerusalem via the Old City's Golden Gate, which faces the mount.

Tradition has it that it was through this big double gate that Jesus marched into Jerusalem, just as an earlier Jewish tradition says that this is how the Messiah will enter the city in the End of Days. The gate, however, is tightly sealed. It is said that either Saladin or

Graceful but empty arches span the Cenacle.

Suleiman decided to have it bricked up to prevent any Messiah from arriving in Jerusalem and wresting the city from Muslim hands.

The reverence for this most sacred of mountains is generally reflected in a spirit of mutual tolerance and understanding. In recent years, however, some ultra-Orthodox Jews have protested against any expansion of Christian presence in the area. Their attention lately has focused on a branch of the Mormons' Brigham Young University, which is being built between the Mount of Olives and the neighbouring Mount Scopus, and zealots periodically post notices around Jerusalem warning of "foreigners encroaching on our time-honoured cemetery."

And as to why the Mount of Olives is so bare and rocky: tradition has it that the Romans cut down all the olive trees to build the siege machines used in the destruction of Jerusalem in AD 70 – but that with the resurrection, the trees will flourish again.

On the far side of the mount, with a view of the Judean Desert and the red hills of Edom across the Jordan, is the **Bethpage Chapel**, from where the Palm Sunday processions to Jerusalem begin. At the crest of the hill is the Russian Orthodox **Church of the Ascension** with its landmark bell tower. Nearby, the small octagonal **Dome of the Ascension** marks the traditional site of Jesus's ascent to heaven. Converted to a mosque with the Muslim conquest of the city in 1187, the structure is said to have been the architectural model for the Dome of the Rock. From this area, several paths lead down to the city. Walks, especially at dawn or sunset, are some of the loveliest experiences Jerusalem offers.

Among the most notable churches on the way down are the **Pater Noster Carmelite Convent**, with the Lord's Prayer in numerous languages on its interior walls, and the **Church of the Eleona**, on the site where Jesus revealed the mysteries to his followers. The small but entrancing Franciscan **Basilica of Dominus Flevit** marks the site where Jesus paused to weep over Jerusalem; built over Canaanite burial caves and a ruined Crusader church, the lovely, tear-shaped chapel was designed by Franciscan architect Antonio Barluzzi, in 1953. The Russian Orthodox **Mary Magdalene Church** further down, easily identifiable by its golden onion-domes, was built by Czar Alexander III in 1873.

At the foot of the mount is the handsome **Church of All Nations**, noted for its fine Byzantine-style mosaic facade. Also known as the Basilica of the Agony, it, too was designed by Barluzzi; its 12 cupolas represent the 12 nations that contributed towards its construction. Its adjoining garden is the largest of several identified as **Gethsemane**, where Jesus was betrayed. The olive grove here has been verified as being 2,000 years old – not remarkable for olive trees. It has been suggested that Judas hanged himself from one of these trees.

Next to the garden is **Mary's Tomb**, deep within the earth and illuminated by candles of a number of Orthodox Christian churches. Midway down the stairs

Shoe-shine man near Jaffa Gate.

to the 5th-century chapel are niches that are said to hold the remains of Mary's parents, Joachim and Anne, and her husband Joseph.

Muslim monuments: The Muslim impact on Jerusalem came essentially in three stages. The first was shortly after the death of Mohammed, when his successors spread the faith out of Arabia and wrested Jerusalem from the crumbling Byzantine Empire in AD 638. In this period the Caliph Omar built a mosque on the Temple Mount which was later expanded to the Dome of the Rock, and in the 8th century the Al-Aksa Mosque was constructed nearby.

The second Muslim phase followed the brief Crusader occupation of the Holy Land. The Europeans were defeated by Saladin, and with the recovery of Jerusalem in 1187 the Muslims began a major reconstruction of the city and especially of the mosques. As of 1249, the dominant Muslims were the Mamelukes, former slaves from Asia Minor who were highly accomplished architects and artisans. Much of the beauty of Islamic Jerusalem today is attributable to the Mamelukes.

But corruption and dissolution marked the Mameluke regime, and by 1516 they were easy prey for the invading Ottoman Turks. For the next 400 years, Jerusalem was ruled from Constantinople. Early in this period (1520–66), Suleiman I built the city ramparts that we see today, the Damascus Gate and the greatest water system in the city from the time of Herod to the present.

After Suleiman, however, the city simply festered until the collapse of the Ottoman Empire in World War I.

Today mosques and shrines dot the various quarters of the Old City, and most of the gates exhibit Islamic calligraphy. But the glories of Islamic Jerusalem are on the Temple Mount, which Muslims refer to as **Haram esh-Sharif**, the Venerable Sanctuary.

The mount is also the most disputed portion of this contentious city. The Arab nations are determined that an Islamic flag must fly over the site. In deference to the local Muslim authori-

Watching the sun set from the Mount of Olives.

ties, Israel leaves the administration of Haram esh-Sharif entirely to Muslim officials. Israeli Border Police provide security in the area, but in cooperation with Arab policemen.

Israel's Chief Rabbinate, meanwhile, has banned Jews from visiting the Temple Mount. The reason is that somewhere on the hill is the site of the ancient temple's Holy of Holies, the inner sanctuary which only the High Priest was allowed to enter, and even then only on one day of the year, Yom Kippur. Nevertheless, certain ultra-nationalist Israelis calling themselves the "Temple Faithful" periodically attempt to hold prayer services on the mount, an act that invariably incenses both the Arab community and other Jews.

The most eye-catching structure on Haram esh-Sharif is the **Dome of the Rock**. The outside of the mosque is a fantasia of marble, mosiacs and stained glass, painted tiles and quotations from the Koran, all capped by the gold-plated aluminium dome. Notable, too, are the curved pillars at the top of the steps, from which, according to tradition, scales will be hung on Judgement Day to weigh the souls of mankind.

The inside of the Dome of the Rock focuses on the huge boulder called the **Kubbet es-Sakhra**. This is the sacred rock on which Abraham was said to have prepared the sacrifice of Isaac. It is also the rock from which, during his mystical journey to Jerusalem, Mohammed is said to have mounted his steed and ascended to heaven.

Appropriately enough, the heavenly interior of the famous golden dome shines down from above, a truly joyous achievement in gold leaf, mosaic and stained glass. Beneath the rock, meanwhile, is a crypt where the spirits of the dead are said to gather.

The silver-capped mosque at the southern end of the mount is **Al-Aksa**, a vast complex that can accommodate as many as 5,000 worshippers. Serving essentially as a prayer hall, Al-Aksa is more functional in design than the Dome of the Rock. Probably built on the remains of a Byzantine basilica, Al-Aksa

Dome of the Rock.

also straddles vast underground chambers known as Solomon's Stables.

Al-Aksa features prominently in the modern history of the region. It was on the doorstep of this mosque in 1951 that a Muslim fanatic murdered Jordan's King Abdullah in sight of his little grandson, the current King Hussein. In 1969 a deranged Australian set fire to the building, causing extensive damage (reconstruction is still under way) and inflaming calls throughout the Muslim nations for *jihad*, or holy war, against Israel. It was at Al-Aksa, too, that Egypt's president, Anwar Sadat, prayed during his peace mission in 1977.

The **Islamic Museum** adjoining Al-Aksa has interesting exhibits covering the centuries of Muslim life in Jerusalem, including lamps, weapons and ancient Korans. Also noteworthy are the mount's elaborately carved fountains, intricate wrought-iron gates, the miniature Dome of the Chain and the marble-and-stone *minbar*, or preaching pulpit, outside of Al-Aksa.

Finally, it should not go unremarked that this area, which can ignite so much political passion throughout the Middle East, is marked by placid, sunny plazas and quiet gardens where the wind sighs through the trees.

Old City atmospherics: For those who thrive on crowds, people-watching in the Old City offers the enthusiast wave after perfect wave. The tradition that Jerusalem is the centre of the world certainly seems borne out by the variety of humanity that daily passes through its portals. Best spots for observing this continental drift are at the outdoor cafés at Jaffa Gate, on the steps leading to Damascus Gate, or at the Western Wall.

Alternatively, you can take in the view of the Old City from the **Ramparts Walk** which can be accessed from Jaffa Gate, Zion Gate, Lion's/St Stephen's Gate and Damascus Gate. Due to religious and security reasons, the section around the Temple Mount is prohibited. For a small charge, tickets allow you to enter four times over two days, thereby allowing you to walk the ramparts of the city at your own pace.

Left, in an Old City market. **Right,** a goat enjoys a rooftop snack.

For a view from the other side, climb the metal stairway on the corner of St Mark's Road and Habad Street, and enjoy a rooftop view that only gets better and better as the daytime colours fade into gentle orange and pink pastels and the clear glistening moonlight replaces the fierce sun. To the east, is the unmistakable Temple Mount and to the north are the domes of the Church of the Holy Sepulchre. Don't forget that beneath you are the mazes of the **market**.

The diversity of Jerusalem's humanity is nearly matched by its wide variety of architecture. Indeed, history lurks amid the hurly-burly of the shopkeepers' displays. A butcher's shop has Roman columns in its corners; a café where Arab and Jewish kids play video games has Byzantine arches; a furniture workshop is obviously part of a Crusader palace. Roman numerals incised on a lintel? Probably by one of Titus's legionaries. A wavelet cornice on a house? Definitely Mameluke work. One needn't be expert to spot these things, just alert.

When buying souvenirs, shoppers should take time to distinguish the quality from the trash, because both forms abound. Palestinian pottery and Armenian tiles are attractive items, but the cheaper varieties have little glazing and will fade. Brass items such as coffee servers and tables should be judged by their weight: too light and it's probably plated tin. Too shiny is also suspect; a little tarnish suggests authenticity. Sheepskin jackets, gloves and slippers are popular, but bear in mind that in time these often smell too much like sheep.

Bargaining is the accepted practice, but not for trinkets costing a dollar or two. If the quoted price for a piece of carved olivewood or a *keffiyah* (Arab head-dress) sounds high, the shopper should walk on; 50 other shops will be offering identical items. Arguing about prices should be saved for more expensive items.

The authorised antiquities dealers are the place for old coins, glass, pottery and so on. Antiquities offered by street urchins are rarely counterfeit; so many real artifacts are unearthed every day that forgery is unnecessary. But the kids' items are hardly museum quality – and, in any event, such trade is illegal.

Similarly, the authorised money changers are generally reputable, and all give about the same exchange rate. None of this applies to the types hissing *psst* from the alleys.

The most popular places to eat are the cafés on David Street and the funky sweet shops along **Souk Khan ez-Zeit**. Wildly popular with Israelis are the pastry shops offering *kanaffi*, a hot cheese and honey dessert, and the *houmous* at Abu-Shukri's on **El-Wad Street**, right near the Fourth Station of the Cross. Yet another favourite treat is *sachleb*, a pudding made with the essence of orchids and sold by street vendors.

Amid the crowds and the noise, the Old City has pleasant corners for rest and reflection. Among these are the **gardens** on Mount Zion, the park-like area between the mosques on the Temple Mount, the sunny Batei Machasei plaza in front of the Rothschild House in the Jewish Quarter and, of course, in many of the church courtyards.

Left, Zion Gate, reportedly riddled with bulletholes. **Right**, Arab shopkeeper.

Jerusalem

875 yd / 800 m

Nablus, Ramallah

Ramat Eshkol

Sderot Eshkol

Hadassah Hospital

Tombs of the Sanhedrin

Ammunition Hill

Mount Scopus

Sanhedria

Shmuel Hanavi

Derekh Shechem

Ma'alot Dafna

Or Samayach Yeshiva

Sheikh Jarrah

Hebrew University

Shimon HaTzadik

Tomb of Simon the Just

American Colony

American Colony Hotel

Bukharin Quarter

Yirmiyahu

Yehezkel

Ge'ula

Beit Yisrael

St. George

Tombs of the Kings

Wadi El Joz

Malchei Yisrael

Mandelbaum Gate

Mea Shearim

Salah Ed-Din

Rockefeller Museum

Mount of Olives

Romema

Nathan Strauss

Mea Shearim

Shivtei Yisrael

Tourjeman Post

Shechem

Garden Tomb

Suleiman

Tomb of the Virgin Mary

Church of Mary

Central Bus Station

Tel Aviv

Jaffa

Israel Center

Ethiopian Church

HaNeviim

Hatzanhanim

East Jerusalem Bus Station

Derekh

International Conference Center (Binyanei Ha'Uma)

Agrippas

Mahaneh Yehuda

Ticho House

Russian Cathedral

Church of All Nations

Mary

Magdalene Church

Holiday Inn

Nahla'ot

Jerusalem Tower

Kikar Tzion

Italian Synagogue

Jaffa

Central Post Office

Notre Dame de France

Absalom's Pillar

Jericho

Yad Laanim (Soldiers Memorial)

Bezalel

Shlomzion

City Hall

The Old

Tomb of Hezir

Tomb of Zachariah

Bank of Israel

Bezalel Academy

Hillel

Beit Agron

St. Vincent de Paul Hospice

City

City of David

Gihon Spring

SACKER PARK

INDEPENDENCE PARK

Hebrew Union College

Arts & Crafts Lane

Supreme Court

WOHL ROSE GARDEN

Ussishkin

Ratisbonne Monastery

King George

Gershon Agron

Mamilla Pool

Mamilla

Sheraton

Yeshurun Synagogue

YMCA

King David Hotel

David Hameleh

Yemin Moshe

Hezekiah's Tunnel

Silwan

Kiryat Ben Gurion

Ruppin

Ben Zvi

Hechal Shlomo & Great Synagogue

Kings

Keren Hayesod

Moriah

Herod's Family Tomb

Mount Zion

Siloam Pool

KIDRON VALLEY

Bloomfield Museum of Science

Knesset

Terra Sancta College

Ramban

King Solomon

Kikar Plumer

Montefiore Windmill

Cinemateque

VALLEY OF HINNOM

Bible Lands Museum

Monastery of the Cross

Jason's Tomb

Aza

Sderot Hazaz

Rehavia

Van Leer Foundation

Jabotinsky

St. Andrew's Church

Khan Theater

Shrine of the Book

Israel Museum

German Colony

LIBERTY BELL GARDEN

Railway Station

Abu Tor

Hebrew University

Neveh Granot

Presidential Residence

Chopin

Jerusalem Theater

L.A. Mayer Museum of Islamic Art

Natural History Museum

PEACE FOREST

Givat Ram

Hapalmach

Emek Refaim

Katamon

Emek Refaim

Derekh Bethlehem

Sderot Herzog

Gonen

Talpiot

UN Headquarters

Sherover Walkway

Mount Herzel, Yad Vashem, Ein Kerem

Pierre Koenig

Yad Harutzim

Derekh Hevron

Holyland Hotel (Model of Ancient Jerusalem)

Bethlehem

Diplomat

Pater Noster

Church of

172

JERUSALEM: THE NEW CITY

If I forget thee, O Jerusalem,
Let my right hand forget her cunning,
Let my tongue cleave to the roof of my
*   mouth, if I remember not thee;*
If I set not Jerusalem above my chiefest joy.
                                —137th Psalm

Next year in Jerusalem!
                    —traditional Jewish prayer

Throughout the ages Jews have wept over, sang and prayed for Jerusalem. Above all, they prayed that one day they might return to their holy city. Yet the Jerusalem that confronted the first waves of Jews who did return to start new lives here in the mid-1800s was a dismal rejoinder to the ideal spiritual capital they had dreamt of for so long. A backwater of the Turkish Ottoman Empire for 400 years, the city by 1917 had been left behind by time. It was filthy, decrepit and unsanitary, cramped within the confines of its great protective wall.

Even the founder of Zionism, Theodor Herzl, during his 10-day sojourn in Palestine in 1898, noted his disgust for its squalid conditions, writing: "When I remember thee in days to come, O Jerusalem, it will not be with delight. The musty deposits of 2,000 years of inhumanity, intolerance and foulness lie in your reeking alleys. If Jerusalem is ever ours, I would begin by cleaning it up. I would tear down the filthy rat-holes, burn all the non-sacred ruins, and put the bazaars elsewhere. Then, retaining as much of the old architectural style as possible, I would build an airy, comfortable, properly sewered, brand new city around the holy places."

No visitor today would doubt the prophecy of Herzl's words. The capital of the Jewish State since 1950, and one united city since 1967's Six Day War, Jerusalem is today every bit as sophisticated as its 19th-century predecessor was provincial. Bold geometric architecture erupts from every hillside; sleek thoroughfares lead into tree-lined boulevards; high-rises tower over church steeples and elegant city parks. There are bars, theatres and luxury hotels.

Yet the city that inspired so much Jewish yearning and Christian passion over the centuries is no less reverent for its modernity; the Christian visitor today will be struck by the vast array of churches and hospices of every conceivable denomination spread across the streets and hilltops of the city. But it is the tremendous blossoming of Jewish spirituality here that is most amazing. Yeshivas, synagogues and cultural institutions abound, the places of worship each reflecting the specific religious or ethnic colouring of its congregants.

Shabbat is observed scrupulously; from dusk on Friday to Saturday evening all stores and buses cease their service, the streets empty, and unprepared visitors may well find themselves without food or transport, save that provided by their hotel, as Jerusalemites go to join their families for the holiday.

Yet as the capital of the State of Israel, Jerusalem – *Yerushalayim* in Hebrew – holds special meaning even to its secu-

The Menorah adorning a window at Hechal Shlomo.

lar residents, who gripe that the city is far less cosmopolitan and lively than not so far-off Tel Aviv.

The new city is still not exceptionally wealthy or grand, and many of her structures exude a symbolic significance that outstrips their otherwise modest aesthetic merits. The domineering presence of a few undistinguished high-rises over the skyline, in particular, is jarring – if nonetheless useful for navigating one's way around. But from other perspectives, the new city can be magical: old and new merge seamlessly and Jerusalem seems as unearthly and splendid as any image its name evokes.

Another integration of old and new, considered by many to be the most lasting legacy of the British Mandate era, is the 1918 declaration forbidding all new construction to employ any material but the city's famous sandy-gold Jerusalem stone. While this has partially tied architects' hands creatively, the result has been a unique sense of visual harmony in the physical surface of the city, enhancing its unity while at the same time moderating the damage of its less successful architecture.

No event has had more influence on the shape of the city in recent years than its unification in the 1967 war. Not only did this clear away the barbed wire and concrete that separated east and west, it also, for a time, took Jerusalem off the front line of the Arab-Israeli conflict. As a result, since the late 1960s there has been an explosion of development.

Presiding over much of this process was one man, Teddy Kollek, Mayor of Jerusalem from 1965 to 1993. The attraction of new institutions into the city, the conservation of Old City landmarks, the colourful sweeps of new public art and hideous behemoths of rapidly erected housing are all, in the end, attributable to his office.

Today, the limits of Jerusalem enclose nearly 600,000 residents, and the city continues to grow, balancing, with mixed grace and awkwardness, the calls of the past and future.

Navigating the city: Cleft by the undulating crests and valleys of the Judean

High-rises surround the Knesset.

Hills and by equally deep political boundaries, Jerusalem is united but disparate, and not always the easiest place to get around in.

Downtown West Jerusalem, however, is compact and easily navigable by visitors. The heart of this area is defined by the triangle of Jaffa Road, King George V Street and Ben Yehuda Street; Jaffa Road then continues to the northwest and the Central Bus Station, located at the gateway to the city, while King George arcs southwards, eventually becoming Keren Hayesod Street and curving back towards the Old City and Mount Zion.

Around Jaffa Gate: As the main portal between the Old City and West Jerusalem, the **Jaffa Gate** acts as a pivot to the new city grid. The site offers a number of contemporary attractions. These include the **Museum of the City of Jerusalem** (Sun–Thurs 10am–4pm, Fri–Sat 10am–2pm) inside the body of the Citadel, which contains displays describing the tumultuous history of the city, figurines of Jerusalem characters, and the multi-layered ruins of the structure itself. A multimedia show with a separate entrance describes the various moods of Jerusalem via numerous slide projectors. The walls themselves are the palette for the sound and light show presented here in a host of languages most evenings from April to October. The Government Tourist Office just within the gate serves as a popular starting point for walking tours.

Old-new Jerusalem: Twisting away from the Old City walls to the left of Jaffa Road, **Mamillah Road** was at one time the big commercial strip of the Jewish city. An expensive residential, tourist and shopping complex is under construction.

During his brief visit to Jerusalem at the turn of the century, Theodor Herzl stayed in a room at 18 Mamillah, the **Stern House**. For years the family kept the room at the back of the postcard/antique shop open to the public at odd hours. It's worth a visit if the place is still standing; in 1985 the government unveiled a plan to level the left-hand

Tourists (below) at Jaffa Gate (right).

side of the street (preserving the more interesting architecture on the right) to make way for a new residential-commercial complex. Somewhat ironically, Moshe Safdie, the visionary Israeli architect who designed Habitat at the 1967 Montreal World's Fair and had several radical plans for the modernisation of Jerusalem, now has his offices in one of the remaining old buildings above the empty store-fronts of Mamillah Road.

Until the 19th century, the Old City walls effectively served as the city limits for Jerusalem's Jews – outside, intolerant Muslims and Bedouin raiders posed a threat to any adventurous stragglers. Opposite the Old City, between the Jaffa Gate and Mount Zion, the first Jewish suburb to penetrate this barrier remains in situ. Wishfully called **Mishkenot Sha'ananim** (Dwellings of Tranquillity), the long, block-like structure was built in 1860 by English philanthropist Sir Moses Montefiore, with the bequest of Judah Touro, a New Orleans Jew.

In the next four years, Montefiore bought an adjoining plot of land and expanded the quarter, calling it **Yemin Moshe**. In the wake of the 1967 war, Yemin Moshe was revitalised as an artists' colony, and today its serene walkways and stone houses command some of the highest rents of any neighbourhood in the city. Montefiore built the landmark windmill at the edge of the quarter to provide flour for the settlement, and in 1948 it served as an important Israeli observation post. It now houses a modest museum.

Between this residential enclave and the Old City walls is the **Sultan's Pool** – long ago a reservoir, today a theatre for outdoor concerts. An ornate Mameluke drinking fountain (*sabil*) sits on the roadside bridge nearby. Just below the Jaffa Gate, half-hidden in the greenery, lies the **Khutzot HaYotzer** (Arts and Crafts Lane), which houses the studios and shops of artisans.

Russians and Prussians: Jaffa Road has long been the prime entranceway to Jerusalem. It was paved in 1898 for the visiting Prussian Kaiser, Wilhelm II –

Left, Montefiore Windmill. Below, a street musician in the Russian Compound.

for whose procession, as well, the wall between the Jaffa Gate and Citadel was rent open. Today Jaffa Road remains the main axis for new city traffic, meandering from the gate to the northern bounds of the city, passing Mahane Yehuda, the Jewish food market that is a colourful attraction in its own right even if you don't want to buy food, before reaching the central bus station.

Leaving the Old City behind, Jaffa Road enters the fabric of the new at **Zahal Square** (Allenby Square until 1948 and afterwards renamed to honour the Israel Defence Forces). The small street to the right hosts another noted crafts area, while behind them to the right loom the massive French hospices of St Louis and Notre Dame de France. This plateau, overlooking the city walls from the north marks the most vulnerable spot in the city's defensive barrier and over the ages served as the launching spot for most of its assaults, including the Assyrians' in 701 BC and Titus's victorious siege in AD 70.

Further up Jaffa Road is the new **City Hall** municipal complex and plaza. Nearby is **Gan Auster**, with bronze plaques describing the growth of Jerusalem's population in modern times. On the left-hand side of the street are two notable buildings: the city's **Central Post Office** and, next door, Erich Mendelsohn's Anglo-Palestinian Bank, now **Bank Leumi**. With its torch-like window grilles and airy, cool interior the 1938–39 building marks a graceful union of Levantine and Bauhaus themes.

The **Russian Compound**, which covers a territory of several blocks to the right of Jaffa Road ahead, was purchased by Tsar Alexander II in the wake of the Crimean War as a refuge for thousands of Russian pilgrims who flocked to the city every year, often dirt-poor and under considerable duress from their trip. Started in 1860, this complex marked the first notable presence outside the Old City; most of the buildings, including the handsome green-domed Cathedral and the Russian consulate, were completed by 1864. The compound has been largely bought by the

Israeli government, and the buildings now house law courts, a police station and part of Hadassah Medical School by day and a plethora of bars, cafés and restaurants by night. The **Hall of Heroism** is a small museum at the back of the complex, within what was once a British prison; it is dedicated to the Jewish underground resistance of the Mandate period.

Rehov Hanevi'im (Prophets' Street) runs from behind the Russian Compound to the Damascus Gate and is one of the main thoroughfares in Jerusalem; because of its congestion, planners propose to add a third traffic lane. However, windows to the past will be sacrificed if the plans go ahead, since this street is fabled for its historic architecture and beautiful buildings. Where the road meets Shivtei Yisrael Street, the **Italian Hospital** was once home to Zionist leader Menachem Ussiskin and author S.Y. Agnon. Today this beautiful 16th-century building houses the offices of the Ministry of Eucation. The **Rothschild Hospital** at the corner of Rav Kook Street, was built in 1887 and is now occupied by students of Hadassah Hospital for paramedic training.

On the corner of Ethiopians' Street is **Tabor House**, built in 1889. Since 1951 it has been home to the Swedish Theological Seminary. The beautiful courtyard is open to visitors daily. The street itself has many architectural wonders which make a stroll down the Street of the Prophets an adventure. Off its course lie several religious institutions, including the **Ethiopian Coptic Church**.

Downtown: Continuing towards Zion Square, Jaffa Road begins to take on the bustling atmosphere of an urban centre. On the right, pleasant cafés are interspersed with various stores: a French-language bookstore, a photocopying shop, a city tourist office, numerous banks. A hop, skip and short walk up Queen Heleni Street takes you to a small **Agricultural Museum** and the Jerusalem offices of the Society for the Protection of Nature, whose Hebrew and English-language tours of the country are widely praised.

Jerusalemites are seldom people of few words.

178

On the other side of Jaffa Road are the winding lanes of **Nahalat Shiva**, Jerusalem's second oldest residential suburb, now delightfully renovated. Founded by Joseph Rivlin in the early 1860s, the enclave has grown to hold some 50 families by the end of that decade. Now Rivlin Street and Salomon Street cross the old neighbourhood and, despite their decidedly narrow girths, these pedestrian avenues house quite a few of the city's favourite restaurants as well as much of its nightlife. At the end of Nahalat Shiva, next to the car park, artisans sell their wares during the summer months.

At the hub of it all is **Zion Square** – always crowded, always crazy. It was so dubbed for the Zion Cinema, now long gone, a rallying spot for young Zionists in the 1930s. A bulky glass tower stands on the site now.

A block up **HaRav Kook Street**, on the left, is one of Jerusalem's most unexpected little nooks – the newly restored **Ticho House**. In the early part of the century it was the home and office of Avraham Ticho, Jerusalem's humanitarian eye doctor, and in more modern times of the artist Anna Ticho.

The Jerusalem café scene gets into its stride at **Ben Yehuda Street**, the five-block long pedestrian avenue that begins at Zion Square. This is the place that everyone comes to see (and be seen), drink and get drunk, sip cappuccino, sample pastries and mingle with friends and strangers alike. Musicians, young couples and would-be prophets are always out in force, and several local characters have established their reputations here. You either love it or hate it.

Marking the city's main north–south axis, **King George V Street**, too, has its share of hubbub. The contrast between old and new is most vivid at the plaza in front of the City Tower, where the preserved doorway facade of an earlier building stands oblivious to its new surroundings. **Hillel Street**, leading back down towards the Old City is the site of the lovely, ornate **Italian Synagogue**, transported from Conegliano Veneto, near Venice, in 1952 and dating origi-

Ben Yehuda Street.

nally from 1719; it is once more in use today. The **Beit Agron**, or press building, is further on, opposite the park and an ancient reservoir, **Mamillah Pool**.

The **Bezalel Academy** on the other side of the Tourist Office is Jerusalem's premier arts and design college and was founded in 1906.

Religion dominates King George Street further on. The **Yeshrun Synagogue** across from the park is followed, further down the block, by the **Jerusalem Great Synagogue**. It aspires to be a third Temple, with a massive entranceway, and adjoining **Hechal Shlomo**, seat of the chief Rabbinate of Israel.

King David Street: Between King George and Mamillah Road, **Gershon Argon Street** rims the final edge of Independence Park; this quiet avenue boasts the world's only **Taxation Museum**.

Nearby **King David Street** hosts two of Jerusalem's most celebrated edifices. The **YMCA**, constructed 1928–33, came from the firm of Shreve, Lamb & Harmon, who at the same time were designing the Empire State Building. Its 36-metre (120-ft) tower offers an outstanding view of Jerusalem and its environs and with its symmetrical rotundas reflects an elegant harmony of modern Middle Eastern form. The **King David Hotel**, directly opposite, was built with old-world grandeur by Egyptian Jews in 1930. It served as a British base of command in the Mandate period and the entire right wing of the building was destroyed in a famous raid by the Jewish underground in 1946. The hotel in recent years has become known for hosting Israel's most famous visitors, including Anwar Sadat in 1977.

Below the hotel, Swiss sculptor Max Bill's **geometric cubes** face the Old City and lead to the Khutzot HaYotzer.

Beyond the King David, an airy park holds the cavern of **Herod's Family Tomb**, where the stormy monarch buried his wife Mariamne and two sons after murdering them in a paranoid rage.

Opposite Mount Zion: Heading down the road between this park and Liberty Bell Garden on the right, the modern city once more opens onto the old. Em-

The King David Hotel (top right of the picture).

180

bedded on the side of the **Valley of Hinnom** like a rugged gem, the **Cinematheque** is the secular set's favourite new landmark. Its theatres screen a wide variety of foreign and alternative films.

Above the cinema, the Scottish **St Andrew Church** has a well-regarded hospice, and a memorial for the Scottish king Robert Bruce who, on his death in 1329, requested that his heart be taken to Jerusalem (the heart was waylaid en route in Spain and never made it). Around the corner, the **Khan Theater**'s atmospheric archways host folklore and jazz performers alike, and the popular Poire & Pomme Restaurant. The train station a block further on dates from 1892 and still offers a daily service to Tel Aviv and Haifa.

While the area is quite serene today, the Valley of Hinnom is historically the site of human sacrifices to idolatrous gods during the reign of King Solomon.

Tree-lined boulevards: Stretching due east from Hinnom are 2 sq. km of tree-lined boulevards and peaceful homes. The area immediately east, called the German Colony, was founded in 1873 by German Templars and still has a subtle European air. In the centre of the neighbourhood is an island housing several important institutions: the **Van Leer Foundation**, the **Israel Academy of Arts & Sciences**, the **Presidential Residence** and the city's new **Cultural Centre**. This complex includes the handsome **Jerusalem Theatre**, home to the Jerusalem Symphony Orchestra, and a multi-theatre complex.

Nearby is the **L.A. Mayer Museum of Islamic Art**, as well as and some of the city's most expensive addresses. Tucked away in the greenery of a sidestreet stands the modest **Natural History Museum**.

The neighbourhood of **Rehavia**, just across Azza Street, is also lovely. In between the apartment homes is an ancient burial chamber known as **Jason's Tomb**, containing Roman-era inscriptions; it was discovered by chance in 1956. The neighbourhood was the home and haunt of many early Zionist leaders, including Levi Eshkol, Ephraim Katzir,

The
Biblelands
Museum.

Golda Meir, Menachem Ussishkin and Eliezar Sukenik.

Religious enclave: Across Jaffa Street again, the mood is far more intense and unworldly. Over a quarter of all Jerusalem citizens are *haredi*, or ultra-Orthodox, and these neighbourhoods reflect the rigorous religious lifestyles of their inhabitants. The most famous Orthodox community is **Mea Shearim** – literally "a hundred gates" – built as early as 1875 as a refuge for Hassidic families. The neighbourhood has retained much of the intimacy and flavour of a European *shtetl*. The Orthodox Jews who live here wear the traditional styles – *peot* (sidecurls), heavy, black garments for the men and shawls for the women. Signs surrounding the community warn that secular fashions, especially "immodest" female dress, is offensive and not tolerated.

Recently, more and more of these settlements have sprung up, such as the Orthodox community of **Har Nof**, on a hill just at the entrance to the city. Since 1988, the religious parties have held the balance of power and, in the light of their new political power (as of the 1996 elections), the Orthodox community has been flexing its muscles iabout issues concerning the preservation of Shabbat. **Bar-Ilan Street**, a major entry route to the city, is home to thousands of ultra-Orthodox Jews who protest about the passing of traffic during the Sabbath. There were clashes between the ultra-Orthodox and the police in 1996.

The **Bukharian Quarter**, to the northwest, dates from the 1890s and houses the descendants of this Central Asian Jewish group. Once quite wealthy, the community fell into decline after the Soviet annexation of the territory brought an end to emigration there.

North Jerusalem, arching from here out across the hills, holds one of the city's more contemporary monuments: **Ammunition Hill**, the scene of a bitter five-hour battle between Israelis and Jordanians in 1967. Today, the trenches and bunkers are preserved and a memorial museum honours the soldiers who died here.

Aerial view of Mea She'arim.

182

In nearby Sanhedria lie the **Tombs of the Sanhedrin**, who were the judges of ancient Israel's highest court. The highway passing by the crypts leads out of the city proper to the village of **Nebi Samuel**, and a mosque marking the spot where the great prophet Samuel is said to be buried. The highway continues to Tel Aviv. The bizzare hexagonal housing units of Ramot and clusters of other new apartment blocks all around mark Jerusalem's new residential frontier.

East Jerusalem: The infamous "green line" that split the city into Israeli and Jordanian sectors wound snake-like across the north of the Old City from just east of the New Gate. While the no-man's land that separated the two areas has officially been cleared away, the gap remains: East Jerusalem is still Arab territory at heart and Arabic-language, music and mosques grace its streets. Much of the population is Christian by faith, however, and middle-class too, and many of the homes, hotels and avenues here are lovely, if not ritzy.

Off **Chail Handassa Street** at the brink of the old border, the **Tourjeman Post** is a fascinating museum documenting the division of the city, within a house that served as an Israeli border post. Nearby is the site of the **Mandelbaum Gate**, which has been taken down, but was from 1948 to 1967 the sole crossing from east to west. The **Damascus Gate**, the grandest entryway to the Old City, marks the hub of the Arab part of the city. Newly landscaped, its plaza offers one of Jerusalem's best forums for people-watching. The **Roman Square Museum** beneath the gate examines the Roman era of the city from the lower-level portal of that period. Also under the Old City walls close by are **Solomon's Quarries**, an ancient mine which tunnels deep below the alleys to Mount Moriah.

The **East Jerusalem Bus Station** just opposite operates buses to points in the West Bank, using an independent Arab line. The **Rockefeller Museum**, further on, has a stately octagonal tower, a gracious courtyard and an extensive collection of archaeological finds; battle-

The *haredim* of Mea She'arim.

scarred from 1967, it is now part of the Israel Museum.

From alongside the Old City, East Jerusalem's two main avenues, **Nablus Road** and **Saladin Street**, lead into a busy cobweb of traffic. Among the best-known restaurants here are the Sea Dolphin on Rashid Street, and Philadelphia, Dallas and Café Europa on Az-Zara Street. The **Garden Tomb**, the Protestant Golgotha (*discussed on page 165*), is off Nablus Road.

Golgotha aside, the whole of East Jerusalem is in fact something of a vast necropolis, and is rife with caves and burial crypts. These include **Jeremiah's Grotto**, where the prophet supposedly wrote lamentations over Jerusalem, and the **Tomb of Simon the Just** – a Jewish high priest from the 3rd century BC. The most awesome chamber is **Tomb of the Kings** – although it is misnamed, being in fact the tomb of Queen Helena of Mesopotamia, who converted to Judaism in 54 BC.

In that part of the eastern city known as Sheik Jarrah, the **American Colony Hotel** is a luxurious Arab villa that in times past greeted such travellers as Mark Twain and Herman Melville and recently housed many "secret" meetings between Jews and Palestinians.

Potent peaks: Isolated and aloof atop a ridge north of the city, **Mount Scopus** holds a special place in Jerusalem history. Its prime importance is as the site of the **Hebrew University**, inaugurated here under the vision of Chaim Weizmann in 1925. It was cut off from the rest of Jewish Jerusalem during the 1948 War of Independence, after a Hadassah Hospital convoy of scientists and staff were massacred in April of that year. Re-absorbed into the city since 1967, the university has enjoyed spectacular modernisation of its campus, which is still continuing. Among the most impressive sites here today is the classical amphitheatre, which hosts concerts and lectures and, when empty, offers an awesome view of the rolling Judean Hills. Other notable monuments include the modern pylon and a British cemetery dating from World War I.

Contemporary synagogue at Mount Scopus campus.

Southern Jerusalem has its own fateful sentinel in the **Hill of Evil Council**. This overlook is where tradition has it that Judas Iscariot received his 30 pieces of silver. The **UN Headquarters** now stands here in the castle that was the seat of the British Mandate government after 1917. The **Peace Forest** and new **Haas Promenade** and **Sherover Walkway** deck the highway leading past here to Talpiot; industrial and commercial **Yad Harutzim Street** is an Israeli Soho, housing many artists' studios. **Kibbutz Ramat Rachel** marks the city's southern tip. To the west, across Derech Hebron and Derech Bethlehem lies **Emek Refaim Street**, where a pleasant village awaits you with up and coming galleries, shops and restaurants

The capital: The open expanse smack west of Central Jerusalem holds the new city's most important landmarks. Ironically, these contemporary forms hover over the eerie 7th-century **Monastery of the Cross**, just below Rehavia, and the juxtaposition of the styles can provide one of the city's most vivid contrasts. (The church marks where the tree for Jesus's Cross was felled.)

The **Israel Museum** on Ruppin Boulevard (Sun, Mon, Wed, Thurs 10am–5pm, Tues 4–10pm, Fri 10am–2pm, Sat 10am–4pm) is one of those institutions that is so acclaimed it has become beyond reproach. Opened originally in 1965, its boxy structure has allowed it to expand over the years; its collection today bridges ethnography, period rooms, history, Jewish culture, coins and modern art, with the Isamu Noguchi-designed **Billy Rose Art Garden**. The nipple-shaped **Shrine of the Book** displays the Dead Sea Scrolls in a chamber nearby.

Opposite are two museums. The **Bible Lands Museum** in Granot Street (Sun–Thurs 9.30am–5.30pm, Fri 9.30am–2pm) displays artifacts from the Middle East in biblical times. The hands-on **Bloomfield Science Museum** is popular with children.

The **Knesset**, the nation's Parliament Building, is the symbol of Israel's democratic system. Be sure you take the tour of the interior. The carved Menorah was

Bloomfield Science Museum.

presented by the British Parliament and depicts scenes from Jewish history. The **Wohl Rose Garden** above is sweetest in the spring. Also in the area is the Hebrew University campus of **Givat Ram**, built to substitute for Mount Scopus between 1948 and 1967, and a pyramidal memorial to Israel's fallen soldiers.

Biblical retreat: Looping westward from the south, you can seek out two unusual sites: a unique scale model of **Solomon's Jerusalem** at the **Holyland Hotel** and the "**Monster**", a sensuous, creature-faced playground by artist Nikki de Saint Phalle at Kiryat Ha Yovel.

The **Malkah Valley** beneath Kiryat Ha'Yovel has been transformed into a leisure and commercial centre. Most conspicuous are the **Teddy Soccer Stadium**, home of Betar Jerusalem, and the adjoining **Malkah Shopping Mall**. Nearby is the newly located **Biblical Zoo**, a beautifully landscaped zoo featuring the animals of the Bible. Also worth visiting, further into the valley, is the **Ein Yael Living Museum**, which offers a hands-on biblical experience as visitors can create their own mosaics and practise other ancient carfts.

Ein Kerem, the biblical small town nestling in a valley to the west of the city proper, is as timeless as the hills and well worth an afternoon itself. Rich in religious history, its most renowned sites include the Franciscan **Church of the Visitation**, designed by architect Antonio Barluzzi in 1956, on the spot where Elizabeth hid John from Herod's soldiers, and the central **Spring of the Vineyard** (also known as Mary's Fountain), which gave the town its name. At the **Church of St John**, mosaics and a grotto mark the traditional birthplace of the Baptist. The **Hadassah Hospital** complex just above the town holds Marc Chagall's stained-glass windows depicting the 12 tribes of Israel. The town also has galleries and restaurants.

A few kilometres south of Ein Kerem are two contemporary sites: the **Kennedy Memorial**, shaped like a giant tree trunk, and the **Artur Rubinstein Memorial Viewpoint**, shaped like a huge piano keyboard.

Left, the Shrine of the Book. **Below**, the Monster.

Remembrance: Remembrance is a key theme of modern Judaism, and Jerusalem has no shortage of memorials. The two most potent of these lie side-by-side on the western ridge of the city, and provide powerful testimony to the two events which altered the course of Jewish history in the 20th century: the Holocaust and the creation of Israel.

Yad Vashem is the official memorial to the 6 million Jews who died at the hands of the Nazis between 1933 and 1945. It is profoundly moving.

The central chamber, **Ohel Yizkor**, or the Hall of Remembrance (Sun–Thurs 10am–4pm, Fri 9.30am–2pm), sits on a base of rounded boulders; inside, an eternal flame flickers amid blocks engraved with the names of 21 death camps: Auschwitz, Buchenwald, Dachau, Bergen-Belsen, Sobibor, Treblinka…

Other structures include the simple shaft of the **Pillar of Heroism**, an art museum of the work created by concentration camp inmates, an extensive archive, the **Hall of Names**, in which the personal records of over 2 million of the murdered are preserved, a valley dedicated to the communities destroyed by the Nazis, and several works of expressive statuary. The permanent exhibit, "**Warning and Witness**", documents the horrors of the era. The **Avenue of the Righteous** leading to the memorial is lined with trees planted in honour of individual Gentiles who helped Jews during the Nazi regime.

Mount Herzl honours the Viennese journalist who founded the Zionist movement between 1897 and 1904. His remains were transported to Jerusalem in 1949, and his simple black granite tomb marks the summit of the mount. Also buried here are Vladamir Jabotinsky and other Zionist visionaries, and most recently, the late Prime Minister Yitzhak Rabin. A **museum** about Herzl stands at the entrance to the mount. In the **Military Cemetery** on the northern slope of the ridge lie graves of Israeli soldiers who died defending the state.

All around them, the stark, rolling Judean Hills and new apartment blocks bear mute witness to their sacrifice.

Below. old Jerusalem modelled at the Holyland Hotel. Right, a statue expresses grief at Yad Vashem.

THE GOLAN HEIGHTS

The **Golan** is a brooding and sombre massif doomed by history and bloodied by nearly ceaseless war. It is a great block of dark grey rock lifted high above the Upper Jordan Valley, and those who have the Golan have the power to rain misery upon their neighbours.

The Golan is a mighty fortress created by the hand of nature. During the Tertiary Age, geological folding lifted its hard basalt stone from the crust of the earth. Today it is a sloped plateau, rising in the north to heights greater than a full kilometre above sea level. It is 67 km (42 miles) from north to south and 25 km (15 miles) from east to west.

Israel considers the Golan Heights to be part of its territory (in 1981 Israeli military occupation of this former Syrian territory was replaced with civil law and administration), although few other countries are willing to accept this *fait accompli*. Israeli justification for absorbing the Golan focused on Syria's belligerence, and the fact that, when it was in Syrian hands, it was used as a base for frequent artillery shelling of the Israeli settlements below.

Since the start of the peace process there has been much talk of territorial compromise over the Golan, but many in Israel vehemently oppose such a move, especially the 13,000 Golan Jewish settlers. A pressure group, Ha'am Im Hagolan (the Nation with the Golan) sprung up as an opposition to any negotiations over the Golan Heights as part of the peace process. In June 1994, 40 tractors drove to the Knesset building from the Golan as part of a four-day protest against handing back the land.

Historic redoubt: The Golan has been disputed throughout history. In antiquity, it was the greatest natural barrier traversed by the Via Maris, the "Sea Highway" that led from Egypt and the coastal plain across Galilee and Golan to the kingdom of Mesopotamia.

The Golan was allocated to the tribe of Menasseh during the biblical era, but was frequently lost and recaptured over the centuries. Under Roman rule, Jewish settlement in the Golan increased, and a few generations later, during the Jewish Revolt against Rome, many of the descendants of those settlers met cruel deaths during the epic battle for the fortress of Gamla.

The range changed hands frequently during the following centuries, though archaeological evidence indicates a substantial Jewish population until the time of the Crusades; for the next eight centuries, the area was largely desolate.

At the end of the 19th century the Ottoman Turks tried to re-populate the Golan with non-Jewish settlers, to serve as a buffer against invasion from the south. Among those who put down roots here were some Druze, Circassians fleeing the Russian invasion of the Caucasus Mountains in 1878, and Turkemans who migrated from Central Asia. A village of Nusseiris (North Syrian Alawites) was also established here.

After World War I, when British General Edmund Allenby drove the Ottomans off the Golan, the region was

included in the British Mandate of Palestine, but in the San Remo conference in 1923 it was traded off to the French sphere of influence.

From 1948 to 1967 the Syrians used the Golan Heights as a forward base of operations against Israel. Jewish villages in Israel's Hula Valley were shelled by Syrian artillery mounted here. Syria continued to install fortifications in the Golan throughout the 1960s, converting the region into a military zone.

War finally broke out on 6 June 1967 with Syrian army attacks on Kibbutz Dan, Ashmura and She'ar Yashuv. The attack was blunted the following day, and on 9 June Israeli troops counterattacked. Within 48 hours, all Syrian units on the Golan had either retreated or surrendered.

The aftermath: Only six inhabited villages, with a total population of 6,400 people, remained on the Golan at the time of the Israeli victory, these including five Druze communities and one Nusseiri village at Ghajar. Within weeks, Israeli kibbutzim began establishing communities in the unpopulated hills, the first being Meron Golan.

In the following years, the region received schools, medical clinics and aid for the old. Modern Israeli agricultural methods vastly increased productivity of many crops, particularly apples, pears, peaches, almonds, plums and cherries, and all residents of the Golan were integrated into Israel's wage scale system.

Syria attacked again on 6 October 1973, the Jewish Day of Atonement, when most Israeli troops were on leave with their families. The next day, Syrian troops occupied nearly half the Golan. Israel responded on 8 October in what was to become the greatest tank battle in history. Within a week, Syria had lost some 1,200 of an estimated 1,500 Soviet-built tanks. By 24 October, Israeli units were within sight of Damascus when the United Nations called for peace, and Israel complied. A dangerous legacy of minefields remains.

In recent years, the Golan has gained a new, more peaceful distinction – as the source and soil of a new Israeli

A destroyed Syrian tank decorates the roadside.

vineyard. The wine, "Yarden", is said to be the best yet produced for export.

Sights to see: The Golan is not a popular tourist attraction. Most Israelis see it as a vital buffer zone between them and Syria, an enormous bunker filling its ancient role of blocking invasion. Visitors usually tour old Syrian battlements. **Nimrod Fortress** on the northern Golan is one of these. From this 13th-century Crusader fortress, one has a spectacular view of the northern Galilee and the Naphtali Hills beyond.

Another often-visited site is **Gamla**, but there is little joy attached to this ruined bastion. Gamla was the "Masada of the North", a fortified town of the south-central Golan which, in AD 66, was the focus of one of the early battles in the Jewish revolt against Rome. Initially, the rebels put Vespasian and three full Roman legions to shame. The over-confident Roman threw his legions against the Jewish bastion only to have them humbled by a much smaller and less professional Jewish force. Recovering, the embarrassed Romans besieged the Jewish town in one of the most bitter battles of the war. Vespasian vowed no mercy would be shown to the defenders.

The Romans gradually pushed the Jews to a precipice on which this mountain top city was built and, when Roman victory appeared imminent, many defenders committed suicide rather than surrender. Four thousand Jews were killed in battle: another 5,000 either committed suicide or were slaughtered by the Romans after Gamla had fallen to them. "The sole survivors were two women," historian Josephus Flavius wrote. "They survived because when the town fell they eluded the fury of the Romans, who spared not even babes in arms, but seized all they found and flung them from the citadel."

The site, reduced to rubble by the Romans, was lost to history for precisely 1902 years. In 1968, Gamla was rediscovered during a systematic Israeli survey of the region. Today it is possible for the visitor to stroll the ancient streets of this community, view the remains of many ancient homes, and even

Ancient dolmen near Gamla.

a synagogue, all built with the Golan's sombre black basalt stone.

The ruins are clustered on a steep ridge and, if the visitor tours the area between late winter and early summer, there is a very good chance of seeing magnificent griffon vultures with a 2-metre (7-ft) wingspan soaring overhead.

In the fields east of Gamla it is possible to find several prehistoric dolmens. These are **stone-age structures** which look something like crude tables, with a large, flat stone bridging several supporting stones. They are generally considered to be burial monuments, and most are dated to about 4,000 BC. Dolmens are found at several other sites around the Golan and the Galilee.

About 6 km (3½ miles) northwest of Gamla, **Katzrin** is the modern "capital" of the Golan and the region's only municipal centre. Established in 1977, it is designed in the shape of a butterfly and is home to the **Golan Archaeological Museum** which exhibits artifacts from the ancient Jewish settlement of Katzrin. Tourists, however, usually prefer to shop in Druze villages, particularly **Majdal Shams** and **Mas'sada**, because of the several shops which specialise in local handicrafts. Majdal Shams is actually the largest town on the Golan and its residents have been separated by the border with Syria since the Six Day War. On Fridays they shout across the border to their relatives on the Syrian side.

Some 15 km (9 miles) south, the road reaches the old Syrian town of **Quinetra**, now a ghost town. The viewpoint here gives a clear view of Syria and the border. Damascus is just 30 km (19 miles) north-east of here.

Ancient baths dating from the Roman period are found on the southern Golan at **Hammat Gader**, near the Yarmuk River. These hot baths were built over springs warmed by volcanic activity deep within the earth; when the waters emerge to the surface, they're steamy hot and rich in minerals. The baths were internationally famous during Roman times, and people came from all over the empire to relax here. Israeli archaeologists have done a fine job of excavating

Skiing on Mount Hermon.

194

and restoring them. Visitors are now invited to take a dip, and to inspect the fine Roman theatre, pools, plazas, mosaics and sundry inscriptions.

Epiphanius, a 4th-century monk, complained about them, noting: "a festive gathering took place at Hammat Gader annually. For several days people from all over came to bathe and wash away their afflictions. But there too the Devil set his snares… since men and women bathe together." They still do – but properly attired, of course.

Mount Hermon: Towering above the north end of the Golan is **Mount Hermon**, (2,814 metres/9,230 ft) with several ranges radiating from it. It occupies an area roughly 40 by 20 km (25 by 12 miles) and is divided between Lebanon, Syria, Israel and several demilitarised zones under UN jurisdiction. About 20 percent of this area is under Israeli control, including the southeast ridge **Ketef HaHermon** (The Hermon Shoulder), whose highest point rises to 2,200 metres (7,200 ft).

The higher areas of Mount Hermon are snow-covered through most of the year, and each winter brings snow to all elevations over 1,200 metres (3,900 ft).

Israeli ski enthusiasts have opened a modest ski resort on these slopes, with a chair-lift, equipment rental shop for skis, boots, poles and toboggans. The slopes are often compared to those found in New England – not particularly lofty, but nevertheless a challenge.

Nature on the Hermon is of particular interest to Israelis because it's the only sub-alpine habitat in the country. Several birds, such as the rock nuthatch and the redstart, are at the southernmost extremity of their range here, while others, such as the Hermon horned lark, are found nowhere else.

Many dolinas are scattered around the Hermon. These are cavities in the surface of the rock formed by karstic action on the mountain's limestone. In the winter, the dolinas fill with snow and they are the last areas to melt in the spring, thus supporting lush green vegetation long after the rest of the slope has dried out under the intense sun.

The spring at **Banias** is among the most popular natural attractions in the country – and has been for many thousands of years. "Banias" is a corruption of the Greek Panaeas, and in a cave near the spring a visitor may find the remains of an ancient temple built in honour of Pan, the Greek god of the forests.

Old Crusader ruins may also be visited in this nature reserve, but the real attractions are the waterfalls and inviting pools.

Before 1967, Banias was located in Syrian territory, but just 4 km (2½ miles) to the west, in Israeli territory, a number of other springs gurgled from the foot of Mount Hermon. The most important of these is the **Dan River**, which provides the greatest single source of the Jordan River – in fact, "Jordan" is a contraction of the Hebrew *Yored Dan* (descending from Dan) and that's precisely what this biblical river does. For its 264-km (165-mile) length, the Jordan flows from the snowy peak of Mount Hermon to the catch basin of the Dead Sea, 400 metres (1,300 ft) below sea level, and the lowest point on the face of the earth.

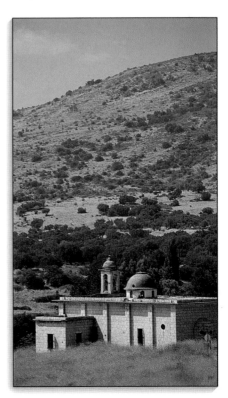

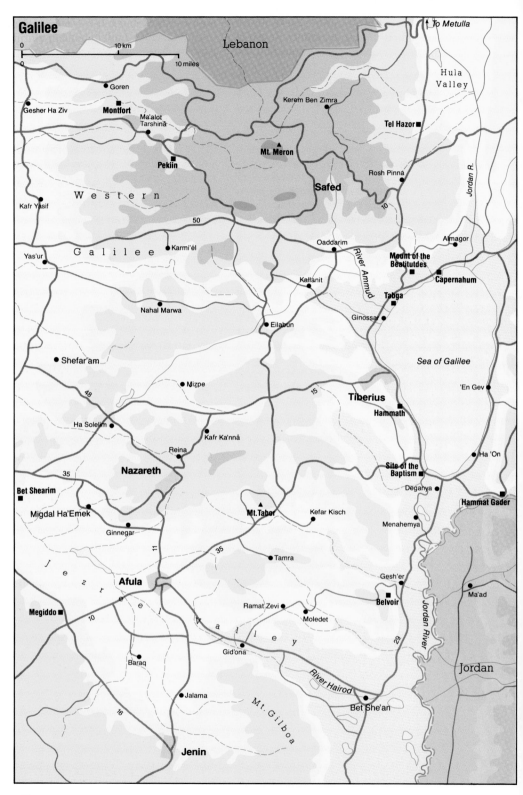

Galilee

0 ___ 10 km

0 ___ 10 miles

To Metulla

Lebanon

Hula Valley

Goren

Gesher Ha Ziv

Montfort

Ma'alot Tarshinā

Kerem Ben Zimra

Tel Hazor

Mt. Meron

Pekiin

Safed

Rosh Pinna

W e s t e r n

Kafr Yasif

50

Almagor

G a l i l e e

Karmi'él

Oaddarim

Mount of the Beatitutdes

Capernahum

Yas'ur

Kallánit

Tabga

Nahal Marwa

Eilabun

Ginossar

River Ammud

Sea of Galilee

Shefar'am

Mizpe

48

'En Gev

15

Tiberius

Hammath

Ha Solelim

Kafr Ka'nnā

Ha 'On

Reina

Nazareth

35

Site of the Baptism

Bet Shearim

Deganya

Migdal Ha'Emek

Mt. Tabor

Kefar Kisch

Hammat Gader

Ginnegar

Menahemya

11

35

Ma'ad

Tamra

Afula

Gesh'er

Belvoir

Megiddo

10

Ramat Zevi

Moledet

J e z r e e l

Jordan River

Jordan

Gid'ona

V a l l e y

29

Baraq

River Hairod

Jalama

16

M t .   G i l b o a

Bet She'an

Jenin

198

GALILEE

A white-robed Druze puffing away on his pipe in a mountain top village; a bikini-clad bather soaking in sulphuric springs at a Roman bathhouse. These are the stark contrasts typical of Israel's dynamically diverse north – the **Galilee**.

Extending from the lush Jezreel Valley to the border of Lebanon, this relatively compact region, at one moment a desolate expanse of bare rock, can suddenly explode into a blaze of blood-red buttercups and purple irises. Here, Christians can retrace the steps of Jesus, while Jews can reflect on the place that produced their greatest mystics.

Lying on the main artery that linked the ancient empires, the Galilee has been a battleground for Egyptian pharaohs, biblical kings, Romans and Jews, Christians and Muslims.

More recently, Jewish pioneers established the country's first kibbutzim here. They have since mushroomed to cover much of this region where tribes of Bedouin still roam and Arab and Druze villages lie nestled in the hills.

The valley: The **Jezreel Valley**, stretching from the Samarian foothills in the south to the slopes of the Galilee in the north, is Israel's largest valley. Because of its strategic location on the ancient Via Maris route, the list of great battle scenes that have scoured this seemingly tranquil stretch is long and colourful. But the greatest battle of all has yet to be fought here. It is the one that the Book of Revelations says will pit the forces of good against the forces of evil for the final battle of mankind at Armageddon. The site referred to is Har Megiddo (Mount Megiddo), a 4,000-year-old city in the centre of the valley.

Even the first written mention of Megiddo – in Egyptian hieroglyphics – describes how war was waged on the city by a mighty Pharaoh some 3,500 years ago. Since then, many a great figure has met his downfall on this ancient battleground. It is said of the Israelite King Josiah, who went down to defeat at the hands of the Egyptians around 600 BC: "And his servants carried him in a chariot dead from Megiddo" (I Kings: 10, 26). In World War I, the British waged a critical battle against the Turks at Megiddo Pass, with the victorious British general walking away with the title Lord Allenby of Megiddo.

In the heap of ruins that make up the mound (*tel*) of Megiddo, archaeologists have uncovered 20 cities. At the visitors' centre, a miniature model of the site gives definition to what the untrained eye could see as just a pile of stones. It is actually a 4,000-year-old Canaanite temple, King Solomon's stables (built to accommodate 500 horses), and an underground water system built by King Ahab 2,800 years ago to protect the city's water source in times of siege. Steps and lighting have been installed to ease exploration of the 120-metre (390-ft) tunnel, along with the almost 60-metre (200-ft) high shaft which was once the system's well.

Afula, the capital and largest city in the Jezreel Valley, is the antithesis of Megiddo. There are no epic dramas to

Preceding pages: a tractor ploughs in Galilee's greenery. Below, Megiddo's underground water system.

be acted out in this sleepy backwater town. Much more in keeping with the larger-than-life dimensions of the valley is **Nazareth**. A strange blend of the timeless and topical, the sacred town where Jesus spent much of his life is today a bustling city of 40,000 Muslim and Christian Arabs – with a communist mayor at its helm.

A water system not quite as historic as Megiddo's but impressive in its own way can be found at **Gan HaShelosha** (The Garden of Three). Modern developers have managed to recreate a tiny piece of Eden in this stunning park. It is also known as Sachne, meaning "warm" in Arabic, because of the warm waters of **Ein Harod** (The Spring of Harod) that bubble up from under the earth to fill a huge natural swimming pool. Around it, exotic flowers and lush forests are interspersed with wide open grassy spaces.

The Spring of Harod actually starts at the foot of the Gilboa mountains, just east of Afula, and flows all the way to the Jordan. But for most of the way, the warm waters are kept underground and diverted for use in local settlements. The only other spot where they surface is at Gidona. The site is named after the Israelite warrior Gideon, who supposedly assembled his forces at this gentle spring 3,000 years ago. In more recent times, it served as the meeting and training spot for the forces of the Palmach, the elite fighting unit of the Jews in pre-state Palestine. There is also a memorial here to Yehoshuah Henkin, a Zionist leader, who purchased hundreds of thousands of acres of land – including this piece – for Jewish settlement.

The Jezreel Valley was, in fact, the first and largest tract of land in what was then Palestine, to be purchased by Zionist leaders close to a century ago. The Arab landowners were only too pleased to rid themselves of what was at the time uninhabitable swampland. In draining the swamps, Jewish pioneers have planted 125 million trees over the years. The act of planting a tree came to symbolise the redemption of the Jewish homeland and has since become a quasi-

Galilee as seen from Tel Hatzor.

religious ritual. Today tree-planting centres in Israel abound, with the largest one located in the Jezreel Valley. The Balfour Forest, named after Lord Arthur Balfour (the British foreign minister whose 1917 speech in favour of a Jewish homeland became known as the Balfour Declaration), has a variety of trees. Balfour's nephew recently added his own sapling to the sprawling forest located 3 km (2 miles) southwest of Nazareth. Aristocratic connections aren't essential however; for a few dollars anyone can plant a tree. The centres are usually open weekdays from 8.30am to 3.30pm, earlier on Fridays.

For an idea of the considerably more gruelling conditions which confronted the original tree-planters, visit the **Museum of Early Agricultural Settlers** at nearby **Kibbutz Yifat**.

To get an overview of the whole Jezreel Valley – a splendid patchwork of gold and green farmland – head up to **Mount Tabor**. This strangely symmetrical hill, shaped not unlike a skullcap, dominates much of the valley. It was here that the biblical prophetess Deborah was said to have led an army of 10,000 Israelites to defeat their idol-worshipping enemies. Two churches commemorate the transfiguration of Jesus Christ, also said to have taken place here.

About a mile west of Gan Hashelosha is **Kibbutz Beit Alpha** where you'll find the country's best-preserved ancient synagogue floor. Discovered when kibbutz members were digging an irrigation channel, the 6th-century floor consists of a striking zodiac mosaic and a rendition of the sacrifice of Isaac.

A particularly remarkable, if eerie, site can be found on the chalky slopes of **Beit Shearim** about 11 km (7 miles) northwest of the Balfour Forest. This is Israel's version of a necropolis. The limestone hills have been hollowed out to form a series of catacombs. Inside the dark labyrinths, vaulted chambers are lined with hundreds of marble or stone sarcophagi (depending on the social rank of the deceased). Each of the often elaborately engraved coffins weighs nearly 5 tonnes. Since the Romans did not allow

Jews to settle in Jerusalem, the centre of Jewish national and spiritual life moved to Beit Shearim. This 2nd-century burial ground became a favourite not only for local residents but for Jews everywhere.

Overlooking the whole length of the Jezreel Valley are the **Gilboa Mountains**. Here King Saul met his untimely end at the hands of the Philistines, causing David to curse the spot forever: "Ye mountains of Gilboa, let there be no dew, nor rain upon you, neither fields of choice fruit" (II Sam 20: 21-23).

The Jordan Rift: East of the Gilboa mountain range is one of the lowest points in Israel: the **Jordan Rift**. Encompassing the Jordan Valley and the Beit She'an Valley, it is part of the same 6,500-km (4,000-mile) rift that stretches from Syria to Africa and is responsible for the lowest point on earth – the Dead Sea. Even here at 120 metres (390 ft) below sea level (it gets to 390 metres/1,280 ft further south), it's like a kiln baking under an unrelenting sun in summertime. By way of comparison, Death Valley, California, the lowest point in the United States, is only 87 metres (285 ft) below sea level. But nourished by the Jordan River, the Yarmuk River, and a network of underground springs (including the Spring of Harod), this remains a lush region, bursting with bananas, dates and other fruit. It is home to some of Israel's most prosperous kibbutzim including **Afikim**, **Gesher** and **Ashdot Ya'akov**.

The ancient *tel* of **Beit She'an** has revealed 6,000 years of civilisation. Near it sits Israel's best preserved **Roman amphitheatre** which once seated 8,000 and there is an archaeological museum featuring a Byzantine mosaic floor. Other structures include a colonnaded street, on the east side of which is a ruined temple which collapsed in an earthquake in the 8th century. Excavations here have revealed 18 super-imposed cities, so if its archaeological intrigue that you are after, Beit She'an is a must. If you're thinking of going to Jordan, there is a crossing here called the **Jordan River crossing**, sometimes referred to as the King Hussein bridge.

The Jordan Valley, at the south end of the Sea of Galilee.

Easily accessible from the highway north of Beit She'an is the impressive Crusader fortress of **Belvoir**. Perched on the highest hill in the region, it offers a superb view of the valleys below and of neighbouring Jordan.

Jewel of the Galilee: Glowing like an emerald, its tranquil surface framed in a purplish-brown halo of mountains, the **Sea of Galilee** is probably the most breathtaking and certainly the largest lake in the country. At 21 km (13 miles) long and 11 km (7 miles) wide, it may not be enormous by global standards, but it has, through some romantically inspired hyperbole, come to be known as a "sea". The Sea of Galilee, the Sea of Tiberias, the Sea of Ginossar are its most popular names. In Hebrew, it's called the "Kinneret" because it's shaped like a *kinnor* or harp.

Not surprisingly, these bountiful shores have been inhabited for millennia, with the earliest evidence of habitation dating back 5,000 years to a moon-worshipping cult that sprouted in the south. Some 3,000 years later, the same lake witnessed the birth and spread of Christianity on its shores, while high up on the cliffs above, Jewish rebels sought refuge from Roman soldiers. The dramas of the past, however, have since faded into the idyllic landscape. Today, it is new water sports, not new religions, that are hatched on these azure shores.

Nowhere is this "fun in the sun" spirit felt more than at the lake's capital, **Tiberias**. A sprawling city of 40,000, halfway down the west coast, it has become one of the country's most popular resorts. On its new boardwalk, lined with seafood restaurants, you can dig into delicious St Peter's fish while enjoying a stunning view of the lake. On the marina you can have your pick of waterskiing or windsurfing, or go for a dip at any of the beaches along the outskirts of the city. (During a typically balmy summer you'll need to dunk yourself in the water one way or another.)

With all the distractions available in this popular playground, it's easy to forget that Tiberias is considered one of the four holy Jewish cities. To remind

you, are the tombs of several famous Jewish sages buried here, including the great 12th-century philosopher Moses Maimonides and the self-taught scholar and martyr, Rabbi Akiva.

When it was founded by Herod around AD 20, Tiberias failed to attract devout Jews and Christians because it was thought to be built over an ancient Jewish cemetery and considered impure. But eventually, economic incentives, as well as a symbolic "purification" of the city by a well-respected rabbi, cleared the way for settlement. During the 2nd and 3rd centuries it reached its zenith. With a population of 40,000, it became the focus of Jewish academic life. It was at Tiberias that scholars codified the sounds of the Hebrew script and wrote the great commentary on the Bible, the *Mishnah*.

By the eve of the Arab conquest of 636, Tiberias was the most important Christian centre outside Jerusalem. A 12th-century battle between the Muslims and Crusaders destroyed the city. After being resettled, it was again re-duced to rubble in 1837, this time by an earthquake. A few devout Jews arrived to rebuild the town and lived there alongside their Arab neighbours until 1948 when the Arabs of the town fled during the War of Independence.

The repeated destruction of the city has, unfortunately, left only meagre souvenirs of its vibrant past. A few remains of Crusader towers dot the shoreline; an 18th-century mosque is crammed in between ice cream stands in the main square.

For historians and hedonists alike, Tiberias's main drawing card is its hot springs situated at the southern outskirts of the city. Legends abound as to the cause of this wonder of nature. In fact, the same cataclysmic convulsions that millions of years ago carved the Jordan Rift also created these 17 springs that gush from a depth of 2,000 metres (6,500 ft) to spew up hot streams (60°C/ 140°F) of mineral-rich water. The therapeutic properties of the springs have been exploited for centuries.

For some contemporary healing, go

By the lake at Tiberias.

to Hamei Tiberias. This hotel-spa offers a range of treatments from whirlpools to "electrohydrotherapy" that are reputed to cure everything from skin ailments to respiratory problems and, claim some, sterility. In the winter, a soak in these mineral-rich jacuzzis can be a soothing respite from the damp Galilee air.

You can see the original **Roman baths** in the National Park across the street in a fascinating little museum devoted to the springs. Next to it, at the site of the ancient city Hammath, archaeologists have uncovered a 2nd-century **mosaic synagogue floor** – undoubtedly the most exquisite ruins you'll find in Tiberias.

Just outside the city are the **Horns of Hittim** where in 1187 the Muslim forces of Saladin defeated the Crusaders in the decisive battle that brought an end to the Crusader Kingdom.

Around the lake: One of the best ways to see the many sites around the lake (if you don't have access to a car) is to obtain a one- or two-day bus pass on Egged's Minus 200 Line (available at most major hotels) which enables you

to get on and off at any of 23 stops. There are also ferry boats that go back and forth regularly from Tiberas to Ein Gev, on the east coast; for the more ambitious, swimming the same route has become a popular competitive sport.

Moving north from Tiberias, you will first come to the towering cliffs of **Arbel**. Today, a rock climbers' haven, during Roman times they served as a hideout for Bar Kochba and his Jewish rebels.

Next is **Ginossar**, an especially beautiful kibbutz with a luxurious guesthouse (be sure to ask about the perfectly intact 2,000-year-old boat recently uncovered on the shores of the kibbutz). **Vered HaGalil** is a bit of an anomaly in these parts with its Wild West-style guesthouse-restaurant and horseback tours. At the northern tip of the lake you come to the ruins of **Capernahum**, one of the most important Jewish and Christian sites in the Roman period.

Hovering over the black pebbly beaches on the east coast of the lake are the Golan Heights, which until 1967 were in Syrian hands (*see pages 191–*

Hammath ruins, Tiberias.

95). The few settlements on this side of the lake used to be bombarded regularly by the Syrians, making much of the lake inaccessible. Since the Israeli takeover, the area has developed rapidly and tourism has burgeoned. Of late, however, the Golan Heights have become central in the peace negotiations between Israel and Syria. Until the early 1990s, Israelis of all political perspectives would not have contemplated giving up this strategic region. Now the Golan Heights has become a contentious pawn in a regional peace process. The residents and other hard-liners have formed a pressure group called Ha'am Im Hagolan (the Nation with the Golan) to oppose the return of this area.

Several settlements have guesthouses and camping facilities, including **Moshav Ramot**; **Kibbutz Ein Gev**, site of a gala music festival every spring; **Kibbutz Ha'on**, which had an ostrich farm before they became popular in other parts of the world; and **Kibbutz Ma' Agan**. Also on the east coast is the **Golan Beach** and its water wonderland,

the **Luna Gal**. At **Beit Yerah**, on the southern tip of the lake, are the ruins of an ancient moon-worshipping cult.

Around the point where the lake merges with the Jordan River are three kibbutzim: **Deganya Aleph**, **Deganya Beth** and **Kinneret**. Not having guesthouses, they attract fewer tourists than other kibbutzim around the lake, but it is these that are most worth noting because they were the first. From their ranks sprang many of Israel's legendary leaders, including Moshe Dayan.

At the entrance to Deganya Aleph is a Syrian tank, stopped in its tracks in the 1948 War of Independence.

Cradle of Christianity: It was, of course, on the waters of the Sea of Galilee that Jesus was said to have walked. The coast of the lake is dotted with churches marking the miracles Jesus reputedly performed in this region which was to become the cradle of Christianity.

"Can anything good come out of Nazareth?" (John: 1,46). This rhetorical question might seem puzzling today, particularly to millions of Christians for

Left, House of St Peter, Capernum. Below, an ostrich at Kibbutz Ha'on.

whom Nazareth is equated with Christianity itself. But when it was posed two millennia ago, the one feature that most distinguished this village in the lower Galilee was its very obscurity.

Since then, the quaint town where Jesus Christ grew up has become renowned. Today, of almost two dozen churches commemorating **Nazareth**'s most esteemed resident, the grandest of all is the monumental **Basilica of the Annunciation**. The largest church in the Middle East, it was built 20 years ago, but encompasses the remains of previous Byzantine churches. It marks the spot where the Archangel Gabriel is supposed to have informed the virgin Mary that God had chosen her to bear his son. The event is depicted inside in a series of elaborate murals, each from a different country. In one, Mary appears kimono-clad and with slanted eyes; in another, she's wearing a turban and bright African garb. Not to be outdone, the Americans have produced a highly modernistic cubist version of the virgin.

Some of the simpler churches, how-ever, capture an air of intimacy and sanctity that the colossal Basilica lacks. This is especially so in the Greek Orthodox **Church of St Gabriel**. Upon entering the small dark shrine you hear nothing but the faint rush of water. Lapping up against the sides of the old well inside the church is the same underground spring that provided Nazareth with its water 2,000 years ago. It takes only a little imagination to envision the scene described in the Gospels in which, "Mary took the pitcher and went forth to fill it with water" – at which point the angel Gabriel is said to have descended and informed her of the surprising news.

In the basement of the **Church of St Joseph** (next to the Basilica) is a cavern said to have been the carpentry workshop of Joseph, Jesus's earthly father.

Shortly after Jesus left Nazareth at age 28, he met John the Baptist preaching near the waters of the Jordan. In the river that the Bible so often describes as a boundary – and more figuratively, as a point of transition – Jesus was baptised. Once thus "cleansed", he set out

Nazareth, pastoral in the early evening.

on his mission. Tradition holds that the baptism took place at the point where the Sea of Galilee merges with the Jordan River near what is today **Kibbutz Kinneret**.

A bathing area has been established just outside the kibbutz in order to accommodate the many pilgrims who still converge on the site. (There is a rival "site of the Baptism" further south near Jericho.)

A few miles outside Nazareth, nestled among pomegranate and olive groves, is the Arab village of **Cana**. Shortly after being baptised, Jesus attended the wedding of a poor family in this town. Here, say the Gospels, he used his new-found powers for the first time, making the meagre pitchers of water overflow with wine. Two small churches in the village commemorate the feat.

It was in the numerous fishing villages around the Sea of Galilee that Jesus found his first followers. The village of **Capernahum** on the northern tip of the lake, became a second home for him. Here he is said to have preached

more sermons and performed more miracles than anywhere else.

It was a metropolis of sorts in its heyday, and at least five of the disciples came from this Jewish town. (It is after one of them, a simple fisherman named Peter, that the Galilee's most renowned fish gets its name.) Today the site houses the elaborate remains of a 2nd-century synagogue – said to be built over the original one where Jesus used to preach. There is also a recently completed church shaped like a ship.

It was standing on a hilltop overlooking the Sea of Galilee that Jesus proclaimed to the masses that had gathered below: "Blessed are the meek for they shall inherit the earth." This, but one line of the now famous Sermon of the Mount, is immortalised by the majestic **Church of the Beatitudes**, also near Capernahum.

In the neighbouring town of **Tabga**, he is said to have multiplied a few loaves of bread and fish into enough food to feed the 5,000 hungry people who had come to hear him speak. The new **Church of the Multiplication**, built over the colourful mosaic floor of a Byzantine shrine, stands here today.

When his sermons began to provoke the Romans, Jesus took three of his disciples and ascended Mount Tabor. There, the Gospels say he "was transfigured before them – his face shone like the sun and his garments became white as light." The Franciscan **Basilica of the Transfiguration** commemorates the event which Christians believe was a prelude to his resurrection.

Atmospheric Safed: A few miles northeast of the lake loom the two highest peaks in the Galilee. They are said to exude an air of something eternal and inexplicable that makes them seem even higher than their 1,170 metres (3,840 ft). Known as the **Mountains of Meron**, their mystique is attributed to the legendary town that faces them: **Safed**.

When one of the great 16th-century poets of Safed was returning to his town after a long absence, he was met along the way by a band of robbers who threatened to kill him. When granted a last request, he picked up his flute and be-

Traditional themes are given a contemporary look by a Safed artist.

gan to play a haunting prayer. The melody so enchanted the robbers' camels that they began to dance, sending their bewildered owners fleeing.

Sheltered by the highest peaks in the Galilee, Safed seems also to be sheltered from time itself. Its narrow, cobblestoned streets wind their way through stone archways and overlook the domed rooftops of 16th-century homes. Devout men, clad in black, congregate in medieval synagogues, the echo of their chants filling the streets.

A modern area of Safed, with some 18,000 residents, has sprung up around the original city core.

When the Spanish Inquisition sent thousands of Jews fleeing, many ended up in Safed, bringing with them the golden age they'd left behind in Spain. The rabbinical scholars of Safed were so prolific that in 1563 the city was prompted to set up the first printing press in Israel (or Asia for that matter).

Safed, an Orthodox Jewish town. The Shulchan Aroch, the basic set of daily rituals for Jews, was compiled here. But the real focus of Safed's sages was not the mundane, but the mystical. Many had been drawn to the city in the first place because of its proximity to the tomb of Rabbi Shimon Bar-Yochai, the 2nd-century sage who is believed to have written the core of the Cabala, Judaism's foremost mystical text.

The efforts of Safed's wise men to narrow the gap between heaven and earth left not only great scholarly work and poignant poetry, but also a legacy of legends about their mysterious powers.

At one synagogue (Abohav), an earthquake apparently destroyed almost the entire building but left the one wall facing Jerusalem unscathed.

Every synagogue here is wrapped in its own comparable set of legends which the *shamash* (deacon) is usually delighted to share. Not all the synagogues are medieval, many of the original ones having been destroyed and replaced by more modern structures. But the spirit of old still lingers in these few lanes off **Kikar Meginim**.

The special atmosphere that permeates Safed has captured the imagination

of dozens of artists who've made it their home. Like the rest of the old city, the **artists' quarter** of Safed remains untouched. Nothing has been added for "the benefit of the tourist" – nothing has to be. Winding your way through the labyrinth of lanes, you'll find over 50 studios and galleries as well as a general art gallery and a printing museum.

Towering above the centre of Safed, littered with Crusader ruins, is **Citadel Hill**, an excellent lookout point taking in a panorama that extends from the slopes of Lebanon to the Sea of Galilee.

Like the ripples that form around a stone tossed in a lake, the hills surrounding Safed reverberate with the sacredness the city inspires. Starting at the cemetery at the base of Safed, where the biblical prophet Hosea is said to be buried, the whole area to Mount Meron is dotted with the tombs of rabbis and scholars.

At the base of **Meron**, in the village of the same name, is the tomb of Shimon Bar-Yochai, the revered rabbi who drew Jews to Safed in the first place. On the feast of Lag Ba'Omer, you can still see thousands of his devout followers gather outside Safed's synagogues and make their way in a joyous procession to his grave at the foot of Mount Meron. Ten minutes from Safed, on the road to Meron, is moshav **Kerem Ben Zimra**, better known as the home of the **Dalton Winery**. Open daily for tasting, the winery has an interesting wine list, including a cabernet sauvignon.

A tomb at nearby Amuka is the site of a pilgrimage of another sort. When Rabbi Jonathon Ben Uziel died in the 1st century, legend has it that he confided to his disciples that his greatest regret in life was not having married early enough in life to be fruitful and multiply. "Anyone who truly wishes to marry should pray at my tomb," said the dying rabbi, "And their wish shall be granted within a year." Thousands of marriage-minded people have since taken the rabbi up on his promise.

Also in this region is the mountainside town of **Pekiin**, a quaint Arab village that's noted for being the only place in

An ancient Jewish grave at Safed.

Israel where Jews have resided continuously since Roman times.

At the outskirts of Safed flows **Nahal Ammud**. This river, which brings images of Eden to mind, leads down to the Sea of Galilee. In the summer you can wade through it, plucking pomegranates and figs along the way.

Havens in the hills: The mountains of Meron are but the two highest peaks in the steep slope-ridden region known as the **Western Galilee**. This is rough mountainous country – stretches of bare rock interspersed with patches of pine trees, olive groves and eucalyptus. Canyons, caves and gorges abound. A number of small rivers (*nahals*) cut through this rugged region, flowing from east to west and emptying into the Mediterranean. To get a real taste of this terrain, follow one of them for a stretch. **Nahal Kziv**, which runs parallel to the ancient seaside ruins at **Achziv**, takes you through natural pools and springs to **Montfort**, an immense Crusader fortress that makes a great lookout point.

In touring less accessible spots, you'd be advised to contact the Society for the Protection of Nature, which provides invaluable information, tips and maps as well as English-language tours. (Main offices: 13 Rehov Helene Hamalka, Jerusalem, tel: 02-6232936; 4 Rehov Hashfela, Tel Aviv, tel: 03-6375063; and 8 Rehov Menachen, Haifa, tel: 04-8664136.)

For all its raw beauty – perhaps, because of it – the Western Galilee's most fascinating natural resource may be its people. Each of the hundreds of small settlements is a world unto itself. At **Beit Jann**, the highest village in Israel, you'll find elderly men clad in turbans and white flowing robes – the clothes worn by the scholars in this Druze community of 5,000.

Sporting long sidelocks and clad in black, Hassidim, a particularly religious sect of Jews, have their own village at **Kfar Hassidim** (and are not especially appreciative of visitors). A few miles away, at **Bosmat Tivon**, is an urban settlement of Bedouin. The difficulties these nomadic people face in making

A Druze merchant.

the transition to urban life create some poignant pictures. You'll find the younger generation living comfortably in new suburban homes, while their stubborn parents continue to camp out – in the back yard.

The wide open space of the Western Galilee acts as a haven, attracting various idealists seeking to carve their own small utopias on its slopes. So, in addition to the more common settlements like kibbutzim, Bedouin encampments and Arab and Druze villages, you'll find a community of transcendental meditationists at **Hararit** who've found their nirvana on these secluded slopes. Or a colony of vegetarians at **Amirim** who have set up an organic farm as well as a guesthouse where visitors can indulge in gourmet vegetarian meals.

Karmiel, which has burgeoned into the largest town in the Western Galilee, is itself an unconventional experiment in urban planning – and by all accounts, a successful one. Established in 1964, its population of 50,000 includes native-born Israelis as well as Jewish im-

migrants from 34 countries (including many Americans and, recently, Ethiopians and Russians). Clean, pretty and prosperous, Karmiel is considered a model development town. Near its centre, against a back-drop of desolate mountains, are a series of larger-than-life sculptures depicting the history of Israel's Jewish people.

Karmiel is set in the **Beit HaKerem Valley**, the dividing line between what is considered the Upper Galilee (to the north) with peaks jutting up to almost 1,200 metres (4,000 ft), and the Lower Galilee (to the south), a much gentler expanse of rolling hills, none of which exceeds 600 metres (2,000 ft).

The latest social experiment to be undertaken in this region is perhaps the boldest and broadest yet. In the midst of these isolated slopes, young Israelis are busy polishing synthetic diamonds, making sophisticated electronic components and designing computer software. They have set up schools and stores, clinics and community centres in what they hope will become Israel's own modest version of Silicon Valley. The single-minded ambition that drives California's whiz kids is not found in abundance here. Infused with idealism, the young settlers of these hi-tech havens are not just out to make a buck, or so they say. It's a question of lifestyle, of commitment to shared values that holds their enterprises together.

In some, like **Moresha** (which means Heritage), this takes the form of strictly observing Jewish law. Others, such as **Shoreshim**, share the socialistic principles of a kibbutz, with all members jointly owning the community's means of production and all receiving equal shares of the profits.

Both Moresha and Shoreshim are part of the largest group of new settlements here called the **Segev Bloc**. Set up in 1978 in the hills south of Karmiel, it has several thousand families spread out in 18 communities. One of them, **Manof**, which is made up of mostly English-speaking immigrants from South Africa, offers guest facilities.

Weaving across the northern extremity of the Western Galilee is a highway

A statue at Karmiel celebrates life.

suitably called the **Northern Road**. In addition to providing spectacular look-out points, this route hugs the Lebanese border for over 100 km (60 miles), sometimes running as little as a few yards from Lebanese farmers nonchalantly tending their orchards. While for many years the Israeli settlements along this route were frequently the target of brutal terrorist attacks, the area is today considered safe for residents and tourists alike. A worthwhile stop is **Baram** where the exquisite columns of a 2nd-century synagogue still stand.

The road to Metulla: The land extending north of the Sea of Galilee gradually narrows into what is known as the finger of the Galilee with Metulla at its tip. This is particularly pretty countryside. The east opens up into the sprawling Hula Valley, beyond which hover the Golan Heights. Towering over the valley to the west are the **Naphtali Mountains**, beyond which loom the even higher – and often ominous – mountains of Lebanon. These picturesque peaks were in the past a source of frequent

Katyusha rocket attacks on the Israeli towns below.

Aside from the beauty it offers, the road to Metulla is an odyssey through the making of modern Israel.

The first stop on this trek is **Rosh Pina**. On the rock-strewn barren terrain they found here a century ago, pioneers fleeing from pogroms in Eastern Europe set up the first Jewish settlement in the Galilee since Roman times. They called it Rosh Pina, meaning the "cornerstone" after the Biblical passage: "The stone which the builders rejected has become the cornerstone." The original 30 families who settled here were part of the first wave of Jewish immigration that began in the 1880s.

Rosh Pina, a quaint town of about 1,000, has maintained something of its original rural character. Cobblestoned streets line the old section of town and 19th-century homes, though badly neglected, still stand.

Continuing towards Metulla, the next stop takes one off the road of modern history, exposing instead the far more

Apple harvest marks rebirth of the land.

ancient foundations of the country. **Tel Hazor** is one of the oldest archaeological sites in Israel – and by far the largest. With its 23 layers of civilisation spanning 3,000 years, it was the inspiration for *The Source*, James Michener's epic history of Israel. Across the street at **Kibbutz Ayelet HaShachar** there is a museum housing many of the finds. The kibbutz runs a popular guesthouse.

This is the region of the **Hula Valley**, a stretch of lush land dotted with farming villages and little fish ponds that would seem like a mirage to someone who stood on the same spot 40 years ago. Then you would have seen 4,000 hectares (10,000 acres) of malaria infested swampland – home to snakes, water buffalo and wild boar.

The draining of the valley was one of the most monumental tasks undertaken by the State of Israel in its early days. It took six years – during which the site's workers were often fired upon by neighbouring Syrian forces in the Golan Heights. But by 1957, the lake had been emptied, leaving a verdant valley in its

place. But now the region is being re-swamped as excessive peat in the ground is impeding agriculture. You can get an idea of what the area was like before by visiting the 800 hectares (2,000 acres) of swampland that have been set aside as a reserve. There is also a **museum** devoted to the natural history of the region at Kibbutz Hulata and a guesthouse in the northern part of the valley at **Kfar Blum**, a kibbutz with a distinctly Anglo-Saxon tone.

North of the Hula Valley, you begin to enter the narrow tip of Israel known as the "finger" or "panhandle" of the Galilee. When the end of World War I left its status unclear, Arab gangs attacked the Jews here, forcing them out of their settlements. The settlers at **Tel Hai** and **Kfar Giladi**, though vastly outnumbered, held out under siege for months until their leader, Joseph Trumpeldor, was shot and killed. The incident made the Jews aware of the need to beef up their self-defence and triggered the formation of the Hagganah, the predecessor of the Israel Defence Forces.

The building from which the settlers defended themselves is now a museum devoted to the Hagganah. Nearby is a memorial to Trumpeldor and seven fellow fighters, including two women, who died in the attack. Thousands of Israeli youths converge on the Tel Hai site on the anniversary of Trumpeldor's death. There is also a youth hostel here and a guesthouse at neighbouring Kfar Giladi, today a flourishing kibbutz.

Just before Metulla, in the **Iyun Nature Reserve**, is a picturesque waterfall that flows impressively in the winter months (October–May), but is completely dry the rest of the year. This is due to a longstanding arrangement in which Israel permits Lebanese farmers to divert the water for agricultural use.

The nearby town of **Kiryat Shmona** (Town of Eight) is named after the heroes of Tel Hai and is, in fact, built on the site from where the Arabs used to launch their attacks. It is one of scores of development towns founded shortly after Israel became a state in order to absorb some of the 700,000 Jews who poured into the new country. Kiryat **Kiryat Shmona.**

Shmona, like many "development towns", was hardly a town at all; it began as a series of corrugated iron huts known as *ma'abarot*. Situated close to the border, it was for years the target of rocket attacks from the Lebanese mountains that overlook it. Today, the mountains serve as a scenic backdrop for what is now a peaceful and, if not prosperous, at least developing town of over 20,000 inhabitants.

Some 10 km (6 miles) east of Kiryat Shmona, on the edge of the Golan Heights (and what used to be the Syrian border) is the archaeolgical site of **Tel Dan**. In Biblical times, as now, at the northern tip of Israel, it was founded by members of the tribe of Dan, after quarrels with the Philistines forced them to leave the southern coast. It is also notorious as one of two cities where Jeroboam permitted worship of the idolatrous golden calf.

Today the site includes various Israelite ruins, a Roman fountain and a triple-arched Canaanite gateway. In the summer, volunteers help excavate this active scenic *tel* where the source waters for the Jordan River emerge. The **museum** at Kibbutz Dan nearby describes the geology of the region and the reclamation of the Hula Valley below.

Until the Hermon was captured from Syria in 1967, **Metulla** was the target of rocket attacks from the most northern point in Israel, surrounded on three sides by Lebanese land. Founded in 1896 by the same wave of immigrants that settled in Rosh Pina, it was for two decades the only settlement in the area. Even today, the nearest shopping centre is 10 km (6 miles) away in Kiryat Shmona.

Aside from the fresh mountain air, abundant apple orchards (most of the country's supply comes from here), and charming pensions, what draws tourists to this secluded town of 600 is its now famous border with Lebanon. Every day (except Saturday) hundreds of Lebanese stream through what has come to be known as "The Good Fence". Some, victims of the turmoil in Lebanon, come for medical care, but most are simply labourers commuting to jobs in Israel.

A war memorial at Kiryat Shmona.

THE NORTH COAST

If Israel were ever to name a capital for sheer atmospheric charm, it would have to be **Acco**. The Old City of Jerusalem, of course, is in a class of its own, but, between the purchasing, piety and politics, can be more intense than charming. Old Jaffa, itself a venerable walled city, has been integrated into Tel Aviv as a museum city and crafts centre. Only Acco, battered over the centuries by successive invaders, has held its own against the flow of time and tourism.

The old sea wall, originally built by the Crusaders, still wearily overlooks the expanse of the Mediterranean, on the northern tip of Haifa Bay, while Gothic archways and minarets mingle within. The ancient stone piers still give port to fishermen bringing in the catch-of-the-day; the markets and cafés still overflow with warm service and mysterious faces. Chosen as the key port of the Crusader Kingdom by Baldwin I in 1104, and successfully defended against such diverse notables as Simon Maccabeus and Napoleon Bonaparte, Acco has left behind the glorious fury of its past. Yet if Acco is a backwater, it is a dramatic backwater, as richly eloquent as any in the Holy Land.

Crusader capital: Mentioned 3,500 years ago by the Pharaoh Tutmoses III, Acco is among the world's oldest known seaports. It was already a major population centre when the Phoenicians dominated the northern coast, and it thwarted attempts at conquest by the tribe of Asher, to whom the city was assigned by Joshua. Its ancient industries included its glassware (the Roman historian Pliny credits Acco with the discovering the art of glassmaking), and its purple dyes – an extract from a local variety of snail, which in time gave the colour its name. Around 333 BC, Alexander the Great passed through the city, by then a flourishing Greek colony; Julius Caesar, travelling with his soldiers, came 300 years later, in the process laying the first stones of the first paved road in Roman Judea – from Acco to Antioch.

The Arabs held the city from AD 636 until 1104, fortifying and rebuilding much of it. Yet Acco only hit its zenith during the era of the Crusaders.

The First Crusade was launched with a bang with the capture of Jerusalem in 1099. Five years later, Acco fell too, and the victorious Crusaders immediately realised the value of their conquest as a Mediterranean lifeline. Developed into a major trading centre by Genovese and other port city merchants, the city was redubbed St Jean d'Acre, and in a short time became the principal port on the eastern rim of the Mediterranean.

Many of the most powerful and colourful Crusaders orders – the Knights Templars, the Teutonic Order, the Order of St Lazarus, and the Hospitaller Order of St John – established centres here. In 1187 Saladin defeated the Europeans at the Horns of Hittim, and many Crusader cities fell into Saracen hands. Led by Phillip Augustus of Spain and Richard the Lionheart of England, the knights of the Third Crusade recaptured Acco, and, failing to do the same for

Preceding pages: Al-Jazzar Mosque, Acco. **Left**, aerial view of the mosque. **Right**, board games in Acco.

Jerusalem, made it the capital of the Crusader Kingdom in 1192. Jews as well as Christians returned to Acco, and the remains left from the ensuing century of Crusader rule testify that this was the city's "finest hour" – in 1291, it fell once more into obscurity.

In the mid-1700s, the port was revived by the Bedouin sheik Dahar el-Omar, who was followed by Acco's most notorious prime builder, the Ottoman Pasha Ahmad, affectionately known as "al-Jazzar" (the butcher) on account of his penchant for cruelty. His architectural legacies include Acco's best known landmarks. Also of note was his financial advisor, a flamascene Jew named Ham Farhi, who was later killed by Suleiman. In 1799, aided by British warships, Jazzar accomplished what much of Europe could not: he defeated Napoleon in a two-month siege. Turkish rule and the advent of the steamship tolled the demise of Acco's importance as a port, and the town regained prominence only in the last years of the British mandate, when its prison held hundreds of underground Jewish freedom fighters, including such top Zionist leaders as Ze'ev Jabotinsky, and was the scene of a remarkable jailbreak in 1947. Since independence, the city has retained its portside character while developing its industry, and today holds close to 40,000 residents, some two-thirds of them Jewish immigrants.

Many cities in one: Like so much of Israel, Acco is divided into old and new sections, and it is the **old city** that is of particular interest. Yet it is many cities in one. To enter the old city from the new, one follows either the coastal strip, or, better, the parallel **Weizmann Street**, with its **Tourist Information Office**. Either takes you through the dry moat and city walls, built by the Crusaders and later refortified. It is possible to climb the wall here, and visit the northeastern command post – the Burj el-Kommandar, which has a strategic view, as well as a restored promenade which continues on to Land Gate, at the bay.

As one passes through into the city, the first prominent structure is the ele-

Fishing harbour and mosque, Acco.

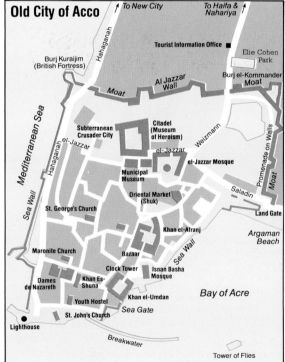

Old City of Acco

To New City
To Haifa & Nahariya
Hahaganah
Tourist Information Office
Elie Cohen Park
Burj Kuraijim (British Fortress)
Al Jazzar Wall
Burj el-Kommander
Moat
Moat
Mediterranean Sea
Hahaganah
el-Jazzar
Subterranean Crusader City
Citadel (Museum of Heroism)
Weizmann
Promenade on Walls
el-Jazzar
el-Jazzar Mosque
Municipal Museum
Saladin
Sea Wall
Oriental Market (Shuk)
St. George's Church
Land Gate
Khan el-Afranj
Argaman Beach
Maronite Church
Bazaar
Sea Wall
Clock Tower
Isnan Basha Mosque
Dames de Nazareth
Khan Es-Shuna
Bay of Acre
Youth Hostel
Khan el-Umdan
St. John's Church
Sea Gate
Lighthouse
Breakwater
Tower of Flies

gant **al-Jazzar Mosque**, built in 1781–82 by al-Jazzar, and today the site of his tomb and that of his adopted son and successor, Suleiman. Ringed with domed arcades and swaying palms, the mosque is considered the finest in Israel, and serves as a primary spiritual centre for Israel's Muslim community (note the modest dress code before entering). Except for a shrine containing a single hair from the beard of the prophet, the interior is as stark as it is magnificent. In fact, the courtyard is built over a Crusader cellar, while the building also covers other Crusader structures. Across the street is the entrance to the most interesting site of all, the dank and dramatic **Subterranean Crusader City**.

While not yet excavated in their entirety, the halls of the sprawling complex contain such unusual historical testimony as carved fleur-de-lis insignia. Now reclaimed, the halls are the venue for the autumn **Acco Theatre Festival**, which brings together the best of the country's experimental companies.

Emerging from the subterranean city, one turns off a small lane into a restored Turkish bathhouse, which is now the **Municipal Museum**. The museum contains exhibits on archaeology, Islamic culture, folklore and weaponry. Abutting both museum and Crusader city, the towering Citadel dominates the old city skyline. Built by al-Jazzar on Crusader ruins, the fortress was used variously as an arsenal and a barracks and, since Turkish times, as a prison. During the British mandate, it became a centre for the incarceration and execution of Jewish underground fighters; the **Museum of Heroism** within the citadel documents this unsettling period.

Wandering deeper into the maze-like streets of Acco, you may stumble across the **Sand Mosque**, off the main market. It bears an inscription beseeching the reader to pray for the soul of its builder. Further in is the Greek Orthodox **St George's Church**, dedicated to two British officers who fell at Acco in 1799 and 1840. Of special interest are the *khans* (inns) that grace the portside area. These include the imposing **Khan el-**

Calling the faithful to prayer.

Afranj (Inn of the Franks), near the Bazaar, and the unequalled **Khan el-Umdan** (Inn of the Pillars). A handsome caravanserai, the khan's lower storeys were used as stables and its upper ones as lodgings. Its geometric courtyard is memorable, and its clock-tower (minus the clock in recent years) offers a glimmering view of the port.

Beneath the tower, wander by the fishing port, and up along the sea wall, which houses one or two lovely cafés among its layered arches. The **youth hostel** is here, and, further on, the lighthouse, and from this corner you can take in the sunset view of the sea wall heading north to the new city, the old stone houses huddled in its tired embrace.

North to the border: Arching north from Acco along the coast lies the final architectural gift from al-Jazzar, the austere, self-contained spine of the **Turkish Aqueduct**, which when new ran 15 km (9 miles) to the spring at Kabri, now a picnic and camping site.

Further on, the **Bahai Tomb and Gardens** marks the burial site and villa of Mirza Hussein Ali, an early leader of the Bahai faith, known also as Baha Ulla – Glory to God. Surrounding the tomb is a lovely formal Persian garden.

From the east, stretching down to Acco, lies a string of Crusader fortresses – the most important of which, **Montfort**, is located 15 km (9 miles) east of the coast, atop a steep ridge, accessible only by footpaths.

Just north of the gardens is **Nahariya**. A clean and modest resort community founded in 1934 by German Jews, it offers many amenities for water sports, and a fine coastline on which to enjoy them. Its most noticeable landmark is the quiet stream, the **Ga'aton**, which flows down the centre of the main street. Nahariya has built an image as the national honeymoon hideaway, and in spring offers discounts to newlyweds, and occasionally other couples. Its reputation is rooted in its association with a Caananite fertility goddess.

The honeymooning really gets into high gear during the celebration of Lag b'Omer – the one day in the six weeks

Coming home from school.

following Passover that Jewish law allows couples to wed. Some 5 km (3 miles) northward along the coastal road are the ruins of **Achziv**, once a thriving Phoenician port, now a thriving **Club Med** resort. For non-members, there is also a holiday village, a campground, and a sparkling beach, equipped with shower facilities. The site is excellent for underwater fishing, and contains small tidal pools to explore. During the summer, the beach hosts an annual all-night reggae festival.

From here continue northwards, passing the **Achziv Bridge**, or Gesher Haziv (Bridge of Glory), where 14 young Hagannah men were killed in 1946 while trying to blow up the bridge in order to cut British communication links. The tragedy is memorialised in the name of both the local kibbutz and youth hostel and a monument stands by the road.

Inland at the Shlomi junction, lies an intriguing piece of nature. The **Rainbow Arch** was formed when a section of the cliff edge dissolved, leaving a large, almost perfect arch. Today, ab-

seilers rappel down this beautiful natural arch into the lush valley below. From the roadside, the marked footpath is a gentle uphill stroll to the arch and a panoramic view.

Some 9 km (5 miles) north of Nahariya towers the rocky border point of **Rosh HaNikra**, Israel's dynamic coastal limit and northernmost seaside tourist spot. While the view from the chalk-white cliffs set off against the crashing azure waves below is itself entrancing, it is Rosh HaNikra's unique grottoes that are the prime attraction. Formed by millennia of erosion, the grottoes offer a dim, damp, splashy and surprisingly placid sojourn in an underground labyrinth of stone; a new cable car takes you down over the pounding tide, and a footpath is also there for the determined.

Atop the cliff, the southernmost edge of the range known as the **Ladder of Tyre**, is a cafeteria, and a view out over the now walled-up railway tunnel that in the days before independence led to Lebanon. On a clear day, looking south, one can make out the port of Haifa.

Rosh HaNikra: the grotto and the snowy white cliffs.

HAIFA

In a fit of pique, a Bedouin sheik destroyed a squalid coastal village because its inhabitants neglected to pay homage. The town lay in ruins for eight years, until 1758, when, having made his point, Sheik Dahr Al-Omar rebuilt it, and improved its natural harbour. **Haifa** grew from that unpropitious beginning, and, in the years since its rebirth, has evolved into a bustling port city and maritime centre.

Today Haifa is Israel's third-largest city, and the centre of the nation's renowned high-technology industries. From its original cradle on the narrow coastal strip between the Mediterranean and the biblical Carmel Range, Haifa has marched up the mountainside, settling itself lazily among the gentle slopes. The city is essentially built on three levels, rising from its first location along the **waterfront**. The second level, in the Carmel foothills, is Hadar, the central business district and the oldest residential area. The newest neighbourhoods have climbed all the way to the crests of the peak, and cling to its sides, connected by a network of excellent roads. At the very apex is the **Carmel Center**, where some of the city's most attractive homes and classiest hotels and shops are located

Historic port: Since the 2nd century, Haifa had been known as a safe haven for passing ships, situated as it was along one of the Mediterranean's oldest sea lanes. But the village itself was little more than an assemblage of wretched huts, at the time of its premature destruction in the mid-18th century having less than 250 inhabitants. Reborn, it thrived, and by 1890 Haifa had some 8,000 people living within its limits. Yet it took a combination of railroads and war to catapult the city into significance and the 20th century.

The two causes were interlinked: under the impending pressures of World War I, the Ottoman Turks built the Hejaz Railroad connecting Haifa to Damascus in the north, while at the same time the British started the Sinai Military Railroad, which was later to link Haifa to Qantara on the Suez Canal. Haifa was now, by land as well as sea, a prime stopover. At the end of the war the British controlled all of Palestine under a League of Nations mandate, and they gradually began to modernise Haifa's port. With a steady increase in maritime traffic, and a continuing stream of Jewish immigrants, the population had reached 25,000 by 1918. By 1923 it had more than doubled, and by 1931 it had doubled again to exceed 100,000.

Although it was now a city, Haifa was still a modest enclave, clinging to the shore, and extending only as far as the Carmel foothills. After Israel's independence in 1948, however, further development of the port became essential. Israel's land borders were sealed, and Haifa's port became the Jewish state's only opening to the world.

Blue-collar city: Today the port, monitored by a centralised computer system, bristles with massive electronically operated cargo-handling equipment, berths

Preceding pages: bird's-eye view of Haifa. **Left**, the Bahai Temple on Mount Carmel. **Right**, Haifa is a thriving port.

the world's seagoing mammoths, and is Israel's premier maritime centre. But Haifa has grown beyond the limitations of a port city to become a versatile industrial centre as well. Known affectionately as the "Red City" because of its long-standing identification with the nation's labour movement, Haifa is a blue-collar town, and Haifites proudly explain that, while Tel Aviv plays and Jerusalem prays, Haifa works.

The evidence is everywhere. At the northern edge of the city, an industrial zone accommodates a very extensive petrochemical industry, oil refineries, and many small manufacturing units. Israel's high-technology companies are centred in a new science-based industrial district at the southern entrance to the city. According to the Haifa labour council, 70 percent of the area's 120,000 wage-earners are employed in industrial enterprises, excluding civil service and tourist-related jobs.

Haifa's blue-collar character is mitigated by the presence of two major academic institutions, the **Technion** and the **University of Haifa**, whose faculties and students total about 40,000.

Covering 6,000 hectares (15,000 acres), with a population of over 250,000, Haifa is known not only as the city that works but also where everything can be worked out. The amiable atmosphere is due in part to the sensible implementation of a policy promulgated in 1947 by David Ben-Gurion. Known as the Status Quo Agreement, the policy guarantees the preservation of the status quo on religious issues as it was at the time the state was established in 1948.

In other municipalities, the amorphous agreement has become a platform for squabbling, but prosaic Haifa managed to transform it into a political instrument which assures that everybody gets something.

Religious communities: Haifa's religious population lives in distinct communities contiguous with secular neighbourhoods in the heart of the city, near **Hadar**. The atmosphere around **Yosef Street**, near the municipal theatre, around **Geula Street**, near the Glory of

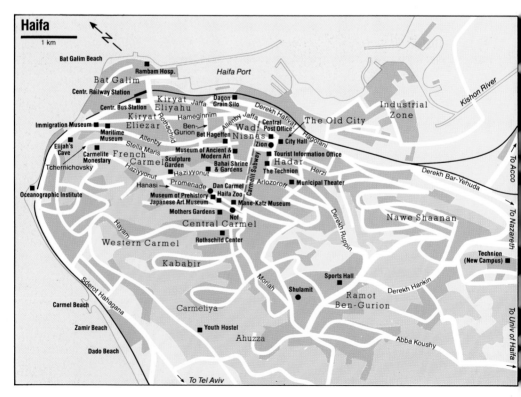

Israel religious school or in **Ramot Wishnitz**, just below Rupin Road, is as rich in intensity and devotion to tradition as comparable communities elsewhere in Israel. But in Haifa they never throw stones.

For tourists, this amicability means that, although movies are closed on Friday evenings, theatres, discos, restaurants and nightclubs operate as usual. Haifa's zoo and most museums are open during the Sabbath, but are not allowed to charge admission fees, and hotels request that their departing guests pay their bills before Friday evening.

Arab communities: Haifa's Saturday bus service is unusual in Israel. It reflects the formative influence of its Arab citizens on the city's social patterns. There has always been a significant Arab presence in Haifa, and Jews and Arabs here have a long history of mutual give-and-take. The buses ran on Saturdays to accommodate Haifa's Arabs in pre-state days, and they still do. Today Israeli Arabs constitute about 10 percent of Haifa's population, and the city attracts thousands more every day from the surrounding villages, coming to take advantage of the work opportunities and to share the amenities of the city with their Jewish fellow-citizens.

Although there are some mixed areas, most Arabs have remained in their own neighbourhoods, in many cases in the same place where their families have lived for generations. There are two distinctive, venerable and easily accessible Arab communities in Haifa.

Wadi Nisnas is one of the area's oldest neighbourhoods, and is adjacent to Hadar, near Bet Hageffen, Haifa's Arab-Jewish community centre. A visit to the community centre is a useful prelude to touring here; telephone in advance to assure the availability of an English-speaking staff member.

The Wadi Nisnas, with its buildings of massive sandstone blocks, its window grilles and arched doorways, its prevalence of Arabic and Middle Eastern music, and the gamut of exotic food and clothing for sale in the shops, is a graphic reminder that Haifa – micro-

Sharing opinions.

chips aside – still stands with one foot firmly planted in the Levant.

In sharp contrast to Wadi Nisnas, **Kababir**, perched high on a ridge overlooking the Mediterranean, is an Arab neighbourhood of sumptuous dwellings and lush gardens. Established as an independent village in 1830, the community opted for annexation to Haifa when the state was established in 1948, anticipating the benefits of schools, health services, water and sewage systems.

The majority of residents are Ahmdya Muslims, a small Islamic sect distinct from the larger Shiite and Sunni groups in Wadi Nisnas. Although fully integrated into the Haifa municipality, Kababir is administered locally by a committee of six elders elected annually by the men of the community. The committee deals with everything from bloc-voting in national elections to problems of interpersonal relations. A new mosque, completed in 1984, is the only one of its kind in the Middle East.

The Carmel Center: The **Carmel Center** is where most of Haifa's hotels are located. Here, atop towering **Mount Carmel**, panoramic scenes of the city, sea and mountains burst into view at every turn. Modern shops line **Hanassi Street** along with sidewalk cafés and restaurants specialising in kosher, Chinese, Italian and Middle Eastern foods. Israel's only museum of Japanese art, the **Tikotin Museum**, is in the heart of the Carmel Center, at 89 Hanassi Street.

A few blocks from Hanassi Street, a half-mile long **Promenade** at the edge of the precipice reveals the city scrambling across the side of the mountain all the way down to the sea. The view from the Promenade is dominated by the **Bahai Shrine and Gardens** halfway down the slope. Founded in Persia by Mirza Ali Mohammed, the sect was proscribed and its leader publicly executed there in 1850. Claiming over 3 million adherents worldwide, the Bahai faith is based on brotherhood, love and charity. Its followers view Moses, Christ, Buddha and Mohammed as messengers sent by God to different parts of the world in different eras, but all preaching

Haifa from the gardens of the Bahai Temple.

more or less one philosophy, and they advocate a common world language and religion. With its unusual dome and Corinthian-style columns, the shrine is probably Haifa's best-recognised landmark, and the world centre of the Bahai faith. Both the building and the lovely gardens are open to the public. From above the shrine, **Panorama Road** now leads either outward towards the sea and the Promenade view, or back in towards the city centre.

Carmel slope retreats: Tucked within the mountainous folds of upper Haifa are a number of hidden treasures. Hugging the slope near the Promenade, the **Mane Katz Museum** is housed in the building where the Jewish-French expressionist lived and worked in his later years. Besides his paintings and sculptures, the display also includes his personal collection of Judaica and antique furniture. A short distance away is the **Edenic Mothers' Garden**, the biggest of Haifa's nearly 400 parks. Among curving paths, flowers, and picnicking families, is the city's **Museum of Pre-history**, displaying finds of the Carmel area, which way back then was home to Neanderthal Man.

A little farther is the pleasant, well-maintained **Haifa Zoo**, and in the far corner of the park, an open-air restaurant specialising in Middle Eastern foods.

Atop the crest of Mount Carmel, marking the end of one's ascent, loom the contemporary features of the **University of Haifa**, its distinctive tower thrust resolutely against the sky. Founded in 1972, the university serves the entire northern district, and operates branches in some of the region's more remote areas. The 25-storey **Eshkol Tower**, designed by Brazilian architect Oscar Niemeyer, is said to straddle a mild fault and offers an unparalleled view of northern Israel. To the east, one can make out the fertile valleys of the Galilee and the brooding outline of the Golan Heights beyond, while down below miles of yellow-sand beaches stretch like satin ribbon along the Mediterranean shore. To the north, are Haifa Bay, Acco, and the white cliffs of Rosh HaNikra. On a

Haifa University.

clear day it's all visible: a living map, sparkling with sun and sea. At night, harbour lights vie with the stars, and the city marks its place with a million glinting shadows.

Returning back down the slope, continuing past the promenade, you reach that part of the city known as **French Carmel**, an expensive but cosy residential district. At the end of this area, Mount Carmel levels off into a promontory, and this is the site of the **Carmelite Church**, the world centre of the Carmelite Order. Situated at the end of the mountain, along Stella Maris Road, the church commands one of the most spectacular views of the city. The site was selected in the 12th century by a small band of Crusaders who settled there to devote themselves to asceticism, solitude and prayer. The order which grew from that beginning was officially founded by St Brocard in the 13th century. The church edifice was built in the 18th century, over a grotto associated in the Christian tradition with the prophet Elijah and his disciple Elisha. The inte-

rior dome depicts events in their lives and a small museum displays local archaeological discoveries.

Along the seaside: Opposite the church entrance, a sinuous platform marks the upper terminal of Haifa's **cable car system**. Delayed for more than a year due to controversy surrounding its intended operation on the Sabbath, the system ferries passengers from the Carmel heights down to the seaside Bat Galim Promenade. It is an easy walk to the **National Maritime Museum** and the **Clandestine Immigration Museum**. The immigration museum includes the tiny ship in which Jewish immigrants sought to evade the British Mandatory government's blockade in the years before the state of Israel was declared.

A little way up the hill from the museums is **Elijah's Cave**, where the prophet is said to have rested and meditated in the 9th century BC, before his momentous encounter with the Baalists on one of the peaks of the Carmel Range. After leaving the cave, Elijah is said to have climbed to the top of Mount Carmel,

Elijah's Grotto at Carmelite Church.

where an altar had been erected by the worshippers of Melkart and other Phoenician deities. Elijah challenged their priests to light a flame under a sacrifice by means of their religious rites.

According to tradition, the pagan priests failed; Elijah called upon the Lord and the flames were instantly ignited. Ahab, the Jewish king who had angered the Lord by worshipping Baal, was witness to the event. Rejecting paganism, he ordered the massacre at the Kishon River of all the Baalists. The event is recorded in detail in I Kings: 18, 17-46. Christians believe the cave to have sheltered the Holy Family on their way back from Egypt, and know it also as the Grotto of the Madonna.

Adjacent to the port area, a short bus ride from the prophet's retreat, is the **Dagon Grain Silo** – probably one of the only architecturally pleasing silos in the world. Besides its commercial use for receiving and storing grain from ships anchored in the port, the silo houses a museum depicting the history of bread and beer making. Ancient implements are displayed with explanatory photographs, murals and mosaics, and there is a working model of the silo's own mechanised operation system.

Hugging the waterfront, the **Railroad Museum** opposite 40 Hativat Golani Street is a tribute to the importance of the railway in Haifa's history. Steam engines that hauled freight from the hinterlands to Haifa's port are preserved there along with luxury passenger cars, ornate bedroom cars, and wood-panelled dining cars. Visitors are encouraged to climb aboard, try out the accommodations, and toot the engine's whistle.

Hadar: In **Hadar**, the level above the waterfront, the original edifice of the country's preeminent Institute of Technology, the **Technion**, has been preserved as an architectural landmark and is now the home of the unique touch-and-feel **Museum of Science and Technology**. The magnificent old building, constructed in 1924, was designed by Alexander Baerwald, combining European lines with an eastern dome, crenelated roofs and intricate mosaics. The

Laser testing at the Technion.

Technion recently expanded into a large new campus in the Neve Shannon neighbourhood; free tours are offered daily.

The city's **Museum of Ancient and Modern Art**, at the southern edge of Hadar, on 26 Shabtai Levy Street, is crammed with displays. Comfortable viewing from vantage points isn't always possible, but the variety and quality of the collections make a visit worth the effort. Special exhibitions are infrequent but excellent. Contemporary Israeli artists exhibit their work at Chagall Artists' House at 24 Hazionut Blvd. It is open daily and admission is free.

Food and fun: Sidewalk cafés are everywhere in Haifa. They range from a couple of tiny tables crowded against a storefront on a sidestreet where excellent *coffee afuch* (Viennese coffee) can be bought, to the umbrella-shaded elegance near the **Cinématique** at the **Rothschild Center** on Hanassi Street in the Carmel Center. Haifa also boasts a wide variety of other dining facilities, ranging from dinner-and-dancing in the Rondo Grill of the Dan Carmel Hotel to a Middle Eastern evening of folk-dancing at Al-Pasha on Hamman-al-Pasha Street.

More local flavour can be sampled at The Pleasant Brothers, an unassuming place on the corner of Moriah and Pica streets in the Ahuza neighbourhood, and is a long-time local favourite: its shish kebab, shishlik and salads are a Middle Eastern version of down-home cooking. After dinner, have a cup of coffee with German or Middle Eastern pastries in the coffee houses around the corner on **Pica Street**.

For informal eating, the favourite of Jewish and Arab Haifaites alike are the felafels bought at any of the kiosks lining **Hehalutz Street** in Hadar. Standing up alongside the kiosk, people help themselves to hot peppers, fiery sauces, olives, pickles and eggplant as space and palate permit. At night, unpretentious Hehalutz Street, with its strolling crowds munching felafels under the glare of unshaded light bulbs, is a typical Haifa scene.

Evening entertainment in Haifa is often a matter of luck. There are the usual discos, pubs and bars but the most popular places depend on their patrons to join in the singing and dancing. When that happens, the evening takes on a special Haifa quality. An evening stroll along Panorama, also known as **Yefe Nof Street**, in the Carmel Center, or along Balfour and Herzliya streets in Hadar, will reveal where the fun is.

Israel's only subway: One block up the hill from the felafel stands of Hehalutz Street is the Hadar entrance to the **Carmelit**, Israel's only subway. While most visitors are accustomed to travelling in subways, the Carmelit is truly one of a kind. Its tunnel, hacked through the interior rock of the mountain, operates on the same principle as San Francisco's cable cars: one train hurtling down from the Carmel Center at the top of the mountain hauls the other train up the steep incline from sea level. Even the cars themselves are designed at an angle. From top to bottom, the trip takes seven minutes.

The Carmel Range: The **Carmel Range**, which runs about 25 km (16 miles) northwest–southeast along the coast,

Decorative plates for the tourists.

rises to some 500 metres (1,650 feet) and falls steeply to the Mediterranean. The **Kishon River**, known since biblical times, flows at its feet. The range takes its name from the words *Kerem-El*, meaning "Vineyard of God".

Carmel's traditional association is with ripeness. Today, at the southern limit of the city, it contains **Mount Carmel National Park**, Israel's largest national forest preserve, which is lush with hilly woodlands, well-marked hiking trails, picnic facilities and breathtaking vistas. The 8,500-hectare (21,000-acre) park includes an 800-hectare (2,000-acre) Nature Preserve where deer and gazelle roam freely. The park was badly burned by a fire in 1993 but much of the greenery has since grown back.

Just beyond the park, tucked among the slopes and valleys of the Carmel Range are the Druze villages of **Daliyat el-Carmel** and **Isfiya**. The Druze, a distinctive Islamic sect, are a well-respected and integral part of the state. Surrounded by tawny precipices plunging to verdant valleys carpeted with tangled foliage, the villages are easily accessible by car or bus. The market places offer traditional handicrafts and pleasant cafés where Turkish coffee and succulent pastries can be enjoyed under the trees.

The **Carmelite Monastery** at **Muhraka**, nearby, stands over the site where Elijah defeated the Baalists.

The aura of sanctity of the Carmel Range has been recognised since ancient times. Successive waves of conquerors set up their altars on its wooded peaks and hillsides. Tutmoses III mentions it as holy. The Greeks dedicated a temple to Zeus here. The prophet Elijah wandered its slopes, honing his faith. Jewish, Christian, Muslim and Druze traditions revere the region. King Solomon sang of it in the Song of Songs (7:5) and Isaiah extols its glory (33:9).

For modern Haifaites, the gentle slopes and softly rounded ridges of the Carmel Range hold their neighbourhoods, define their lifestyles, and establish an enduring link between them and their ancient roots.

A Druze musician in a Carmel shop.

THE CENTRAL COAST

From Ashkelon in the south to the environs of Caesarea in the north, Israel's central coast is citrus country – the fertile **Sharon Plain**. In Hebrew, the word for citrus, *hadar*, is the same as the word for "splendour", and in the proper season both meanings are equally appropriate as the entire strip from seashore to foothills becomes lush with orchards and ripe, hanging fruit.

It is one of Tel Aviv's greatest ironies that its development as a city came at the expense of its initial drawing point – its fine, sandy soil, perfect for growing citrus – and today the metropolitan area continues to sprawl out over thousands of acres of prime citrus land. Yet the crop was never indigenous to the area, and, in fact, well into the 19th century the central coast was generally regarded as a miasma of swamps and malaria, avoided even by the roadway, which twisted northward along higher ground further inland.

By the turn of the century, however, the development of pumps which could raise the buried groundwater to the soil surface suddenly harnessed the land to the desires of its pioneer settlers, who set about draining the marshes and cultivating new orchards.

Exporting their crop to Europe via the central port of Jaffa (hence Jaffa oranges), the industry hit a high in the 1930s; World War II and the ensuing struggle for independence hindered its development in the decade following. But in the 1950s and 1960s the industry once again blossomed, and the 1970s witnessed another doubling of exports.

Today, citrus is Israel's most valuable agricultural export, making up a large share of the nearly half-billion dollar-a-year market. The variety of citrus under cultivation runs the spectrum, including all sorts of offshoots and varieties, with the sweet "Jaffa" oranges and their kin dominating along the coast, and the grapefruits mainly thriving in the thicker, river-washed soil closer inland. The citrus gathering season is in the winter, from mid-December to April, and this is when the fruits are at their most intoxicating, swinging ripely off their evergreen branches, their scent wafting out over the road, to the Mediterranean.

Cities of wealth and taste: From Tel Aviv and Ramat Aviv, the coastal highway winds past modest memorials on its route northward. On the shore side of the highway, approaching Herzliya, is a metallic rectangle standing upright atop a layered curve of a pedestal: this commemorates the 34 people killed in a 1978 sea-launched terrorist attack. A short way further on, a faded ship's hull commemorates those would-be immigrants who died attempting to gain refuge in Palestine in the final years of the British mandate.

A fascinating monument lies a short distance to the east in **Ramat HaSharon**, the Memorial to the Fallen Members of Israel's Intelligence Community, inaugurated in 1985.

The city of **Herzliya** (pop. 90,000) includes among its inhabitants the elite of Israeli society, and, for that matter,

just about anyone else who has money to play with: from wealthy real estate developers to industrial moguls to members of the intelligentsia such as Abba Eban. It is a favourite with diplomats and ambassadors, who are only too happy to take advantage of the stylish beaches and company, and whose posh villas stud the slopes above the shore amid such ritzy five-star hotels as the Sharon, Accadia and Daniel.

Reflecting the general opulence, some of the nicer beaches charge an admittance fee. This is the scheme in **Herzliya-by-the-Sea**, at the town centre. Along the highway, the city puts on a different face: a haven for high-tech entrepreneurs. Numerous well-known company names – Scitex, Elbit, Digital – glow brightly with futuristic logos, their office complexes complementing the city's reputation as the base of Israel's communications industry.

Just north of the seaside resort city, the ruins of a **Crusader fortress** and ancient Hellenistic city, **Apollonia**, overlook the water, and it is said the beach still contains visible remnants of the ancient coloured glass that was once produced here. All but disappeared are traces of the battle fought in this area between Richard the Lionheart and Saladin during the twilight years of the Crusader Kingdom.

Approaching Netanya, we pass over the **Nahal Poleg** (Poleg River), at one time an unpleasant morass, since tamed as a nature reserve. Close by stands the **Wingate Institute**, Israel's premier centre for sports and physical training instruction. It is named after Charles Orde Wingate, a British officer who served in Palestine from 1936 to 1939, and who helped instruct the Jewish policemen in defensive fighting techniques that would later prove invaluable in the War of Independence. Wingate reputedly carried a Bible with him, reinforcing the Jews' knowledge of their land through appropriately quoted passages.

Some 20 km (12 miles) north of Herzliya, lies **Netanya** itself, the capital city of the Sharon region. Founded as a citrus colony in 1929, the settlement

The beach at Herzliya.

was named after American millionaire Nathan Strauss, as a potential encouragement for him to contribute to the town's development (supposedly he was unmoved). Netanya has proved to be just as well off without, boasting a charming beach and promenade, a population upwards of 150,000 and a galaxy of expensive and not-quite-so-expensive hotels, often filled to capacity with vacationing Europeans and in-the-know Israelis. Most of the hotels are clustered along King David and Machnes streets, by the beachfront, while the bus station is situated on the main thoroughfare, **Herzl Street**, a few blocks walk away.

All three avenues come together at **Independence Square** (Kikar Ha'Atzmaut), where a kiosk at the southeast corner houses the Tourist Information Office. Their offerings include regular performances of Israeli folk dancing, information about horseback riding and various recreational sports, visits to a citrus packing plant (in season, of course) and a "Meet the Israeli" programme in which the tourist can drop by the home of a native Netanyan for an informal cup of coffee and exchange of views. All in all, the boldly modernistic concrete beach facilities and pleasantly landscaped greenery make Netanya a fine place to spend a lazy afternoon.

Netanya also happens to be the hub of Israel's formidable **diamond industry**, the country's second most important export next to the ubiquitous citruses. Inaugurated by immigrants from Belgium and the Netherlands in the early years of the state, the business has grown to the extent that, since 1974, Israel has held the title of world's number-one exporter of polished diamonds (the raw stones being imported from Asia and Africa).

Several companies offer opportunities to buy. Taub & Company, the largest, selling over $20 million worth of stones from their Netanya offices each year, operates an expansive showroom of precious stones. Female guides take visitors on a tour of the facilities, which includes a brief video presentation, a chance to see craftsmen in action and a stop-off in their showroom. There is

Eyeing diamonds, a big export.

also a modest museum with information on the history of diamonds.

The region just north of Netanya is the **Valley of Hefer** (Emek Hefer, in Hebrew), and although it isn't really a valley the area gets a mention in the Old Testament. This marshy plain is inextricably linked to the efforts of the pioneers of the 1930s, whose sweat and foresight revitalised the land, enabling it to be as productive as it is today. Kfar Vitkin was among the first of these new settlements and today it is among the largest moshavim (collective farming settlements) in the country.

A little way further on, less than 10 km (6 miles) from Netanya, is **Mikhmoret beach**, as lovely as its city cousin, but a lot less crowded. Still further is **Habonim** (the builders) beach, next to the moshav of the same name. At Habonim, you can find small sandy coves to nestle in and extraordinary sunsets from atop the small cliffs. **Hadera**, the city inland of the beach, derives its name from the Arabic word for green (nothing to do with the Hebrew word for citrus), and serves as a transfer point for visitors to the northern Sharon.

Crusaders at their best: Although its greatest historical importance was as a Roman colony, it is the Crusader ruins at **Caesarea** that tourists flock to by the busload today, and truly, they are as impressive as any in Israel. It takes a good half a day just to take in the site, while the visual impact of Crusader arches, crumbling walls and smashed Roman pillars is constantly disarming, and attests to the layered history of habitation here. Despite its being one of Israel's most lauded archaeological sites, Caesarea is still difficult to reach via public transportation, which means that individual tourists must either rent a car, stay overnight nearby, or join a tour.

While settlements in the region date back as far as Phoenician times, the history of the city only really begins with the Romans in 22 BC, when royal master-builder Herod the Great founded it, naming it in honour of the emperor Augustus. Around the year 6 BC it was

Sculpture at Caesarea.

MEDITERRANEAN SEA

Crusader Castle

Old harbour

Herod's Wall

Greek Wall

Wall

Roman Wall

Tower

Swimming baths

Haifa, Tel Aviv

Caesarea

500 m / 547yds

Sedot Yam

designated the official residence of the governors of Judea, and for some 500 years Caesarea was to remain the capital of Roman administration in Palestine. At the time of Jesus, Pontius Pilate lived here, and St Paul was imprisoned here for two years before being sent to Rome from this port.

The great Jewish Revolt in AD 66 was set off in Caesarea initially, and in the struggle that followed the city's prisons saw the torture and execution of many captive Jewish zealots. In AD 70, the Roman general Vespasian was crowned emperor here. With the Bar Kochba uprising, many notable Jews once again met their deaths here, among them the great sage and spiritual leader Rabbi Akiva, in AD 135. (The rabbi is commemorated in the nearby community of Or Akiva.)

During the period of Pax Romana, the city was a centre of Hellenistic and, later, Christian culture. Among the most notable of the early Christians was Eusebius, one of the founding fathers of the Christian Church, who became the first bishop of Caesarea in the 4th century, and who was responsible for codifying Christian religious law, and outlining the geography of the Bible in his book *Onomastikon*.

The Crusaders, under Baldwin I, captured the city in 1101, and during the next 200 years Caesarea changed hands so often it could make a camel cross-eyed. King Baldwin treasured the city, believing it to hold the Holy Grail which Jesus sipped from at the Last Supper, but the massive fortifications that so commend it today were only added after 1254, with the reconquest of the city by Louis IX, "the Holy". Muslim forces captured the city in 1265 (and again in 1291), and Caesarea never again regained importance, its fine marble pillars and carvings being pillaged over the centuries by successive rulers.

The contemporary visitor to Caesarea enters the city through a vaulted **Crusader gatehouse**, after passing over a bridge across a wide moat. The walls around the city, which slope down precipitously from an imposing height, are

Crusader ruins, Roman pillars at Caesarea.

perhaps the most awe-inspiring monument here; walking the breadth of this imposing redoubt, imaginative tourists can easily sicken themselves picturing the spectacle of hand-to-hand combat that took place here time and again. Inside the city are numerous ruins of Crusaders' homes and streets. Along the waterfront, Roman pillars used as foundation stones by the Crusaders jut out among the waves. If the postcard shops and restaurants within the Crusader city limits jar your sense of decorum, you may want to remind yourself that the Israeli economy is always in need of spirited help.

Outside the entrance to the Crusader city, a Byzantine **Street of Statues** represents the far larger Byzantine city that preceded the Crusaders, its headless figures (Roman dignitaries) pondering, like Ozymandius, the passing of their power. A half-kilometre south of the city walls is the restored **Roman amphitheatre**. This arena witnessed mass executions in Roman times; it has recently hosted popular summer concerts by such virtuosi as Pablo Casals and Issac Stern and rock stars such as Eric Clapton.

The handsome Roman aqueducts stretching north from the city once conducted fresh spring water; today they provide shade for lounging bathers.

Inland from the ruins is the only **golf course** in Israel, on the grounds of the elegant and pricey Dan Caesarea hotel.

Martyrs and benefactors: Kibbutz Sdot Yam, just south of Caesarea, is worth special note as the former home of Jewish poetess-martyr Hannah Sennesh. Joining the young kibbutz after escaping Hungary for Palestine at the outbreak of World War II, she parachuted back behind Axis lines in 1944 to fight the Nazis; soon after, she was caught and tortured and executed at the age of 23. The modest archaeological museum here is named in her honour.

Heading north from Caesarea, one immediately enters the area of the **Kabara marshes**, which hosted some of the early Zionist settlements at the turn of the century and is excellent birdwatching country. The **Crocodile**

Caesarea's amphitheatre is still impressive.

River bears testimony to the once intimidating nature of the terrain; the last croc, however, bid life adieu in 1910.

A short distance inland, is the town of **Binyamina**, named after the great benefactor of Israel's first settlers, Baron Edmond (Benjamin) de Rothschild. (This lower portion of the Carmel Range bears the title Ramat HaNadiv – Benefactor's Heights.)

Two kilometres (1¼ miles) further north is **Rothschild's Tomb**, built in the 1950s to house the remains of the Parisian banker and his wife Adelaide. Situated amid a fragrant garden of date trees, sage, roses and all varieties of flowers, this sensuously designed landscape opens up to a magnificent panorama of the upper Sharon, while a concrete map indicates the locations of the many settlements made possible by Rothschild (whose generosity lingers today in the bar-room phrase "put it on the Baron's account"). The crypt itself is contemporary and tasteful; the site, all told, is one of the most significant in Israel.

A minute's drive north, the town of **Zichron Yaakov** was established in 1882 in memory of Rothschild's father James (Jacob). The **Aaronson House and Museum**, just off the main street, describes the lives of Aaron and Sarah Aaronson. Aaron was the botanist who in the early 1900s isolated durable strains of wheat for cultivation in Palestine; he and his sister are enshrined in legend because of their role in organising the pro-British "Nili" spy ring during resistance to the oppressive Turkish regime. Caught by the Turks, and afraid she'd give away information, Sarah shot herself in her home in 1917.

Like Rishon LeZion further south, Zichron Yaacov is one of the original homes of the Carmel Oriental winecellars, and interested tourists are welcome to take a free tour of the facilities, capped off with a complimentary winetasting break.

Heading back toward the coast, a road passes the gentle, slope-hugging Arab town of **Faradis** (Paradise).

The Carmel Coast: One of Israel's most active on-going archaeological sites is

Below, ruins at Caesarea. Left, archaeologists sift through the rubble.

Tel Dor. The excavations as yet have only unearthed a fraction of this sprawling ancient city, but the ruins on display, dating from Canaanite to Israelite to Hellenistic times, give indications of a vast ancient metropolis of tens of thousands of inhabitants. Archaeology aside, this is a site of enormous natural beauty, the lagoons and water washing against the cliffs complementing the rolling hills of Mount Carmel inland.

Abutting the *tel* just to the south is a lovely beach, **Nasholim** (Breakers), and a kibbutz of the same name which offers a roomy guest house and friendly atmosphere. On the grounds of the kibbutz you will find an illuminating **Maritime Museum**, housed in a turn-of-the-century building which was a glass factory under Rothschild. This rocky portion of the Carmel coast just south of Haifa, along a major ancient shipping lane, is the site of hundreds of undersea wrecks, which were the focus of a major underwater excavation in 1985. The museum holds a selection of these treasures culled from the depths, and their exhibits range from Phoenician catapult balls to ancient bronze anchors and coins, to relics dating from Napoleon's naval misadventures off this shore in 1799.

Along the length of the northern coast, rows of vegetables sheathed in white plastic dot the roadsides, often under the stately presence of towering cypress or eucalyptus trees. Towards evening, when the hues in the sky drift into violet, lilac and pale orange, the landscape looks as if it had been painted by Claude Monet, an unreal, curvaceous Impressionist silhouette.

Continuing past the beach of **Neve Yam** is the imposing Crusader fortress of **Atlit** perched wearily on the rocks above the Mediterranean. At the time of writing the ruins are off-limits to the general public, although a modern-day fortress, the prison in which Israel held Shi'ite prisoners during its war in Lebanon, is visible in the shadow of the highway.

Heading upwards and eastwards into the twisting greenery of Mount Carmel, the wildness of the scenery is echoed by the primal nature of the site: prehistoric caves, inhabited by Neanderthal Man some 50,000 years ago. Discovered in 1929, the three cliffside caves were found to contain flint tools and dozens of skeletons that provided anthropologists with revelations about the lifestyle of these early hunters, and their place in the chain that led to the proficient homo sapiens we know today.

Ensconced introspectively amid gnarled olive trees and Moorish arches, the artists' colony of **Ein Hod** was conceived of in 1953 as a rugged oasis of creativity, and today holds the living and working space for some 200 artisans. The gallery and restaurant in the town centre warmly welcome company.

Winding deeper into the mountainside, the road arcs through gorges and allows for a severe, often astonishingly attractive, landscape: the region is known as Little Switzerland. (**Kibbutz Bet Oren** tucked between the pines here operates a guesthouse.) At the crest of the ridge lies the ultimate view of the Carmel coast, and the gateway to Israel's ebullient third-largest city.

Below, the Tel Dor coast. Right, paragliding at Netanya.

stained-glass windows each portray a different chapter in the town's history. Opposite the tower, past an arched entranceway, is a large inner courtyard, once the Armenian Hostel which served as a "central station" for travellers and convoys going to and from Jewish settlements throughout the country. Walk past the police station and, on your right, a large entrance leads to the **Mahmoudia Mosque** (the actual entrance is around the back), built in 1812 and named after the city's Turkish governor.

Turning right from Yefet Street onto **Mifraz Shelomo Street**, towards the renovated section of Old Jaffa, one passes the **Jaffa Museum of Antiquities**, where archaeological exhibits from more than 20 years of excavations trace the city's development. Erected in the 18th century, the building was once the Turkish governor's headquarters and the local prison. In a later reincarnation, it won acclaim throughout the Middle East as the soap factory of the Greek Orthodox Damiani family.

The Franciscan **Saint Peter's Church**

is further along, on one side of Keddumim Square. The **Saint Louis Monastery** in the courtyard was named after the French king, who arrived at the head of a Crusade, and stayed here in 1147. The monastery later served as a hostel for pilgrims to Jerusalem and was known in the 17th century as "The Europeans' House." Napoleon also relaxed here after conquering Jaffa.

A little way north and towards the sea is the minaret of the **Jama El-Baher Mosque**, located next door to the first Jewish house in Jaffa. Built in 1820, the house was also a hostel for Jerusalemites who came to swim off Jaffa's beach. The **Armenian Convent** and church here mark the site of a large Armenian pilgrims' inn from the 17th century. A magnificent, renovated Turkish mansion behind the museum, once a Turkish bath house, has been converted into a nightclub and restaurant, El-Hamam.

At the top of the hill, past the Pisgah Park, **Horoscope Path** begins to wind its way through the Jaffa wall. It goes all the way to the lighthouse at the wall's

Stone heads at Jaffa.

southern entrance, on the corner of Shimon Haburski Street. At the centre of the renovated section is a square called **Kikar Kedumin**, in which the Jaffa excavations present a reconstruction of the city's multi-faceted history; this is also one of Tel Aviv's most popular evening spots.

On the southern side of the wall, along **Pasteur Street**, a modern structure mars the beauty of the ancient (renovated) walls. This is the **Israel Experience**, a new tourist centre comprising an auditorium for a multimedia show, a shopping area and a restaurant. The main show combines computerised projection systems on giant screens by means of 40 slide projectors, accompanied by special light and sound effects, for those who like that sort of thing.

Further along Pasteur Street is the **Horace Richter Gallery**.

Back on Yefet Street, turn left and walk down the hill crossing the road. Just before the traffic lights is Jaffa's first pitta-bread establishment (dating back to the 1880s) called **Abu Elafiah**;

it reputedly does its briskest business on Passover and Yom Kippur, when droves of bread-craving Israelis queue outside. The area is especially lively after dark, and Tel Aviv's night owls descend on Jaffa after the parties in town begin to wind down.

Jaffa's famous **flea market** lies in the next complex of alleys just east of here. It specialises in antiques, copperware ("antique" specimen made while you watch), jewellery and second-hand junk, but isn't open on Saturdays.

The city's growth: Tel Aviv sprang out of the desolate sand dunes north of Jaffa almost overnight, when a group of Jewish Jaffa residents purchased some land and raffled it off among themselves in 1909. They intended to build a garden suburb in which to find respite after a day's work in noisy, crowded Jaffa. But they also had hopes of creating the first new Jewish city in 2,000 years.

They named it Tel Aviv (Hill of Spring) – a name symbolising hope for a new future to be built on the ruins of **Jaffa's** the past. A *tel* in Hebrew is an artificial **old port.**

hill, created on the accumulated debris of past, abandoned cities; *aviv* means spring, connoting new life. First mentioned in the book of Ezekiel, Tel Aviv was the name of a town in the exile in Babylon where the prophet went for his dry bones prophecy. Tel Aviv was also the name given the Hebrew translation of Herzl's book *Alteneuland (Old-New Land)*, in which he predicted and conceived of the Jewish State.

The first houses were completed before the year was out. By the eve of World War I, the suburb had grown to 20 times its original size, and Jaffa's Jewish institutions began draining one by one into the new city to the north. When World War I began, the Turkish rulers expelled the Jewish population of Jaffa and Tel Aviv to other parts of the region, but after the British occupation in 1917, the settlers drifted back into their homes. They continued laying out their city, and by 1984 there were already some 230,000 Tel Avivians.

Architecture and navigation: In the city's early days, people built their own dwell-ings, infusing their own vision and hope into the city they were moulding. The first residents built houses to remind them of their origins in Europe, inspired by neo-classical buildings in Vienna, Odessa or Warsaw. Local architects tried to introduce European styles by softening the symmetrical corners with rounded balconies, or by adding domes, arched entranceways, and wall decorations depicting biblical motifs. In the 1920s and '30s, Tel Aviv became an eclectic collection of styles and influences. Its staid neoclassical structures were jazzed up with art nouveau, Middle Eastern and kitsch elements.

In the 1930s, the new or International building style, inspired by the Bauhaus in Germany and such architects as LeCorbusier and Erich Mendelsohn, took over. The symmetry and colonnades made way for clean, minimalistic lines, and severe functionality became the name of the game. Tel Aviv became the only city in the world to be dominated by the International style. In later years, the "White City", as it was dubbed

Bakery in the old city.

by poet Nathan Alterman, was peeling and its buildings were repainted in various colours, partly in reaction to the severe style. But city streets are still characterised today by apartment blocks raised up on columns and the roof gardens introduced by that school of architecture, and many of the newer apartment complexes going up are once more sparkling white.

Orientation: The most important streets to get to know are Ben Yehuda Street, which goes parallel to the shoreline and serves the various hotels along that strip, and Dizengoff Street, which runs from the Mann Auditorium complex and the famous café hub of Dizengoff Circle down to the intersection with Ben Yehuda at the northern tip of the city. These routes are both conveniently serviced by the number 4 and 5 buses, respectively, which in turn run all the way to the Central Bus Station, an all-new, six-storey building to the southeast of the city, replacing what was arguably the ugliest, seediest bus station of them all. Allenby is the final important connecting street, passing through most of the downtown area, to Ben Yehuda, where it turns left for two blocks before terminating at the beachfront.

Near the Shalom Tower: The tallest building in the Middle East, the **Shalom Tower** on Herzl Street soars 35 floors – and 140 metres (460 ft) – above the city, an austere white rectangle. Its main significance lies in its location. For on these premises stood one of the very first buildings to be erected in Tel Aviv – the Herzliya Gymnasium (High School). Built in 1910 on the new town's first thoroughfare, the school was a symbol of pioneering and became the cultural and economic nucleus of the embryonic town. The building was torn down in 1959. All that remains of it is a huge fresco on the wall of the tower, created by artist Nahum Gutman.

The tower consists of some 34 office floors. Its top floor is open to the public and presents a multimedia information system on the history of Tel Aviv/Jaffa and a magnificent view of the area, reaching on a clear day from Mount

The Shalom Tower.

Carmel in the north to the Negev in the south, with Jerusalem visible to the east.

The **Wax Museum** on the third floor displays figures from a century of Jewish history (1867–1967). There are wax likenesses of former prime ministers David Ben-Gurion and Golda Meir, and even Nazi war criminal Adolph Eichman. A chamber called "The Enchanted World" intermixes Neil Armstrong on the moon, Hansel and Gretel, the Manson murders and Michael Jackson (next to Israeli pop star Ofra Haza).

Right behind the Shalom Tower's sharp modernism is an entirely different world. The **Yemenite Quarter**'s exotic winding streets are a jolt back in time, preserving the look and feel of the Yemenite community which settled here 100 years ago. This is the best place to sample the spicy, pungent Yemenite cuisine, in authentic, Arab-style stone houses. Pundak Shaul, Zion, Pninat Hakerem and Maganda are among the best Yemenite restaurants in the country.

One of the most impressive old buildings remaining in Tel Aviv, although in a sorry state of disrepair, is the **Pagoda House** in King Albert Square. The square, once destined for the site of city hall, had the town's prettiest buildings erected around it. Located across Allenby Street, at the intersection of Nahmani, Montefiore and Melchet streets, the Pagoda House was built in 1925 for an American, Joseph Bloch, who lived in it six months a year. The house had a pagoda-like structure at the top of its three floors, and boasted the first passenger elevator in Tel Aviv. It is currently under renovation.

Opposite is a fantastic restaurant/bar named by its address, **Nachmani 22**.

Continue down Nachmani, passing the **Gesher Theatre** on your left. Founded in 1991, it is Israel's first Russian-speaking theatre and is testament to the growing influence of the 800,000 or so immigrants from the former Soviet Union. The building was also used, in pre-state days, as a centre for the Hagannah forces (Jewish underground).

Turn right and first left until you reach **Allenby Street**, named after the British

general who liberated Tel Aviv from the Turks in 1917.

Turn left and cross over the road, continuing on Allenby until you reach the impressive **Great Synagogue**, built by Rav Kook, first Chief Rabbi of Tel Aviv/Jaffa. Interestingly, he boycotted the placing of Tel Aviv's foundation stone on the grounds that they had not located a site for the synagogue. He made it his personal mission to get the project accomplished and within a few years it was the dominant building on Allenby Street. On Yom Ha'atzmaut (Independence Day), there is a massive service in the presence of the Chief Rabbi, the Mayor, Prime Minister and other dignitaries.

Indeed, although fully secular at face value, Tel Aviv is home to a large Orthodox community. Unlike Jerusalem, there is no segregation in living quarters and therefore very little antagonism between secular and religious residents. For example, the headquarters of the **Lubavitch** (ultra-Orthodox movement originating in Poland) is situated on **Sheinkin Street**, possibly the epitome of the modern secular Israeli.

Rothschild: Built in 1910 over a dried riverbed, **Rothschild Boulevard** was once Tel Aviv's most elegant address. It's still lovely, its central promenade dotted by trees, benches and refreshment kiosks, and its buildings embrace a jumble of styles. At number 13 is the Bezalel style (named after the Bezalel Art School in Jerusalem), combining European and Oriental design.

The public museum **Independence Hall** is at number 16, the former residence of Tel Aviv's first mayor, Meir Dizengoff. Israel's Declaration of Independence was signed in this building on 15 May 1948 and it was also the initial home of the Knesset (parliament) until it moved to the Opera Tower building on the beach before moving to Jerusalem. The second and third floor comprise the **Bible Museum**.

Across the road is the **Israel Defence Force Museum**, located in the former residence of Hagannah (pre-State forces) commander, Eliahu Golumb. Here, and

Four wheels on Rothschild Boulevard.

dotted around the city (for example, outside the old Davar Rishon building on Sheinkin Street, corner of Melchett, and on the Gesher Theatre on Nachmani Street) are brown square signs that refer to the original use of the building. Before Israel's independence, the resistance forces fought underground from these very positions, against both the British and the Arabs. To this day, the IDF (Israel Defence Forces) headquarters are located in Tel Aviv at the Kirya (originally a German Templar settlement, turned by the British into their headquarters, and then by Israel into the headquarters of the IDF). This explains where Saddam Hussein was aiming for when his forces fired Iraqi missiles at Tel Aviv in the 1991 Gulf War.

Breuer House at number 46 was built in 1922; it has tiny, decorative balconies, a slanting, pagoda-like wooden roof, a minaret, and a large, enclosed garden. On the verge of demolition in 1948, the building was saved when the Soviet ambassador requested it for his headquarters. It served as the Soviet Embassy until 1953, when diplomatic relations with the USSR were severed.

Typical **Bauhaus buildings** may be observed at numbers 89, 91 and 140, and on nearby **Engel Street**, recently converted into a pedestrian mall.

A walk on Bialik Street: Further west along Allenby, **Bialik Street** is another pleasant street left over from the city's early days. At number 14 is the **Rubin House**, the former residence of noted Israeli artist Reuvin Rubin; a short walk from here is the **Bialik House**, once the home of Israel's national poet, Haim Nahman Bialik. Built in 1925, it has a little tower and dome, a prominent pink balcony and arched columns, like those of the Doge's Palace in Venice.

At the end of the street is **Skura House**, containing the **Museum for the History of Tel Aviv-Jaffa**. Built in 1925, this house never became the hotel it was supposed to be, instead housing the Tel Aviv municipality from 1928 to 1968, when the City Hall moved north to Ibn Gvirol Street.

Next to the building, stairs lead down

Soldiers are a commonplace sight.

to Idelson Street, near Gan Meir (Meir Garden), one of the prettiest in town. Across the park, and a little way up King George Street one reaches Tel Aviv's shortest street. This is **Anonymous Alley** (Simta Almonit), sister to the nearby **Unknown Alley** (Simta Palmonit). These two tiny alleys were built as academics' residences in American Colonial style for American and British immigrants in the 1920s. Inside the buildings' curved facade stands the faded, peeling statue of a lion. Its eyes, destroyed long ago, were once glowing electric torches which shone at night.

Neve Tzedek: The oldest quarter in the city, **Neve Tzedek** was founded in 1887 as a suburb of Jaffa, and is a picturesque maze of narrow streets flanked by low-built Arab-style houses. At the time, the quarter was considered a luxury suburb, despite the crowded housing and less-than-sanitary conditions. In recent years, the quarter's quaint old dwellings have taken the fancy of artists and well-to-do families, who restored them and re-planted the inner courtyards.

The **Neve Tzedek Theater**, otherwise known as the Suzanne Delal Center, which specialises in avant-garde drama, opened in the building of the city's first girls' school, which was also the first all-Hebrew school in Israel. This is also the home of the Batsheva Dance Company and the Inbal Dance Company. With the theatre's opening in a magnificent plaza dotted with orange trees, several colourful galleries, restaurants and nightclubs popped up, lending a new vitality to the century-old streets.

On the border of Neve Tzedek and Tel Aviv, at the intersection of Lillienblum and Pines streets, stands Israel's first cinema. The **Eden Cinema** was built in 1914, seating 600 wide-eyed movie viewers who marvelled at the silent movies accompanied by a not-always-synchronised orchestra. When talking pictures arrived towards the end of the 1920s, the cinema management was successfully pressured by the powerful Labour Federation to continue paying the unemployed orchestra members' wages for a year and a half.

Between Neve Tzedek and the sea, on the fast road to Jaffa, is the **Hassan Bek Mosque**, contrasting sharply with the contemporary high-rise near it. Built in 1916 by Jaffa's Turkish-Arab governor of the same name, the mosque was intended to block development of Tel Aviv towards the sea. Supposedly, Hassan Bek had robbers pilfer building materials from Tel Aviv in order to construct the mosque. During the War of Independence, the mosque served as an outpost for Arab snipers who would shoot at the Jewish population.

Levantine markets: If Tel Aviv is often noted for its European air and lifestyle, its market-places are an inseparable part of the Levant. The biggest and best known of these is the **Carmel Market**, on and around Hacarmel Street, off Allenby. Always crowded with shoppers and hagglers, the market is a medley of colours, smells and sounds. A large variety of fruits, vegetables and herbs can be found here, as well as underwear, clothes, shoes, pickled foods and pitta bread at bargain prices. Exotic anonas, fijoyas, persimmons and star **Modern style.**

fruit are piled alongside more prosaic fruits like bananas and oranges.

To the left of the entrance to the Carmel Market on Allenby street, is a pedestrianised street called **Nahalat Binyamin**. Here, on Tuesdays and Fridays, arts and crafts traders bring their wares to parade and sell. A great place for present-shopping, as the artisans combine jewellery with juggling; cactus plants with camel bags; and wood carvings with wonderful art. The nearby **Bezalel Market**, off King George Street, is reputed to have the best felafels in Israel, as well as the usual discount quality fashion items and second-hand bric-a-brac.

Tourists have not yet discovered **Sheinkin Street**, the local equivalent of London's Soho or New York's Village, tinged with Lower East Side. Stretching from Allenby all the way east to Yehuda HaLevi Street, Sheinkin is one street that has it all. And on Fridays the street is closed to traffic to allow shoppers to buy wallpaper, furniture or home appliances; discover a second-hand Georgian fake-fur coat; bind a book; buy eggs in a shop which sells only farm-fresh produce; have their hair done; and wind up over coffee in a Bohemian café that has trees growing in it.

The latter, by the way, is **Café Tamar**, a veteran establishment facing the old editorial offices of *Davar* (and the Labour Party newspaper). Nobody remembers exactly how old the café is; old-timers affirm it has always been there. Most importantly, Sheinkin is renowned for its leading fashion designs, and hip Tel Avivians who can be seen flaunting and flirting their funky outfits and their latest chic hairstyles.

Gateway by the beach: Most tourists spend at least their first and last nights at one of Tel Aviv's hotels. These establishments, concentrated along the beach promenade, have inevitably become the gateway to Israel.

From the north of the city to the south, the coastline is dominated by an imposing row of **hotels**, lined up like dominoes, their number including the Hilton, north of Arlozorov Street, and working down through the Carlton, Moriah,

Carmel Market.

Holiday Inn, Ramada, Sheraton and Dan. In the middle of these is the **Opera Tower**, a terraced apartment building overlooking the sea with a mall on the ground floor including restaurants, shops, jewellery stores and a cinema.

The seaside **promenade** is dotted with cafés, restaurants, ice-cream parlours and the like all offering free sea air and costly refreshments. On summer nights the promenade is clogged with people on foot and in cars, manoeuvring for some sea breeze after the day's humid, oppressive heat or queueing up outside the new Planet Hollywood restaurant or the Yotvata dairy restaurant, a commercial outlet of the kibbutz-based dairy factory that is synonymous with chocolate milk and great dairy products.

In front of the Carlton and Marina hotels is Tel Aviv's large **seawater swimming pool**, maintained at 24°C (70°F) year-round. Aerobic exercise sessions are held on the beach in the summer, and, if this is *passé*, a **roller-skating rink** operates at evening hours near the pool. The **marina** next door, largest in the Middle East, rents out sailing and motor-boats, and equipment for windsurfing, seasurfing, waterskiing and other water sports.

You can't get away from **Kikar Namir** (still known locally by its former name, Kikar Atarim), a concrete monstrosity squatting over the marina, at the end of Ben-Gurion Boulevard. This is an open-air square and mall, offering concrete mushroom sunshades, tourist items and a chance to lose one's way. Its cafés, pizzerias and restaurants, tolerable in the sunlight, turn seedy at night.

Each hotel has its own beach strip (the beaches are all public), most of them quite civilised, with showers, easy chairs and refreshment facilities.

Marking the end of the hotel line to the south, across from the Dan Panorama, is the **Dolphinarium**, a white elephant, now unused, obscuring the magnificent view of Old Jaffa from Tel Aviv's coast. There is, however, an outdoor (and free) reggae gig every Friday, Saturday and Sunday in summer.

Dizengoff's cafés: Café-going is a ma-

Kikar Atarim at dusk.

jor part of any self-respecting Tel Aviv-ian's way of life. Some people go to cafés for their first coffee of the day; others conduct business meetings or entertain guests; senior citizens spend their mornings over cappuccino and croissants at their regular haunts. On a sunny day, a newcomer may get the impression that the entire city is on holiday, sipping coffee at sidewalk cafés.

The bulk of Israeli café activity takes place along the city's main drag, **Dizen-goff Street**, an indigenous cross between the Via Veneto and Fifth Avenue. Young, upbeat and action-packed, this street is a constant parade of beautiful people, window shoppers, tourists, actors and models and in-vogue popstars, vagabonds, soldiers and business people. A seat in a Dizengoff café is an excellent vantage point for observing the multifaceted human panorama.

At no time is Dizengoff more glamorous or crowded than on Friday afternoons, when groups of Tel Avivians congregate to unwind from the long work week with friends, try to chat up girls, catch up on gossip, and learn of the night's best parties.

The café scene begins in the north of Dizengoff with "respectable" veteran establishments like Café Afarsemon and Batya. Eminent literary figures and the Austro-Hungarian set used to favour the former Café Stern a little way down, today the Stern-Dolphin Fish Restaurant. On the corner of Ben-Gurion Boulevard is Café Cherry, particularly crowded on Fridays when singles come to meet and greet each other.

A short walk west on Ben-Gurion brings you to the former **David Ben-Gurion House**, today a public museum housing his personal mementos and a 20,000-volume library.

The next street to cut across Dizengoff is Gordon, known as **Gallery Street**. Works of the great masters, such as Picasso and Chagall, are displayed here beside paintings by leading Israeli artists like Agam, Gutman and Kadishman. Those who like to combine sightseeing with food can then eat their way down Dizengoff, which, as it proceeds south-

People-watching from a Dizengoff café.

wards, gets crowded with snack bars and restaurants, offering everything from fruit juice, pizza and hamburgers to Hungarian blintzes and shwarma.

The raised piazza with the sculpture-fountain spouting in its centre is **Dizengoff Circle**. Originally a traffic circle for the streets converging on Dizengoff, the pedestrian level has since been lifted above the street, creating a peculiar urban hub, but allowing for the free flow of people and traffic.

A block further south is the **Dizengoff Center**, a modern multi-level shopping complex offering everything from off-beat pets to carpets, complete with cinemas, restaurants, sport shops and banks.

Bring on the night: Tel Aviv is one of the few large cities of its kind which is relatively safe at night, and its main streets throng with activity well past midnight. Pubs and nightclubs, which according to municipal law should close down by 1am, usually stay open much longer, although they invariably look shut from the street.

In recent years, the evening action has

gravitated to north Tel Aviv, at the converging point of Dizengoff, Ben Yehuda and Hayarkon streets, where a night-time eating and entertainment centre has blossomed. Dozens of Chinese, French, Japanese, Hungarian and Oriental restaurants illuminate the streets.

Yirmiyahu Street, which cuts across the three north–south streets, leads from the Peer Cinema to countless eating establishments, adding to the general atmosphere of culinary well-being. Equally, the industrious area of **Florentine**, just south of the centre, opens up at night into a bohemian array of pubs, cafés, bars and clubs.

Two of its quirkier locations are a bar called Hamachbesa (The Laundrette), which is actually a bar and a laundry facility in one; and, close by, a funky hairdressers called Vittrio, noted for its opening hours – from the afternoon until 2am. The Ministry of Sound and the Nanna Bar are other venues – not forgetting the Café With No Name.

Apart from the many nightclubs, discotheques and bars dispersed throughout the city, the remaining nightlife focuses on **Old Jaffa**. Popular **clubs** here include El Hamam and The Cave, specialising in Israeli folklore, and Ariana for Greek music and dancing.

Independence Park hides among its shrubbery various archaeological finds, but in the evenings the park is the gathering spot of the city's gay community. From here they may go on to Divine, a gay-oriented nightclub on Dizengoff Street, or another (mixed) club.

The modern city: During the Russian Revolution, a group of young Russian-Jewish actors formed a collective and dreamed of a Hebrew theatre. The dream came true in Tel Aviv, dozens of years later. The **Habima Theater**, built for the company in Habima Square (*habima* means "the stage" in Hebrew) originally had creaking wooden chairs and lousy acoustics: today it has two theatre halls (one seating 1,000 and a smaller seating 300), revolving stages, orchestra seats and simultaneous translation into several languages during the high season. The square itself fronted by Dizengoff Street in the north, Huberman

Dizengoff Circle.

Street in the east, and Tarsat Boulevard in the west, also holds a large abstract sculpture by Menashe Kadishman and has become synonymous with Tel Aviv's performance prowess.

Just next to the Habima Theater is the **Mann Auditorium**, the home of the Israel Philharmonic Orchestra. Tickets here are always highly prized. The third building in this complex is the **Helena Rubinstein Pavilion**, a branch of the Tel Aviv Museum, which specialises in modern art exhibitions. The little park in the middle of the complex hides the chic, brass and chrome Apropos Café.

From here, the new part of the city splays out northwards, along a network of tree-lined residential boulevards, bisected by the main strip of **Ibn Gvirol Street**, and the central square of the city, next to the headquarters of the municipality. It was here, at **Kikar Malchei Yisrael** (the Square of the Kings of Israel), on 4 November 1995 that Prime Minister Yitzchak Rabin was assassinated after a huge demonstration in support of the peace process.

The square was immediately renamed **Yitchak Rabin Square** and there is an unusual memorial close to the spot where he fell, at the northern end of the square, just behind the steps to the municipality building. Portraits, paintings and graffiti cover the area as the people's memorial to a man respected by many of differing political and religious convictions. The assassin, Yigal Amir, intended to destroy the authors of the peace process – Rabin and Peres – and thus peace itself. His bullets killed Rabin and, six months later, Peres and the Labour-led government were voted out.

Further north lies the luxuriously wide circle of **Kikar Hamedina**, a shoppers' paradise for those who can afford the fashion labels from London, Paris and New York.

At the corner of **Shaul Hamelech Street** (King Saul) and **Weizmann Street**, are the most striking modern edifices in the city. The most unusual of these is **Asia House**, created by architect Mordechai Ben-Horin in gleaming white to resemble a horizontal series of

Asia House and the IBM Building.

giant, rolling waves, taking a morphological cue, perhaps, from the amoeba. Its entrance holds a permanent exhibit of sculpture under a pastel-coloured mosaic ceiling. The building houses embassies, offices and restaurants.

The **IBM Building** next door towers above, a three-sided cylinder supported on a mushroom-like shaft. Designed by Israeli architects Yasky, Gil & Silvan, it creates a handsome profile for the city skyline. Across the street, the red slated roofs of the **German Templar Colony** (1870–1939) provide one more architectural contrast in a city of contrasts.

Located at **Golda Meir Square** further in on King Saul Boulevard, the **Tel Aviv Museum of Art** (Sun–Thurs 10am–9.30pm) has four central galleries, an auditorium which often features film retrospectives, numerous other halls, a statue garden, a cafeteria and a shop. The museum has exhibitions of 17th-century Dutch and Flemish masters, 18th-century Italian paintings, Impressionists, post-Impressionists, and a good selection of 20th-century art from the US and Europe, in addition to a collection of modern Israeli work.

North of the Yarkon: Defining the northernmost limit of the city proper is the **Yarkon River**, which once marked the border between the tribes of Dan and Ephraim. Today, it is lined with rambling parkland and serves to accommodate scullers who row along it in the cooler hours of the day. Near the western rim, across the river, can be seen the dome and chimneys of the **Reading Power Station**, while the greenery of the city's exhibition grounds marks the river's eastern limit.

Across the river in **Ramat Aviv**, the sprawling **Eretz Israel Museum** on University Street (Sun–Fri 9am–1pm) comprises the most comprehensive storehouse of archaeological, anthropological and historical findings in the region. Its spiritual backbone is **Tel Quasile**, an excavation site in which 12 distinct layers of civilisation have been uncovered, its finds including an ancient Philistine temple and Hebrew inscriptions from 800 BC. The museum complex consists of 11 pavilions, including glassware, ceramics, copper, coins, folklore and ethnography museums, and a planetarium. In the section entitled "Man and his Toil", staff members demonstrate ancient methods of weaving, jewellery and pottery making, grain grinding and bread baking.

No visit to Israel would be complete without calling at least once at the **Beth Hatefutsoth** on the Tel Aviv University campus. Founded in 1979, the **Museum of the Jewish Diaspora** (Sun–Thurs 10am–5pm) is known throughout the Jewish world. It is also, in concept and methodology, a radical departure from the accepted notion of a museum, for apart from a few sacramental objects, Beth Hatefutsoth contains no preserved artifacts. Its principal aim is reconstruction.

The body of the main exhibit is handled thematically, focusing on general themes of Jewish Life in the Diaspora: Family Life, Community, Religious Life, Culture, Interrelations with the Gentile Environment and the Return to Zion. Its striking displays include a col-

The Opera House, Shaul Hamelech Street.

lection of beautifully intricate models of synagogue buildings from across the globe. A memorial column in the central atrium commemorates Jewish martyrdom through the ages.

An audio-visual depiction of the migrations of Jews in relation to world history is presented in the hall known as the "**Chronosphere**". Four video "study-areas" enable visitors to view documentary films selected from a catalogue, while a computer system allows them to trace their own lineage. Special exhibitions highlight topics related to Jewish communities around the world.

North, east and south Tel Aviv is surrounded by what Tel Avivians refer to as the "bedroom suburbs", whose residents commute to the city for work, shopping and social activities. On Tel Aviv's southern border are the Sephardi-dominated communities of **Holon** and **Bat Yam** (literally, Daughter of the Sea); in the north are the slightly more affluent areas of **Ramat Aviv** and **Shikun Lamed**. To the east, as well as Ramat Gan and its diamond exchange –

which handles around $3 billion worth of stones a year – is **Giv'atayim** and a **Safari Park**.

Still further east are the religious town of **Bnei Brak**, established in 1924 by Orthodox Jews from Poland, and **Petach Tikva** (meaning Gate of Hope, from Hosea: 2,17). Petach Tikva was known as the "Mother of Settlements", for it was founded in 1878, the first Jewish settlement of modern times. The town's emblem is an orange tree and a plough.

The original founders would be shocked at the contemporary metropolis that is now Tel Aviv. Intended as a "garden suburb" of Jaffa, Tel Aviv has become "The Big Orange" – an Israeli attempt to match New York's "Big Apple", complete with McDonald's, Pizza Hut and Planet Hollywood. Yet the urban sprawl is, without doubt, the pulse of the nation. If it's happening, it's in Tel Aviv. Jerusalem, just 40 minutes' drive away, is so near – and yet so far from the secularised, hedonistic lifestyle that draws over a third of the nation to Tel Aviv's beaches and environs.

THE INLAND PLAINS

It is not the most acclaimed tourist area in the Holy Land, nor is it the most famous for its ruins. Odds are, in fact, the average visitor to Israel will pass through this region, from Tel Aviv to Jerusalem and back, never bothering to venture from the main roads.

And they won't be the first – the main historical routes between the ancient empires of Egypt and Mesopotamia passed through this region thousands of years ago, and the centuries following continued the pattern. In more recent years, this area – spanning from the fringes of Samaria above Tel Aviv in the north to the uppermost sands of the Negev to the south, and to the besieged citadel of Jerusalem in the east – became a strategic wedge of supplies and habitation during the War of Independence, connecting the coastal plain and the state's new capital city. Yet the consistent flow of conquerors, immigrants, wayfarers and settlers have left their mark on the landscape, and today the area – still the central crossroads of the nation – is rich in history.

Rising from the flat coastal plain into the gently rolling Judean foothills, this area has always been one of the most densely populated in the country. Controlled by Egypt until the 13th century BC, it was the scene of some of Joshua's toughest battles during the conquest of Canaan. It became a flourishing community of villages during the time of the Israelite kingdom, but was devastated with the fall of Jerusalem at the end of the 6th century BC. Alexander the Great swept through in the 4th century BC and it was from here that the Hasmoneans launched their revolt against the Syrian-Greek empire.

Some of the first modern Jewish settlements in the 1880s and 1890s were established here. Today several of these villages have grown into small towns; others, with their lush vegetation and smell of cow dung, convey an air of tranquillity at odds with the hectic pace of so much of modern Israel.

A haven for immigrants: Some 60 km (35 miles) south of Tel Aviv, at the edge of the Judean foothills, is the development town of **Kiryat Gat**. Founded in 1954 as the centre of the Lachish Region, the city marked Israel's first attempt to deal in an organised way with the immigrants who poured into the country in the late 1940s and early 1950s from Europe and the Middle East.

Earlier settlement had been realised haphazardly; for Lachish, planner Lova Eliav assembled a team of experts who created a whole area of coordinated settlement. The new immigrant villages were integrated with existing kibbutzim, grouped around four regional centres providing various facilities and services. In the centre was Kiryat Gat, with cotton mills, sugar refineries and other industries based on local agriculture.

Southeast, near the moshav (collective farming village) of Lachish, is the ancient mound of **Tel Lachish**, which was a fortified city throughout the Bronze Age (4000–1200 BC). Captured by Joshua, it became a city in the tribe of

Judah until destroyed by the king of Assyria in 701 BC. Rebuilt, it was destroyed again by Nebuchadnezzar of Babylon in 598 BC and never regained prominence. The most important find was 21 Hebrew *ostrocons* (ink inscriptions on pottery fragments) from the time between the city's two destructions.

About 35 km (22 miles) north of Kiryat Gat, just inland of Yavne, is the town of **Rehovot**, home of the **Weizmann Institute of Science**, Israel's well-known research and development centre, named after Chaim Weizmann, Israel's first president. Weizmann was also an organic chemist of international renown, and for many years the leader of the Zionist movement. His scientific research assisted the British war effort during World War I, toward the end of which he was instrumental in securing the Balfour Declaration. Founded in 1934, the Weizmann Institute originally concentrated on local agriculture and medicine, but in 1949, following the establishment of the state, it was transformed into a world-class research institute. Today it has a staff of 1,500 researchers and graduate students, with over 400 research projects in the pipeline, in such fields as cancer cures, hormones, immunology, ageing, cell structure, computer science, geophysics, lasers, atomic particles and astrophysics.

The centre's moving spirit in its early years was Meyer Weisgal, an American showbiz impresario who, in addition to raising millions of dollars for the institute, used to pace the grounds picking up discarded cartons, plastic bags, and even matchsticks. The institute is still one of the tidiest places in Israel. There are daily guided tours of the grounds.

Apart from the laboratories, other sites worth seeing include the view from the top of the futuristic atomic particle accelerator, and Weizmann's house, designed by Erich Mendelsohn in 1936–37. Weizmann's tomb is in the gardens of his former home.

Opposite the Weizmann Institute is another prestigious academic campus: the Hebrew University's **Faculty of Agriculture**, one of the world's leading research centres in this discipline, which has played an important role in the development of the country's leading edge farming capability.

North and inland from Rehovot, are the towns of Ramla and Lydda. They were originally Arab communities, but many of their inhabitants fled in the War of Independence in 1948; today they are two of the few mixed Jewish–Arab communities in Israel. **Ramla** has three important mosques: the **White Mosque**, dating to the 8th century; the **Mosque of the Forty**, built by the Mamelukes in 1318; and the **Great Mosque**, built on the site of the Crusader Cathedral of St John. The **Vaulted Pool**, an underground water cistern in the centre of town, dates from the 9th century. Finally, the **Open House** is a joint Jewish–Arab co-operative, organising activities for both Jewish and Arab youth in an attempt to bridge the gap between the cultures.

North of Lydda (Lod in Hebrew) is **Ben-Gurion Airport**, the country's busy international terminal, named after Israel's first prime minister. **Lydda**, today in the shadow of soaring jetliners,

Chaim Weizmann (left) at his home at Rehovot in 1937 with a US diplomat, Henry Morgenthau.

was an important town during the Biblical and Second Temple periods. Visit the ancient **Sheikh's Tomb** built over the ruins of a 12th-century Crusader church, in the basement of which is the legendary **Tomb of St George**.

The Judean foothills: East of Ramla, in the Jerusalem foothills, is the site of **Modiin**, birthplace of the Hasmonean family, leaders of the great 2nd-century BC revolt against the Syrian-Greek empire which controlled Judea. The revolt actually started in Modiin, when an official of the empire came to the village to order the people to sacrifice a cockerel on a pagan altar, in accordance with the policy of fostering Hellenisation and repressing Judaism.

Mattitiahu, a local priest, and his five sons killed the official and his military escort, triggering the conflict. The revolt, led by Judas Maccabeus, the third son, expanded all over Judea, resulting in the recapture of the Temple and the restoration of Jewish worship in Jerusalem.

Not much remains of ancient Modiin, but an attractive **park** has been laid out, with a model of a village of the period of the revolt. If they like, visitors can bake pitta bread in the ancient-style ovens, handle replicas of ancient agricultural implements and spin yarn.

At Channukah, the festival commemorating the revolt, a torch is lit at Modiin and carried in relays to Jerusalem to light candles at the Western Wall. Today, Modiin is being built into a major city to help house Israel's growing population.

Some 15 km (8 miles) southwest of Modiin is **Neve Shalom**, a unique experiment in Jewish–Arab coexistence. The only settlement founded specifically for people of the two groups to live together, it runs special courses, where Jewish and Arab schoolchildren learn about each other's cultures. Nearby is the **French Trappist Monastery of Latrun** (just across the old border with Jordan). The remains of a 12th-century Crusader fortress called Le Toron des Chevaliers, and an almost perfectly preserved Roman villa and bath house is also located nearby.

A little to the north is the **Canada Park**, a recreation centre with vineyards, almond orchards, ancient fig trees and adventure playgrounds. In the park are the ruins of a village thought to be the **Emmaus** of the New Testament, where the risen Jesus was seen, according to St Luke's gospel. Emmaus was also the site of one of the greatest victories of the Hasmoneans.

Less than 30 km (16 miles) to the south is the ancient site of **Beit Guvrin**, opposite a modern kibbutz of the same name. There are ruins of many historic periods, notably the Crusader ruins on either side of the road, but it is the **caves** that are of special note. There are hundreds of bell-shaped caves in the area, caused by ancient Roman quarrying operations. Some of them are even earlier, dating to Greek and even Phoenician times. There are daily tours of the caves.

The Jerusalem corridor: About 20 km (13 miles) west of Jerusalem, on a secondary road between the town of Beit Shemesh and Moshav Ness Harim, is a different type of cavern: the spectacular **Sorek Cave**, which extends across some 6 hectares (15 acres) of the **Avshalom**

The greenhouse effect.

Nature Reserve. Discovered by chance during routine quarrying, it is by far the largest cave in Israel and contains stalactites and stalagmites of breathtaking beauty. Tours operate daily.

Just to the south is the **Valley of Elah**, where David killed Goliath, the Philistine from Gath. According to the Book, David rejected the armour given to him by King Saul, "and chose him five smooth stones out of the brook," one of which he slung at the giant warrior, killing him. The battle is described in I Samuel: 17. The actual site of the encounter is not marked; today a kibbutz and a TV satellite receiving station stand in the valley.

The main road to Jerusalem enters the gorge of **Shaar Hagai** west of Latrun, then climbs steeply through the wooded hills. They weren't always so green; when the first Jewish pioneers arrived to make their settlements they saw a hilly desert, stripped of trees by centuries of abuse. Much of the forest here, though, was destroyed by fire in 1995.

The early forests were made up almost entirely of indigenous Jerusalem pine – and this tree still dominates – but modern planters are diversifying for both ecological and aesthetic reasons. Among the newcomers are cypress, acacia, eucalyptus, pistachio, carob, and many varieties of the local scrub oak.

Visitors may be surprised to see dozens of ruined vehicles by the roadside, painted brown to prevent them from rusting. They are the remains of burnt-out armoured vans and buses which carried supplies to besieged Jerusalem in the 1948 war, and which sit permanently at the spots where they were destroyed, as monuments to those who tried to run the siege. Jutting out from a hilltop farther ahead is the more formal **Monument to the Road Builders**, its aluminium spars pointing compellingly to the capital beyond.

The nearby settlements of **Shoresh**, **Neve Ilan**, **Kiryat Anavim** and **Maale Hahamisha** offer guesthouses with stunning views of the Judean hills; all of them have attractive swimming pools and comfortable accommodations.

Also in this area are three Arab vil-

Roman-era cave at Beit Guvrin.

274

lages, each of them with features of interest. The largest, **Abu Gosh**, is named after the Arab family which still comprises the majority of its inhabitants. It has two fine churches and a French Benedictine monastery. A sacred spring, where Jesus is said to have drank, is situated in a garden of towering pines and old palm trees. Some great local Arab restaurants offer tasty spiced pitta bread, hummous and tahina.

Nearby **Ein Nekuba** is the only Arab village built by the State of Israel from scratch; it was constructed for villagers whose homes were taken over by new immigrants, after they fled from their village of Beit Nekuba in the 1948 war.

Although most of its fruit trees and vegetable plots are watered by modern methods, neighbouring **Ein Rafa** has an irrigation system that dates back to biblical times. Some 4 hectares (10 acres) of village land are watered by a natural spring, which is allowed to flow into the individual plots according to a traditional eight-day rota system, stringently observed by the villagers.

Between the two villages and the main road is **Ein Hemed** (or Aqua Bella), a landscaped camping site and nature reserve, with a stream flowing through it and a restored Crusader farm. Up the hill is the suburb of **Mevasseret Zion**, formerly Kastel, an important Arab town and the site for one of the key battles for Jerusalem in 1948. Part of the village has been preserved as a memorial to soldiers who died here, and some bunkers and pillboxes have been restored. There are magnificent views of the surrounding Judean Hills, and the gleaming expanse of Jerusalem to the southwest.

One last stop on the road to the capital is the village of **Motza**, and the stump of **Herzl's Cypress**. Planted by the founder of modern Zionism on his visit to the Holy Land in 1898, the tree became a place of pilgrimage, and was later cut down as an anti-Zionist gesture. A glass case has been built around the stump, and it has become traditional for presidents of Israel to plant a tree in the surrounding garden as a symbol of the continuing growth of Zionism.

Stalactites form veils at Sorek Cave.

THE SOUTH COAST

The Mediterranean coast means many things to the Israelis. It is, foremost, the spine of the country, in terms of population as well as geography, with over half of all Israelis living along its vital and accommodating lowlands. The coastal plain is the site of the country's most luxurious hotels, as well as some of its most important ruins. It is a prime transportation corridor and is the location of the fertile Sharon Plain, the source of Israel's renowned citrus industry. Its harbours service industry, military and tourist needs alike.

But for the average Israeli, the Mediterranean coast really means one thing: recreation. From April to October, from Yad Mordechai to Rosh Hanikra, thousands of bronzed sabras flock in droves, day after day, to the glimmering sands at the western rim of their country, to bake in the sun, play paddle-ball along the water's edge, swim, wade, run, sail, tan, and then in turn watch everyone else do the same.

While many of the best-known beaches are a kaleidoscope of human activity in the summer, there are quite a few lesser known beaches as well, which offer fewer facilities, but equally pleasant access to sun and sand. Similarly, because of the density of resources, it's not unusual to take a dip against a backdrop of an ancient aqueduct, or the looming grey silhouette of a power plant.

With so much vitality in unlikely co-existence – orange groves and vacation villages, minimal bikinis and Philistine *tels* – the coastal plain is as unexpected as it is inviting. With all the various civilisations whose pillars and monuments have crumbled into the waves here, one can't help wondering if even the sand underfoot is a uniquely Israeli blend.

Israel's beginnings: Israel's southern coast begins just north of the Gaza Strip, with the kibbutz of **Yad Mordechai**. Named after Mordechai Anilewitz, who died leading the Jews in their uprising against the Nazis in the Warsaw Ghetto in 1943, the kibbutz was founded the same year by Polish immigrants, and played a pivotal role during the Israeli War of Independence. Attacked by the Egyptian army on its way northward in May 1948, the settlement managed to hold out against vastly superior forces for six days, thereby allowing for the adequate defence of Tel Aviv. Several structures commemorate this event. The morbid but effective battlefield reconstruction includes cut-out figures of advancing Egyptian soldiers, and a taped narration of the course of events.

Close by, the imposing **museum** houses displays about the fighting, the four kibbutzim that stood together here, and a memorial to the Polish-Jewish community which was annihilated during the Holocaust. On a ridge nearby are the graves of those who fell defending the young settlement.

Overlooking today's community, the **statue of Anilewitz** stands in defiant pose, grenade in hand, while behind him rests the fallen watertower, its rutted surface preserved in commemoration of all it withstood. The overall

effect of Yad Mordechai is unquestionably sobering rather than joyful, yet it does provide a potent insight into the mentality of this small nation, time and again besieged by hostile forces.

Slightly to the east lies the sister kibbutz of **Negba**, which was not taken by the Egyptians and which, throughout 1948, served as Israel's main supply line to the Negev and the south.

Philistine cities: Some 16 km (10 miles) to the north of the kibbutzim sit the time-washed stones of **Ashkelon**, one of the world's oldest cities. Situated on a crest of dunes above the sea, Ashkelon is an amalgam of industrial plants, contemporary apartment towers and lovely beaches. But it is the archaeological part that makes it special, and thoughtful preservation has made this erstwhile Philistine city accessible to visitors.

The multi-layered ruins of this strategic harbour city attest to the diversity of peoples who have made their habitation here over the centuries. Lying along the famous Via Maris, the roadway linking Egypt and Syria, the city was a trading centre from its earliest days, its exports including wine, grain, and a variety of local onion now known as a scallion after its place of origin. In the early 12th century BC, the town was conquered by the Philistines, in their sweep of the southern coast, and in the following years grew to become one of the five great Philistine cities – the others being Ashdod, Gaza, Gath and Ekron.

The next two centuries witnessed bitter rivalry between the Philistines and the Israelites, and, although the Jews never took the city, it filtered into Jewish history in the story of Samson, whose exploits included his victory with the jawbone of an ass, the episode in which he set fire to the Philistine fields by tying torches to foxes' tails, and his famed ill-fated romance with the Philistine barber-girl, Delilah.

When King Saul died at the hands of the Philistines, it prompted David's oft-quoted lament: "Tell it not in Gath, publish it not in the streets of Ashkelon, lest the daughters of the Philistines rejoice" (II Sam: 1, 20). Three centuries

<u>Left</u>, fallen Roman pillars in surf at Ashkelon. <u>Below</u>, brilliant blooms on a kibbutz.

later, Ashkelon was still a Philistine stronghold, provoking the wrath of the prophet Zephaniah, who, in the final pages of the Old Testament, proclaims "For Gaza shall be forsaken, and Ashkelon a desolation: they shall drive out Ashdod at the noonday, and Ekron shall be rooted up" (Zeph: 2, 4).

Eventually, of course, all were. Taken in the ensuing centuries by Assyrians, Babylonians, and the like, Ashkelon once more realised growth in the years of Greek and Roman rule. Herod the Great was supposedly born here, and contributed by adding greatly to the city. Ashkelon fell to the Arabs in the 7th century, and briefly to the Crusaders in 1153, and, in the process, was pillaged of its monuments and stones. In 1270 it was destroyed completely by the Sultan Baibars, from which time on it remained largely ignored by all.

Today, most of the city's antiquities are encompassed within the **National Park**. Here, one can ramble by the ruins of Herodian colonnades and ancient synagogues, a Roman avenue presided over by the headless statue of Nike, goddess of victory, and a long-abandoned Roman amphitheatre. The site is surrounded by a grass-covered Crusader wall, while on the beach below, fallen pillars rest forlornly against the pressing of the tides. Nearby are a camping area and holiday village.

The modern city consists of two distinct residential areas: **Midgal**, a former Arab town, to the east, and **Afridar**, a newer suburb along the shore, founded in 1955 by Jews from South Africa. Distinguished by its tall, fenestrated clock-tower, Afridar holds Ashkelon's pleasant downtown, where one can find the commercial centre and information office, and two preserved Roman sarcophagi. There are a number of hotels here as well, including the fancy King Saul and Swissotel, and the affordable self-contained Dagon, which means "mermaid". The beaches are fine for bathing, and enjoy such biblical sobriquets as Samson Beach, Delilah Beach, Bar-Kochba Beach, and so on.

Other notable sights include the Ro-

Sunset at Ashkelon.

man-era **Painted Tomb**, and, in **Barnea** to the north, the remains of a Byzantine church and 5th-century mosaic. Continuing up the coastal highway, leaving Ashkelon behind, one passes an access road to **Nizzanim**, a settlement founded by South American immigrants, which boasts a fine strip of beach.

Some 40 km (25 miles) north of Ashkelon, the concrete skyline of **Ashdod** comes into view. Its Philistine history now long behind it, Ashdod is a burgeoning man-made harbour, Israel's most important port, and, if not much of a gift to tourism, a striking example of commercial success.

Founded only in 1957, Ashdod has grown in four decades to a city of over 120,000 people, and is virtually bursting at its seams with rugged vitality. With its prospering economy based on the new deep-water port, Ashdod is a major immigrant absorption centre. Its populace includes Arabic-speaking Jews, Indian Jews, sabras, and Soviet Jews, among them a large community from Soviet Georgia, "Gruzinim". From

Memorial Hill, just below the lighthouse, is a clear view of the port, with great ships lined up to carry away exports such as potash and phosphates.

Outside the city, to the southeast, lies the grave of the ancient metropolis, **Tel Ishdud**. The site is quite literally a *tel* (mound), as little remains of its previous incarnation other than a hillock and the scattered shards of Philistine pottery. Returning towards the highway, keep an eye out for the sycamore trees which dot the environs, and which bear a sometimes edible fruit.

Ashdod marked the official northernmost advance of the Egyptian army in 1948, and supposedly hosted Gamal Abdel Nasser himself, then a young officer. At the point where the roadway crosses the streambed, just east of the city, two relics of that period can be found. The first, the **railroad bridge** parallel to the road, is a reconstruction of the original, which was blown up by the commandos of the Israeli Givati Brigade, whose nickname – the Foxes of Samson – recalls earlier history. To

Tetrapods lend support in Ashdod port.

the west of the bridges, a small white **pillbox**, built by the British in World War II, stands by in lonely vigil.

First in Zion: To the north of Ashdod, the quiet town of **Yavne** proffers a rich history. The legend goes that in AD 70, when the fall of Jerusalem seemed imminent in the war against Rome, the renowned Rabbi Yohanon Ben Zakkai appeared before the Roman general Vespasian, to request permission to found an academy here, predicting that one day the general would become emperor. The prophecy came true shortly afterwards, and the request was granted. Regardless of the tale, Yavne did become the site of a great academy in the years following, and is known as the site where the Mishnah, the great commentary on the Bible which adapted Judaism to a modern framework, was started.

The *tel* of Yavne today consists of a lone **Mameluke tower**, built on Crusader ruins on top of a ridge. More recently, Yavne is notable as the site of a small atomic research reactor, Israel's first, built in 1960 by architect Philip Johnson. Just north of here, where the Sorek River winds into the sea, is the site of the ancient port of Yavne, **Yavne-Yam**, and the swimming beach of **Palmakhim**, said to offer Israel's finest surfing as well as the site where Judas Maccabeus marked a victory over Greek forces in the 2nd century BC.

The area from Ashdod to Tel Aviv is historically known as Darom (the South). In ancient times it was a seat of wisdom, thanks to Yavne, and in the 20th century it became the location of some of the new country's first, and southernmost, communities.

Continuing towards Tel Aviv, the road passes through two of these. **Nes Ziona**, founded in 1884, is said to have been the first place where the now familiar blue-and-white flag of Zion was unfurled; **Rishon LeZion**, meaning "First in Zion", was founded in 1882 by Polish and Russian Zionists.

After struggling for five years, the community was given new life in 1887 by the Baron Edmond de Rothschild who, in one of his first acts as Israel's benefactor, established vineyards here. He imported shoots of grape vines from Beaujolais, Burgundy and Bordeaux, and the vineyards flourished, producing mainly sweet wines for Jewish ceremonial occasions. After years of Rothschild ownership, the company reverted to co-operative ownership in 1957 and today the **Carmel Oriental Vineyards** produce a variety of lovely dry whites and table wines as well. After touring the wine cellars and the old Rothschild offices, the visitor can enjoy a free wine-tasting, courtesy of Carmel.

Another bonus is the small garden, which contains all seven of the trees mentioned in the Bible – fig, date, grape, pomegranate, olive, palm and carob. Also to Rishon LeZion's credit are the first synagogue built in Israel in modern times (1885), the first kindergarten to teach in Hebrew, and the first Hebrew cultural centre, where Israel's National anthem *HaTikva* (The Hope) was composed and sung for the first time.

From Rishon LeZion, it is only 10 km (6 miles) to the resort-suburb of **Bat Yam** and the outskirts of Tel Aviv.

Mameluke tower at Yavne.

"We are trying to
show that these are
wondrous animals."

THE DEAD SEA

Over the centuries, Christian pilgrims travelling here were aghast at the lifelessness they encountered and gave the **Dead Sea** its name. It's an apt one, for the most saline body of water on the face of the earth contains no life of any sort, and for most of its history there has been precious little life around it either.

Yet today it is a source of both life and health: the potash contained in its bitter waters is an invaluable fertiliser, exported all over the world, while the lake and the springs that feed it have cured everything from arthritis to psoriasis since ancient times. Sun worshippers from Scandinavia and health fanatics from Germany fill its spas and hotels, seeking remedies and relaxation. Many tourists and even Israelis come here to breathe in the abundant oxygen, float on the water's salty surface, and marvel at the rugged panoramas.

Situated some 400 metres (1,300 ft) below sea level in a geological fault that extends all the way to East Africa, the Dead Sea is the lowest point on the face of the globe, and is surrounded by the starkest scenery that Israel, and indeed the world, has to offer. Steep cliffs of reddish flint rise sharply to the west, contrasting with beige limestone bluffs and the blinding white salt flats of the plain. Across the shimmering gold surface of the water to the east, the mauve and purple mountains of biblical Moab and Edom are almost indistinguishable in the morning, gaining visibility through the day. In late afternoon, their wadis and canyons are heavily shadowed, forming a spectacular backdrop of ragged earth.

Mild and pleasant in winter time, the Dead Sea basin is an oven in summer. The hot air has an almost solid presence and the glare from the sun makes everyone, including sunglass-wearers, screw up their eyes.

The southern part of the Dead Sea has partly dried up, due to the use of the waters of the River Jordan by both Israel and Jordan. On the Israeli side, dykes built for the potash plant form a network of artificial lakes, designed for the extraction of chemicals, but also made use of by bathers.

The **Judean desert**, the area between the hills of Judea and the Dead Sea, was traditionally a region of hermits, prophets and rebels. David hid there from Saul. The Hasmoneans, who raised the banner of Jewish independence from the Syrian-Greek empire in the 2nd century BC, regrouped there after their initial defeat. Jesus retired to the desert to meditate and the Essenes established their community in its desolate wastes. The Jewish War against Rome of AD 66–73 started with the capture of the Judean desert fastness of Masada.

Israel's pre-1967 border with Jordan ran just north of **Ein Gedi**, about halfway up the western shore of the Dead Sea, which meant that only the southern half of the Judean desert was in Israel proper. Some of the sites described here thus became accessible to Israelis only after 1967's Six Day War, and may revert back to Arab administration in the future.

The scrolls of Qumran: On the northwest shore of the Dead Sea is the Essene settlement of **Qumran**, where the Dead Sea Scrolls were found. The Essenes, an ascetic Jewish sect of the Second Temple period, deliberately built their community in this inaccessible spot. It was destroyed by the Romans in AD 68.

In the early summer of 1947, a Bedouin shepherd was looking for a goat which had strayed by the shores of the Dead Sea. He threw a stone into one of the caves in the cliff side and heard a sound of smashing pottery. Later, it transpired that he had made the most exciting archaeological discovery of the century: scrolls, dating to the first centuries BC and AD, preserved in earthenware jars.

Some of these documents were acquired by Israel in rather dramatic circumstances. Eliezar Sukenik, professor of archaeology at the Hebrew University, was offered the chance of buying a collection of ancient scrolls by an Armenian dealer. He was shown a fragment briefly and was impressed by its antiquity but, to see the collection, he had to travel to Bethlehem where they were stored. It was the period just prior to the establishment of the State of Israel, and Jerusalem was a war zone; Bethlehem was in the Arab-controlled area, and dangerous for Jews. Sukenik approached his son Yigael Yadin for advice. Yadin, an archaeologist himself, and at that time chief of operations of the new Israel Defence Forces, replied: "As an archaeologist, I urge you to go; as your son, I beg that you do not go; as chief of operations of the army, I forbid you to go!" Sukenik did go to Bethlehem, at considerable personal risk, and managed to buy three scrolls. He could not complete the purchase of the other four, which were eventually taken to the United States and later repurchased for Israel by Yadin.

Subsequent searches of the caves unearthed other scrolls and thousands of fragments, most of which are now on display in Israel, either in the Shrine of the Book, at the Israel Museum in Jerusalem, or at the Rockefeller Museum in the formerly Jordanian part of the city.

Left, Qumran Cave. **Below**, local transport.

288

They have revolutionised scholarship of the Second Temple period and thrown new light on the origins of Christianity, indicating that Jesus may have been an Essene, or at least was strongly influenced by the sect. The scrolls have revealed the mood of messianic fatalism among the Jews of that time, explaining both the emergence of Christianity and the fervour of the Jewish rebels in their hopeless war against Rome. The scrolls have also disclosed much about the nature of the Essene way of life and the beliefs of the sect, as well as revealing details of temple ritual and worship.

The partly reconstructed buildings of Qumran are on a plateau some 100 metres (330 ft) above the shore and are worth a visit. Numerous caves, including those where the scrolls were found, are visible in the nearby cliffs, but these are not accessible to the tourist.

The oasis of **Ein Feshkha**, where the Essenes grew their food, is 3 km (2 miles) to the south. Today it is a popular bathing site, where visitors can swim in the Dead Sea and later wash off the salt in the fresh water of the springs. Bathing in the Dead Sea is a unique experience: the swimmer bobs around like a cork, and it is possible to read a paper while sitting on the surface. The salinity of the water – 10 times as salty as the oceans – can make it very painful if the bather has a cut or scratch.

The Emperor Vespasian threw manacled slaves into the sea to test its buoyancy. Most modern bathers go into the water voluntarily. Non-swimmers can float easily, but they must be careful to maintain their balance. The bitter taste of even a drop can linger all day and a mouthful of Dead Sea water is an experience that should be avoided.

Some 19 km (12 miles) south of Qumran is the new kibbutz of **Mitzpe Shalem**. The original site, on a cliff overlooking the sea, has been converted into a field school, **Metzoke Dragot**, which offers desert safaris in jeeps, rock climbing and rappelling. Past the school there is access to the steep-sided **Murabbat Canyon**, which contains caves where other 1st- and 2nd-century scrolls were discovered.

Ruins of an ancient Essenes village.

The canyon descends to the Dead Sea, but at that point it is sheer and unclimbable. A walk down the canyon from the field school is a memorable experience, but not to be undertaken alone. Would-be hikers are advised to go in a group from the school, with expert guides.

Also found in the Murabbat caves were fragments relating to a later revolt against Rome in AD 132–135, led by Simon Bar-Kochba, including a letter written by Bar-Kochba himself to one of his commanders.

Where David hid from Saul: Less than 15 km (8 miles) further south is the lush oasis of **Ein Gedi**, site of a kibbutz, a nature reserve and another field school. A particularly beautiful spot, with the greenery creeping up the steep cliffs beside the springs, Ein Gedi is the home of a large variety of birds, and animals, including gazelles, ibex, oryx, foxes, jackals and even a few leopards.

The most popular site for hiking and bathing is **David's Spring**, which leads up to a beautiful waterfall, fringed in ferns, where tradition says David hid from King Saul, when he was the victim of one of the king's paranoid rages. "Then Saul took three thousand chosen men out of all Israel, and went to seek David and his men upon the rocks of the wild goats." (I Sam; 24, 2) According to the biblical account, Saul went into the very cave where David was hiding and, as Saul slept, David cut off a piece of the king's robe, proving he could have killed him but desisted. A tearful reconciliation followed.

On most days, summer and winter, the area around David's Spring is thronged with visitors, so the more energetic may prefer to hike along the course of Nahal Arugot, a kilometre south. This canyon is full of wildlife and has several deep pools for bathing. Both Nahal David and Nahal Arugot are nature reserves.

Kibbutz Ein Gedi runs a guesthouse and a spa for bathing in Dead Sea water and nearby sulphur springs. A camping site, youth hostel and restaurant are situated on the shore below the kibbutz.

A little further south is the canyon of **Nahal Hever**. Of particular interest here

Left, cooling off at Ein Gedi. **Below**, free-roaming ibex.

are the **Cave of Horror**, where 40 skeletons of men, women and children from the time of the Bar-Kochba revolt were discovered; and the nearby **Cave of Letters**, in which 15 letters written by Bar-Kochba to his commanders were found. As with Murabbat, visitors are not advised to climb to the caves alone.

Masada: About 20 km (12 miles) south of Ein Gedi, towering almost 300 metres (1,000 ft) above the Dead Sea shore, is the rock of **Masada**, the most spectacular archaeological site in Israel. Part of the line of cliffs which rise up to the Judean desert plateau, Masada is cut off from the surrounding area by steep wadis to the north, south and west.

It was on this desolate mesa that Herod the Great built an impregnable fortress as a retreat from his potentially rebellious subjects. Visitors to the site can wander through the magnificent three-tiered palace which extends down the northern cliff; the Roman bath house, with its ingenious heating system; the vast storehouses; the western palace with its fine mosaics and the huge water cisterns hewn in the rock. They can appreciate the remarkable desert landscape from the summit, which can be climbed easily from the west via the Roman ramp, ascended by cable-car from the east, or more energetically climbed via the "Snake Path", also from the east.

These features alone make the fortress worth a visit, but it is the story of the epic siege of the fortress in the Jewish War against Rome which has made Masada a place of pilgrimage second only to the Western Wall.

In AD 66, a group of Jewish rebels called the Sicarii – named after the *sica* (dagger) their favourite weapon – seized Masada from its Roman garrison, triggering the Jewish War against Rome. Securing their base there, the Sicarii proceeded to Jerusalem, where they took over the leadership of the revolt. In the bitter infighting between the rebel groups, their leader was killed and they returned to Masada to regroup.

The new Sicarii leader, Elazar Ben-Yair, waited out the war at Masada, joined from time to time by other groups.

Masada.

He was still in possession after the fall of Jerusalem in AD 70. In AD 73, the Roman Tenth Legion arrived to put an end to this last Jewish stronghold.

With its auxiliaries and camp followers, the legion numbered over 15,000. Defending Masada were fewer than 1,000 Jewish men, women and children. Herod's store rooms were still well supplied. The Romans destroyed the aqueduct feeding the cisterns from dams in the wadi, but the cisterns had enough water for a prolonged period and were accessible from the summit.

The legion constructed a wall around the rock, reinforced by camps, which blocked the main possible escape routes and then built an earth ramp, reinforced by wooden beams and shielded by stone, which pointed like a dagger at the perimeter wall of the fortress.

The final defences were set on fire, and when the blaze died down, the Romans entered Masada to discover the bodies of the defenders laid out in rows. Repudiating defeat and refusing slavery, the men had first killed their own families and then themselves, drawing lots for a final 10 to carry out the act, one last electee killing the other nine and finally committing suicide.

This account in *The Jewish War* by Flavius Josephus has become one of the legends of modern Israel. In recognition of the symbolic importance of the site, young soldiers being inducted into the armoured corps today swear their oath of allegiance atop the fortress and vow: "Masada shall not fall again!"

The excavations by Yigael Yadin in the 1960s uncovered the magnificence of Herod's fortress and palaces, but the most moving finds were of the Zealots' living quarters in the casement wall, their synagogue and ritual baths, the remains of the fire, and, in some cases, bits of their final meal. The skeletons of a man, woman and child were uncovered in the northern palace; more were found in a nearby cave, where they had apparently been thrown by the Romans.

The country caught its collective breath when the discovery was announced of a set of inscribed pottery shards,

The cistern at Masada.

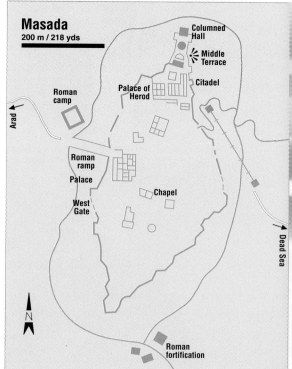

Masada
200 m / 218 yds

Columned Hall
Middle Terrace
Citadel
Palace of Herod
Roman camp
Arad
Roman ramp
Palace
West Gate
Chapel
Dead Sea
N
Roman fortification

which might have been the lots cast by the defenders to decide which of them would kill the others. One of them was inscribed "Ben-Yai".

Sodom's soothing spas: Ensconced along the shore just north of biblical Sodom, the resorts of **Ein Bokek** and **Neve Zohar** attract health-seekers from across the globe, with a wide range of accommodations based around their fabled mineral springs. Famous since the 1st century AD, the healing waters are believed to cure a spectrum of ailments, from skin disease to lumbago, arthritis and rheumatism. The clinics, run by medical staff, offer sulphur baths, mineral baths, salt baths, mud baths, massage and exercise programmes. The prices range from reasonable to five-star hotels, where the spas are actually on the premises.

Don't miss the mud if you do stay; Cleopatra is said to have sent slaves here to fetch it for her, and even today Dead Sea Mud has become a sought-after export as a natural moisturiser.

There is a peaceful atmosphere about modern **Sodom** which, despite its oppressive heat, makes it an unexpectedly calm place to swim, stroll or sunbathe. This is in stark contrast with the legendary "cities of sin", Sodom and Gomorrah, which in the Bible were destroyed with fire and brimstone for the decadence and sexual perversion of their inhabitants. The Bible is rather coy regarding the exact nature of these "sins", but homosexuality and buggery are implied (originating the term "sodomite").

According to the story, Lot, Abraham's nephew, pleaded with God to spare the cities and was allowed to escape with his family, but his wife looked back to view the destruction, having been told not to do so, and was turned into a pillar of salt. On the Dead Sea shore there is a cave with a hollow tower. Called **Lot's Wife**, the pillar is said to be the remains of that illustrious lady. Take a walk inside, lick your finger, and taste the salt.

Further south, looking like a moon base, the conveyor belts, funnels and ovens of the **Dead Sea Mineral Works** grind and roar day and night. Around

Left, Ein Bokek. Right, dramatic cave formation at Ein Bokek.

them rises an eerie skeletal scaffolding. Huge articulated trucks move ponderously out of the yard, hauling the potash, magnesium and salt down the Arava to Eilat, or up the ridge to the railway and Ashdod port.

Arad, old and new: Between the spas and the chemical plant, a road wends westward into the mountains, climbing over 1,000 metres (3,300 ft) in less than 25 km (15 miles), to **Arad**, Israel's first planned town.

Arad has a history of human habitation going back 5,000 years, but while modern Arad is constructed on an elevation near the Dead Sea to ensure a mild climate, the historic settlement is set in farming land, 8 km (5 miles) further west. The ancient mound of **Tel Arad** has been excavated and partly reconstructed. Sections of a Canaanite town of the 3rd millennium BC have been found, with pottery from the First Dynasty in Egypt, indicating trade between the two nations at that time.

A 10th-century BC fortress of the time of King Solomon was the next settlement. Far smaller than the original Canaanite city, the Israelite enclosure contained a sanctuary modelled on the Temple in Jerusalem, with a courtyard, outer chamber, and Holy of Holies, the only one of its kind ever discovered.

Archaeologists found the remains of a burnt substance in two smaller altars inside the Holy of Holies. Analysis showed it to be traces of animal fat, indicating sacrifices. This is consistent with the denunciations of the prophets, recorded in the Bible, of continuing sacrifices on the "high places". King Hezekiah, who ruled Judah from 720 to 692 BC, heeded the advice and "removed the high places and broke the images."

Modern Arad, founded in 1961, was the most ambitious "new town" project of its time. It was meant to provide housing, health services and tourism facilities plus regional industries. It was well-placed to utilise the natural reserves, archaeological sites and mineral spas at the Dead Sea, and offered dry desert air, suitable for asthma treatment.

Architecturally, Arad was conceived as a fortress against the desert: the buildings were grouped around squares; the paved walkways were shaded by houses; greenery was planted in small concentrations which did not require too much water. The six basic neighbourhoods and the town centre were less than a mile across. Arad is an interesting example of theory being changed by practice. It was initially assumed that the inhabitants would wish to cluster together in the desert environment, but this did not prove to be the case and the planners were forced to modify their designs to meet demand for more space.

The opposite of improvised Beersheba, Arad is the epitome of planned pioneering: the rational creation of a town, adapted to the desert and utilising its resources.

King Uzziah, the Bible records, "built towers in the wilderness." Constructed only a few miles from where the king's buildings stood, Arad's apartment blocks are Israel's new towers in the desert. The two Arads are a symbol of today's Israel: a modern community arising where an ancient one used to exist.

Below, cult basin at Tel Arad. Right, visiting the caves at Ein Bokek.

אגן פולחני
CULT BASIN

THE NEGEV

The very name "Negev" conjures up an image of the rugged outdoors, jeeps, camels, frontiersmen – an unforgiving expanse of bleak wastes, sunlight and sharp, dry air. In fact, it is every bit as vast and intimidating as it sounds, containing 60 percent of Israel's land area, but holding less than 10 percent of its population. Yet the Negev is far from barren: it supports successful agricultural communities, a sprawling "capital", a complex desert ecosystem, and – since Israel relinquished the Sinai in 1982 – a variety of defence activities.

The Hebrew word means "parched", and the Negev is indeed parched, with rainfall varying from an annual average of 30 cm (12 inches) in the north to almost zero in Eilat. But don't expect expanses of white sand and palm trees, like in old Rudolph Valentino movies; Israel's desert is entirely different.

The northern and western Negev is a dusty plain, slashed with wadis, dried-up riverbeds which froth with occasional winter flash floods. To the south are the bleak flint, limestone, chalk, dolomite and granite mountains, with the Arava valley to the east dividing them from biblical Edom, today part of Jordan.

Although a desert, the Negev, like the rest of Israel, is saturated with history. In prehistoric times, the area was well watered and settled. It was subsequently desiccated; but by the Chalcolithic period, in the 4th millennium BC, communities had sprung up in the wadis around Beersheba.

At the time of Abraham, around 2,000 BC, the area was inhabited by nomadic tribes. When the Children of Israel left Egypt in the 13th century BC, the warlike Amalekites blocked their path to the Promised Land, setting back their settlement by decades. Joshua eventually did conquer Canaan and awarded the Negev to the tribe of Simeon, but only the northern part was settled.

King David extended Israelite rule over the entire Negev in the 10th century BC and his son Solomon constructed a string of forts to defend it. Solomon also developed the famous copper mines at Timna, and his southern port of Etzion Geber, today's Eilat. After the division of the kingdom into Israel and Judah, the area was occupied by the Edomites, who were expelled by the Nabateans in the 1st century BC. In the Middle Ages, it was an important Byzantine centre.

In the following centuries the Negev remained the domain of nomadic Bedouin tribes, until the start of Zionist immigration to Palestine in the 1880s. However, it was not until 1939 that the first successful kibbutz, **Negba**, northwest of Beersheba, was established. Three other outposts were created in 1943, also in the western Negev, and a further 11 were thrown up on a single day in 1946.

The Jews fought hard for the inclusion of the Negev in the new State of Israel, and the UN partition plan of 1947 awarded most of the area to the Jewish state. The rest was won in the War of Independence of 1948, when the Egyp-

Preceding pages: stark hills mark the Judean desert. **Left**, the visitor centre at Mitzpe Ramon. **Right**, the desert blooms.

tian and Transjordanian armies were expelled in the fighting.

David Ben-Gurion, Israel's first prime minister, was a passionate believer in the development of the Negev, and went to live in what was then a tiny, isolated kibbutz, Sde Boker, in the heart of the desert, when he retired from politics. He was buried there in 1973.

Capital of the Negev: Although it has become comparatively civilised, **Beersheba** still possesses something of its old frontier atmosphere: brash, bustling, and bursting with energy. Big trucks park in the main streets; open jeeps drive through the centre; sunburned men with scuffed boots and dust in their hair drink beer in the sidewalk cafés; young soldiers sip their colas, wait for rides and monopolise the public telephones. You don't see too many suits or ties here, even in winter.

Despite planners' efforts to create a new centre further east, the **"old city"** remains the real centre of town. The unusual rectangular formation of its streets was the work of a German engineer, who served with the Turkish army in the years before World War I. The rest of Beersheba is more spread out, a monument to the great improvisation phase of Israel's development, laid out as if it were an English garden city, without consideration for the special climatic and topographical condition.

But the town, thrown up hastily while Israel was doubling its population with an influx of Jews from Europe and the Middle East, couldn't have been built any other way. There was no time for proper planning. Today, with a population of 150,000, a flourishing industrial base, a university, hospital, medical school, music conservatory, dance school, orchestra and arts centre, Beersheba is Israel's fourth largest city. If it's a mess, it's a triumphant mess.

Beersheba is the capital of the Negev, providing services for the surrounding population. The regional offices of the companies extracting potash, phosphates, magnesium, salt and lime are all located here, alongside new factories for everything from ceramics to pesticides.

Left, the Ben-Gurion graves. **Right**, Bedouin trader.

An immigrant community in every sense of the word, Beersheba accommodates people from more than 70 countries, the earlier immigrants from Romania and Morocco rubbing shoulders with more recent arrivals from Argentina and the former Soviet Union. An Arab town until 1948, it is today a predominantly Jewish community; but several hundred Bedouin have moved here from the surrounding area and form an important part of the population.

Every Thursday morning, there is a **Bedouin market** on the southern edge of town, for which a special structure has been built. The Bedouin still trade their camels, sheep and goats here; but in recent years it has become primarily a tourist attraction, providing opportunities to purchase of all kinds of Bedouin arts and crafts.

The name Beersheba means "well of the swearing", in memory of the pact sworn between the patriarch Abraham and Abimelech, a local ruler, in which Abraham secured the use of a well to water his flocks. There is a dispute as to the location of the actual **Well of the Swearing**. The traditional site is at the bottom of the main street in the old town; but more recently archaeologists have suggested it to be the 40-metre (130-ft) well excavated at the site of **Tel Beersheba**, some 6 km (4 miles) east of the modern city.

The **Ben-Gurion University of the Negev**, founded here in 1969, is one of Israel's largest universities with a student population of 10,000 studying courses in humanities, sciences, engineering and medicine, amongst others. In this respect, the university has transformed the town from a desert backwater into a modern community, with its own sinfonietta orchestra and light opera group. Its contribution to the surrounding environment should not be overlooked. Impressively, the university is researching projects on water resource management, and carrying out magnesium research, and arid zones studies. The **Beersheba Museum**, housed in a former mosque in the old town, has a good display of archaeo-

The futuristic library at Beersheba's Ben-Gurion University.

logical artifacts. The city has a youth hostel, hotels of all standards and several good restaurants, including ones specialising in Moroccan, Romanian and South American cuisine, which reflects the makeup of the population.

About a mile to the east, overlooking the city, is the **Memorial to the Negev Brigade of the Palmach**, which captured Beersheba in the War of Independence. Designed by sculptor Dani Karavan, who spent five years on the project, its trenches, bunkers, pillboxes and tower (through which visitors are encouraged to climb and crawl) create a claustrophobic atmosphere evocative of a siege. The sinuous concrete edifice is a worthy commemoration of the bitter battle for the Negev between the Egyptian army and the fledgling Israeli forces backing the kibbutz outposts during the 1948 war.

South of the monument is the country's only **animal hospital**, which is attached to the life sciences department of Ben-Gurion University. It includes a camel clinic.

Southeast of the hospital, next to ancient Tel Beersheba, is **Tel Sheva**, a modern village built for the local Bedouin. It is the first of five Bedouin villages in the Negev gradually replacing the traditional tented camps of the nomads which, as a rule, are spread out over a large area. In the village, high-walled courtyards separate the houses, in an attempt to preserve as much privacy as possible.

The concept was developed by an Arab architect and its logic seems unassailable, but in fact the Bedouin were not keen on Tel Sheva initially, and subsequent development has encouraged the former nomads to build their own homes. Israel's Bedouin claim large tracts of the desert over which they formerly grazed their herds; but the lands were never registered, and this has led to disputes with the government. In most cases, the Bedouin have been given title to the land around their camps. Where the land has been appropriated by the government, as in the case of the **Nevatim Airforce Base** east of Beer-

Camels quench their thirst.

302

sheba, monetary compensation has been awarded in its stead.

There is a Bedouin school at Tel Sheva, and nearly all the children receive elementary education. More recently a Bedouin high school was built and there are a number of Bedouin students at Ben-Gurion University. The first Bedouin doctor to graduate in Israel, Yunis Abu-Rabia, is now in charge of the region's health services.

There are three main routes leading south from Beersheba to Eilat, Israel's pleasure resort on the Red Sea. The main highway leads down the eastern side of the Negev, through the **Arava Valley**, and that is the one to take if your aim is simply reaching the sunny beaches. A narrow, beautiful, scenic road goes through the middle of the desert; a third road, the most recently constructed, travels along the Sinai border with Egypt to the west.

Harvesting wheat in western Negev.

The traveller may well feel that the Negev between Beersheba and Eilat is a mythical badland dividing Israel from the Red Sea paradise to the south, an impression reinforced by a rapid drive (or flight) to Eilat; but there is plenty to see on all three routes.

The Arava: The eastern route takes you past the moshav of Nevatim, settled in the early 1950s by Jews from Cochin in southern India. Even within the Israeli population kaleidoscope, these beautiful, dark-skinned people stand out as "more different" than the others. In the past few years, they have become famous for growing winter flowers, exported by air to Europe. This industry, which takes advantage of the mild desert climate, has been taken up by others and become a major Israeli export.

Further east, the development towns of Yeroham and Dimona, built in the mid-1950s, were settled primarily by immigrants from North Africa. **Yeroham** has a new park, 10 km (6 miles) south of the road, which should one day become a startling green patch in the arid grey-brown wasteland; but so far the dust tends to dominate the man-high trees. Nearby is an artificial lake, created by a dammed wadi, fed by the

winter rains. A huge variety of birds migrate across the Mediterranean coast from Africa to Europe in the spring and return in the autumn; Israel is one of their favourite way stations.

Dimona is home to the fierce harsh desert climate which many thought would prove to much for people to live and work in. The few original settlers have now blossomed into a town of 28,000. Called the "Flower of the Desert", Dimona is known more for its nuclear plant and Black Hebrew community than for its flora. A small Indian Jewish community also resides here, and their small delicatessens supply great Indian spices and popadums.

Between Yeroham and Dimona, the dome of Israel's **Atomic Research Station** looms in the plain behind its numerous protective barbed-wire fences.

Just past Dimona is the ancient site of **Mamshit**, called Kurnab by the Arabs. A fine example of a Nabatean site of the 1st century AD it contains the remains of two beautiful Byzantine churches, and a network of ancient dams. Nearby is the

Camel Farm of Mamshit, home to the original ships of the desert. It is still worth a visit even if this alternative mode of travel is not particularly to your taste. Safaris, four-wheel-drive tours, rappelling and hiking are among the other options.

South of the road is the **Machtesh Gadol** (Large Crater) a spectacular geological fault, and, further east, the **Machtesh Katan** (Small Crater): less extensive, but more beautiful, with geological layers exposed in some locations like a rainbow cake. Their origin is unknown. One theory ascribes the Negev craters to volcanic activity; another suggests the fall of large meteors in the distant past.

The old road south – today a dirt-track – cuts through the desert south of the small crater, connecting with the Arava valley via **Scorpions' Pass**. The most spectacular road in the southern desert, it plunges down a series of dizzying loops that follow each other with frightening suddenness. To the right are the heights of the Negev, great slabs of **Overnight stop on a camel trek.**

primeval rock, slammed together in a giant's sandwich. Below are the purplegrey lunar formations of the **Valley of Zin**, with the square-shaped hillock of **Hor Hahar** rising up from the valley floor. Be warned: the rusty metal drums that line the road have not been able to prevent accidents. It should be negotiated slowly with a four-wheel-drive vehicle, or on foot.

The main road reaches the Arava Valley south of the Dead Sea, opposite the moshav farming village of **Neot Hakikar**. Situated in the salt marshes and utilising brackish water, it has become one of the most successful settlements in Israel, exporting a variety of winter vegetables to Europe.

In the 1960s Neot Hakikar was settled by an eccentric group of desert lovers, who established a private company. As initial attempts at farming the area proved less than successful, they set up a desert touring company for trips by camel and jeep to the less accessible locations of the Negev. Those initial settlers eventually abandoned the village, but their company (still called Neot Hakikar) continues to thrive, with offices in Tel Aviv and Eilat.

Similar tours are run by the Society for the Protection of Nature in Israel, which, among its noteworthy spectrum of activities, offers a four-day camel tour starting at **Ein Yahav**, a *moshav* some 80 km (50 miles) south.

The road through the Arava is bordered by the flint and limestone ridges of the Negev to the west; 19 km (12 miles) to the east tower the magnificent mountains of **Edom** in Jordan, which are capped with snow in winter. These mountains change colour during the day from pale mauve in the morning, to pink, red and deep purple in the evening, their canyons and gulleys etched in grey.

About 130 km (80 miles) further south, past another dozen moshavim and kibbutzim, and a small "snake zoo", is kibbutz **Yotvata**, with its unique **Hai-Bar Nature Reserve**. At this unusual game park, conservationists have imported and bred a variety of animals mentioned in the Bible (which had be-

The mushroom rock.

come extinct locally): wild asses, os- triches and numerous varieties of ga- zelle. A holiday village, with modest but comfortable accommodations, swimming pools and a mini-market is available for visitors. Also at the site is the **Arava Visitors' Centre** with a mu- seum and audio-visual display of the desert. **Ketura**, a kibbutz 16 km (10 miles) to the north, offers riding.

Timna, 24 km (15 miles) further south is the site of **King Solomon's Mines**, a little to the south of the modern copper mine. The ancient, circular stone ovens for roasting the copper ore look simple enough, with stone channels to the col- lection vessels for the metal, but the air channels were skilfully angled to catch the prevailing north wind, which comes down the Arava. The late archaeologist Nelson Gleuck, who excavated the mines, called the ventilation system "an ancient example of automation".

The area surrounding the mines is being developed as a national park, with an artificial lake and a network of roads – including a fine scenic route in the northeast of the park to facilitate tour- ing. Highlights include the massive **Pil- lars of Solomon**, a natural formation of Nubian sandstone, and the redoubtable **Mushroom Rock**, a granite rock shaped like a mushroom. Also here are the time-worn remains of a settlement, a fortress and two Egyptian sanctuaries used by the ancient mine workers.

The western Negev: West from Beer- sheba the desert is flat and dull, more for settlement than for tourism. It is an area of cotton and potatoes and extensive wheat fields, irrigated by the run-off from the National Water Carrier, which ends in this area, and Beersheba.

The first Negev kibbutzim were built in this region in the 1940s and, after the peace treaty with Egypt, some of Isra- el's northern Sinai settlements were moved to **Pit'hat Shalom** (the Peace Region) next to the international border in 1982. East of these communities lies the **Eshkol Park**, 300 hectares (750 acres) of trees, lawns and playing fields with an amphitheatre, swimming pool and a natural pond, surrounded by cat-

King Solomon's Mines, Timna

tails and cane and stocked with fish.

The **Western Negev road**, which goes south from this region, is designated as a military area, as it is right on the Egyptian border and travellers using it have to fill in forms provided by the military. Since the peace treaty with Egypt in 1978, it is not regarded as dangerous, but the army wants to know who is using it so that travellers are not stranded there after dark. The southern sector of the road winds attractively through the Negev mountains, providing some spectacular views of Sinai to the west and the Negev to the east.

The Negev Plateau: The most interesting route south is also the oldest and least convenient; but it passes a number of interesting sites, the first of which is **Sde Boker**, some 49 km (30 miles) south of Beersheba. The kibbutz was the final home of David Ben-Gurion, Israel's first prime minister, and his wife, Paula. Their simple, cream-coloured tombstones, which overlook the Wilderness of Zin, is a place of pilgrimage for Israeli youth movements and foreign admirers. The old man is said to have personally selected his burial place with its view of beige and mustard limestone hills, the flint rocks beyond, and the delicate mauve of Edom in the hazy distance.

The **Sde Boker College**, south of the kibbutz, is divided into three sections: the **Institute for Arid Zone Research**, which coordinates desert biology, agriculture and architecture; the **Ben-Gurion Institute**, which houses all the first prime minister's papers and records, and the **Center of the Environment**, which runs a field school and a high school with an emphasis on environmental studies.

South of the college is **Ein Avdat**, a steep-sided canyon with freshwater pools fringed with lush vegetation. Rock badgers, gazelles and a wide variety of birds inhabit this oasis, where the water is remarkably cold even in the heat of summer. A swim can be refreshing, but the water is deep and sometimes it is difficult to climb out on the slippery rocks. Lone hikers should not take the

Ruins of a Roman villa at Avdat.

risk, and a party of visitors should take it in turns, leaving some out of the water to haul out their companions. There are paths up the sides of the cliffs, with iron rungs and railings in the difficult parts.

A few miles further south is **Avdat**, site of the Negev's main Nabatean city, built in the 2nd century BC. Situated on a limestone hill above the surrounding desert, Avdat was excavated and partly reconstructed in the early 1950s. With its impressive buildings, burial caves, a kiln, workshop and two Byzantine churches, it is one of the most rewarding sites in the country; but what makes it fascinating is the reconstruction of the Nabatean and Byzantine agriculture.

An Arab tribe, the Nabateans dominated the Negev and Edom in the first centuries BC and AD. With their capital at Petra (today in the Kingdom of Jordan), their achievements in farming the desert are unsurpassed. Their technique was based on the run-off systems of irrigation. Little rain falls in this part of the desert, but when it does, it is not absorbed by the local loess soil; it cuts gulleys and wadis, running in torrents to the Mediterranean in the west and the Dead Sea and the Arava in the east. The run-off system collects this water in a network of fields and terraces, fed by dams, channels and slopes.

Variations include gently sloped fields in which each tree has its own catchment area. A botanist, Michael Evenari, working with archaeologists and engineers, has reconstructed Avdat and two other farms, growing a variety of crops without the help of piped water: fodder, wheat, onions, carrots, asparagus, artichokes, apricots, grapes, peaches, almonds, peanuts and pistachios are among them.

What started as research into ancient agriculture has proved to be relevant to the modern era as the system could provide valuable foodstuffs in arid countries of the third world using only existing desert resources, thus preserving the delicate ecological balances. Indeed, although the ancient Nabateans managed to grow grape vines here 2,000 years ago, they didn't irrigate them with **Sharing a snack.**

salt water. New scientific research using saline water, has begun to reap rewards in the form of cabernet sauvignon and sauvignon blanc.

Some 45 km (28 miles) west of Avdat is **Shivta**, another Nebatean city later rebuilt by the Byzantines in the 5th century. Although less accessible, it is still relatively well-preserved with three churches, a wine press and several public areas still intact.

Nizzana, 25 km (16 miles) further west at the intersection of the western highway, is one of three active border crossings to Egypt.

The youth village also located at Nizzana – a desert outpost which now boasts a thriving seminar centre about desert flora and fauna – was founded in 1987 and lies just next to the border. It was here that the government issued a proposal for a new settlement to encourage some 50,000 or so of the bulging population to settle part of this vast uninhabited desert. Ben Gurion was firm in his belief that "unless we conquer… the desert… we cannot succeed in the tasks of immigration and re-settlement". Some 50 years on, it seems that the call is finally being heeded – although the plan is still in its infancy.

Further into the desert, and further back in time, lie the venerable walls of some 40-odd strongholds built by King Solomon to guard his route to Timna and his port of **Etzion Geber**. After the peace treaty with Egypt, 20 of these fortresses were partly excavated in a "rescue operation" mounted by the Department of Antiquities, in advance of the redeployment of the army in the Negev. Sustained by Solomon's decisive authority, the fortresses were destroyed shortly after his death, and never rebuilt. The one exception is **Kadesh Barnea**, some 35 km (21 miles) west of the road, rebuilt in the 8th century BC during the temporary resurgence of Judea under King Uzziah.

A number of the strongholds are close to the road, including **Ritma** and **Halukim**, north of Sde Boker, and **Mishor Haruh**, further south. In general, it is advisable to visit such sites in the company of a trained guide.

A half hour south of Avdat is the development town of **Mitzpe Ramon**, perched at an elevation of 1,000 metres (3,300 ft) along the northern edge of the **Machtesh Ramon** – the largest of the three craters in the Negev, at 40 km (25 miles) long and 12 km (7 miles) wide. Despite its enormity, the crater comes into view quite suddenly: an awesome sight. Among the finds here have been fossilised plants and preserved dinosaur footprints, dating back 200 million years to the Triassic and Jurassic periods. The town has an observatory connected with Tel Aviv University, which takes advantage of the dry desert air. In the Ramon crater, a geological trail displays the melting pot of minerals in the area, evident from the patches of yellow, rush, ochre, purple, and even green that tint the landscape.

To the south lies the **Paran Valley**, the most spectacular of the Negev wadis, which runs into the Arava. The road twists through the timeless desert scenery, before joining the southern part of the Arava road on its way to Eilat.

The astro-observatory at Mitzpe Ramon.

EILAT

Eilat is remote. It is searing hot and parched dry. The cultural diversions are negligible and a geological fault runs through town. There's neither casino, nor racetrack nor concert hall.

Nevertheless, Eilat is one of Israel's most popular tourist resorts. Vacationers migrate instinctively, like tens of thousands of lemmings, to its sunburnt shores and soothing seas. What's more, a good percentage of them are Israelis who know the best places in the country for spending a holiday.

Some Israelis going to Eilat claim they're vacationing *hutz l'aretz* (abroad). Others simply say they're off to *sof olam* – the end of the world. And anyone who drives from the populated central part of Israel across that "Great Bald Spot" known as the Negev Desert, might be inclined to agree with them.

Eilat is Israel's southernmost community. It is the Jewish State's flipper-hold on the Red Sea. It is also a mecca (if such a word might be used in Israel) for snorkellers, scuba-divers, windsurfers, water-skiers, swimmers, sailors, sandcastle builders, bikini-watchers, sun worshippers, tropical-fish fanatics and bird watchers.

Eilat's single significant industry lies in assisting visitors to do nothing productive. It is a sensual city which caters to people who like magnificent natural beauty, lazy afternoons, spicy food and cold beer.

First city: Eilatis whimsically call their town Israel's "First City", because it was the first piece of modern Israel's real estate to be occupied by the Children of Israel after the Exodus from Egypt (Deut: 2, 8). Like most Eilatis, though, Moses was only a tourist; he moved north to find milk and honey soon afterwards.

A few centuries later, King Solomon built a port here and called it Etzion Geber. With the help of his friend, King Hiram of Phoenecia, the wise monarch sent a fleet of ships eastward, to the land of Ophir, "and fetched from thence gold, four hundred and twenty talents, and

brought it to King Solomon." (I Kings: 9, 26). Since there were about 3,000 shekels to the talent, and about a half-ounce to the shekel, those sailors must have lugged something like 20 tons of gold back via Eilat to Jerusalem.

Eilat changed hands many times during the following centuries. The Edomites grabbed it for a while, and then King Uzziah grabbed it back for the Israelites. The Syrians later wrested it away from him. A succession of conquerors marched through – Nabateans, Greeks, Romans, Mamelukes, Crusaders, Ottoman Turks and a bunch of others. (The Crusaders left behind their 12th-century fortress at Coral Island, just south of Taba.) The celebrated colonel T. E. Lawrence, popularly known as Lawrence of Arabia, trekked through here after his conquest of Akaba across the bay.

The most recent army to "conquer" Eilat was the Israel Defence Forces which swooped down on this exotic pearl during Operation Uvda in March 1949, and scared the dickens out of several sleepy lizards and a cranky tor-

Preceding pages: Eilat's Dolphinarium. **Left**, diving in the Red Sea. **Right**, Eilat's north beach.

toise inhabiting the ruins of Umm Rashrash, an uninhabited mudbrick "police station" which stood all alone in what is now the centre of town.

Although the United Nations had allocated Eilat to Israel in its partition plan, the War of Independence capture of this corner of the Promised Land was so hastily organised that the Israeli troops arrived without a flag to proclaim the land as part of their new state. Thus, a soldier with artistic talent was issued a bed sheet and a bottle of blue ink with which to produce one Israeli flag of appropriate dimension and design.

Development town: The new flag didn't fly over very much, but Israeli authorities knew that Eilat was located in a very strategic position and quick steps were taken to create a town. It was strategic because it provided Israel's only access to the Indian and Pacific oceans, and trade with Asia, East Africa, Australia and the islands, including vital oil supplies from pre-revolutionary Iran. Holding on to Eilat also meant a break in land continuity between Egypt and Jordan, thus offering a military advantage to the defence forces.

In the rush to create a city on the Red Sea, Eilat's builders didn't invest much in fine architecture. Instead, they wanted fast, simple, sturdy construction of apartments to house immigrants trickling in from the horrors of Nazi-occupied Europe, and the expulsions by Arab states such as Iraq and Yemen. Visitors to Eilat can see some of the older 1950s apartment buildings still standing like concrete bastions on the hillside. They're still quite serviceable and occupied by Eilati families who have affectionate nicknames for them, such as "Sing Sing" and "La Bastille".

As the city expanded, other neighbourhoods grew further up the slopes of the Eilat Mountains. Improved architecture didn't spare them from satirical nicknames. One neighbourhood built about a kilometre up a steep hill west of the centre of town is locally know as the "Onesh" district. In Hebrew, *onesh* means "punishment" and anybody who walks this distance from the centre of **Eilat, the "First City".**

314

town on a hot day will appreciate the appropriateness of this sobriquet. In recent years, prosperity has produced colonies of villas around town, unleashing a new generation of cognomens which are still to stand the test of time.

Crisis and boom: Egypt's Gamal Abdel Nasser realised the strategic value of Eilat and its potential for becoming a multi-million-dollar tourist playground. He planned that Eilat would be one of his first conquests in the 1967 War.

In May of that year, he again imposed a blockade on Eilat and shut down its shipping – including the vital oil supplies from Iran. Next, he ordered the UN peace-keeping forces out of Sinai, and moved his own army into the mountains northwest of Eilat, within clear view of Jordan. With one quick push, he could have cut off Eilat, linked-up with the Jordanian Arab Legion, and created a solid, integrated southern front against Israel. Eilat was in an extremely vulnerable position for a few days, until the Israeli pre-emptive strike against Egyptian air fields deprived Nasser of the vital air cover his troops would need. The following six days witnessed Israel's lightning conquest of Sinai and the removal of military threats against Eilat.

Shortly after the Six Day War, terror infiltration from Jordanian territory near Eilat caused apprehension. There were several incidents and people were killed. Eilat remained unattractive for tourism, immigration and development until the charismatic Moshe Dayan flew there to make a speech intended for the ears of Jordan's King Hussein. Further infiltration of terrorists from Jordan would indicate to Israel that the Jordanian armed forces were incapable of maintaining a secure border, Dayan said. If this became the case, he added, the Israel Defence Forces would have to do the job for them by entering Jordanian territory – including the port city of Akaba – to stem the incursions.

The Jordanian monarch got the message and border security improved immediately. Assured of security, Eilat blossomed. The past decade has catapulted the city into success, with an

ever-expanding tourist business, a population of close to 50,000 and a busy downtown, with its modern art museum, a sheltered lagoon and marina, and a shorefront of hotels.

Most of the tourists are Israelis who drive the six-hour trans-desert trek from Jerusalem, Tel Aviv and Haifa for their holiday. But many, especially in winter, are foreigners who take charter flights from Europe directly to Eilat. Arkia, Israel's domestic airline, also operates several flights a day from here to Israel and the Sinai.

Plenty of rocks: An adage grew up among Eilatis: "If we could export rocks, we'd all be millionaires!" The key to Eilat's tourism has been to twist the adage to bring the foreigners to the rocks. Nearly all of these rocks are pre-Cambrian, formed by the forces of the earth in the epochs before the beginning of life on the planet. Aeons ago, they were beach-front real estate facing to the north, where the ancient Tethys Sea flowed over what is now the state of Israel. To the south extended the pri-

mordial megacontinent of Gondwanaland. (Gondwanaland eventually drifted apart to form India, Africa, South America, Australia and Antarctica, and the bed of the Tethys Sea was pushed up to form the bedrock of Israel.)

Geologists are forever pottering about the Eilat Mountains, picking at chunks of granite, gneiss, quartz-porphyry and diabase. In some places, they are after an attractive rock called $CuCo_3.Cu(OH)_2$. Merchants in town call this bluish-green malachite Eilat Stone, a type of copper ore which can be shaped and given a high polish. In fact, this stone has been used in jewellery-making in the region for thousands of years, and is still very evident in many Eilat tourist shops.

For those who like to see their rocks in the rough, there are has the **Eilat Mountains**: spectacular ascents of colourful stone. In some areas, it appears as if their volcanic genesis was quick frozen, and their flowing magmas interrupted in full flood. Erosion here has taken some bizarre and incredibly beautiful courses. In places, it is possible to walk

Left, windsurfing. Below, camping out at Taba.

through narrow canyons, with walls towering hundreds of metres vertically, but just a metre or two apart. The harsh desert wind has carved monumental pillars among the mountains, particularly in the sandstone regions such as the **Pillars of Amran** (named for the father of Moses), some 9 km (5½ miles) north of Eilat and 3 km (2 miles) west of the main highway. The site is laced with lovely ravines and clusters of imposing natural columns.

About 4 km (2½ miles) south of Eilat, along the coast highway leading to Sinai, is the entry to **Solomon's Canyon**, a popular hiking area. A dusty granite quarry at the mouth of the canyon tends to obscure the formations lying beyond, but those following the Nature Reserves Authority path markers will be treated to an exotic geological adventure. Entering the canyon, **HaMetsuda** (the Stronghold) rises to the left. This great rock was vital to Eilat's defences against invasion from the Sinai coast. The path then leads another 16 km (10 miles) up into the mountains, twisting and turning along

the route of the canyon. Hikers pass beneath **Mount (Har) Yehoshafat**, then **Mount (Har) Shlomo** and next **Mount (Har) Asa**, all of which tower more than 700 metres (2,300 ft) overhead.

Eventually, the trail crosses the paved **Moon Valley Highway** which leads into central Sinai. Across the highway, the trail continues on to the spectacular cliffs and oasis at **Ein Netafim** (the Spring of the Drops) which trickles across a barren rock into a picturesque pool at the foot of an imposing cliff. Further along is **Red Canyon**, another impressive natural wonder of erosion-sculpted sandstone.

Seaside sojourning: Beaches are a year-round attraction in Eilat. Even in the summer, when temperatures can range well above baking at 40°C/l05°F, the waters of the Red Sea are cool and soothing. Mid-winter swimming, however, is usually left to the Europeans and Americans, while native Eilatis stare from the shore, bundled up in parkas to dispel the wintery gusts, which usually hover at around 15°C (roughly 60°F).

Eilat offers five distinct, attractive

beaches, spanning 11 km (7 miles), ranging from fine sand to gravel. **North Beach**, close to the centre of town, is the local hangout for sun worshippers. The bay is protected, the swimming is easy and dozens of hotels line the shore. The eastern end of North Beach also has inexpensive bungalows and even camping facilities for the economy-minded.

About 6 km (4 miles) down the coast, past the navy station and port facilities, is **Shmurat Almogim** (the Coral Reserve). This Israeli nature reserve includes a fine sandy beach and a truly spectacular coral reef. Here, visitors can rent diving masks, snorkels and flippers from the reserve's office and swim along any of three marked routes which lead over different parts of the coral reef. Special markers set into the reef itself identify different types of corals and plants growing there, as well as some of the more common fish. The reserve also has changing rooms, showers, snack and souvenir stands and other tourist amenities. Nevertheless, this is a strictly monitored nature reserve. Removal of

any corals will result in the culprit paying a visit to the local judge.

Further south is the **Coral World Underwater Observatory**, an unusual commercial aquarium and undersea observatory. Here, the visitor walks out on a long pier to the observatory building, which is set into the reef itself. Descending the spiral staircase within the observatory, one emerges into a circular room with windows facing out into the coral reef at a depth of 5 metres (16 ft). All sorts of fish swim freely about outside the window, and the many colours and shapes of the living reef are astonishing sights which should not be missed. Nothing quite as lovely has been seen since Captain Nemo retired the *Nautilus*.

Those who abjure actually going into the water might be more inclined to ride on it instead. A large marina and lagoon at North Beach is the mooring for many boats and yachts, from expensive charter schooners to more affordable windsurfing craft. There are also several glass-bottom boats for reef-viewing, and a number of water-skiing speed boats available for charter. Licensed diving clubs which will rent diving equipment and offer diving courses include Lucky Divers, Red Sea Divers, and Eilat Aqua Sport.

For the birds: Birdwatching too, is a year-round attraction in Eilat, and several dozen species of resident birds can be found in the mountains and deserts, by the seashore and among the fields of neighbouring **Kibbutz Eilot**.

The spring migration season, however, is particularly dazzling and is the best time to be here. Millions upon millions of migratory birds fly across the Eilat region on their northward journeys from warm wintering havens in Africa to their breeding grounds scattered across Eurasia. Great waves of eagles and falcons often fill the sky – and highly respected ornithologists keep producing reports giving strangely precise figures such as 19,288 steppe eagles, 26,770 black kites and 225,952 honey buzzards in the course of a single migration season.

Sharp-eyed birdwatchers will also pick out booted eagles, snake eagles, lesser spotted eagles, imperial eagles, marsh harriers, sparrowhawks and os-

The world of coral.

prey. And then come the pelicans and storks in their tens of thousands.

As an assistance to birdwatchers, the Nature Reserves Authority has established special **hiking trails** and **observation hides** in the region to help spotters. A special information centre is maintained by the Nature Reserves Authority in the King Solomon Hotel to provide up-to-date information for bird watching, registration for tours, rental of field glasses, sale of literature and nightly lectures and nature films about the Eilat region.

For those looking for a leisurely holiday, there are scores of restaurants ranging from inexpensive pizza parlours and felafel stands to high-priced haute cuisine in the Eilat Center, the New Tourist Center and the Hotel District. Several hotels also have night clubs, discos and other social entertainments. The Red Sea Jazz Festival, has become an annual summer fixture, drawing thousands of jazz fans and others to several nights of live entertainment by local acts and international stars.

Eilat is also a free trade zone with no sales tax. As a result, many items are cheaper than elsewhere in the country. For the tourist, however, this will probably be offset by the not-so-cheap hotel and restaurant prices.

Eilat is in addition the departure point for several expeditions into the vast and barren waste land of **Sinai**. Most of the tour agencies in town can book arrangements to visit Santa Katarina, Sharm El-Sheikh and other Sinai attractions and, for a moderate fee, the Egyptian consulate in Eilat provides the required visas.

Moreover, after the signing of a peace agreement with Jordan in 1994, a new border crossing, the **Arava Checkpoint**, was opened just north of Eilat. Travel companies began offering itineraries which begin in Eilat and include visits to Petra (the ancient Nabatean city carved in red rock) in Jordan, the Sinai coast and even Cairo. Marketed as a "Middle Eastern French Riviera," the region's tourist industry mushroomed as a by-product of the peace agreements between Israel, Egypt and Jordan.

Two ways of hitting the water.

Jericho, City of Palm

THE WEST BANK

Hugging the Jordan River to the east and the amber-hued walls of Jerusalem to the west, stretching out over the cities and valleys of Samaria to the north, and the tumbling Judean Hills to the south, the West Bank is perhaps the geographic centre of the Middle East, and the epicentre of all the tensions that area has come to represent. It lies at the very heart of the Holy Land, holding such revered names as Bethlehem, Hebron, Shiloh and Jericho within its domain.

For centuries, Jews, Christians and Muslims have paid homage here, and today pilgrims from around the world still flock to its shrines. Scattered throughout the region, these places are often claimed by more than one religion, and today such spots lend a physical immediacy to age-old conflicts. More than a millennium has not erased the tension in this contested land.

The West Bank was occupied by Israel in 1967. In 1994 the first tentative steps were taken to restore the Occupied Territories to the Palestinian people, beginning with the town of Jericho and the Gaza Strip. Since then, and in accordance with the Oslo Agreement (the peace treaty signed by Israel and the Palestinians in September 1993), Israel has handed over all of the major Arab towns in the West Bank, save Hebron. Owing to its place in Jewish history – it is the site of the Cave of Machpelah (Tomb of the Patriarchs), resting place of Abraham, Isaac and Jacob – fierce Jewish opposition has complicated the retreat of Israeli forces there.

Political history: In 1947, there were 1.3 million Palestinians living under the British mandate in Palestine. Within two years 700,000 had fled to other areas of the Middle East or beyond, some to the area, later known as the West Bank, earmarked by the United Nations to be an independent Palestinian state. But in 1948, after Jordan, Egypt, Iraq, Syria and Lebanon declared war on the newly established State of Israel, East Jerusalem and the Arab areas west of the Jordan River fell to Jordan. In 1950, Jordan annexed the region, hence the name "West Bank". In the same year, the United Nations Relief Works Agency (UNRWA) took on the responsibility of "overseeing and furthering the well-being of the Palestinian refugees until a political solution to the Palestinian displacement could be found."

The 1967 war: The strategic value of the West Bank was clearly evident in the 1967 war. Its location in the centre of Israel made transportation to such Israeli communities as Ein Gedi, on the Dead Sea, and Tiberias in the Galilee time-consuming and posed a difficult strategic problem. The high hills of the West Bank gave the Jordanians a clear view and access to the lower regions of Israel, and at places along the coast just above Tel Aviv, Israel's territory was a slim 15 km (9½ miles) wide.

Preceding pages: shepherd at work in the West Bank. **Left,** a Jericho tourism official tries to be optimistic.

On the night following the outbreak of the 1967 War, Tel Aviv was shelled from the Jordanian-controlled town of Kalkilya, just across the border. As a result of the week-long war that followed, Israel gained control of the region. Capturing the former Arab strongholds, the mountains dominating the Jordan River Valley, was a stupendous strategic gain. Following Israel's victory over Jordan, a further 300,000 Palestinians became refugees for the first time, while another 150,000 picked up their belongings for a second time. Many moved to Jordan.

After the war, as well as constructing an intricate electronic defence system in the Jordan Valley, the Labour-led coalition installed numerous defence outposts, which soon evolved into settlements. These pockets of Jewish presence quickly became precedents for further settlement based upon religious and nationalistic claims dating back to 1900 BC, when the Patriarchs inhabited Canaan. Later, Israelis were drawn to the area for less ideological reasons: financial incentive. State subsidisation of settlements made living here much more affordable for the inflation-strapped Israeli than housing costs permitted within the "green line".

In 1977, the new Likud coalition decided to populate the West Bank, particularly Samaria, where there were sizeable Arab populations. When the Labour government took office in 1992, however, the growth of new settlements was halted, although some already planned or under construction were completed. It is still possible to drive along a road and see, towering over a hill bordering an Arab village, a huge billboard announcing plans for new co-op apartments complete with swimming-pool, tennis courts and a modern shopping centre. In fact, the Israeli settlements – built with predominantly Arab labour – are comprehensive residential centres replete with shopping, schooling and recreation facilities.

During the Intifada, the stone-throwing rebellion begun by Palestinians in 1987, tensions ran high, and such conflicts remain the greatest threat to the peace process. Atrocities on both sides continue to occur. One of the worst – during the period leading up to peace – was the Hebron Mosque massacre in February 1994, in which 30 Palestinians were shot by an Israeli settler.

Travelling in the West Bank: Before venturing into the West Bank check on the prevailing political climate. Modest dress (no shorts) is recommended. Several companies offer group tours of the region, though these invariably express a Jewish nationalistic theme.

Between the army outposts, Jewish settlements and refugee camps, a trip to the West Bank necessarily provokes political cognisance. But much of the landscape appears unchanged since the days of Abraham, David, or Jesus. With the political and spiritual each so firmly entrenched here, your sense of wonder is sure to be heightened. However, in this period of negotiations, and especially since the return of the Likud Party to power in 1996, the area is to be approached with caution.

Right, homeward bound in the Judean desert.

SAMARIA

Leaving Jerusalem along the Jerusalem–Jericho highway, signs of successive civilisations abound in the hills of Samaria, which are stone white by day and gleaming bronze at sunset.

The road winds through the slopes of East Jerusalem by the congested quarters of its residents. Women are outside scrubbing clothing; children run up and down stairs and in and out of courtyards. Playing marbles on level slabs of stone is a widely enjoyed game among small Arab boys and is fun to watch. Heading into Samaria, the main Arab towns of Ramallah, Jericho and Nablus are now under the control of the Palestinian Authority as a result of a treaty signed by Israel and the Palestinians in 1993.

Refugees and ruins: Heading north, a few kilometres from Ramallah, **Shuafat** is the largest Palestinian refugee camp in the territories. It bustles with activity. Some of the Arab homes here, with their contemporary architecture and well-manicured gardens, are palatial, but for the most part the housing, medical, social and educational aid given by the United Nations Relief Works Agency (UNWRA) is essential. Among its offerings are vocational training centres, such as the Ramallah Women's Training Centre, where courses are tailored to the demands of the Middle Eastern economy. Ramallah exemplifies the problems of the Israeli presence. For many of the Palestinian Arabs here, it is a hotbed of anti-Israel sentiment. Countless tyre burnings, school closures, and Israeli-imposed curfews have occurred here over the years.

Twelve km (7 miles) northwest, **Bir Zeit** is the largest of the five major Palestinian universities in the West Bank. Constructed by the Israelis in 1972, it is an active centre of hostility to the Israeli government; Israeli and self-imposed closures occur often.

Travelling north of Ramallah en route to Nablus, limestone terraces climb up and down the hills, retaining all the mineral-rich soil they can. Knotty olive trees edged with flora grace the landscape. These olives are harvested by the local farmers who transport them to the villages for pressing.

Just above the city, two towns atop nearby hills serve as natural landmarks: Bethel and Ai. **Bethel** is prominent in early biblical narratives as the site where Jacob dreamed of a ladder ascending to Heaven. At this spot he made an altar and called it Beit El, or House of God. This is also where the Ark of the Law remained until the time of Judges. **Ai** was one of the earliest cities captured by Joshua and the Israelites during their military conquest of Canaan.

The ancient city of **Shiloh** stood equidistant between Nablus and Bethel. According to the Bible, it was at Shiloh that the land of Israel was divided among the 12 tribes and where the cities were delegated. In the 11th century BC it was the religious centre for the Israelite tribes, and for over 200 years it was the sacred ground for the Ark of the Covenant. And it was in the city of Shiloh that the great prophet Samuel was born, and "grew before the Lord" (I Samuel: 2,

Left, harvesting wheat in Samaria. Right, Yasser Arafat has a permanent presence in Jericho.

21). In time, the Philistines defeated the Israelites, captured the ark, and burned Shiloh to the ground. Today, the *tel* of Shiloh spans less than 3 hectares (8 acres), although archaeologists have unearthed remnants of civilisations dating to the Bronze Age (1600 BC).

Some 48 km (30 miles) north of Ramallah is **Nablus** (Shechem in Hebrew), which is many things to many people. The largest city in the West Bank, with an estimated population of over 100,000, it is chock-full of sites with biblical resonance. From a distance, Nablus looks like a pointilist painting. Innumerable blue doors dot houses neatly spread across a hillside. Within earshot there's a cacophany of sounds: honking car horns, the majestic mu'ezzin calling the Muslim faithful to prayer, and the ululations of Arab women.

Rich in history, the area just outside today's city centre is mentioned in Genesis as the place where Jacob pitched his tents. **Jacob's Well**, located here, is still in use by Nablus residents. According to the Gospel, John (4: 25–26), Jesus stopped here for refreshment, weary from his travels. He spoke to a Samaritan woman who drew water from the well. "I know that the Messiah cometh, which is called Christ," she told him, whereupon Jesus responded: "I that speak unto thee am he." Adjoining this structure is a Greek Orthodox convent built on the remains of a Crusader church.

Nearby, the Tomb of Joseph is a Muslim shrine reputed to hold the great man's bones, "in a parcel of ground which Jacob bought of the sons of Hamor the father of Shechem" (Josh: 24, 32). (Defying scripture, there is another cenotaph for Joseph at the Tomb of the Patriarchs in Hebron.)

Other archaeological discoveries in this proximity include foundations of Canaanite temples, and an ancient *yeshiva*, now guarded by Israeli soldiers.

During the time of the Judges, Abimelech, the son of Gideon, had himself proclaimed king here; some 200 years later, in 928 BC, the 10 northern tribes called on Jeroboam to be king from Dan to Bethel and for several years Shechem

Samaritans celebrate Passover atop Mount Gerezim.

served as the capital of the new northern kingdom of Israel. Going farther back into biblical history, Abraham probably stopped in Shechem just after he arrived in Canaan, and some believe this was the place where he founded the covenant between God and man.

In Roman times, Shechem was renamed Neapolis (New City), laying the root of the name it finally gained when it was taken by the Arabs.

The Samaritans: Standing like two gate posts at the southeastern entrance to Nablus are two historic sister peaks, **Mount Ebal** and **Mount Gerezim**. Moses spoke of them, blessing Mount Gerezim and cursing Mount Ebal. After the conquest, Joshua built an altar on Mount Ebal and from this point read the law to the people.

Mount Gerezim today is the centre of the Samaritan religion. The sect's origins date back to when Assyria swept through the northern kingdom in 720 BC. Returning from exile in 538 BC, the Jews shunned the Samaritans for their intermarriage with their conquerors, although the Samaritans claimed strict adherence to Mosaic Law. Today, approximately 250 of the remaining 500 Samaritans (they were tens of thousands strong during the Middle Ages) celebrate the Passover holiday.

Omri's stately capital: A little over 10 km (6 miles) northwest of Nablus is the site of one of the most impressive ruins of the Holy Land: **Sebastia**. Once called Samaria, it was the capital of the northern Kingdom of Israel upon Omri's accession to power in 887 BC. He and his son, the ill-tempered King Ahab, built magnificent palaces and temples inside a circular protective wall. Ahab also added embellishments and temples to Baal and Astarte, cult figures favoured by his wife and queen, Jezebel, from Sidon. This departure from monotheism incurred the wrath of the Lord and the flight of Elijah, which was to terminate eventually on Mount Carmel.

The remains of **Ahab's Palace** adjoin the impressive steps which led to Herod's Temple of Augustus, constructed in roughly 30 BC. Herod's grandiose style

Pillars at Sebastia.

The West Bank

25 km / 15 miles

Atlit
Nazareth
Umm Qais
Afula
Zikhron
Ya'aqov
En Harod
Zabda
Deir Abu Said
Binyamina
Umm el Fahm
Bet-She'an
Hadera
Jenin
Ya'bad
Qabatiya
Halawa
Netanya
Tulkarm
Tubas
Ajlun
Anabta
Sabastiya
Qalqiliya
Nablus
Rajib
Herzliyya
Azzun
Khallat el Fula
El Ardah
Massu'a
Damiya
Tel Aviv-Yafo
Betah Tiqwa
Marda
Salt
Arura
Qusra
ISRAEL
Bet'Arif
WEST
Karama
Rishon le Zion
Ramala
Allenby
Bridge
Rehovot
Ramallah
Yavne
Jerusalem
Jericho
Ashdod
(Al Quds/Ur Shalem)
(Palestinian Autonomy)
Bet
Qiryat
Shemesh
Beit Jala
Mal'akhi
Ashqelon
Agur
Bethlehem
Qiryat Gat
BANK
Tarqumiya
Ataruz
Gaza
Hebron (Al Khalil)
Bet Qama
Dura
Sederot
Yatta
Netivot
Edh Dhahiriya
Es Samu
Faqu
Ofaqim
Beersheba
Arad
Al Mazra'a
Dead Sea
JORDAN

is certainly not lost in the rubble. Many of his massive constructions still stand in part, testimony to his naming the city in honour of the Emperor Augustus (Sebaste in Greek) and his marrying the beautiful, doomed Mariamne here.

In addition to Herod's work, Sebastia's ruins include an enormous hippodrome, the acropolis, a basilica, and many remains of Israelite and Hellenistic walls. The colonnade-lined street is a majestic reminder of Sebastia's opulence.

In the Arab village of Sebastia just outside the Roman wall, lie the ruins of a 12th-century **Crusader cathedral**. It is reputed to stand over the tombs of the prophets Elisha and Obadiah and St John the Baptist. This site is included in the **Mosque of Nabi Yaya**, in which a small chamber is believed to hold the head of John the Baptist.

Among the parched hills and occasional discarded soda cans that compose the less populated regions of the West Bank, you are likely to spot a Bedouin with his flock on the hillside. While these nomads usually live in clusters in the Judean Desert and Samaria, it is equally common to see a lone Bedouin tent with an incongruous TV antenna protruding from its centre and a pick-up truck parked outside. Young Bedouin children clad in colourful garments can be affable photographic subjects.

Hidden hermitage: On the road southeast of Jerusalem to Wadi Kelt, the silence is so pure that it creates a ringing in your ears. For 1,600 years, since the age of the Patriarchs, monks have inhabited this surrealistic place, where the **Wadi Kelt River** meanders through a dramatic gorge in the canyon between Jericho and Jerusalem. This 35-km (22-mile) stretch includes ruins on top of ruins, monasteries, eerie hermit caves and surprising watering holes. These sights appear as adornments on the earth's crust, which projects every which way to form hills, cliffs and ravines – a photographer's delight. Honeycombing the rockface are hollowed-out niches which serve as isolation cells for monks, who live off the fruit of the land from a garden by a stream. The Greek Orthodox Monastery

Monastery of St George clings to Wadi Kelt.

of St George is just over a century old, but its community long precedes it. Hasmonean, Herodian and Roman remains line this circuitous course.

South of Jericho, off the Jerusalem-Jericho highway, is the **Mosque of Nabi Musa**, astounding to the eye. It appears out of nowhere in the middle of nowhere. Here, Muslims worship the Tomb of Moses. Deut: 34, 1–6 states that Moses was "buried in a valley in the land of Moab, but no man knoweth of his sepulchre unto this day." But an old tradition dating back to Christian pilgrims places it here. The Mamelukes constructed the mosque in the 13th century, providing a high cenotaph for Moses.

Today the mosque is open during the times of Muslim prayer, and all day Friday. Only Muslims are admitted in April, when thousands of Muslims make their pilgrimage to Nabi Musa. The Muslims take a route that intersects the procession of Christians making their Easter pilgrimages to al-Maghtes on the Jordan River, and clashes have resulted from the coinciding celebrations.

The walls of Jericho: Jericho must have been a prime spot for the earliest city dwellers on earth some 10,000 years ago. Widely considered to have sprouted the first agricultural community, the town today is once more centred on agriculture, although on a less historic scale. Ensconced in an oasis in the midst of barren land, Jericho's greenery is nurtured by underground springs, the secret of its endurance. Jericho was the first Arab town in the West Bank that was handed over to the Palestinian Authority.

In times past, rulers used this spot as a warm-weather retreat. One such vacationer was Hisham, the 10th Ummayid Caliph, who built the fabulous **Hisham's Palace** in the 8th century, about 3 km (2 miles) from the city. An enormous aqueduct supplied water from the nearby Ein Dug Springs to a cistern, which then doled it out to the palace as needed. The carvings and monumental pillars are awesome, and the palace floors contain examples of the finest Islamic mosaics.

A few kilometres south of the palace is **Elisha's Spring**, a fountain which the

Hisham's Palace.

Jews believe was purified by the prophet after the populace claimed it was harmful to crops: it is referred to by Arabs today as Ein-es-Sultan.

Nearby is the preserved floor of a 6th-century **synagogue**, featuring a mosaic menorah in its centre, within the walls of a Jericho home.

Ancient Jericho, which lies under Tel es-Sultan, is where the walls came tumbling down on the seventh day after they were encircled by Joshua and the Children of Israel. Archaeological excavations confirm that settlements here date to 8,000 BC, when the early population of hunters and gatherers completed here the transition to sedentary life, becoming the earliest practitioners of agriculture and animal husbandry.

Jericho today is a sleepy town of 7,000 people, with most of the activity confined to its centre. Here, men and women gather to sit on rattan stools, talk, sip coffee, or play backgammon. The markets are ablaze with the earth's fruits and vegetables, and huge bunches of dates and bananas swing from their beams, fresh and delicious. The cafés here offer authentic Middle Eastern foods and refreshment.

In the stark wilderness outside this small town, Jesus encountered the devil's temptation, on a peak the Bible calls the Mount of Temptation. Hinged to the rockface here is a **Greek Orthodox monastery**, constructed in front of the grotto where Jesus was said to have fasted for 40 days and nights.

Along the river Jordan: Some 10 km (6 miles) east of Jericho at a ford north of the Dead Sea known as **al-Maghtes**, Jesus was baptised at age 30: "and it came to pass in those days, that Jesus came from Nazareth of Galilee, and was baptised by John in Jordan," (Mark: 1, 6–9). Not surprisingly, this traditional Site of the Baptism is favoured today by Christians as a place of christening.

Mark Twain described the Jordan River as "so crooked that a man does not know which side of it he is on half the time. In going 90 miles it does not get over more than 50 miles of ground. It is not any wider than Broadway in New York." Indeed, the symbolism attached to this stream – its muddy waters barely flowing in winter – far exceeds its actual size.

The **Allenby Bridge** is the river-crossing from the West Bank to Jordan's Hashemite Kingdom. During the 1967 War, the bridge, reduced to scaffolding, was jammed with Palestinians fleeing the West Bank into Jordan. Since then it has been rebuilt and its traffic is strictly monitored by Israeli security. It is the gateway for West Bank produce into the market places of the Arab world. Visits are exchanged by families and friends on both sides of the Jordan, and many West Bank residents go to Amman to do banking and preserve commercial links.

Although Israel and Jordan are officially at peace, the Palestinian community living between them still constitutes a security threat and therefore, stationed at the bridge's western side are young Israeli soldiers, who meticulously search the sacks, parcels and personal belongings of all travellers. Similarly, the Jordanian armed checkpoints at the border just beyond are potent reminders that peace remains tentative.

Left, the Palestinian flag. **Right**, intricate embroidery in Ramallah.

JUDEA

There is no clear boundary marking the transition of the hills of Samaria to those of Judea, as both are part of the same central range of high ground, reaching from above Ramallah in the north through the Judean cities of Bethlehem and Hebron. Yet the **Judean Hills** have sustained a body of legend, as a well-spring of both the Old and New Testament. To the east, marking the descent of the range into the Jordan Rift Valley, lies the **Judean Desert**, which over the centuries served as a place of refuge for prophets, monks and kings.

Judea is as elusive as it is revered; all around, the arid rolling hills remind you that this is the land of the Bible, and belie the tensions below the surface.

The approach to **Bethlehem**, just south of the border with the Palestinian autonomous zone, holds **Rachel's Tomb**, where the wife of the Patriarch Jacob and mother of Benjamin is said to be buried. The shrine is one of the holiest in Judaism, and is a place of worship for Jews and Muslims alike. The modest dome over the site was rebuilt by the British philanthropist Sir Moses Montefiore in 1841, at the place where it is said "Jacob set a pillar upon her grave."

Shrines of Bethlehem: Centuries after Rachel, during a Bethlehem field harvest, the widowed Ruth fell in love with Boaz. Their great grandson David, chosen from these same fields (and born in Bethlehem), became the famous poet-king of Israel. On the eastern edge of Bethlehem lies the **Field of Ruth**. It is near the Arab village of **Beit Sahur** (House of the Shepherd), and is believed to be the Shepherds' Field where the angel appeared before the shepherds "keeping watch over their flock by night," to announce the birth of Jesus.

On **Manger Street**, which leads directly into the hub of town, up a flight of stairs, you'll find three huge water cisterns hewn out of rock, said to be David's Well. When he was battling the Philistines, David was in their garrison here when thirst prompted him to cry "Oh,

that one would give me water to drink of the well of Bethlehem, which is by the gate!" But, offered the water drawn from the well of his enemies, "he would not drink thereof, but poured it out unto the Lord." (Sam II: 23, 16).

Today, music, bells and churches grace the town. The area teems with pilgrims during the holidays, and the festivities don't stop after Christmas and Easter. The great pomp, ornate decor and beautiful displays continue year-round.

Christ was born in Bethlehem. The exact route of the Nazarene in life remains unknown, and the Gospels do not even agree on chronology. But over the ages there has been a broadening consensus on the exact site of His birth. Following the road into Manger Square, is the hub of Bethlehem, the wide plaza before the **Church of the Nativity**, entered by stooping through a small entranceway, reduced to such scale by the Crusaders for defence purposes, and again made smaller in later years. The original basilica here was built in the year 325 by the Emperor Constantine.

The foundation for the structure is the cave revered in Christian tradition as the place where Jesus was born, and which is mentioned in the writings of St Justine Martyr just 100 years after Christ.

Beyond the vestibule is the nave; much of this interior, including the towering wooden beams, dates from the Emperor Justinian's rebuilding the church in the 6th century. At the front of the church, down some stairs, is the **Grotto of the Nativity**, where the altar features a barely discernible 12th-century mosaic. But the eye is riveted to a gleaming silver star on the floor of this small space, inscribed in Latin, *Hic de virgine Maria Jesus Christus natus est* (Here Jesus Christ was born of the Virgin Mary). Next to the ornate and gilded grotto is the **Chapel of the Manger**, where Mary placed the newborn.

The Church of the Nativity is adjacent, diagonal and adjoined to several churches of varying Christian denominations. The most celebrated on Christmas Eve is **St Catherine's Church**, from which Bethlehem's annual midnight mass is broadcast worldwide.

A few minutes' walk down Milk Grotto Street will take you to the **Milk Grotto Church**. Its milky white colour lends the name; the legend is that while nursing the newborn Jesus, some of Mary's milk splashed to the stone floor and permanently whitened it. Today stone scrapings are sold to pilgrims to improve breastfeeding. From this spot, the Field of Ruth and the expansive Wilderness of Judah are in clear view.

Outside of the churches and shrines, countless self-appointed tour guides promise to show you all you wish to see. Often, they know some interesting tidbits about the history of the town, but expect to pay for this "freely" offered information or be hounded around Manger Square and its environs.

All over town, but particularly in the area of the square, Bethlehem vendors offer a wide array of religious articles and artifacts. They are freshly minted, but traditionally inspired, often of olive-wood, ceramics or Jerusalem stone. If you are persistent but not too pushy, you can bargain with these people and

Milk Grotto Church.

take care of all your Christmas shopping in one go.

Looking into the town of Bethlehem to the north, steeples rise from the hillside maze of houses, proclaiming the city's continued sanctity to the 20,000-odd Arab Christians who live here. Among the various religious institutions here is an Arabic-language university directed by the Catholic Order of the Brothers of Christian Schools; known as **Bethlehem University**, it was established with Israeli assistance.

Castles in the wilderness: Some 8 km (5 miles) east of here is the desert citadel of **Herodian**, perhaps the most outstanding of Herod's architectural conceits. As a result of all his conquests, Herod felt he needed a safe haven from those seeking revenge, and Herodian is nothing if not aloof. A monstrous circular protective wall struck with four equidistant watch posts guards, Herod's ample living space and bath house; included in the layout were hot baths, arcades, a synagogue, and numerous other luxuries. The banquet hall of the palace is as immense as a football stadium, and the structure caps an elevation of 800 metres (2,500 ft) above sea level or 100 metres (330 ft) above the desert floor.

The view from Herodian is a kaleidoscope of the region; Jerusalem lies north, Bethlehem to the west, while the Dead Sea glistens beyond the Judean wilderness to the south and east. According to scholars, just as in Masada, the Jewish uprising resulted in this mountain's defenders taking their own lives before the Romans could. But like the zealots of Masada, the bearers of this fortress were among the last to fall.

Even more remote, dug into the canyon walls overlooking the **Kidron River** to the northeast, is the blue-domed **Mar Saba Monastery**. In years gone by, St Sabas used this serene niche in the desert as a retreat for study and worship and in AD 492 he established the monastery named after him. In the 7th century, Persians and Arabs ruined the monastery and murdered the monks; it was rebuilt, however, and early in the 8th century John of Damascus came to the

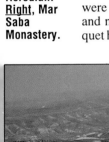

Below, Herodian. Right, Mar Saba Monastery.

site. The writing he did here was an important contribution to Christianity and representative of Christian/Islamic differences at the time. Today, the most prominent feature of the hermitage, from first approach, is the huge protective wall that surrounds the complex. Among the finds inside are the robed remains of St Sabas himself, returned here from Venice in 1965, where they had been stored for over 700 years for preservation. Also on display are the skulls of the hundreds of monks killed by the Persians in 614. Women are not allowed entrance to the monastery.

The area is inhabited by Bedouin, who claim to descend from the monastery's ancient caretakers, who travelled from Byzantium.

Along the path to Mar Saba is the **Church of St Theodosius**, where the three wise men rested after paying homage to the infant Jesus, and where St Theodosius died in 529 at the age of 105. Back on the road above Bethlehem is another fortress-like monastery, **Mar Elias**. Built on a spot where the prophet Elijah slept when fleeing Jezebel, it was restored by the Crusaders in the 11th century and was an important border post in the years the West Bank was Jordanian – between 1948 and 1967.

Roughly 25 km (15 miles) from Bethlehem, heading south towards Hebron, lie the dark-green cisterns known as **Solomon's Pools**. Tradition attributes them to the workers of the great Jewish king in the 10th century BC; archaeology suggests they date from Roman times. In either case, an aqueduct carried water from here to the population of Jerusalem, and today they still serve as a source of water for the city.

Passionate Hebron: Close to 16 km (10 miles) south from Bethlehem lies the ancient city of **Hebron**. While Hebron represents layers of history, its agriculture and urban community is progressive. Farmers, goat and sheep herders, and food packers have made great strides in production by mechanising.

The town also boasts a major **Islamic University** which enrolls nearly 2,000

Left, Tomb of the Patriarch, Hebron.

Arab students. In existence since 1971, this institution is noted for promoting Palestinian culture and nationalism, much to the chagrin of the Israeli authorities who close the facility every so often, citing anti-Israel activity.

Hebron is definitely not the place to sport your knowledge of Hebrew – but any attempt to speak a few words of Arabic is appreciated by the local Arabs. Chances are that you'll be beckoned into a web of merchants' stalls or to a private home for a cup of tea. Turning down such an invitation will offend, but steer clear of controversy. Debating the merits of Israel's presence on the West Bank, for example, is ill-advised especially since this is the last Arab town, under the Oslo Agreement, that Israel has not retreated from. Hebron, today, remains volatile.

Meander through the criss-cross of alleyways in the Hebron casbah. Here you will find a variety of artisans crafting pottery, compressing and sculpting olivewood, and of course blowing the colourful glass for which Hebron is widely famed. A variety of fresh fruits can be bought all along the roadsides and in the shuk. Hebron-grown peaches, pale and sweet, are in demand all over the Middle East. Hebron's produce, including dried and fresh fruits as well as different types of vegetables, are transported to Arab countries by way of the Allenby Bridge with Israeli agreement.

Jewish presence in Hebron dates back to when God bestowed upon Abraham the father-role over the descendants of monotheism, Israel and Ishmael. He chose this airy hill as the burial ground for his family, and today the Tomb of the Patriarchs dominates the city, and is visited by both Jews and Muslims. According to the Pentateuch, Abraham bought the Cave of Machpelah from Ephron the Hittite as the burial site for his wife Sarah.

Here, all three Patriarchs and their wives are believed to be buried, and their cenotaphs compose the centre of the edifice: Abraham and Sarah in the centre, Jacob and Leah on the outer side of the enclosure, and on the other side, inside the mosque area, Isaac and Rebecca. More expansive folklore fur-

ther contends the site to hold the graves of Adam, Eve, Esau, and all 12 sons of Jacob as well (Cain, Abel and the snake not being included).

Standing just outside the structure is **Joseph's Tomb**, at least by name; according to the book of Joshua (24, 32) Joseph's bones were laid to rest instead at Shechem (Nablus today) after their transport from Egypt.

The entire rectangular building gives the impression of a massive fortress, and was built with typical architectural confidence by Herod the Great. The Arabs later made a mosque of it, and the Crusaders made it a church during their stay, adding the roof-top crenellations. In 1188 it was taken by Saladin and once more converted into a mosque.

Eight hundred years after Abraham, David was crowned King of Israel in Hebron, and he ruled from the city for several years before making it his capital. Among his sons born here was Absalom, his favourite, who was to lead a futile rebellion against his father years later. With David's capture of Jerusa-

Blowing glass at Hebron.

lem from the Jebusites in 1000 BC the capital was also shifted, although Hebron would remain one of the four holy cities of Israel, along with Jerusalem, Tiberias and Safed.

The city's Jewish community survived the destruction of both Temples, and remained until the year 1100, when it was expelled by the Crusaders. The population resurfaced and dwindled alternately over the centuries. In 1929 and again in 1936, the community was wiped out in anti-Jewish Arab riots, and it was not until 1967 that Jews re-entered Hebron. In 1968, a group of Jewish settlers gained *de facto* rights to settle the area, although not in Hebron's Arab centre. The result today is a suburb called **Kiryat Arba** (Hebron's name in biblical times), overlooking the city from a nearby hill.

Both Jews and Muslims claim descent from Abraham, and the Hebron area (and particularly the Tomb of the Patriarchs) is a centre of separate worship and mutual confrontation. Adding to the friction is the fact that a mosque now covers part of the site, which had at one time been a synagogue.

The situation in Hebron has been tense ever since the 1967 War, and Israeli soldiers are on constant patrol in the area. Violent clashes among Jews, Arabs and Israelis have riddled the town. During the summer of 1985, a few Likud-supported Knesset members staged a sit-in at an apartment opposite the Arab shuk. They were protesting the halt of settlement expansion and were evicted on the order of Israel's Defence Minister.

Due to sporadic unrest here, it is best to consult the Israeli Government Tourist Office in Jerusalem before travelling to Hebron. Be sure you plan your return trip in advance, however: Hebron is the one place in the West Bank where you should not spend the night.

On the outskirts of Hebron stands the gnarled but living **Oak of Abraham**, believed to be some 600 years old. It is reputed to be the site where Abraham was visited by three angels who told him of Isaac's impending birth. It is owned by Russian monks, who have a small monastery here. The ancient name for this place is Mamre; Abraham supposedly built an altar and a well here, and Herod's structure on the site was where Bar Kochba's defeated troops were sold into slavery.

North of Hebron, along the road to Bethlehem, lies the **Etzion Bloc**, where the agricultural-religious community of Kibbutz HaDati was founded in 1926. Abandoned in the Arab riots of 1929, it was resettled only to be thwarted again in the riots of 1936–39. In 1948 its persistent settlers were wiped out in Israel's War of Independence. The Etzion Bloc and the surrounding Hebron Hills were retaken by the Israeli army on 7 June 1967 and several months thereafter **Kibbutz Kfar Etzion** was resettled by the children of the original kibbutzniks. Today, the Etzion Bloc symbolises the perseverance of Jewish settlement in a hostile environment.

From Kfar Etzion, the highway leads directly back to Jerusalem some 14 km (8 miles) away through a newly constructed series of tunnels and bridges that bypasses Bethlehem.

Politically correct vegetable seller.

GAZA

The sandy strip of **Gaza**, only 6 km wide and 45 km long (4 miles by 28), is home to over 800,000 Palestinians, and thus one of the most densely populated areas in the world with one of the world's highest birth rates. It begins at the **Shikma River** in the north and extends to the Egyptian border at Rafa. Once a part of the seafaring Philistine federation, it was here that the illustrious Samson met the beguiling Delilah, who turned out to be his nemesis.

According to Arab tradition, Samson is buried under the site of the **Great Mosque**, a structure built by the Crusaders in 1150 and transformed into a mosque by the Mamelukes. Gaza has hosted Muslims, Crusaders, Turks, the British, even Napoleon's soldiers, since Samson's time. In 1948 Egyptian soldiers were perched on this gateway to Palestine, and Egypt retained control after Israel's independence.

About a fifth of the 800,000 Palestinian Arabs who were displaced in the fighting before and after 1948 ended up in Gaza. Egypt's President Nasser organised the first *fedayeen* (underground fighters) and encouraged their terrorism against Israel. Israel responded in 1956 with the Sinai Campaign, during which it briefly occupied the Sinai Peninsula and the Gaza Strip. In 1967, Israel seized the territory from Egypt again.

In May 1994 Gaza at last gained self-rule in areas of civil government, the first of the Occupied Territories (along with Jericho) to benefit from the Middle East Peace Accord. Subsequently, the PLO moved its headquarters from Tunis to Gaza, and its chairman, Yasser Arafat, is based there. But the prospects for this impoverished strip of land did not turn round overnight, in spite of the tremendous optimism of the inhabitants and promises of investment by international organisations. For close to 40 years, Palestinian refugees had lived in UNRWA camps, designed for temporary accommodation, and although 90 percent of households have electricity, conditions remain squalid. Some 60 percent of the 800,000 or more residents are unemployed. All this creates fertile ground for Hamas, the Islamic Resistance Movement fiercely opposed to the PLO–Israeli peace accord and a rival to the PLO for control of the area. One of the biggest challenges for Palestinian security forces is to prevent further acts of terrorism by Hamas members.

Before travelling to Gaza, it is important to keep abreast of current political events there and heed security measures. There is little to see in the way of pleasing tourist sights, but the street life itself is an attraction here. Arab women in long black robes, plastic baskets balanced atop their heads, walk through the streets and camps, passing by children in crisp school uniforms, these days emblazoned with the Palestinian flag. The city centres are busy with merchants selling a variety of wares: cotton clothing (the word "gauze" comes from Gaza), terracotta pottery (a speciality), wicker furniture and mounds of camel-hair carpets.

Left, Arab boys selling pottery in Gaza. **Right**, the city of Khan Yunis.

INSIGHT GUIDES
Travel Tips

Your vacation.

Your vacation after losing your wallet in the ocean.

Lose your cash and it's lost forever. Lose American Express® Travelers Cheques and get them replaced. They can mean the difference between the vacation of your dreams and your worst nightmare. And, they are accepted like cash worldwide. Available at participating banks, credit unions, AAA offices and American Express Travel locations. *Don't take chances. Take American Express Travelers Cheques.*

do more

Travelers Cheques

Getting Acquainted

Area: 21,000 sq. km (8, 110 sq. miles) including administered territories and Palestinian autonomy
Capital: Jerusalem
Highest mountain: Mount Hermon (2,766 metres/3,962 ft)
Longest river: River Jordan (264 km/ 165 miles)
Population: 5.8 million
Language: Hebrew and Arabic
Religion: 80 percent Jewish, 15 percent Muslim, 5 percent Christian and Druze
Time zone: GMT plus 2 hours
Currency: New Israeli Shekels
Weights & measures: Metric
Electricity: 220 volts AC, single phase, 50 cycles
National anthem: *Hatikva* (The Hope)
National emblem: The Star of David
International dialling code: 00 972 (2 Jerusalem; 3 Tel Aviv; 4 Haifa; 6 Galilee; 7 Eilat and the South)

Climate

Israeli summers are long (from April to October), hot and virtually rainless. During these months, the atmosphere in the hill towns such as Jerusalem is drier and cooler while Tel Aviv and the coast are humid. The winter season (from November to March) is generally mild but quite cold in hilly areas. Spells of rain are interspersed with brilliant sunshine. During this period, the Tiberias area on the Sea of Galilee, the Dead Sea and Eilat (all of which are searingly hot in the summer) all have ideal warm, sunny weather.

The weather in Israel allows for year-round bathing: from April to October along the Mediterranean coast and around the Sea of Galilee; and throughout the year, though especially enjoyable in winter, along the Dead Sea shore and the Gulf of Eilat.

MEAN TEMPERATURES

Minimum–Maximum

	January	April	July	October
Jerusalem				
°C	6–11	12–21	19–29	16–26
°F	43–53	53–69	66–84	60–78
Tel Aviv				
°C	9–18	12–22	21–30	15–29
°F	49–65	54–72	70–86	59–84
Haifa				
°C	8–17	13–26	20–30	16–27
°F	46–63	55–78	68–86	60–81
Tiberias				
°C	9–18	13–27	23–37	19–32
°F	48–65	56–80	73–98	65–89
Eilat				
°C	10–21	17–31	25–40	20–33
°F	49–70	63–87	78–103	69–92

ANNUAL RAINFALL

Jerusalem and Tel Aviv: 550mm (22 inches)
Galilee: 650mm (26 inches)
Eilat: 20mm (0.79 inches)

All rain falls between October and April, with most rain concentrated in December, January and February.

The best time to visit is early spring, when the hillsides are ablaze with flowers and the weather is still mild. Late autumn is also very pleasant, while Eilat and the Dead Sea are best appreciated in the winter. The hot summers are strictly for those who enjoy high temperatures and know how to handle the heat (i.e. drink lots of liquid, use sunscreen, move slowly and stay in the shade).

The Economy

Israel's biggest exports are polished diamonds, high-tech and electronics equipment, fruit and vegetables, petrochemicals and minerals from the Dead Sea. Exports amount to over $20 billion a year. In addition, Israel receives nearly $2 billion a year from tourism, a further $2 billion from donation by World Jewry and other supporters of Israel, and over $3 billion from US aid. Israelis receive around $500 million a year from Germany in compensation for Nazi atrocities.

Imports comprise mainly manufactured goods (from cars to compact discs) as well as oil, coal and raw dia-

monds. Since 1990, the gross domestic product has been rising by about 6 percent a year, while inflation averages 10 percent. Despite mass immigration, unemployment is only 6 percent.

The Government

Israel is a democracy with a 120-member single chamber Knesset (parliament) elected every four years by all citizens aged 18 and over. Seats are allocated by proportional representation. For the first time in 1996 the Prime Minister was elected directly by the voters but must still command a majority in the Knesset. The President, elected every five years by a secret ballot of Knesset members, is a titular head of state like the British monarch. Israel has no formal constitution but the Supreme Court has the power to interpret Knesset legislation.

Etiquette

After receiving some service or purchase, it is polite to say *toda* (thanks) or *toda raba* (thanks very much). Often the response will be *bevakasha* (please) or *alo davar* (it's nothing). The standard hello or goodbye is *shalom*. "How are you?" is *Ma Shlomcha?* to a man or *Ma Shlomech?* to a woman. "See you" is *lehitra'ot*.

But generally Israelis can be curt, not bothering to say please or thank you, though increasingly greater efforts are being made to be polite to tourists. This is all part of the Israels' famous informality, in which formalities are often dispensed with. Do not judge Israelis harshly by their lack of courtesy. If you are really in trouble, Israelis will surprise you by their painstaking and generous efforts to help.

Israelis can be very physical, looking strangers hard in the eye and doing a lot of touching. This is usually out of friendliness rather than sexual forwardness but the situation can be confusing for a female tourist coming into contact with a strange man.

Of obvious sensitivity is religious etiquette. When visiting holy sites, women should dress conservatively (no bare legs or shoulders), and men should wear shirts and pants. When visiting Jewish shrines or memorials it's also standard for men to cover their heads; if you don't have a *kepah* or hat, a cardboard substitute is often provided. In some religious neighbourhoods, especially in Jerusalem, these conservative rules of dress apply as general practice. While not all Israelis are observant, you should be aware that religious Jews see the Sabbath as a holy day and smoking or other behaviour can be considered offensive.

Ten facts about Israel

1) More Israelis have been killed on the roads (over 20,000) than in all its wars.
2) There are 37 newspapers printed in Russian every week in Israel.
3) Rarely will you see a man wearing a suit, tie and carrying a briefcase – and if you do it's probably a foreign businessman.
4) Jerusalem is the only city in the world with a fax number direct to heaven: c/o The Western Wall, tel: (02) 5612222. (The telephone company places your fax into the cracks of the wall.)
5) Black signs stuck to tree trunks around town inform the community of a death and of the time, date and place of the funeral.
6) On Holocaust Rememberance Day and Memorial Day for Israel's Fallen Soldiers (April/May) the country grinds to a halt for two minutes' silence – no matter where they are, even on the highway. Everybody pays their respect.
7) The Kibbutz and Moshav are two forms of collective settlement unique to Israel. Tourists should visit them in order to understand their purpose.
8) On any Egged Bus, on the hour, the chatter will die down and the driver will turn up the radio. National news is a national priority.
9) The Dead Sea is the lowest point on earth – 392 metres (1,286 ft) below sea level.
10) The national greeting, *Shalom*, means hello, goodbye and, most fittingly, peace. It is also a popular name.

Planning the Trip

What to Bring

Dress in Israel is informal by Western standards. Few people wear jackets and ties in the summer except for business occasions. However, even in the summer Jerusalem can get quite cool in the evenings. Be sure to bring some conservative clothes for visiting religious sites.

Suggested packing lists might include the following:

Summer (April to October): slacks, shorts and open-neck shirts for men; plenty of light cotton daytime dresses and an afternoon dress for more formal occasions for women; light shoes, sandals and closed shoes for touring; sunglasses, hat, suit and beachwear; a light coat, jacket or sweater for cool evenings in the hills.

Winter (November to March): warm coat, sweaters, raincoat and hat, walking shoes, overshoes; shirts, slacks, sports jacket; woollen or heavy suit, blouses, skirts and slacks, long dress or evening skirt for women; lighter clothing and swimsuit for Eilat and the Dead Sea area.

If you forget anything, you will find that the shops in Israel have high quality clothes for all occasions.

Everything is available in Israel but the cost of living is high, roughly 10 to 20 percent more expensive than in Western Europe so it is advisable to bring film and other holiday necessities with you.

Note: the sun's rays are extremely powerful in Israel even in the winter so bring a broad-brimmed hat, lots of sunscreen and a water canteen.

Entry Regulations

Visas & Passports

Tourists are required to hold passports valid for Israel. Stateless persons require a valid travel document with a return visa to the country of issue.

Citizens of the US, Canada, the European Union, Australia and New Zealand do not need a visa to enter Israel, only a valid passport.

Landing-for-the-Day Card

If you visit Israel on a cruise ship, you will be given a Landing-for-the-Day card, which permits you to remain in the country for as long as your ship is in port, and you need not apply for a visitor's visa.

This applies only to people wishing to enter Israel for travel purposes.

Visa Extensions

Those entering Israel on vacation can only stay for three months and are not allowed to work for money. Anyone wishing to enter for work, study or permanent settlement must apply while still abroad to an Israel Diplomatic or Consular Mission for the appropriate visa. Due to a rise in illegal workers in Israel even visitors from North America and Western Europe may be refused entry if they do not have a return ticket, sufficient funds for their stay or an Israeli citizen to vouch for them.

Entry & Exit Formalities

All visitors to Israel, including diplomats, are required to fill an entry form, AL 17, upon arrival.

Visitors who intend continuing to Arab or Muslim countries (except Egypt and Jordan) after their visit to Israel should ask the frontier control officer to put the entry stamp on this form instead of in their passports, as they may subsequently be refused entry into countries hostile towards Israel if an Israeli stamp appears on the passport itself.

Extensions of Stay

Tourists who wish to stay in the country for longer than three months must obtain an extension of stay. This applies also to citizens of those countries which are exempt from entry visas and generally requires the stamping of your passport. The extension may be obtained through any district office of the Ministry of Interior.

The main offices are located at:
Jerusalem, General Building, Rehov Shlomzion Hamalka, tel: (02) 6290222.
Tel Aviv, Shalom Meyer Tower, Visa Department, 9 Rehov Ahad Ha'am, tel: (03) 5193333.

Haifa, Government Building (opposite Municipality), 11 Hassan Shukri, tel: (04) 8616222

Customs

Every adult tourist may bring into the country without payment of duty the following articles, provided that they are for personal use: eau de Cologne or perfume not exceeding 0.2 litres (0.44 pint), wine up to 2 litres and other alcoholic drinks not exceeding 1 litre; tobacco or cigars not exceeding 250 grams or 250 cigarettes; gifts up to $200 in value, including assorted foodstuffs not exceeding 3 kg (6½ lb), on condition that no single type of food exceeds 1 kg (2.2lb).

Gift parcels sent unaccompanied – by post or by any other means – are liable to full import duties and Value Added Tax.

Portable, expensive electronic items such as cameras, video cameras and lap-top computers may be taken into the country duty-free on condition that they are taken out on departure. These are meant to be for your use in Israel. You may have trouble explaining why you need to use a fax machine, or VCR and there are stiff fines (usually equal to the value of the item) for those attempting to smuggle such goods into Israel.

The red-green customs clearance system is in operation at Ben-Gurion Airport. Tourists bringing in goods mentioned above may choose the Green Channel and leave the Airport. Tourists bringing in other goods, even if they are exempt from duty, must use the Red Channel.

The following articles are subject to declaration and deposits of duties and taxes and the Red Channel must be taken: professional instruments (which can be held in the hand during operation) up to a value of $1,650; boat (rowing, sailing or motor) and a caravan trailer; scuba-diving equipment portable and appreciably used; records in reasonable quantity.

CUSTOM DEPOSITS

The custom authorities are entitled to demand deposits or guarantees on any article brought in by the tourist or sent separately. This is usually enforced only for very expensive professional equipment or other expensive items. The guarantee or deposit is re-turned to the tourist when he leaves the country and takes the articles out with him. Since the formalities take some time, it is advisable to make all arrangements a day or two before departure, and preferably at the port of entry of the goods, so that the return of the guarantee can be carried out more conveniently.

Further information contact:
The Department of Customs and Excise, 32 Rehov Agron, POB 320, 91000 Jerusalem, tel: (02) 6703333.

Health

There are no vaccination requirements for tourists entering Israel except if they are arriving from infected areas. By far the biggest health problem affecting visitors stems from a lack of respect for the sun. Sunburn and sunstroke afflict bathers, while dehydration plagues those who over-exert themselves sightseeing. Tourists should acclimatise gradually, apply suntan lotions, keep indoors or in the shade between 10am and 4pm in the late spring, summer and early autumn, and wear light, comfortable clothes that cover both legs and arms and use a hat and sunglasses.

Most importantly of all, it is vital to drink continually even if you do not feel thirsty. Research has shown that the average person who is exerting themselves in the heat of the day during an Israeli summer needs to drink one litre (over 2 pints) every hour to replace the body liquids lost through sweat. The first symptoms of dehydration are tiredness, headache and lack of appetite. Advanced dehydration can express itself in unpleasant symptoms, from migraines and fever to diarrhoea and vomiting. Medication will not help. Recovery will come about through rest and sipping water, possibly with some salt added, though it is probably best to consult a doctor to ensure that the problem really is dehydration.

Upset stomachs are also common. Here, too, rest and a diet of water are the best medicine. Tap water is as drinkable as anywhere in the developed world, though mineral waters are available everywhere.

Aids: The number of cases of Aids in Israel is considerably lower than in other countries in Western Europe, but is nevertheless on the increase. The Ministry of Interior requires all visitors seeking to extend their stay beyond three months to take an Aids test.

Money

Tourists may bring an unlimited amount of foreign currency into Israel, whether in cash, traveller's checks, letters of credit or State of Israel Bonds. They may also bring in an unlimited amount of Israeli shekels but upon departure are allowed to take out only $500 worth, though nobody ever checks this. They are not required to declare, upon arrival, the amount of foreign currency in their possession and currency exchanges are not recorded.

Tourists who have changed foreign currency into Israeli shekels, may rechange their money by presenting the receipt of the transaction up to a maximum of $500. This may be done at any bank in Israel during the course of one's visit. However, upon departure from Israel, a maximum of only $100 may be exchanged at Ben-Gurion International Airport. This can be done after going through customs and passport control. Generally Israel's economy is undergoing rapid liberalisation so these rules are not always enforced. However, it is not a good idea to change too much money into shekels because of the problems of converting back, though this can be done on the black market.

Local Currency

The currency is the New Israeli Shekel (NIS) which officially succeeded the old Israeli shekel in 1985. The shekel is divided into 100 agorot. Bills are issued in four denominations: 10 NIS (orange with a portrait of former Prime Minister Golda Meir – now virtually faded out in favour of a coin), 20 NIS (grey with a portrait of former Prime Minister Moshe Sharett), 50 NIS (purple with a portrait of Nobel Prize winner Shmuel Agnon), 100 NIS (grey with a portrait of former President Yitzhak Ben Zvi), 200 NIS (reddish-brown with a portrait of former President Zalman Shazar). Change comes in coins of 5 agorot, 10 agorot, ½ shekel, 1 shekel, 5 shekels and 10 shekels.

Exchange rates are the same in all banks and *bureaux de change*. The NIS is stable and floats freely agianst the world's major currencies, with a revised exchange rate each day according to supply and demand. Vendors are prepared to accept the world's better known currencies but offer inferior exchange rates.

Credit Cards & Cheques

Visa, MasterCard/Euro Card, American Express and Diners Club are honoured virtually everywhere. The cash machines outside almost every Israeli bank will dispense money against these cards (so remember your personal identification number); this can save waiting around in crowded banks. Traveller's cheques and Eurocheques are widely accepted, though banks take a commission on each cheque so it is cheaper to bring them in higher denomination.

Should your credit card get lost or stolen, telephone one of the following numbers immediately:
American Express, tel: 03-5242211
Visa & Diners Club, tel: 03-5723572
EuroCard/MasterCard, tel: 03-5764444

Public Holidays

Public holidays fall on the Jewish holidays listed. On Rosh Hashanah (New Year), Yom Kippur (Day of Atonement), the first and last day of Succot (Tabernacles), the first and last day of Pesach (Passover) and Shavuot, all shops and offices are closed and there is no public transport. On Holocaust Day, Memorial Day and Tisha B'Av all places of entertainment and restaurants are closed. In Arab areas such as Nazareth and Bethlehem Christian and Muslim festivals are observed, though most shopkeepers remain open on Friday and Sunday, the Muslim and Christian sabbaths.

The Sabbath & Festivals

Israel observes a solar-lunar year in accordance with Jewish religious tradition, with the New Year occurring in September/October, with the holiday of Rosh Hashana. But the standard Gregorian system is also in daily use everywhere.

The working week runs from Sunday to Thursday, and most businesses are also open Friday mornings. From sunset Friday to sunset Saturday, however, everything shuts down in observance of the Jewish Sabbath, or

Shabbat. This includes all banks and public services, including buses and other forms of transportation. In Tel Aviv and Haifa, however, small minibuses run along the main bus routes and inter-city *Sheruts* also run some services. On Saturday evening, most of these services resume.

The Hebrew calendar is a lunar calendar with a leap month added every two to three years to ensure that the year is also a solar one. Jewish holy days, therefore, fall on different dates in the general calendar each year.

CALENDAR OF JEWISH HOLIDAYS

Festival	Month
Rosh Hashana	Sept/Oct
Yom Kippur	Sept/Oct
Succot	Sept/Oct
Simhat Torah	Sept/Oct
Chanukka	Dec
Tu B'Shevat	Jan/Feb
Purim	Feb/Mar
Pessah	Mar/Apr
Independence Day	Apr/May
Lag Ba'Omer	May
Jerusalem Liberation Day	May/June
Shavuot	May/ June
Tisha B'Av	July/Aug

Rosh Hashana & Yom Kippur

Rosh Hashana (the Jewish New Year) and Yom Kippur (the Day of Atonement) are known as the "Days of Awe". On these days a Jew is called upon to give an accounting of himself before God. These festivals are purely religious in character and are observed principally in the synagogue.

Yom Kippur ends the 10-day period of penitence which begins on Rosh Hashana. For the observant Jew this is a 25-hour period of complete fasting and prayer. On this day the entire country comes to a standstill. All public and commercial services shut down and there is no traffic either public or private. There are no organised tours for tourists on this day. Tourists who do not fast are advised to check with their hotels for arrangements about meals.

Succot (Feast of Tabernacles) & Simchat Torah (Rejoicing of the Law)

The Succot Festival has a dual significance – religious and agricultural. Observant Jews dwell, or at least eat, in *succot* (booths) erected near their

homes to commemorate the Israelites dwelling in the wilderness after the Exodus from Egypt. Some hotels and restaurants also build a *succot* on their premises.

The agricultural significance of the festival is symbolised by the "four species"–the palm branch, the myrtle, the willow and the citron, over which a special blessing is recited on each day of the festival.

Simchat Torah is on the eighth day of the Feast of Tabernacles and on this day the annual cycle of the reading of the Law (Torah) is completed and another cycle begins. This festival is an extremely joyous one and is marked by singing and dancing in the streets as well as in the synagogues.

Chanukah (Festival of Lights)

Chanukah is an eight-day celebration recalling the successful revolt of the small Jewish community in the Land of Israel in the year 167 BC against the Syrian Hellenistic Empire.

During Chanukah, each night for eight days a light is lit on an eight-branched candelabrum. This is to commemorate the miracle of the burning oil in the Holy Temple which occurred after the revolt. When the victorious fighters came to cleanse and re-dedicate their temple, which had been polluted by idolatry, they found that the supply of ritual oil, sufficient for one day, miraculously burned for eight days – the length of time needed to prepare a new supply of the special oil.

During Chanukah, large electric lamps are lit outside public buildings and many shops display eight-branched candelabra in their windows. Hotels conduct candle-lighting ceremonies for their guests, after which traditional Chanukah fare, such as doughnuts and potato pancakes, is served.

Tu B'Shvat (The New Year of the Trees)

On this day, which is also considered the awakening of spring, children all over Israel carry tree saplings which they plant in special planting areas, singing traditional Tu B'Shvat songs. Fifteen species of fruit are tasted and a blessing said over them.

Purim

This festival commemorates the events which took place in Shushan in ancient Persia, when the wicked chancellor Haman persuaded Ahashverus, king of Persia, to kill all the Jews in his domain. Through Queen Esther and her uncle Mordechai, the plot was foiled and the Jews were saved. The festival takes its name from the Hebrew word *purim*, meaning lots, which Haman cast to determine the day to carry out his terrible plan.

On the eve of the festival, the Scroll of Esther, which relates the tale, is read in every synagogue. Throughout the festival children and adults dress up in colourful costumes and masks and eat triangular-shaped pastries filled with fruit or poppy seeds, known as "Haman's Ears".

Pesach (Passover)

One of the main festivals in the Jewish calendar, joyously commemorating the Exodus of the Jews from Egypt and the miracles that preceded it (including the last plague, which struck the first-born sons of the Egyptians but "passed over" the Israelites).

The centre of festivity is the home, where the ritual Passover meal (*Seder*) takes place on the eve of the festival, accompanied by the reading of a special text (Haggadah) which recounts the historical events that Passover commemorates through ritual questions and answers, blessings and songs.

During the time of Passover (seven days in Israel and eight abroad) only unleavened bread (*matza*) is eaten and there is abstention from all fermented foods. Jewish hotels do not serve bread during this period. It is also a time for pilgrimage to Jerusalem, as are Shavuot (Pentecost) and Succot (Feast of Tabernacles). In the Christian tradition, the Last Supper was a Passover meal, and Easter Sunday is determined as the first Sunday in the Passover period.

Shavuot (Pentecost)

This ancient holiday is mentioned in the Holy Scriptures as the "Feast of the Giving of the Law (Torah)", commemorating God giving Moses the Ten Commandments, which he in turn gave to the Children of Israel; the "Feast of Ingathering", marking the end of the wheat harvest; and the "Feast of the First Fruits", for in ancient days first-fruit offerings were brought to the Temple in Jerusalem as an expression of gratitude to God.

In Israel, Shavuot is observed with prayer and public celebrations. School children can be seen with fresh flower garlands on their heads, carrying baskets of fruit as they parade. The entire night preceding the festival is devoted to the study of the Law (Torah), and the next day special prayers are recited in the synagogues, which are decorated with flowers, fruit and greenery.

It is customary to eat dairy foods and honey during this time.

Tisha B'Av (the 9th of Av)

Commemorating the destruction of the First and Second Temples, and other tragedies that befell the Jewish people in later history, Tisha B'Av is a traditional day of mourning and fasting.

Muslim Holy Days

Friday is a holy day for Muslims and places of worship are closed to visitors during prayers on that day, as they are on all holy days. The Muslim calendar comprises 12 lunar months, so that, say, the month of Ramadan, rotates backwards through the seasons. Muslim holy days are decided in accordance with the appearance of the new moon, thus falling on different dates in the general calendar each year. The most important are:

Id el Adha, Sacrificial Festival (four days).

New Year.

Mohammed's Birthday.

Feast of Ramadan (one month).

Id el Fitr, Conclusion of Ramadan (three days).

Christian Holy Days

Sunday is, of course, the Christian sabbath, but different Christian denominations celebrate festivals on different dates. For example the Catholic and Protestant Christmas is 25 December, the Orthodox Christmas 6 January, and the Armenian Orthodox Christmas 14 January. During some years all denominations celebrate Easter together, while other times the Orthodox Easter falls a week after the Western Easter.

By Air

Ben-Gurion International Airport is situated in Lydda (*Lod* in Hebrew) near the Mediterranean coast, 20 km (12 miles) southeast of Tel Aviv, 50 km (30 miles) west of Jerusalem and 110 km (68 miles) southeast of Haifa, and is the main hub for international air traffic. Its facilities include a Government Tourist Office, open around the clock, providing information and helping to arrange accommodation, tel: (03) 9711485). The airport also has a bank and post office, both open 24 hours except for holidays and *Shabbat*, plus a cafeteria, shopping area and First Aid post. The El Al Lost & Found department, also open 24 hours, can be reached at tel: (03) 9712541. Airport arrivals information in English on tel: (03) 9723344.

About 40 percent of the international flights in and out of Ben-Gurion International Airport are operated by the government-owned El Al Israel Airlines, which carries over 2 million passengers a year.

Other major airlines with regular flights to Ben-Gurion International Airport include Air France, Alitalia, Austrian Airlines, British Airways, Delta, Iberia, KLM, Lufthansa, Sabena, SAS, South African Airways, and Swissair.

There are also regular charter flights to Ben-Gurion International Airport by El Al, by Arkia, another Israeli carrier, and by overseas companies including Monarch and Tower.

By Sea

The main ports are Haifa and Ashdod. The Stability Line and Sol Line offer sailings from Greece and Cyprus to Haifa port, and many Mediterranean cruises include Israel in their itineraries. Official ports of entry for foreign yachts and boats in addition to these include Eilat and the Tel Aviv Marina.

By Bus

There are services from Cairo to Tel Aviv and Jerusalem and to the Taba border point near Eilat. There are also services from Amman to the three border crossings with Israel which meet up with buses from Jerusalem and Tel Aviv. A direct service is planned between Amman and Israeli cities.

By Road

FROM JORDAN

Following the signing of a peace agreement between Israel and Jordan in 1994, communications between the two countries have improved considerably (Israel now recognises Jordanian stamps in passports and visas and vice versa). Visitors now have several border crossings to choose from: the Allenby Bridge, the Jordan River Crossing (near Bet Shean) and the Arava Checkpoint (between Eilat and Aqaba).

Note: It is advisable to check the advice given here before travelling. Israel's Ministry of Tourism can provide the latest information, tel: (02) 7548111.

Allenby Bridge, near Jericho, some 40 km (25 miles) from Jerusalem, is the main crossing-point. For information, tel: (02) 9941038

The visa requirements are the same as those at any other point of entry into Israel (it is not possible to get an Israeli visa upon arrival at the Bridge and, as yet, it is still not possible to get one in Jordan).

The Bridge is open Sunday–Thursday 8am–4pm and on Friday and the eves of holidays 8–11am. It is closed on Saturday and on Jewish holidays. At Allenby Bridge a Tourist Information Office is open at the same time as the Bridge. Other facilities are: currency exchange, post office, public telephones, cafeteria, toilets, porters and *sherut* (service) taxis to Jerusalem, Jericho, Bethlehem, Hebron, Ramallah and Gaza.

For opening hours and restrictions at other points of entry between Jordan and Israel check the latest details with Israel's Ministry of Tourism, or contact the border itself:

Jordan River (near Bet She'an): (06) 586448.

Arava Checkpoint (near Eilat): (07) 6336812.

FROM EGYPT

Points of entry open between Israel and Egypt are Nizzana, Rafiah, and Taba, open 363 days a year (exceptions are Yom Kippur and the first day of Id el Adha).

Nizzana, which is the main point of entry, is about 60 km (37 miles) southwest of Beersheba, and is open between 8am–4pm.

Rafiah, 50 km (30 miles) southwest of Ashkelon, is open between 8.30am–5pm.

Taba, just south of Eilat, is open between 7am–9pm.

By Car

Israel has good roads but most of them are packed with traffic. Drivers, as elsewhere in the Mediterranean, are fast and discourteous and specialise in overtaking on the inside. Pedestrians tend to meander in the road. Car hire is expensive and is probably not necessary for the centre of the country which has good bus and taxi services. Parking is difficult and expensive in the city centres. However, it is worth hiring a car for touring the Galilee or Negev.

Specialist Tours

So much history gets missed without an expert guide to explain the significance of each site, so it is well worth joining an organised tour. Major tour bus companies include:

Egged Tours, tel: (02) 5304868.
United Tours, tel: (02) 6251287.
Galilee Tours, tel: (toll free) 177-022-2525; fax: (02) 6231341.
Camel Riders, tel: (07) 6373218; fax: (07) 6371944. Desert sites by camel; Bedouin-style accommodation.

Accommodation

There is a wide choice of accommodation from de luxe suites in high class hotels through to budget hotels and youth hostels. Unique Israeli forms of accommodation include kibbutz guest houses (relatively expensive rural retreats) and Christian hospices (more luxurious than they sound, usually with a 19th-century European ambience).

On Departure

By Air

CONFIRMING RESERVATIONS

You must confirm your scheduled departure with your airline at least 72 hours in advance.

PROCEDURES ON DEPARTURE

Departing passengers should arrive at the airpor 2–3 hours prior to their flight's departure time and prepare the following documents: a valid passport,

flight tickets and money (Israeli currency preferred) for payment of the airport tax, which is obligatory for every passenger over the age of two, and which costs the equivalent of $10. This tax is usually included in the price of the air ticket.

PORTER SERVICE

If you are flying El Al, you can check in your luggage at their office in Haifa, Jerusalem or Tel Aviv the evening before departure (except on Friday, holy days and the eves of holy days). It will be taken straight to your plane and you need only arrive at the airport 1 hour before departure.

The following El Al offices are open for check-in services:
Tel Aviv Railway Station, North Tel Aviv, tel: (03) 6917198. Open: 1pm–midnight.
Center One, Jerusalem, tel: (02) 5383166. Open: 4–11pm.
6 Hanamal Street, Haifa, tel: (04) 8677036. Open: 6.30–10pm.

SECURITY CHECKS

These are for your protection. Be prepared to unlock your luggage and submit yourself and carry-on bags to a careful but courteous examination. To avoid spoiling any precious records of your visit, make sure to empty your camera of film.

GETTING TO THE AIRPORT

From Tel Aviv: By United Tours Bus No. 222 from Railway Station, Rehov Arlosorov to Ben-Gurion Airport every hour, year round, from 4am–noon. For details tel: (03) 7543410.

By Egged Buses, every 15 minutes, 6am–11.30pm.

From Jerusalem: By Egged Buses, from 6.15am–7pm, approximately every 20 minutes. By Nesher *sherut* taxi: book in advance at 2l Rehov Hamelech George, tel: (02) 257227.

From Haifa: By Egged Buses, from 7am–6pm, approximately every 45 minutes. By Aviv *sherut* taxi service, at 5 Rehov Allenby, tel: (04) 666333, approximately every hour from 6am–5pm.

Travelling On

To Jordan

When crossing from Israel to Jordan the tourist must possess a passport valid for at least six months, a Jordanian visa (obtainable at the Jordanian checkpoint) and pay an exit tax. This is levied in the form of a revenue stamp which can be purchased at any post office in Israel as well as at the Bridge. Private vehicles (including cycles) may not cross the Bridge (the Arava Checkpoint is open to vehicles).

BORDER CROSSINGS

Allenby Bridge:
From Jerusalem: By *sherut* taxi service from Damascus Gate.
From Jericho, Bethlehem, Hebron, Ramallah and Gaza: By *sherut* taxi service from the centre of each town. Tourists who wish to leave by other means of transportation must coordinate their departure with the Tourism Staff Officer, Judea and Samaria, tel: (02) 9955318 or with the Allenby Bridge Tourist Information Office, tel: (02) 9941038.
From Tel Aviv: A Dan bus now runs direct from the Central Bus Station in Tel Aviv to Amman twice daily (except Saturday) at 7am and 2.30pm. Contact Dan Buses for the latest information (03) 6394444.

Jordan River Crossing:
From Bet She'an: By bus No. 16 – daily (except Saturday) – departing 8.20am; 9.20am; and 2.20pm.

Arava Checkpoint:
From Eilat: By bus No. 16 departing daily from the Central Bus Station every hour.

To Egypt

Passengers to Egypt pay a tax of $8. Visitors departing via the land crossing point to Egypt at Nitzana pay a tax approximately equivalent to $2. The tax is paid at the Bank Leumi branch at the terminal. Visitors departing via Rafiah pay a tax approximately equivalent to $8. It can be paid at any branch of Bank Hapoalim to the order of the Israel Airport Authority, account number 566-05-39710.

Tourists crossing from Taba to Egypt can obtain a visa on presentation of a passport. The Egyptian visa, valid up to seven days, is free, but there is a $5 tax. Travel is permitted to the tourist sites in Southern Sinai only, and visitors must return to Israel via Taba. The AL-17 entry form into Israel is required.

With the exception of those entering Southern Sinai (through Taba) an Egyptian visa must be obtained in advance. In addition to your valid passport, the AL-17 entry form must be presented. Private vehicles may be driven into Egypt, and documentation must be obtained from the automobile clubs in your country. Rented cars are not permitted to cross. Southern Sinai may also be entered by sea through Sharm el Sheikh only. Free visas are obtainable in advance, for a 48-hour stay, from the Egyptian Consulate in Eilat.

GETTING TO THE BORDER

From Jerusalem: By *sherut* service from Damascus Gate.
From Tel Aviv: By *sherut* service from the Central Bus Station.

In addition to these shuttles, tourist agencies in Israel offer inexpensive round-trip bus service in air-conditioned buses, leaving daily except on *Shabbat* (Saturday).

Both El Al and Air Sinai also offer several flights to Cairo per week, which although much more expensive than the bus, cut the travel time down from 10 hours to less than 55 minutes.

The Egged Bus Co-op runs a regular service from Tel Aviv to Cairo. Buses depart daily (Sunday–Thursday) from the Central Bus Station at 8.30am. Visas for Egypt cost approximately $15 and can be obtained by visiting the Egyptian Consulate in Tel Aviv, at 54 Rehov Basel, Tel Aviv 62744, tel: (03) 5464151.

Rented cars are not permitted to cross the border. As at the airport, all visitors leaving through the land borders are expected to pay a transit tax.

Useful Addresses and Information

Canada: Suite 700, 180 Bloor Street West, Toronto, Ontario, tel: 416-964-3784.

United States: 350 Fifth Avenue, 19th Floor, New York, New York, tel: 212-560-0650.
United Kingdom: 18 Great Marlborough Street, London W1V 1AF, tel: 0171-434 3651.

Backpacking

Israel is a backpacker's paradise. It is customary for Israelis after completing their army service to spend six months, or even a year, backpacking around the world, and so backpackers are generally warmly received in Israel and rarely frowned on as undesirables.

Hitchhiking is as common as catching a bus and hitchhiking stops, rather like bus stops, can be found at every major junction. But competition is tough, especially in urban areas where dozens of Israelis vie for car space, including many soldiers who receive priority. Buses are relatively cheap and there is a 10 percent discount on inter-city routes for holders of international students cards.

Youth hostels abound and their representatives often wait at bus stations to approach backpackers. Sleeping on the beach or in public parks is also usually permitted. Eating is incredibly cheap and healthy at *felafel* stalls where you can take as much salad as you want along with your pita bread and *felafel* for just $2.

Backpackers also like Israel because there is usually plenty of casual employment. Strictly speaking, this is illegal, and wages are poor, but a week or two's pay for washing dishes or working on a construction site can be useful for those travelling around the world on a shoestring budget.

Travelling with Children

Israelis love children, who are expected to be seen and heard. Restaurants, hotels and cafés are very flexible in meeting children's fussy food needs and many hotels operate babysitting services.

Children under five travel free on buses. Children under four must be harnessed into special seats when travelling in cars (except taxis).

Gay Travellers

Homosexuality is illegal in Israel, but no prosecution has ever been brought for relationships between consenting adults. Independence Park in Tel Aviv is the country's main gay pick-up point and the city abounds with gay clubs. Jerusalem also has a scene, albeit smaller.

Students

Youth Tours: The Israel Student Tourist Association (ISSTA) arranges low-cost flights to and from Israel and offers young visitors a variety of tours including safaris and work camps. The association also issues and renews International Student Identity Cards. The ISSTA representative at Ben-Gurion Airport answers queries on kibbutzim, archaeological digs, hotels and hostels, buses, taxis, inland flights, and discounts.

ISSTA offices are located in Israel's three main cities:
Tel Aviv: 109 Rehov Ben Yehuda, tel: (02) 6247164/5.
Jerusalem: 5 Rehov Elishar, tel: (02) 6225258.
Haifa: Hakranot, Rehov Herzl, tel: (04) 8669139.

Practical Tips

Business Hours

Banks: Sunday, Tuesday and Thursday from 8.30am–12.30pm and 4–5.30pm. Monday and Wednesday 8.30am–12.30pm only. Friday and eves of holy days 8.30am–12 noon.

Branches in the leading hotels usually offer convenient additional banking hours.
Offices: Sunday–Thursday 8am– noon.
Stores: Sunday–Thursday, Friday mornings only and sometimes Saturday night. Some smaller stores may, however, take a siesta.

Tipping

In restaurants if a service charge is not included then 10–15 percent is expected. Israelis do not tip taxi drivers but taxi drivers will expect a small tip from tourists. Hotel staff such as porters (bell hops) will be happy with a few shekels for each item of baggage.

Religious Services

Jews and Muslims will have no problems finding synagogues and mosques which are virtually on every street corner in some neighbourhoods.

Jewish

Jerusalem Great Synagogue, 56 King George Street, tel: (02) 6247112.
Chabad Synagogue, 16 Yermiyahu Street, Jerusalem, tel: (02) 5814755.
Centre for Conservative Judaism, 4 Agron Street, Jerusalem, tel: (02) 6223539.
Union for Progressive Judaism, 13 David Ha-Melekh Street, Jerusalem, tel: (02) 6232444.
Tel Aviv Great Synagogue, 110 Allenby Street, tel: (03) 5604905.
Beit Yisrael, Independence Square, Netanya, tel: (09) 8624345.
Haifa Central Synagogue, Rabbi Herzog Street, tel: (04) 8660599.

Muslim

The best known mosques in Israel are the El Aksa Mosque (tel: 02-6281248) on Jerusalem's Temple Mount, the Al-Jazzar Mosque in Akko and the White Mosque in Ramla. There are also many mosques in Arab towns and villages throughout Israel.

Christians

While Israel has much to offer every tourist, for the Christian pilgrim a trip to Israel is more than just a journey because here the pilgrim has the unique opportunity of tracing the footsteps of Jesus and the early Christians and visiting sites significant to the life and teaching of Jesus: Bethlehem, his birthplace; Nazareth, the town of his boyhood; the Sea of Galilee, scene of miracles and his ministerial teaching; Mount Tabor, site of the Transfiguration; the Garden of Gethsemane and Jerusalem, where he spent his last hours of prayer and agony; and Latrun, now the site of a Trappist monastery,

where Jesus appeared before his disciples after the Resurrection.

JERUSALEM

Armenian Cathedral of St James, tel: (02) 6284549. Monday–Friday 3am–3.30pm, Saturday and Sunday 2.30am–3.15pm.
Cenacle Chapel Franciscans, tel: (02) 6713597. 7am–noon, 3pm–sundown. Ring bell.
Christ Church – Office, tel: (02) 6282082. 8–10am, 4.30–6pm.
Dominus Flevit, tel: (02) 6285837. 6.45am–11.30am, 3–5pm.
Ein Karem: St John's, tel: (02) 6413639. 5.30am–noon, 2.30–6pm (winter 2.30–5.30pm).
Ein Karem: Visitation, tel: (02) 6417291. 9am–noon, 3–6pm.
Flagellation, tel: (02) 6282936. 6am–noon, 2–6pm (winter 2–5.30pm).
Garden Tomb, tel: (02) 6283402. 8am–1pm, 3–5pm (winter 8am–12.30pm and 2.30–4.30pm). Sunday closed.
Gethsemane, Church of Agony and Grotto, tel: (02) 6283264. 8.30am–noon, 3pm–sundown (winter 2pm–sundown).
Holy Sepulchre, tel: (02) 6273314. 4am–8pm (winter 4am–7pm).
Lithostrotos-Ecce Homo, tel: (02) 6282445. 8.30am–4.30pm. Sunday closed (winter 8.30am–4pm).
Lutheran Church of the Redeemer, tel: (02) 6282543. 9am–1pm, 2–5 pm, Friday 9am–1pm. Sunday for services only.
Monastery of the Holy Cross, tel: (02) 5634442. Irregular hours – phone ahead.
Russian Cathedral, tel: (02) 6284580. By appointment.
St Mary Magdalene, tel: (02) 6282897. Irregular hours – phone ahead.
St Ann's, Bethesda, tel: (02) 6283258. 8am–noon, 2.30–6pm (winter 2–5pm).
St George's Cathedral, tel: (02) 6282253 or 282167. 6.45am–6.30pm.
Dormition Abbey, tel: (02) 6719927. 7am–12.30pm, 2–7pm.
Abu Gosh Crusader Church, tel: (02) 6539798. 8.30–11am. 2.30–5pm.

OUTSIDE JERUSALEM

Bethlehem Nativity Church. 6am–6pm.
Bethlehem St Catherine, tel: (02) 6742425. 8am–noon, 2.30–6pm.

Bethlehem Shepherd's Field, tel: (02) 6742423. 8am–11.30am, 2–6pm (winter 2–5pm).

Capernaum "City of Jesus", tel: (06) 6721059. 8.30am–4.30pm.

Emmaus Qubeibeh, tel: (04) 9952495 ext: 4. 6.30–11.30am, 2–6pm.

Latrun Monastery, tel: (08) 9420065. 7.30–11.30am, 2.30–5pm.

Mount of Beatitudes, tel: (06) 6720878. 8am–noon, 2–4pm.

Mount Carmel Stella Maris, tel: (04) 8523460. 6am–noon, 3–6pm (winter 3–5pm).

Nazareth: Basilica of the Annunciation & St Joseph's, tel: (06) 6572501. 8.30–11.45am, 2–6pm. Sunday 2–6pm (winter 2–5pm).

Tabor Transfiguration, tel: (06) 6567489. 8am–noon, 3–5pm.

Tabgha: Multiplication of the Bread, tel: (06) 6721061. 8am–4pm.

The Christian Information Centre, inside the Old City's Jaffa Gate, opposite the Citadel (tel: 02-6287647) offers information on all churches, monasteries and other Christian shrines. The office also issues certificates of Christian pilgrimage.

Baptismal Sites

An organised baptismal site has been erected at the mouth of the River Jordan, 8 km (5 miles) south of Tiberias. There are three levels of platforms in the water and descent is by steps or a wheelchair-accessible ramp. There is ample space for groups. The site is open during daylight hours.

Media

Access to news is very important for Israelis, due to their unique geopolitical situation. Listening to hourly news updates on the radio in taxis, buses, as well as in private homes is part of the daily routine. There is censorship but only in security matters.

Print

Israelis are prolific newspaper readers. With several dozen daily newspapers and countless weekly and monthly magazines, they read more newspapers per head of the population than almost any other country in the world. Most of these newspapers are in Hebrew, the two largest being the afternoon journals Yediot Ahronot and

Ma'ariv, which each sell over 500,000 copies of their Friday (weekend) edition. Remember there are only 5.8 million Israelis.

The Jerusalem Post is published in English six days a week (except Saturday). Founded in 1932, the paper was originally owned by the Histadrut Trade Union Movement and supported the Labor Party. But in 1990 it was sold to Conrad Black's Canadian-based Hollinger Corporation for $17 million. Hollinger also owns Britain's Daily Telegraph group. Under new management, the Jerusalem Post supports the right-wing Likud. The Time Out section of the Friday paper is the only English listings of what's going on in the arts, music, theatre, television and radio. The paper also carries useful information about medical services and religious services, etc.

The Jerusalem Report is an English language fortnightly magazine that gives comprehensive news and features insights into Israeli life. It offers a more centre-left alternative to the Jerusalem Post.

There is also a dynamic Arab press with over 20 publications including six dailies and six weeklies. The Israeli Arab press is based in Haifa, while journals printed in East Jerusalem are aimed at a readership in the West Bank and Gaza.

The size and impact of the recent waves of immigration from Russia can be measured by its press. There are a dozen national papers printed in Russian, most of which are dailies. In addition there are several weeklies in French, Spanish, Amharic, Hungarian, Romanian and many other languages.

Many of the leading newspapers and magazines from Western Europe and North America are available at newsagents the day after publication.

Broadcast Media

The Israel Broadcasting Authority (IBA) is a government-run organisation modelled on Britain's BBC and has two channels. Programmes include a 15-minute news bulletin in English (currently at 6.15pm). Channel 2 is a commercial station, and then there is cable television which offers subscribers 30 channels including BBC World Service, CNN and Sky. In addition, Israelis can receive the broadcasts of all its neighbours including two English lan-

guage stations, Middle East Television from Lebanon and Jordan's Channel 6.

The IBA has a comprehensive radio service broadcasting on six networks. On the foreign language service there are English language news bulletins at 7am, 1pm and 5pm. Other Israeli stations include the BBC World Service, Voice of America and Jordan's English language radio station.

Post & Telephone

Postal Services

Israel's post offices have many branches and can be identified by a logo of a white stag leaping across a red background. Post boxes are red for out of town and international mail, and yellow for letters within the city. Letters take 7–10 days to reach Europe and America. Express service takes half the time and super Express (very expensive) about one-third of the time.

Post office hours are from 8am–12.30pm and 3.30–6pm. Major post offices are open all day. On Friday afternoon, Saturday and holidays post offices are closed all day.

Telephone

Phone books are only in Hebrew. Numbers can be obtained from Information (tel: 144) which operates an English language service, though callers are charged the cost of one unit for each enquiry.

Public telephone booths can be found throughout the country. Most function when telephone cards are inserted. These cards can be bought at post offices and newsagents. Restaurants, cafés and bars usually have coin-operated phones which are more expensive than card-operated phones. At major tourist sites, some telephones accept international credit cards and this can be a convenient way of making overseas calls. Many private companies lease out cellular phones for about $5 per day but the cost of calls on cellular phones is much cheaper than in Western Europe and North America.

Domestic regular phone calls are most expensive between 8am and 1pm. There is a 25 percent reduction from 1–8pm and a 50 percent reduction from 8pm–8am. There is also a 50 percent reduction from Friday at 1pm through Saturday.

02 – Jerusalem
03 – Tel Aviv
04 – Haifa
06 – The Galilee and north
07 – The South including Eilat, Beersheba and Ashkelon
08 – Ashdod, Rehovot
09 – Herzlia, Netanya
050 – Pelephone cellular phone network
052 – Cellcom cellular phone network

Overseas calls can be booked through post offices listed below, or the international operator 188 or through 03-622881. International phone calls from hotels are often very expensive (perhaps three times the actual price). Alternatively, using the 177 toll-free number you will be connected to an operator abroad who can place reverse charge calls or debit your credit card or subscriber account.

The numbers to call are:
Canada: tel: 177-430 2727.
UK: British Telecom, tel: 177-440 2727.
US: AT&T, tel: 177-100-2727; MCI, tel: 177 150-2727; Sprint, tel: 177-102-2727.

To dial abroad first dial 00, then the country code (44 for Britain, 1 for the US and Canada and 61 for Australia), then the area code (but omitting any initial zeroes) followed by the number.

International phone calls are most expensive (except for North America) on weekdays from 8am–10pm. There is a 25 percent reduction from 10pm–1am and all day Saturday and Sunday, and a 50 percent reduction from 1–8am.

To North America the most expensive rate is from 1pm until midnight. There is a 20 percent reduction from 8am until 1pm and all day Saturday and Sunday, and a 45 percent reduction from midnight until 8am.

Post offices with international telephone call facilities:
Jerusalem: 3 Rehov Koresh, tel: 02-6249858
Tel Aviv: 13 Rehov Frishman, tel: 03-5244365
Eilat: The Old Commercial Center, Hatamarim Boulevard, tel: 07-6372323
Tiberias: Pedestrian Mall, tel: 06-6739218

USEFUL NUMBERS

Police: tel: 100.
Ambulance: tel: 101.
Fire Service: tel: 102.
Collect calls: tel: 142.
Information: tel: 144.
Telephone Repairs: tel: 166.
Overseas Operator: tel: 188.
Overseas Collect Calls: tel: 03-622881.
Direct Dialling Information: tel: 195.
Telegrams, tel: 171.

RECORDED MESSAGES

By dialling (03) 5160259 tourists can receive information on events in the Tel Aviv area. Tourists can also leave a message if they have any questions, and they will have their call returned the next day by a member of staff. This service operates after 6pm Sunday–Thursday and Friday after 3pm.

Jerusalem has a similar service. Dial (02) 6754863 after 6pm Sunday–Thursday and after 2pm on Friday.

Haifa has a 24-hour telephone service to hear "What's on in Haifa", tel: (04) 8640840.

Internet Information

Israel's Ministry of Tourism has an excellent site offering information about the country, accommodation, restaurants, transport etc. at: http://www.israel-mfa.gov.il/sites.html (under "sites" choose "tourism").

Information about Israel can be found from the Foreign Ministry's site. URL:http//www-mfa.gov.il

Alternatively information about Israel and Jerusalem can be found at the following Jewish net sites: http://www1.huji.ac.il/jeru/moreinfo.html and http://www1.huji.ac.il//jerusalem.html

Tourist Information

Akko, Municipal Building, tel: 04-9910251.
Allenby Bridge, tel: 02-9922471.
Arad, 28 Ben Yair Street, tel: 07-9954409.
Ben Gurion Airport, tel: 03-9711485.
Bethlehem, Manger Square, tel: 02-9711485.
Eilat, Yotam Street, tel: 07-6372111.
Haifa: 106 Hanassi Avenue, tel: 04-8374010; 20 Herzl Boulevard, tel: 04-8666521/2.
Jerusalem: 17 Jaffa Street, tel: 02-6258844.

Jaffa Gate, tel: 02-6280382.
Nahariya: City Hall Building, tel: 04-9879800.
Nazareth: Casa Nova Street, tel: 06-6573003.
Netanya, Haîatzmaut Square, tel: 09-9573003.
Safed, 50 Yerushalayim Street, tel: 06-6920961.
Tel Aviv, New Central Bus Station, tel: 03-6395660.
Tiberias, 23 Habanim Street, tel: 06-6725666.

Embassies & Consulates

Most embassies are closed on Sunday.
Australian Embassy, 37 Shaul Hamelekh Boulevard, Tel Aviv, tel: (03) 6950451.
Canadian Embassy, 220 Rehov Hayarkon, 63405 Tel Aviv, tel: (03) 5272929. Visa section, 7 Havkuk Street, tel: (03) 5442878.
Embassy of The Republic of South Africa, Dizengoff 50 (Dizengoff Tower), tel: (03) 5252566; fax: (03) 5253230.
UK Embassy, 192 Rehov Hayarkon, Tel Aviv 63405, tel: (03) 5249171. Consular Section, 1 Ben Yehuda tel: (03) 5100166; fax: (03) 5101167.
Embassy of The United States of America, 71 Rehov Hayarkon,Tel Aviv 63903, tel: (03) 5197575; fax: (03) 5103830.

In Jerusalem

UK: 19 Nashabibi Street, Sheikh Jarrah, tel: (02) 5828281/5828482; fax: (02) 5322368.
US: 16 Agron Street, tel: (02) 6253288 (West Jerusalem); 27 Derech Shechem, tel: (02) 6282452 (East Jerusalem).

OTHER USEFUL ADDRESSES

American Cultural Center, Keren Hayesod Street 19, Jerusalem, tel: (02) 6255755.
British Council Library, 3 Abu Ovadia Street, Jerusalem, tel: (02) 6283021; 140 Hayarkon Street, Tel Aviv, tel: (03) 5222194.

Emergencies

Security & Crime

Israel has a high rate of non-violent crimes (theft of homes, cars, property, pickpocketing, etc.) but little violent crime (mugging, murder and rape). So do not leave valuables in hotel rooms, or cars, or wallets sticking out of pockets. Take all usual precautions.

In terms of violent crime the security situation is the most pressing problem but incidents are few and far between. Under no circumstances leave unattended baggage lying around in a public place. Police sappers will blow it up within a few minutes. You should report all suspicious packages.

Before taking trips to the West Bank or Gaza you should ask about the prevailing security situation there.

To contact the police, tel: 100.

DRUG OFFENCES
Hashish is illegal but prosecutions are rarely brought. Because neighbouring Lebanon supplies much of the world's hashish, the drug is widely available in Israel with peddlers frequenting bars. Heroin, also grown in Lebanon, is taken much more seriously by the Israeli authorities.

Legal Representation
If you need a lawyer there are bound to be many who have emigrated to Israel from your country of origin and most lawyers speak English. Your consulate can probably suggest some names.

Lost Property
Egged Lost Property (buses), tel: (02) 5304766. Otherwise phone the local police station (tel: 100).

Medical Services
Visitors are advised to have medical insurance because in a worst case scenario hospital bills can reach astronomical levels. Israel has a developed medical system in which the most advanced techniques from laser surgery to laparoscopic procedures are routine. Even before the recent influx of new immigrants, Israel had the highest ratio of doctors in the world.

MEDICAL EQUIPMENT
Visitors temporarily in need of such medical equipment as oxygen tanks, wheelchairs, vaporisers, and a large number of other items can obtain them on loan, at no charge, at the Yad Sarah Organization for the Free Loan of Medical Equipment, Jerusalem. Book at least two weeks before your visit, Yad Sarah, 43 Haneviim Street, 95141 Jerusalem, tel: (02)-6244242; fax: (02) 6244493.

EMERGENCY TREATMENT
Dial 101 to summon an ambulance or for information about the nearest hospital receiving casualties. If you want to see a doctor urgently, you can go to a Magen David Adom ambulance station at night, or the emergency room of any hospital (remember 101 will give you details).

Most doctors will be happy to see patients privately for about $40 a consultation. The tourist magazines are usually filled with adverts for medical services provided by US- and Europe-trained doctors.

If in pain, Israelis tend to be expressive. So if you are sitting in the emergency room of a hospital with an appendix that is about to burst, go ahead and yell. If you stoically play the strong silent type, then staff will tend to assume you are not really in pain and others will be treated before you.

DENTISTS
If you stroll around the area near your hotel you are bound to come across dental surgeries.

PHARMACISTS
Most pharmacists are helpful and used to dealing with tourists. The *Jerusalem Post* will tell you which pharmacy is on all night or weekend duty. Routine prescription drugs like antibiotics are frequently sold over the counter even though this is illegal.

Getting Around

From the Airport
An El Al airport bus leaves Ben-Gurion Airport Terminal in Tel Aviv (some 20 minutes away) approximately every hour from 6am–10pm and in accordance with the arrival of planes at other hours.

Egged buses leave for Tel Aviv every 15 minutes 5am–11.10pm; for Jerusalem (one hour away) about every 20 minutes from 7.15am–6pm; for Haifa (1½ hours) from 7am–6pm approximately every 20 minutes.

United Tours Bus No. 222 travels between the airport and the Railway Station, Rehove Arlosorov, Tel Aviv, every hour year-round. The service operates from 4am–midnight. The bus stops at the Palace, Diplomat, Sheraton and Dan hotels. For further details, tel: (03) 7543410.

Sherut taxis (Nesher), in which each passenger pays for his own seat, take less than an hour to reach the centre of Jerusalem.

Ordinary taxis are available to almost any point in the country. The fare is fixed and the tourist may ask to be shown the official price list. The cost of a taxi to Tel Aviv is about $10–15, or $22–30 to Jerusalem. *Sherut* service is considerably less expensive.

Internal Flights
Arkia Israel Airlines Ltd operate the following scheduled flights:
From Jerusalem–Tel Aviv–Haifa–Rosh Pinna–Eilat.
From Tel Aviv–Jerusalem–Rosh Pinna–Eilat.
From Haifa–Jerusalem–Tel Aviv–Eilat.
From Eilat–Jerusalem–Tel Aviv–Haifa.

A number of other companies operate charter flights (3–10 passengers) to various parts of the country. Further particulars may be obtained from travel agents. El-Rom Airlines operate air taxi services from Beersheba to Tel Aviv, Eilat, Jerusalem and Haifa and from Tel Aviv to Mitzpeh Ramon and Sodom.

For further information:
Arkia Israeli Airlines Ltd, Sde Dov Airport, Tel Aviv, tel: (03) 6992222.
El-Rom Airlines Ltd, Sde Dov Airport, Tel Aviv, tel: (03) 5412554.

AIRPORTS
Ben-Gurion International Airport, tel: (03) 9710111.
Eilat, tel: (07) 6373333.
Haifa, tel: (04) 8722084.
Herzliya, tel: (09) 9502373.
Jerusalem, tel: (02) 5850980.
Rosh Pinna (North), tel: (06) 6936478.
Sde Dov Tel Aviv, tel: (03) 6991058.
Uvda, tel: (07) 6339442.

Public Transport

Buses
Buses are by far the most common means of transportation for both urban and inter-urban services. Services are

regular and the fares are reasonable though prices have risen substantially in recent years due to the withdrawal of government subsidies.

Most buses in Israel are operated by the Egged Bus Cooperative, one of the largest bus companies in the world. Buses are air-conditioned and Egged operates all urban and inter-urban services except within Tel Aviv. Services are punctual and, if anything, impatient drivers tend to leave half a minute before time. If travelling to Eilat, it is advisable to reserve seats several days in advance.

An intra-urban flat fare ticket costs about $1.25 and a Jerusalem–Tel Aviv ticket costs $6. Tel Aviv–Eilat costs $25. Return tickets are cheaper, and there are tickets allowing unlimited travel anywhere in Israel over a period of 7, 14, 21 days or a month.

Buses do not run from Friday before sundown until Saturday after sundown. Inter-urban bus services start around 6am and finish in the early evening except for the Tel Aviv–Jerusalem and Tel Aviv–Haifa lines which continue until midnight. Urban services run from 5am–midnight.

Egged Information:
Jerusalem: tel: (02) 5304555.
Tel Aviv: tel: (03) 5375555.
Haifa: tel: (04) 8549555.
Eilat: tel: (07) 6373148.

The Jerusalem Central Bus Station is in Rehov Jaffa near the western entrance to the city. The Tel Aviv Central Bus Station is a vast shopping mall complex on Levinsky Street in the south of the city and the Haifa Central Bus Station is on the Tel Aviv highway at the city's southern entrance.

For information about Dan bus lines in Tel Aviv: tel: (03) 6394444

Trains

Israel Railways run from Haifa and Nahariya in the north and from Tel Aviv to Jerusalem, on a daily basis. Fares are considerably lower than bus fares, and seats can be reserved in advance for a small extra charge.

Most of the trains are rather old, but all of them have a buffet car and service. The trip from Tel Aviv to Jerusalem is a particularly lovely train route, winding through the scenic Sorek valley.

There is no train service on the Sabbath, or on Jewish holidays.

Train information: tel: (03) 6937515.
Main Train Stations:
Haifa: Bat Galim, tel: (04) 8564564.
Jerusalem: Kikar Remez, tel: (02) 6733764.
Tel Aviv: Central Station, Rehov Arlosorov, tel: (03) 5421515.
Student Discount: A 10 percent discount on all inter-city Egged Bus Company trips and a 25 percent on Israel Railways is available on presentation of a student card.

Metro

Israel's only subway operates in Haifa. Metro buffs will enjoy this recently renovated system which is in fact an underground cable car. It is also the quickest way of getting about Haifa. The train runs from Central Mount Carmel to downtown Haifa every 10 minutes and makes six stops. The trip takes 9 minutes. It operates Sunday to Thursday 5.30am–midnight and Friday 5.30am to 1 hour before the Sabbath, Saturday from sunset to midnight.

Taxis & Sherut

Taxis offer a quick and convenient mode of travel in Israel. You can phone for a taxi in any major city or hail one in the street.

All urban taxis have meters, whose operation is compulsory. If the driver wants to take it off the meter, he might be trying to take you for a ride in more ways than one. Tipping is not compulsory, but often greatly appreciated.

Prices are pre-fixed between cities, and the driver will tell you your fare ahead of time, or show you the official price list if you ask for it.

The *sherut* is Israel's own indigenous mode of transportation, operating in and between main cities every day but *Shabbat*; some private companies or owners operate on *Shabbat* as well. Individuals share a van or cab, which accommodates up to seven people, at a fixed price usually equivalent to the bus fare for the same route.

Sheruts between cities leave from near the central bus station, and, in Jerusalem, from near Zion Square. In Tel Aviv and some other cities, local *sheruts* follow the main bus routes, making similar stops in quicker time.

Driving

Israelis drive with Mediterranean creativity. There is a lot of horn honking, overtaking on the inside and general improvisation. But life on the road is not as chaotic as in many other Mediterranean countries. With well over one million vehicles on the roads, Israel has one of the world's densest road systems. There are around 500 fatalities each year from road accidents, which is comparable with death rates on Western European roads.

Laws are strictly enforced and it is necessary to wear seat belts at all times and strap children under four into appropriate seats. Speed limits are 90–100 kph (55–60 mph) on highways and 50–70 kph (30–40 mph) in urban areas. Keep your passport, driver's licence and other papers with you at all times. Police tend to be lenient with tourists but can take you straight in front of a judge if they wish.

Fuel is cheaper in Israel than Western Europe but more expensive than America. In Eilat there is no 17 percent VAT charge on fuel.

PARKING

Parking is very difficult in the major city centres and it is best to look for a parking lot. These can cost $1.50 an hour in Jerusalem, and up to $3 per hour in parts of Tel Aviv. If a kerbside is marked in blue and white, you need a ticket which you can purchase in batches of five from kiosks, lottery kiosks and stores. Each ticket costs about 90 cents and allows you to park for an hour. You must tear out the right time, month and day and display the ticket on the kerbside window. These tickets must be displayed from 7am–7pm. Outside these hours, parking is usually free, though it is prohibited in some residential areas of Tel Aviv.

If you fail to display a ticket or the ticket has expired, you are liable for a $20 fine, though this need not be paid for several months.

Do not ignore red and white marked kerbsides or No Parking signs. Here you may be clamped with a "Denver boot" or towed away. In either instance, it will cost you $20 (or more) and a lot of wasted time in redeeming your car.

HIRING A CAR

Many of the world's principal car hire companies, including Hertz, Avis, Euro-Car, Inter-Rent, Budget and Thrifty, have outlets in Israel. Israel's largest car hire company, Eldan, also has offices overseas. These companies can supply you with a car at the airport and allow you to leave it there on departure. They have a network of offices around the country. In addition, if you break down a new car is almost immediately at your service.

But hiring a car is expensive (at least $300 a week for a small 1200cc or 1300cc saloon). Traffic is usually heavy and parking is difficult in Israel's big cities, so for urban travel it is probably cheaper and more convenient to take taxis.

Hiring a car can be cheaper off-season (between October and April) or if you cut a deal with one of the many local, smaller companies. But in general it is much cheaper to book a car as part of a package deal (flight, hotel, car) with your travel agent overseas.

As everywhere in the world, carefully check that there is no damage to the car, that the spare wheel, jack and other equipment is in place and that oil and water are sufficient before accepting a car.

Car hire companies require an international driving licence or will accept national licences if written in English or French.

Hertz: 18 King David Street, Jerusalem, tel: (02) 6256334; 144 Hayarkon, Tel Aviv, tel: (03) 5223332.
Avis: 22 King David Street, Jerusalem, tel: (02) 6249001/3; 113 Hayarkon, Tel Aviv, tel: (03) 6884242.
Eldan: 24 King David Street, Jerusalem, tel: (02) 6252151; Tel Aviv, tel: (03) 6394343. Internet: http://www.eldan.co.il/
Reliable: 14 King David Street, Jerusalem, tel: (02) 6248204/5; 112 Hayarkon, Tel Aviv, tel: (03) 5249764.

On Foot

PEDESTRIANS

Drivers cannot be relied upon to stop at pedestrian crossings. The safest place to cross is at traffic lights but only when the pedestrian light is green. In Jerusalem, police hand out fines to pedestrians who cross at red lights. Beware at right turn filters where the pedestrian light is green but traffic may still pass.

HITCHHIKING

Hitchhiking is a conventional way of getting around in Israel. There are even hitchhiking stations at major junctions that look like bus stops. But hitchhiking can still be difficult because of the fierce competition and the fact that priority is given to soldiers. Women should always be wary of predatory male drivers.

Where to Stay

Accommodation

There is a diverse range of accommodation options in Israel including over 300 hotels and dozens of youth hostels. But there is a certain sameness about Israeli hotels, most of which were built between 1960 and 1980, offering modern comfort and convenience without any character. Kibbutz Guest Houses and Christian hospices offer a unique taste of Israel.

Kibbutz Guest Houses

Visitors wanting an Israeli experience should try a kibbutz guest house. The guest house itself usually offers all the facilities of a luxury hotel plus the chance to get acquainted with kibbutz life at first hand. Though many of these guest houses are in isolated rural areas, especially in the northern Galilee, others are located in the country but just 20 minutes or so by bus or car from Jerusalem or Tel Aviv.

For further information, contact Kibbutz Hotels Chain, 90 Rehov Ben Yehuda, Tel Aviv 61031, tel: (03) 5243358.

Following is a list of recommended kibbutz guest houses (moderate prices):

Mitzpeh Rachel, Kibbutz Ramat Rachel (near Jerusalem), tel: (02) 6702555. Though within the city limits the kibbutz grounds offer a stirring view of the Judean Desert.
Neve Ilan, D.N. Hare Yehuda (near Je-rusalem), tel: (02) 5348111; fax: (02) 5348197. Pleasant country club atmosphere 20 minutes by bus from Jerusalem with view of coastal plain.
Shefayim Guest House, Kibbutz Shefayim, tel: (09) 9523434. Close to the Mediterranean coast and a short bus ride away from Tel Aviv.
Kfar Blum Guest House, Kibbutz Kfar Blum, tel: (06) 6943666. Beneath the snowcapped Mount Hermon in the Upper Galilee. The River Jordan flows through this kibbutz.

Christian Hospices

Another unique Holy Land experience is the broad array of Christian hospices. Originally designed principally for pilgrims and owned by churches, these hospices cater for all comers, including many Israeli Jews on vacation, who enjoy the old-world European charm of these establishments.

The term hospice is misleading. Some, like Notre Dame in Jerusalem, owned by the Vatican, resemble luxury hotels. Others reflect the ethnic origins of their founders. The Sisters of Zion in the Jerusalem suburb of Ein Kerem resembles a pension in Provence, while St Andrew's Church in Jerusalem could be a guest house anywhere in Scotland and even serves mince pies and mulled wine at Christmas.

In Jerusalem

Notre Dame, Opposite the New Gate, tel: (02) 6281223. Luxurious accommodation, splendid 19th-century architecture and one of Jerusalem's best (non-kosher) restaurants. Superbly appointed opposite the Old City walls. Owned by the Vatican. Expensive.
YMCA, King David Street, tel: (02) 6253433. Stylish 1930's building opposite the King David Hotel. Recently refurbished and made more up market. Expensive.
St Andrews Scots Memorial Hospice (opposite the railway station), tel: (02) 6732401. Intimate guest house atmosphere in central location. No kippers but there is sometimes haggis. Moderate.
Our Sisters of Zion, Ein Kerem, tel: (02) 6415738. Delightful Provence-style pension in Ein Kerem. Spacious gardens filled with olive trees and grape vines and comfortable accommodation. Moderate.

Until recently, Israel's Ministry of Tourism graded hotels from one up to five stars according to size, service and facilities. This system has now been discontinued.

Hotels require guests to check out by midday but on Saturday and holidays guests are entitled to retain possession of their rooms until the sabbath or holiday finishes in the evening. Check-in is usually after 3pm.

Hotel prices are high if you simply turn up. It is much cheaper to arrange a package deal before leaving. Whereas a luxury hotel can charge $100 or even $150 a night, a one week package deal at a luxury hotel in Jerusalem, Tel Aviv or Eilat including a return flight from Britain can usually be found for less than $500. Prices can be even more expensive during high season Easter/Passover, July to August, Jewish New Year and Christmas. But there are hotels catering for every pocket down to youth hostels which charge $10–15 a night.

Hotel rates are generally quoted in dollars and include a 15 percent service charge. If you pay in foreign currency you are exempt from 17 percent VAT. In Eilat there is no VAT charge.

Dead Sea

INEXPENSIVE

Tsell Harim, Ein Bokek, Dead Sea, tel: (07) 6584757. Cheap and comfortable the hotel is located by the sea.

Eilat

EXPENSIVE

Princess Hotel, Nr Taba border, Eilat, tel: (07) 6365555; fax: (07) 6376333. Well away from the town near the Egyptian border, this hotel is a self-contained complex of swimming pools and restaurants.
Royal Beach, North Beach, Eilat, tel: (07) 6368888; fax: (07) 6368811. Large hotel with a diverse array of restaurants and pools.

MODERATE

Lagoona, North Beach Eilat, tel: (07) 6332089. Tranquil location north of the city on the lagoona also offers a good view of the Red Sea.

Red Rock, POB 306, Eilat, tel: (07) 6373171. Great location by the beach and near the centre of town; otherwise comfortable but unexceptional.

INEXPENSIVE

Moon Valley, POB 1135, Eilat, tel: (07) 6333888. Cheap, clean and comfortable. It's as well the hotel has its own swimming pool because it is a 10-minute walk from the beach.
Etzion, 1 Sderot Hatamarim, Eilat, tel: (07) 6370003. Far from the beach but in town and by the central bus station.

Haifa

EXPENSIVE

Dan Carmel, 85–87 Hanasi Boulevard, Haifa, tel: (04) 8306211. The city's most sylish hotel located on Mount Carmel with a breathtaking panorama of Haifa Bay and the azure-coloured Mediterranean.

Jerusalem

EXPENSIVE

King David Hotel, 23 King David Street, Jerusalem, tel: (02) 6208888; fax: (02) 6232303. Israel's premiere hotel where political leaders, the rich and famous stay. It has style and an old-world ambience but in terms of quality of service its newer rivals try harder. Has beautiful gardens overlooking the Old City.
Laromme, 3 Jabotinsky Street, Jerusalem, tel: (02) 6756666; fax: (02) 6756777. Overlooking the Liberty Bell Garden, this delightfully designed hotel has attracted some world leaders away from the King David.
Hyatt Regency, 32 Lehi Street, Mount Scopus, Jerusalem, tel: (02) 5331234; fax: (02) 5323196. Stylish interior and external design which blends into the hillside and commands a splendid view of the Old City.
Dan Pearl, POB 793, Jerusalem, tel: (02) 6226666; fax: (02) 6226649. Jerusalem's newest hotel is superbly located opposite the Old City walls near the Jaffa Gate.

MODERATE

American Colony, Nablus Street, Jerusalem, tel: (02) 6285171; fax: (02) 6279779. Jerusalem's oldest hotel has much character and charm and is favoured by the foreign press corps on account of its location between West and East Jerusalem.
Holyland Hotel, Bayit Vegan, Jerusalem, tel: (02) 6437777; fax: (02) 6437744. Away from town near the Second Temple model, the Holyland has a laid-back ambience and great view of West Jerusalem.
Windmill Hotel, 3 Mendele Street, Jerusalem, tel: (02) 5663111; fax: (02) 5610964. Comfortable and convenient and well located for walks into both the new and old City.
Reich Hotel, Bet Hakerem, Jerusalem, tel: (02) 6523121; fax: (02) 6523120. Relch Hotel is located in the salubrious leafy suburbs of Bet Hakerem, the hotel is not far from the city and the bus station.

INEXPENSIVE

Ron Hotel, Zion Square, Jerusalem, tel: (02) 6253471; fax: (02) 6250707. Smack in the centre of West Jerusalem, this hotel has an old world charm. Its balconies are somtimes rented out to politicians for addressing political rallies.
Palatin Hotel, King George Street, Jerusalem, tel: (02) 6231141; fax: (02) 6259323. Clean and comfortable with central location in West Jerusalem.
Caesar Hotel, 208 Jaffa Street, Jerusalem, tel: (02) 5005656. Modern and non-descript but right by the central bus station, this hotel is ideal for itinerant tourists.
Itzik Hotel, 141 Jaffa Street, tel: (02) 6233730; fax: (02) 6243879. Newly opened comfortable and clean with interesting location in the heart of the Mahane Yehuda fruit and vegetable market.

Netanya

MODERATE

King Solomon, 11 Hmaapilim Street, Netanya, tel: (09) 8338444; fax: (09) 8611397. Pick of the budget priced hotels in Netanya. Near the beach and centre of town.

INEXPENSIVE

Yahalom Hotel, 11 Rehov Gad Machness Street, Netanya, tel: (09) 8635345. Located in Netanya's hotel district opposite the sea; makes a pleasant base for seeing the entire country.

Safed

EXPENSIVE

Rimon Inn, Artists Quarter, Safed, tel: (06) 6920665; fax: (06) 6920456; 177-022-7676 (toll free). The best hotel in the Galilee with relaxing hillside views.

INEXPENSIVE

Central Hotel, 37 Rehov Yerushalaim, Safed, tel: (09) 6972666. In the heart of Safed by the quaint artists' colony and synagogue neighbourhood. Makes a good base for seeing the Galilee.

Tel Aviv

EXPENSIVE

Tel Aviv Hilton, Independence Park, Tel Aviv, tel: (03) 5202222; fax: (03) 5272711. Generally accepted as the city's most luxurious hotel. Very fashionable with Tel Aviv high society, with prices to match.

Tel Aviv Sheraton, 115 Hayarkon Street, Tel Aviv, tel: (03) 5211111; fax: (03) 5233322. Challenges the Hilton's claim to be the city's paramount hotel.

MODERATE

Adiv Hotel, 5 Mendele Street, Tel Aviv, tel: (03) 5229141; fax: (03) 5229144. Friendly, comfortable and convenient with self-service restaurant. Situated just over the road from the seafront and beach.

Imperial Hotel, 66 Hayarkon Street, Tel Aviv, tel: (03) 5177002. In the heart of the city's hotel district, this comfortable hotel is well located for the beach and walks to the Dizengoff shopping and nightlife district.

INEXPENSIVE

Deborah Hotel, Ben Yehuda Street, Tel Aviv, tel: (03) 5278282. Pleasant hotel and location in the northern part of the city though its a 5-minute walk from the beach.

Tiberias

MODERATE

Galei Kinneret, 1 Eliezer Kaplan, Tiberias, tel: (06) 6792331. On the lakeside in Tiberias, this is one of the city's oldest and most stylish hotels.

Bed & Breakfast

With the exception on the Galilee, there is a very limited amount of B&B accommodation in Israel, partly because Israelis live in relatively small apartments.

Good Morning Jerusalem, tel: (02) 6511270, located in the International Congress Centre opposite the bus station, gives information on all available B&Bs in the city. Overnight prices are no more than $60 per couple.

Moshav Amirim in the Galilee, tel: (06) 6989572; fax: (06) 6980772, offers B&B with vegetarian meals. In fact, Amirim is a vegetarian village with a great view of the Sea of Galilee.

For Bed & Breakfast in Eilat, try the **Garden of Eden**, 14 Rotemim Street, tel: (07) 6371306.

Holiday Apartments

For a longer stay in one place, it can be very economical to rent an apartment, with its own kitchen, bedroom, living room, etc. For families it can mean a cheap way of accommodating the kids; for couples, individuals or groups it can mean a more natural experience of the country, living as the locals do, away from bellhops and room service.

Here, too, options range from the economical to the luxurious.

Dahum, 6 Frishman Street, Tel Aviv, tel: (03) 5222695.

Bet Rotman, 17 David Remez Street, Nahariya, tel: (04) 9921017.

Nitzan, 704/14, Eilat, tel: (07) 6379037.

Campgrounds

Israel is good for camping, with camp sites providing an excellent touring base for each region. They offer full sanitary facilities, electric current, a restaurant and/or store, telephone, first-aid facilities, shaded picnic and campfire areas and day and night watchmen. They can be reached by bus, but all are open to cars and caravans. Most have tents and cabins, as well as a wide range of equipment for hire. All sites have swimming facilities either on the site or within easy reach.

There is a reception and departure service for campers at Ben-Gurion Airport. By telephoning (03) 944524 on arrival, a camping car comes within a very short time to take participants to the reception camping site at Mishmar Hashiva, about 10 km (6 miles) from Ben-Gurion Airport. A similar service is available from Mishmar Hashiva to the airport upon departure, if you stay the last night there.

Arriving campers can obtain assistance from the Tourist Information Office in the Arrivals Hall of the airport. At the reception camp at Mishmar Hashiva, campers are given maps and folders and are individually advised on touring the country.

Reception Site: Mishmar Hashiva, tel: (03) 9604524.

CAMPING SITES

Bet Zait (near Jerusalem), tel: (02) 5346217.
Ein Gedi (by Dead Sea), tel: (07) 6584342.
Eilot (near Eilat), tel (07) 6374362.
Neve Yam (near Haifa), tel: (04) 8844827.
Kibbutz Maayan Baruch (Upper Galilee), tel: (06) 6954601.

Youth Hostels

There are nearly 30 youth hostels throughout the country, operated by the Israel Youth Hostel Association (IYHA) which is affiliated with the international YHA. They offer dormitory accommodations and most of them provide meals and self-service kitchen facilities. There is no age limit. Some hostels also provide family accommodation. Individual reservations should be made directly with the hostel.

The IYHA arranges package tours, called "Israel on the Youth Hostel Trail" for 14, 21 or 28 days. These include nights in any of the hostels with dinner and breakfast, unlimited bus travel, a half-day conducted tour, entrance to 31 National Parks and numerous museums, a map, and other informational materials.

For further information contact:
Head Office–IYHA, 3 Rehov Dorot Rishonim, POB l075, 91009 Jerusalem, tel: (02) 6252706.
Acco, POB 1090, Acco, tel: (04) 9911982.
Beit Bernstein, 1 Rehov Keren Hayesod, 94266 Jerusalem, tel: (02) 6258286.
Beit Sara, Ein Gedi, 86910 MP Dead Sea, tel: (07) 6584165.

Beit Yatziv, POB 7, Beersheba, tel: (07) 671490/677444.

Carmel, MP Hof Hacarmel, Haifa, tel: (04) 8532516.

Eilat, POB 152, Eilat, tel: (07) 6370088.

Ein Kerem, POB 17013, 91170 Jerusalem, tel: (02) 6416282.

Ramot Shapira, POB 7216, Beit Meir, Jerusalem, tel: (02) 5342691.

Taiber, Poriah, POB 232, Tiberias, tel: (06) 6750050.

Tel Aviv, 32 Rehov Bnei Dan, Tel Aviv, tel: (03) 5441748.

Tel Hai, MP Upper Galilee, Tel Hai, tel: (06) 6940043.

Y.H. Taylor, 86901 MP Dead Sea, Massada, tel: (07) 6584349.

Yoram, MP Korazim, Kare Deshe, tel: (06) 6720601.

Yoseph Mayouhas, POB 81, Tiberias, tel: (06) 6721775.

Eating Out

What to Eat

Eating is a national pastime in Israel, one engaged in as much and as often as possible. On the street, at the beach, in every public place and in every home, day and night – you'll find Israelis tucking in to food.

The biblical residents of the Land of Canaan were nourished by the fertility and abundance of a land "flowing with milk and honey". But the milk was mainly from sheep and goats, and the honey from dates, figs and carobs. Much depended on the sun, the rains and the seasons. Food was simple; feast predictably followed famine. Times have changed – at least in the culinary sense.

Just as Israel is a blend of cultures from all over the world, so its cuisine is a weave of flavours and textures, contrasts and similarities. There is no definitive Israeli fare, just as there is no definitive Israeli. Rather, there is a unique merging of East and West, and the results are a profusion of culinary delights.

The predominant food style reflects the country's geographical location –

somewhere between the Middle East and the Mediterranean. Dining out? Don't be led astray by signs telling you that the establishment serves "oriental" food. "Oriental" refers to the Middle East. "Oriental" Jews are those of Sephardic (Spanish, Italian or Arab) heritage. Each Jewish ethnic group, whether Moroccan, Libyan, Tunisian, Yemenite, Iraqi or native born (sabra) Israeli, has its own special dish and its own holiday fare.

Their food is similar yet distinct from each other. Basic herbs and spices include cumin, fresh and dried coriander, mint, garlic, onion, turmeric, black pepper, and sometimes cardamom and fresh green chilli. Dark, fruity olive oil adds further fragrance.

Arabic food is also considered "Oriental" and both Arabic and Jewish meals begin the same way – with a variety of savoury salads. Humus, ground chick pea seasoned with tahina (sesame paste), lemon juice, garlic and cumin – is probably the most popular dip, spread and salad rolled into one. You'll also find the most astounding variety of eggplant (aubergine) salads you've ever seen; eggplant in tahina, fried sliced eggplant, chopped eggplant with vegetables, chopped liver-flavoured eggplant and more. Assorted pickled vegetables are considered salads as well.

While the waiters may show some sign of disappointment, you can order a selection of these salads as a meal in itself. Or you can follow it with kebab (grilled ground spiced meat), shashlik (grilled sliced lamb or beef with lamb fat), seniya (beef or lamb in tahina sauce), stuffed chicken or pigeon, chops or fish.

Don't expect pork in either a kosher or traditional Muslim restaurant. Both religions prohibit its consumption. Seafood, while forbidden by Jewish and permissible by Muslim law, is widely available. Shrimps and calamari are the predominant varieties.

Do try the fish, particularly in the seaside areas of Tiberias, Tel Aviv, Jaffa and Eilat (there are no fish in the Dead Sea). Trout, grey and red mullet, sea bass and St Peter's fish are generally served fried or grilled, sometimes accompanied by a piquant sauce. Authentic North African restaurants will also feature harimeh – hot and spicy cooked fish fragrant with an

appetising blend of tomatoes, cumin and hot pepper.

And if you still have room, there's dessert. In Arabic restaurants this may mean baklava (filo dough sprinkled with nuts and sweet syrup), some other rich sweet, or fruit. In typical Jewish oriental restaurants it could mean caramel crème custard, chocolate mousse or an egg white confection laced with chocolate syrup and (for some unknown reason) called Bavarian cream. Turkish coffee or tea with fresh mint seals the meal. If you do not want sugar in your coffee, tell the waiter in advance.

Yemenite food is characterised by virtually all the same spices as other Sephardic cuisines, just more of them. Genuine Yemenite restaurants offer rather exotic types of soups for the Westerner, including "foot soup", "tail soup" and "udder soup" among others, though more conservative lentil, vegetable, and beef soups are available. All are aromatic and rich in flavour. Several types of bread are served: mallawah (crispy fried, fattening and delicious), lahuh (light and like a pancake) and jahnoon (slow-baked strudel-like dough). While pitta bread is served automatically with any order, the other breads must be requested. Eat them with a mixed vegetable salad, humus and/or ful (slow-cooked fava beans), haminados (slow-cooked brown and creamy-yolked eggs) or alone with condiments.

Yemenites have their own special spice mixtures and condiments, and believe them to be healthful and a particular aid to digestion. These are hilbe (a bitter but interesting fenugreek preparation) thought to be helpful in the treatment of diabetes, and tzhoug (fresh coriander chopped with hot green or red peppers and spices), considered beneficial for blood circulation. In authentic Yemenite restaurants, these are served along with the meal. You may want to end your repast by ordering coffee with hawaiig, a fragrant blend of spices akin to the Indian garam masala.

If it's Askenazic or Eastern European Jewish cooking you're after, you can find traditional gefilte fish, chopped liver, borscht (beet soup), Hungarian goulash (stew) and Russian peroshki (baked or fried piquant filled pastries), but these are not considered day-to-day fare by most of the populace, and are served only by speciality restaurants.

Due to the influx of Vietnamese Boat People, and former residents of Taiwan, Hong Kong, Thailand and the Philippines, Chinese-style restaurants abound and are much beloved by the native population. Ask the locals for recommendations.

Elegant restaurants are also a part of the local scene, and like their counterparts in other countries, offer a rich selection of gourmet foods, some authentic to the cuisine they proffer, some tailored to local tastes. Thanks to a new generation of young Israeli chefs a new movement is growing, based on an intense desire to create an authentic *haute cuisine* rooted in classic French cookery and personalised with ingredients indigenous to this country.

The results – dishes like "lamb wrapped in bulgar pastry and stuffed with *pâté de foie gras*" or "sweetbreads stuffed with avocado and served in an avocado sauce" blend the foreign and the familiar.

For a real understanding of the country's cuisine, visit supermarkets, vegetable sellers and open air markets, and investigate little out of the way eateries in the Old City of Jerusalem, the Yemenite Kerem Hataymanim and Hatikvah quarters in Tel Aviv, the Jaffa port and little villages.

Snacks

Since Israelis are major league eaters, snacks play a starring role in the day. Favourite munchies include bagel-shaped sesame-sprinkled breads (served with *za'atar* – a wild oregano-based spice mixture available only in "ethnic" settings like the Old City of Jerusalem), nuts and sunflower seeds. Pizza, blintzes, waffles, and burgers all come in and out of vogue.

But the ultimate Sabra snack has to be *felafel* (fried chickpea balls served in pitta bread with a variety of vegetable possibilities). Along the pavements of major streets, you can usually find several adjoining *felafel* stands where you're free to stuff your pitta with salads for as long as your pitta bread holds out.

Tel Aviv's Shuk Betzalel is probably the most famous of the *felafel* centres. Located near the Carmel market,

it features an entire street of *felafel* vendors, with the largest salad selection this side of the Mediterranean.

Fruit & Vegetables

The country's produce is legendary. Fruits and vegetables arrive at market stalls hours after picking, and a trip to the open-air Mahane Yehudah in Jerusalem or the Carmel market in Tel Aviv, will reveal a sumptuous array of everything from apples to artichokes, kohlrabi to celeriac. Sub-tropical fruits include kiwi, mango, persimmon, loquat, passion fruit, cheromoya and papaya. Fresh dates, figs, pomegranates and the world's largest strawberries are seasonal attractions.

Produce is sold by the kilo or gram, and is most reasonably priced at open-air markets. Avoid supermarket produce because it tends to be second rate. Wash or peel everything well before you eat.

Meat & Poultry

Those who prefer fowl will find chicken and turkey, and in more upmarket restaurants, goose and mullard duck (an Israeli hybrid) excellent choices. While much beef is imported, all fowl is domestically raised.

Dairy Products

In days of old, water was scarce and not very palatable, so milk became a major component of the biblical diet. Goat's milk was considered the richest and most nourishing. Next came sheep's milk, cow's milk and finally the milk of camels.

Today's Israel continues the "land of milk and honey" tradition with a wealth of more familiar cheeses (like Swiss, Camembert, Brie and Gouda), double-rich cottage cheese, and a wide variety of goat and sheep yogurt and cheeses (special varieties are found in some health food stores and in Arab villages).

A visit to the supermarket will reveal Israel's wide range of white cheeses. Wrapped in paper or sold in tubs, these are marked with a number signifying their fat content. Try Tov Ta'am, a soft spreadable 5 percent fat white cheese wrapped in paper – if you're looking to lower your fat intake. Or taste *leben* or *eshel* – cultured milk products with approximately the same fat content as yogurt.

Holiday Foods

If there are jelly doughnuts (*sufganiot*) it must be Chanukah, the occasion also for potato *latkes* (pancakes). On Purim you'll find *oznay haman* (filled triangular cookies).

If you're in Israel around holiday time, try to experience some holiday fare. On Passover, it's *matzobrie*, coconut macaroons, and sponge cake. Shavuot is strictly for dairy delights. Sukkot and Tu B'shvat are celebrated with dried fruits and nuts. Every Friday afternoon, there are special braided *challahs* for the Sabbath. And every Sabbath there is *cholent* (*hamin* if you're Sephardic), a baked bean and meat stew set to bake on Friday for Sabbath lunch.

Throughout the world, bread is considered the staff of life. In Israel eating heartily, and often, is a way of life.

Eilat

MODERATE
Lotus Restaurant, by the Caesar Hotel, Eilat, tel: (07) 6376389. Excellent Chinese cuisine with a varied menu.
La Barracuda, Commercial Centre, Eilat, tel: (07) 6376222. The right place to come if you want to know what those peculiar-looking Red Sea fish really taste like.

INEXPENSIVE
Milan Cafe, the Red Shopping Mall, Eilat, tel: (07) 6374487. Serves light dairy meals in pleasant atmosphere.

Haifa

EXPENSIVE
Nof Chinese Restaurant, Nof Hotel, 101 Hanassi Boulevard, Haifa, tel: (04) 8354311. The taste buds are stimulated by an amazing view of Haifa Bay.

Jerusalem

EXPENSIVE
Cow on the Roof, at the Jerusalem Sheraton Plaza Hotel, tel: (02) 6228133. Elegant Western dining by reservation only. Located in the basement and not, as the name implies, on the roof. Culinary emphasis, as the name implies, on beef.

Mishkenot Shaîananim, Yemin Moshe, behind the windmill, tel: (02) 6251042. Excellent French cuisine with a glorious panorama of the Old City walls. Try the filet steak.

American Colony Hotel, Nablus Road, Jerusalem, tel: (02) 6279777. *A là carte* menu and a beautiful courtyard in which to dine.

Valentinos, Hyatt Regency Hotel, 32 Lehi Street, Jerusalem, tel: (02) 5331234. Italian cuisine with excellent choice of pastas and antipastas.

Tandoori, Holiday Inn Crowne Plaza, Givat Ram, Jerusalem, tel: (02) 6588867. One of a chain of Indian restaurants serving delicious foods including a choice of vegetarian dishes.

MODERATE

Philadelphia, 9 Alzahara Street, East Jerusalem, tel: (02) 6289770. The city's most famous restaurant for Middle East cuisine. Excellent choice of *hors d'ouevre* salads.

Shipudei Hagefen, 74 Agrippas Street, Jerusalem, tel: (02) 6253267. The pick of the Middle East restaurants near Mahane Yehuda market.

Mama Mia, 38 King George Street, Jerusalem, tel: (02) 6248080. Jerusalem institution for lovers of Italian food. But no meat served.

Pie House, 5 Hyrkanos Street, Jerusalem, tel: (02) 6242478. Good choice of pie and salads near Zion Square.

INEXPENSIVE

Anna Ticho House, off Harav Kook Street, Jerusalem, tel: (02) 6244186. Dairy garden restaurant which forms part of a museum.

Rimon Cafe, 4 Luntz Street, Jerusalem, tel: (02) 6252772. A popular hang-out by the Ben Yehuda Street Mall with a choice of light meals and cakes.

Cheesecake, 23 Yoel Salomon Street, tel: (02) 6245082. An institution for cheesecake lovers. Try it with blue berries. Serves good salads and soups.

Tmol Shimshon, 5 Shalmon Street, Jerusalem, tel: (02) 6232758. This bookstore café offer delightful light meals combined with a vast library.

Simas, 78 Agrippas Street, Jerusalem. The speed of the service makes this the cheapest steak house in town.

Eucalyptus, 7 Hyrkanos Street, Jerusalem, tel: (02) 6244331. Offers an unusual choice of local foods. Try the sorrel soup.

Tel Aviv

EXPENSIVE

Yossi Peking, 302 Dizengoff Street, Tel Aviv, tel: (03) 5443687. Very good food with all the Chinese favourites.

Takamaru, 4 Haîarbah Street, Tel Aviv, tel: (03) 5621629. This is one of a very few Japanese restaurants in Israel. Will not disappoint.

MODERATE

Ba-Li, 8 Ibn Gvriol Street, Tel Aviv, tel: (03) 6955661. Modest Yemenite restaurants with home-cooked food and authentic Yemenite soups and breads.

Zion, 4 Peduim Street, Tel Aviv, tel: (03) 5178714. The pick of the restaurants in the city's famous Yemenite Quarter (Kerem Hatamanim).

Taboon, Old Jaffa Port, tel: 03-811176. Specialises in oven-cooked Mediterranean fish. Charmingly located in Jaffa's old port.

Tarkari, 68 Hakishon Street, Florentine, tel: (03) 6834702. An Indian vegetarian restaurant offering exceptional value for money.

INEXPENSIVE

The UP Cafe, 56 Sheinkin Street, Tel Aviv, tel: (03) 5606071. In the heart of Tel Aviv's bohemian district serves a wide range of meals.

Lev Harachav ("wide heart"), Rabbi Akiva Street, Carmel Market, Tel Aviv. A no-nonsense, on the street, tasty and cheap authentic Israeli restaurant with excellent *humus*.

Marsala, 15 Yosef Hanassi Street, Tel Aviv, tel: (03) 5256515. Delicatessen and eatery which serves fresh sandwiches and salads.

Tiberias

EXPENSIVE

The House (Habayit), opposite Lido Beach, Tiberias, tel: (06) 6792353. Chinese cuisine. Considered to be one of the best restaurants in Israel. Located in a 19th-century landmark.

Drinking Notes
Soft Drinks

All the usual carbonated drinks such as colas are available. As in Britain, "soda" refers to soda water and not a flavoured carbonated drink. Diet and

regular soft drinks are available. The most delicious and healthiest drinks to try are the wide range of fruit drinks available. For a few dollars, street vendors will squeeze you an orange, carrot, grapefruit, kiwifruit or a dozen other fruits.

Tea & Coffee

Tea connoisseurs will be out of luck. Most Israeli establishments dip a feeble tea-bag into hot water. But they take their coffee seriously. Most popular are Middle Eastern coffee (*botz*), Bedouin coffee (*botz* with *hell*) – a spice known as cardamon in English, Turkish coffee, Viennese coffee (*café hafuch*) and filter coffee. Instant coffee Western style is known as *Nes*. Cafés and *espresso* bars, like the counterparts in Europe, have increasingly become both the centre of social and business life.

Alcohol

Israel has a wide selection of wines, both red and white. Since the 1980s many good quality wines have been produced, but they can be expensive. There are several local beers, both bottled and draft, and a range of imported beers – but ale specialists will probably turn up their noses. There are both home distilled and imported spirits and liquors. The local speciality is *arak*, very similar to Greece's ouzo.

Although Israel has none of the alcoholic inhibitions of its Islamic neighbours, most Israelis consume relatively small amounts of alcohol compared to Europeans and Americans. Excessive drinking is viewed with suspicion by society at large. A person who drinks, say, six bottles of beer (three pints) every day is likely to be branded an alcoholic.

There are plenty of bars and pubs, and all restaurants and cafés serve alcohol. Israelis will often go to a pub and spend the entire night nursing just one or two drinks. By the same token it is acceptable to sit at streetside cafés chatting for several hours over just a coffee and cake.

BARS & PUBS

Finks, corner of King George and Hahistadrut streets, tel: (02) 6234523. Jerusalem's oldest established watering hole. Caters to a more mature clientele. Serves good food.

La Belle, 18 Rivlin Street, tel: (02) 6240807. Favoured by journalists because of its proximity to Bet Agron, the foreign press association building. Also serves good fish and dairy foods.

Glasnost, 15 Helena Hamalkah Street, tel: (02) 6256954. This is one of many bars in the Russian Compound such as Sergei's, Arthurs, Cannabis and Alexander amongst others. Littered along this street and its arterries, Jerusalem's nightlife begins here.

The Tavern, 14 Rivlin Street. Seedy but a veteran Jerusalem bar.

Balcony, 5 Nahalat Binyamin, Tel Aviv, tel: (03) 5162852. Well-appointed bar close to the Nahlat Binyamin pedestrian precinct.

Punch Line, 4 Haíarbah Street, Tel Aviv, tel: (03) 5610785. Remember night life doesn't get going until 11pm.

Nachmani 22 (at the same address), tel: (03) 5661114. Pleasant wine bar near Allenby Street with good food too.

The Stagecoach, 216 Hayarkon Street, tel: (03) 5241703. Near the hotels. Live music Thursday and Friday nights. Offers snacks and light meals.

The Godfather, Red Shopping Mall, Eilat, tel: (07) 6373262. Offers good pub atmosphere.

Culture

Israel has a wealth of cultural and artistic entertainments. Ticket agencies in each city or town sell tickets for concerts, plays and other events. Annual festivals of all art, cultural and musical events are booked up well in advance. Calendars of Events are available at the tourist information offices.

Art Galleries

Jerusalem

Israel Museum, Ruppin Boulevard.
Jerusalem Theater, 30 Rehov Marcus.
Artists House, Bezalel Street.
Anna Ticho House, off Harav Kuk Street.

Tel Aviv

Tel Aviv Museum, 27 Sderot Shaul Hamelech.

Helena Rubinstein Pavilion, Habimah Square.

Haifa

Haifa Museum, 26 Shabbetai Levi Street.
Tikotin Museum of Japanese Art, 89 Hanasi Boulevard.

Other Galleries: There are scores of other museums displaying archaeological finds, ancient glass, coins, folk costumes, natural science collections as well as contemporary art. In addition, groups of artists have formed "colonies" in the village of Ein Hod on Mt Carmel (near Haifa), at Safed and in Jaffa, with picturesque studios open to the public. In Tel Aviv, the gallery scene centres on Gordon Street, also known as "Gallery Street". In Jerusalem, visiting artists from abroad are housed at the Mishkenot and from time to time give performances or speeches for the public. The Aika (Ariel Brown) Gallery in the gritty industrial zone of Talpiot, Jerusalem's artists' work region, displays contemporary art work at 6 Yad Harutzim Street.

Music

There are several orchestras, of which the most famous is the Israel Philharmonic, playing under the baton of the great conductors of the world and featuring distinguished guest artists. The Jerusalem Symphony Orchestra gives a weekly concert in Jerusalem in the winter season.

There are frequent performances by the Haifa Symphony Orchestra, the Rishon Le Zion Symphony Orchestra and the New Israel Opera.

Mann Auditorium (for Israel Symphony Orchestra), 1 Huberman Street, Tel Aviv, tel: (03) 5251502.

Israel Opera (for Israel Opera and Rishon Le Zion Symphony Orchestra), Israel Opera House, Shaul Hamelech Boulevard, tel: (03) 6927707.

Henry Crown Hall (for Jerusalem Symphony Orchestra), Marcus Streeet, Jerusalem, tel: (02) 5610011/5610293.

Dance

Professional dance companies include the Israel Classical Ballet, the Batsheva Dance Company, the Bat-Dor Dance Company, Kol Hademana and the Kibbutz Dance Company. Batsheva

and Bat-Dor are both modern dance groups. All perform regularly in the three main cities, as well as in other towns and kibbutzim.

Suzanne Delal Centre, 6 Yechieli Street, Neve Tzedek, Tel Aviv. For Batsheva and Inbal Dance Troupes, tel: (03) 5171471.

Theatre

The theatre is very popular in Israel and there are many companies performing a wide range of classical and contemporary plays in Hebrew, including original works by Israelis. The best known are the Habimah and Cameri Theatres in Tel Aviv and the Haifa Municipal Theatre, which take their productions all over the country. In Jerusalem, the Centre for Performing Arts includes the Jerusalem Theatre, the Henry Crown Auditorium and the Rebecca Crown Theatre. Also, Sultan's Pool Ampitheatre is a must for a concert, located beneath the walls of the Old City. Smaller companies offer stage productions in English, Yiddish and other languages. One such theatre, Gesher (meaning bridge), founded in Tel Aviv in 1991, is the first Russian-speaking theatre in Israel.

Jerusalem Theatre, Marcus Street, Jerusalem, tel: (02) 5610011/5610293.

Khan Theatre, David Remez Street, Jerusalem, tel: (02) 6718281.

Habimah Theatre, Tarsith Boulevard, Tel Aviv, tel: (03) 5266666.

Carmeri Theatre, 101 Dizengoff Street, Tel Aviv, tel: (03) 5233335.

Bet Lessing Theatre, 34 Weizmann Boulevard, Tel Aviv, tel: (03) 6956222.

Movies

There are cinemas in all the big towns; most have three showings a day, one at about 4pm and two in the evening.

For about $7 you can see the latest Hollywood offerings. You'll also find the latest movies from France, Germany, Italy, Hungary and elsewhere. These films usually have English subtitles but ask at the box office first.

Israel itself produces a dozen or so films a year and these offer an insight into the local culture. These, too, have English subtitles. The local cinematheques show golden oldies as well the more recent movies.

Jerusalem Cinematheque, Derech Hevron, tel: (02) 6724131.

Tel Aviv Cinematheque, 2 Sprinza Street, tel: (03) 6917181.
Haifa Cinematheque, Hanassi Boulevard 142, tel: (04) 8383424.

Festivals

The Israel Festival of Music and Drama takes place in May of each year, with the participation of the country's lead talent and world-famous visiting companies and artists. The Festival centres on Jerusalem.
The Jerusalem Film Festival – June.
The Haifa Film Festival – July.
The Karmiel Dance Festival – July.
The Red Sea Jazz Film Festival – August.
The Acco Fringe Theatre Festival – September/October.

In addition, the **Jerusalem International Book Fair** is held every two years in March. An International **Harp Contest** takes place every three years, drawing young musicians from all over the world, while the **Zimriya**, an international choir festival, is another well-established triennial event. **Spring in Jerusalem** and **Spring in Tel Aviv**, annual festivals, include music, drama and dance, and the **Rubinstein Piano Competition** brings talented young artists from around the world to Israel.

Events in Haifa include the **International Flower Show** (Floris), when hundreds of thousands of flowers from all over the world, typical of their countries of origin, adorn the city.

Nightlife

Nightlife starts late in Israel and is very vibrant. From 10.30pm onwards Israelis are out on the streets of Tel Aviv, and even Jerusalem and virtually every Israeli city. Streetside cafés and restaurants are busy until well after midnight and bars and discos have a brisk trade right through the night. Because Friday and Saturday is the weekend Thursday night is a big night out. **Tel Aviv seafront** and other hotspots are crowded right through the night.

Nightclubs abound in the main cities and resort towns. Many have regular floor shows, while others offer more informal entertainment. Rock, jazz, folk and pop music are the usual fare. Jerusalem and Tel Aviv are the hot spots.

Tel Aviv

Allenby 58, located at the same address in Tel Aviv. This nightclub has been the hottest spot in town for quite some time. A converted cinema, it has a massive sound system and a downstairs bar to cool off when the heat of the beat gets too much. Thursday and Friday nights are the best.
The Minzar, opposite Allenby 58. A small bar with a lively atmosphere. A perfect place to start your night if proceeding to Allenby 58.
Ministry of Sound, 2 Haim Vital Street. A small bar with a cute upstairs, this is one of many new bars that have opened up in the Florentine area, South of the centre. Others are **The Nanna Bar** and the **Laundry**, which is situated in an old laundromat equipped with the machines. In case you suddenly feel the urge during a night out, you can get your hair cut at **Vitt Rio**, also on Haim Vital Street. It's a funky place that opens in the afternoon and closes at 2am.
Porto Loco, The Brazilian Club in Old Tel Aviv Port, Yordei Hasira Street, tel: (03) 6836618.

Jerusalem

Hallelujah, Kibbutz Ramat Rachel near Jerusalem, tel: (02) 6736828. Not as holy as it sounds.
Canaan, tel (02) 6735633. In the heart of Talpiot's discoland,

Attractions

Archaeology

Archaeology is one of Israel's best loved national pastimes, and the opportunities for archaeological exploration here are rich and varied.

There are dozens of major archaeological sites, spanning all time periods of recorded history. The most important – such as Caesarea, Ashkelon, Jericho and Masada – are national parks and open to the public on a regular basis for a modest admission fee. Often these sites include English-language signposts and have informative brochures to explain the history and design of the site.

Gardens

Jerusalem is famous for its parks which as well as the city centre parks include the Botanical Gardens beneath the Givat Ram University campus and the Sherover Walkway from Abu Tor to East Talpiot.

Tel Aviv's Independence Park overlooks the sea while Yarkon Park is a pleasant expanse of greenery by the river Yarkon.

Nature Reserves

There are 280 nature reserves in Israel covering 4,000 sq. km (1,544 sq. miles). Especially worth visiting are the Hai Bar Reserve in the Negev, the Carmel Park nature reserve, the Hula Reserve in the Upper Galilee and the Ramon Crater in the Negev.
National Parks Authority, 4 Rehov M. Makleff, Hakirya, Tel Aviv 61070, tel: (03) 7320333.

Health Resorts

All hotels in the Dead Sea region offer medically supervised facilities. The sea's unique mineral content is beneficial for a range of ailments including psoriasis and rheumatism. Contact the Ministry of Tourism's Health Resorts Authority, tel: (02) 6754811.

Tree Planting

Visitors wishing to plant trees, for a nominal contribution, may do so on their own or as part of tours organised by the Jewish National Fund. Each planter will receive a certificate and a badge to commemorate the event.

Further details: "Plant a Tree With Your Own Hands", Meir Malca Jewish National Fund, 7 Rehov Shmuel Hanagid, Jerusalem, tel: (02) 6241781.

Nature Tours

For those visitors searching for the unusual, the Society for the Protection of Nature in Israel (SPNI) offers fascinating tours combining unique learning experiences in natural settings with touring, hiking and swimming.

These Nature Trails leave the main roads and penetrate into little known and relatively inaccessible areas. Experienced guides explain the natural and human history of the region and point out hidden places of beauty and interest. All the tours include some walking. Depending on the interests and abilities of the group, this can range from a few hours per day to difficult hikes for experienced trekkers. There are a number of English-guided trips to all parts of the country suitable for individuals as well as the entire family (children over 12 years old).

Their shops also have a selection of publications and accessories regarding natural Israel. SPNI has a network of field schools charging about $30 per room per night.

Main offices:

Jerusalem, I3 Rehov Helene Hamalka, tel: (02) 6232936.

Tel Aviv, 4 Rehov Hashfela, tel: (03) 6375063.

Haifa, 8 Rehov Menachen, tel: (04) 8664136.

National Parks

The national parks can include nature sites and sites of historical and archaeological interest. They include Hazor, Achziv, Nimrod Fortress, Caesarea, Ashkelon, Megiddo, Herodian, Masada, Qumran, Jericho, Tel Arad and Ein Avdat. Visitors to sites and parks can buy a ticket for multiple entrance, permitting them to visit all of the sites or parks within a period of 14 days. In the case of groups, the ticket can be used for 21 days. It can also be purchased from the National Parks Authority.

For further information, contact: **National Parks Authority**, 4 Rehov Aluf M. Makleff, Hakirya, Tel Aviv 61070, tel: (03) 6902281.

Kibbutzim

The kibbutz is a communal or collective settlement governed by the general assembly of its members. All property is jointly owned and work is organised on a cooperative basis. Members receive no salary, but in return for their work get housing, clothing, food, medical services, education for their children and other social amenities. Most kibbutzim are agricultural but many

also have sizeable industrial enterprises. There are over 200 kibbutzim in all parts of the country and the number of members ranges from 90 to over 2,000.

Most kibbutzim accept volunteers for varying periods. Volunteers must be between 18 and 32 years of age. Neither children nor pregnant women are accepted. For further information contact any Israel Government Tourist Office or the following organisations:

Hakibbutz Hadati, Zipi Romen Volunteer Department, 7 Rehov Dubnov, Tel Aviv, tel: (03) 6957231.

Ikhud Hakvutzot Vehakibbutzim and **Hakibbutz Hemeyuhad**, Ben Baor, 10, Rehov Dubnov, Tel Aviv, tel: (03) 5452622.

INFORMATION ABROAD

It is best to plan ahead of time as far as possible if you are serious about volunteering:

Australia: Ichud Habonim-Dror, pob I54, Waverley, 2024, Sydney, N.S.W, tel: 389-4993.

France: Sochnut, I7 Vue Forunay, Paris 75017, tel: 766-0313.

Germany: Haus des Kibbuzes, D-6000 Frankfurt/Main, Falkensteinerstr. 1, tel: 0611/556963.

Netherlands (Holland): Ichud Habonim, John Wermeer-Straat 22, Amsterdam, tel: 020-719123.

UK: Kibbutz Representative, 1A Accommodation Road, London NWI, tel: 0181-450-9235.

US: In New York direct enquiries to: The Jewish Agency, Kibbutz Aliyah Desk, 515 Park Avenue, New York, NY 10022, tel: (212) 688-4134.

Ulpan

Ulpan Akiva is a Hebrew language school where Hebrew is taught as a living language in everyday conversation at all levels: reading, writing, speech patterns, drama and idioms. Courses are from 4–20 weeks, for families and individuals of 12 years and up. The school is located at the Green Beach Hotel near Netanya and facilities include a swimming pool, tennis and basketball courts and a lovely strech of beach.

The programme consists of: four or five hours of Hebrew study a day, lectures on the Bible, Jewish history, Hebrew literature and current affairs;

and cultural activities that include folk singing and dancing, and meetings with local personalities. Study side by side with Israelis and new immigrants and experience the culture of Israel.

Tours can be arranged to archaeological sites and other places of interest in the area. Courses are run on a residential, full-board basis.

For further information, contact: **Ulpan Akiva**, International Hebrew Study Center, POB 6086, 42160 Netanya, tel: (09) 8352312/3; fax: (09) 8652919.

Many kibbutzim offer courses which cost $50 in return for participants' part-time work on the kibbutz. The courses last for $5\frac{1}{2}$ months and are open to Jews between the ages of $17\frac{1}{2}$ and 35. Students may arrive at the kibbutz a week before the course begins. Participants must be physically fit for work.

For further details, contact:: **The Ulpanim's Kibbutzim Department**, The Jewish Agency, 12 Rehov Kaplan, Tel Aviv, tel: (03) 5423423.

Zoos

The **Jerusalem Biblical Zoo**, Manhat, tel: (02) 6430111, houses animals mentioned in the Bible. Other zoos are located in Tel Aviv, Eilat and Haifa.

There is a **Safari Park**, a 100-hectare (250-acre) wildlife sanctuary in Ramat Gan near Tel Aviv, where hundreds of animals roam freely. At the Hai Bar Reserve, north of Eilat, many of the animals mentioned in the Bible can be seen. Visitors to the Safari Park and Hai Bar Reserve may tour in closed vehicles only.

Eila has an underwater observatory for watching exotic aquatic life.

Activities for Children

So much religion, archaeology and history can be a bit too much for small children. Aside from the aforementioned zoos the Israel Museum in Jerusalem has an excellent Children's Wing and the nearby Science Museum has plenty of hands on exhibits for the young. Of course in Tel Aviv and Haifa there are wonderful golden beaches and every child falls in love with the fish at Eilat's Underwater Observatory.

Outdoor Activities

Israel is an ideal place for sports enthusiasts. Here they will find excellent facilities and an opportunity to combine interests such as skin and scuba diving, riding, tennis, golf, swimming and skiing with a general tour of the country. The Mediterranean climate guarantees most outdoor sports year round (the exception being snow skiing, which is available only in winter).

Participant Sports

The Mediterranean shoreline and the Sea of Galilee are ideal for water sports: swimming, surfing, sailing and water skiing. The Tel Aviv marina offers yachting as well as sailing. All the large hotels have swimming pools and there are municipal or private pools all over the country. Skin and aqualung diving are especially popular along the Gulf of Eilat; centres at Eilat will rent equipment and provide instruction.

Fishing equipment, both for angling and under water, can be hired along the Mediterranean and the Red Sea, though the latter is now a protected area, with fishing permitted only in certain places.

Tennis courts are available at a number of hotels and the Tennis Centre at Ramat Ha-Sharon, near Tel Aviv, is putting Israel on the international tennis circuit. There is a fine 18-hole golf course at Caesarea. You can find riding clubs in Arad, Beersheba, Caesarea, Eilat, Netanya, Vered Hagalil and other places. Bicycles can be rented in most cities and cycling tours of the country can be arranged. During winter, there is skiing on the slopes of Mt Hermon. Marches, races, and swimming competitions are organised by the HaPo'el and Maccabi sports organisations. The highlight of the year is the annual Jerusalem March, a highly organised event, in which thousands of Israelis from all over the country, as well as overseas visitors, both individually and in groups, make a colourful and high-spirited pilgrimage to the capital. This event is held in spring, usually in April.

A programme of events is published monthly and can be obtained from the Israeli National Sports Association, 5 Rehov Warburger, Tel Aviv, tel: (03) 5281968.

SPORTS CENTRES

Caesarea Golf Club, POB 1010, 30660 Caesarea, tel: (06) 361174.
Haifa Squash Center, MP Hof, Kfar Zamir, Hacarmel, tel: (04) 8539160. Herzliya Squash Center, tel: (09) 8357877.
Ramat Gan, Kfar Hamaccabiah, Sport Center, Ramat Chen, tel: (03) 6715739.
Israel Tennis Center, Ramat Hasharon, tel: (03) 481803/485223.
Hermon Ski Site, tel: (06) 6981339.
Moshav Neve Ativ, 12010 MP Ramat Hagolan, tel: (06) 6981331 (for ski accommodation).
Vered Hagalil Ranch, Mobile Post Korazim, tel: (06) 6735785.
Neve Ilan Ranch, Neve Ilan, Judean Hills (near Jerusalem), tel: (02) 5340535.

Water Sports

Israel is truly a diver's paradise. Its mild climate ensures year-round diving in the crystal clear waters of both the Mediterranean and Red seas, where hundreds of miles of easily accessible coral reefs and spectacular seascapes await the diving enthusiast. A variety of diving experiences include underwater photography, archaeological diving, grotto and cave diving. It should be noted that unless the diver has a 2-star licence, they must take a special diving course, though diving without a licence can be done if you are accompanied by instructors.

SKIN & SCUBA DIVING COURSES

The courses for beginners last about five days and cover the theory of diving, lifesaving, physiology, physics and underwater safety. The only qualifications necessary are the ability to swim, a certificate from a doctor confirming fitness to learn diving, and a chest X-ray. Beginners can also go out on individual introductory dives, lasting from one to 1½ hours, accompanied throughout by an instructor.

It is possible to rent all the necessary skin and scuba diving equipment at the following centres:

Eilat
Aqua Sport, Red Sea Diving Center, Coral Beach, tel: (07) 6334404.
Lucky Divers, Moriah Hotel, tel: (07) 6335990.
Dolphin Reef (dive with the dolphins), tel: (07) 6375935.
Red Sea Divers, Caravan Hotel, tel: (07) 6373145/6.

Tel Aviv
Octopus Diving School, Tel Aviv Marina, Atarim Square, tel: (03) 5271440.
The Federation for Underwater Activities in Israel, POB 6110, 61060 Tel Aviv, tel: (03) 5467968.

WATER SKIING, WIND SURFING, BOARD SURFING

Aqua Sport, Eilat, tel: (07) 633440.
Octopus Diving School, Tel Aviv, tel: (03) 5271440.

SWIMMING

Israel's mild climate allows year-round swimming on all of its coasts – the Mediterranean, the Gulf of Eilat, the Dead Sea and the Sea of Galilee. Qualified lifeguards are in attendance at all beaches and pools.

Swimming is free at most beaches. But beware: the Mediterranean currents are strong and nearly 100 people drown every year. Most hotels have swimming pools, to which guests of the hotel are generally given free entry; many allow use by visitors, for a fee.

Spectator Sports

Soccer is the number one spectator sport with several matches every week. Israeli teams particpate in the major European competitions. Basketball is also very popular and Israelis are especially proud of the Maccabi Tel Aviv basketball team, which has won the European championship twice. There are many international matches during the winter season at stadiums in the Tel Aviv area.

Stadiums
The Ramat Gan National Soccer Stadium, Tel Aviv, tel: (03) 5799966.
Yad Eliahu Basketball Stadium, Tel Aviv, tel: (03) 5272112.

Shopping

What to Buy

Shops in Israel offer a wide variety of merchandise and gifts. These include exclusive jewellery and diamonds; oriental carpets and antiques; fashionable ladies' wear and elegant furs; leather goods; paintings and sculptures; ceramics; silverware and copperware; embroidery and *batiks* and religious requisites. Several hundred shops are approved by the Ministry of Tourism. These shops display a sign stating "Listed by the Ministry of Tourism" and the Ministry's emblem (two scouts carrying a bunch of grapes on a pole between them), which is the symbol of quality merchandise.

In addition, colourful oriental markets and bazaars are found in the narrow alleyways of the old cities of Jerusalem, Bethlehem, Acco, Nazareth, Hebron and Druze villages like Daliyat El Carmel near Haifa. These sell handmade arts and crafts – including olive wood, mother-of-pearl, leather and bamboo items, hand-blown glass and clothing, vegetables and fruit.

Duty-free shops are located at Ben-Gurion and Eilat airports and at most of the leading hotels. Foreign-made articles such as watches, cameras, perfumes, tobaccos and liquors as well as many fine Israeli products may be purchased with foreign currency for delivery to the plane or ship prior to departure.

Judaica

Besides these items, Israel has a unique variety of traditional crafts and Judaica for sale, ranging from religious articles like *Menorahs*, *mezzuzot* and spice boxes to wall hangings and statuary. They range from loving reproductions to stark minimalism.

Centres for buying fine crafts include several locations in Jerusalem, among them the House of Quality, the Khutzot Hayotzer Arts & Crafts Lane, Yochanan Migush Halav Street, and the Mea Shearim area.

Shopping Areas

In the Old City of Jerusalem and other Arab market places bargaining is standard practice. Usually you can buy an item at 25 percent off by starting to haggle at half the quoted price. Avoid haggling if you are not interested in buying or if an item is cheap. Brassware, carvings and fabrics are among the more popular buys.

Other popular shopping places include the weekly Bedouin market in Beersheba on Thursday mornings, the Druze markets in the north, such as Daliat-al-Carmel and Nahalat Binyamin in Tel Aviv, where artesans trade their wares on Tuesday and Friday.

On the other hand, Israel has plenty of Western-style shopping malls. Prices are high but these malls have the advantage of being air-conditioned. Try the Malha Mall in Jerusalem or Dizengoff Centre in Tel Aviv. In malls, stores usually open Saturday night.

Export of Antiquities

It is forbidden to export antiquities from Israel unless a written export permit has been obtained from the Department of Antiquities and Museums of the Ministry of Education and Culture, Jerusalem. This applies also to antiquities which accompany tourists who are leaving the country. Antiquities proven to have been imported to Israel after 1900 are exempted. Antiquities are defined as objects fashioned by man before the year 1700. A 10 percent export fee is payable upon the purchase price of every item approved for export.

The articles must be dispatched by post, with an accompanying check for the appropriate amount, or taken in person to: The Department of Antiquities and Museums, Rockefeller Museum opposite Herod's Gate, POB 586, Jerusalem. It is advisable to telephone (02) 6278627 for an appointment first.

VAT

After your passport has been stamped by customs, apply to Bank Leumi in the exit hall. A refund of VAT (value-added tax) of 17 percent is made at the point of your departure. However, you must make sure that:

1. The total net sum (after the 17 percent reduction) on one invoice is not less than $50. The following items are not included in this scheme: tobacco products, electrical appliances and accessories, cameras, film and photographic equipment.
2. The purchased items are packed in a plastic bag with at least one transparent side.
3. The original invoice (white) is placed inside the bag in such a manner that the entries on it can be read.
4. The bag is sealed or glued shut.
5. The bag must remain sealed during your entire stay in Israel.
6. When arriving at the departure hall on leaving the country, you must present the sealed bag with the purchased goods to the customs official for approval of refund.

After checking and placing the stamp of approval on the invoice, the customs official will direct you to the bank counter where the refund will be made in US dollars.

Note that Eilat is a VAT free zone and these regulations do not apply to goods purchased there.

Also many hotels and stores will exempt you from VAT if you pay in foreign currency.

How to Complain

Be persistent in arguing with shopkeepers if you have a complaint. You cannot expect a shopkeeper to respond to your problem if you do not articulate your grievance. Otherwise contact the Ministry of Industry & Trade's Consumer Protection Service, 76 Mazeh Street, Tel Aviv, tel: (03) 5604611.

Language

Hebrew

Hebrew is the most widely spoken language in the country, and Hebrew and Arabic are the official languages. Although other languages, especially English, are also fairly widely spoken, it is a good idea to know some basic Hebrew words and phrases before coming to the country.

Here are 60 basic words which may help you find the language a little less daunting:

all-purpose greeting, (literally "peace")	shalom
good morning	boker tov
good evening	erev tov
yes	ken
no	lo
please	bevakasha
thank you	toda
very much	raba
good	lov
bad	ra
big	gadol
little	katan
more	yoter
less	pahot
I	ani
you (singular)	m/f ata/at
you (plural)	m/f atem/aten
we/us	anahnu
them	m/f hem/hen
want	m/f rotseh/rotsa
how much?	kama?
too dear	yakar midai
cheaper	yoter zol
bank	bank
restaurant	mis'ada
post office	do'ar
hotel	malon
shop	hanut
taxi	monit
train	rakevet
bus	autoboos
station/bus stop	tahana
Where is?	eyfo?
right	yemin
left	smol
when?	matai?
white	lavan
black	shahor
red	adom
blue	kahol
right, correct	nahon
wrong	lo nahon
straight	yashar
one	ehad
two	shtayim
three	shalosh
four	arba'
five	hamesh
six	shesh
seven	sheva'
eight	shmoney
nine	taysha'
ten	esser
hundred	me'a
thousand	elef
many	harbey
stop, wait a minute!	rega!
cinema	kolno'a
newspaper	iton'
water	mayim
food	okhel
bill	heshbon

Spelling

As of yet, there is no standardised spelling of Israeli place names. Thus one has: "Acre", "Akko" and "Acco"; "Nathanya" "Natanya" and "Netanya"; "Elat", "Elath" and "Eilat"; "Ashqelon" and "Ashkelon"; "S'fat", "Zefat", "Tzfat" and "Safed", etc. As if to purposely confuse the visitor, all such variations are used freely.

Armchair Travel

Films & Videos

Exodus. Paul Newman wins independence for Israel.
Cast A Giant Shadow. Kirk Douglas wins independence for Israel.
The Entebbe Raid. Yet more Israeli heroics.
The Little Drummer Girl. John Le Carre grapples with Middle East intrigue.

Discography

Ahinoam Nini (known as Noa in the West) combines Yemenite and Israeli music with western rhythms.

Ofra Haza, another Yemenite singer with a major following in the West.
Rita, also combines Eastern and Western melodies.
Yehoram Gaon, Israel's number one crooner.

Further Reading

Exodus by Leon Uris.
The Little Drummer Girl by John Le Carré.
Mandelbaum Gate by Muriel Spark.
Smith's Gazelle by Lionel Davidson.
To Jerusalem and Back by Saul Bellow.
My Michael by Amos Oz.
Nine Stories by A.B. Yehoshua.

Other Insight Guides

Other books in the 190-title Insight Guides series which highlight destinations in this region include *Insight Guide: Jerusalem, Jordan, Egypt, Cairo* and *Yemen*.

Apa Publications also produces two other series of guidebooks. Insight Pocket Guides provide detailed itineraries for the short-stay visitor and come with a full-size pull-out map.

Insight Compact Guides

Insight Compact Guides are mini encyclopedias packed with essential facts, while being readable and reliable. Titles include Israel and Egypt.

Photography by

Sammy Avnisan 73, 75, 85, 181, 185, 211, 224/225, 229, 234, 235, 261, 273
Werner Braun 31, 82/83, 94/95, 98, 110, 134/135, 154, 174, 177, 190, 194, 199, 207, 218, 221, 241, 282, 291, 294, 306, 312, 338/339, 342, 343
Central Zionist Archives 37, 40, 43, 45, 46
Bill Clark 81, 117, 120, 275, 328
Joel Fishman 102
Neil Folberg 132/133, 136/137, 270, 320/321
David Harris 27, 72, 92/93, 104/105, 158L, 186L, 186R, 188/189, 206R, 288L, 292L, 302, 309
Beth Hatefutsoth 267
Hebrew University, Mt Scopus 184
Israel Hirshberg 246
Israel Government Press Office 49, 50, 62/63, 89, 169R, 279, 303, 305, 316R, 317R
Israel Government Tourist Office 38R
Israel Philharmonic 103
Jerusalem City Archives 36, 42
Yorman and Jane Korman 108
Lyle Lawson 322, 331, 332, 333, 341
Library of the Jewish Theological Seminary of America 1, 29, 38L, 112, 272
George Melrod 24, 47, 280L, 280R
National Library, Givat Ram 22/23
Gary-John Norman 54/55, 56, 57, 70, 87L, 87R, 121, 126, 127, 141, 150, 151, 152, 156R, 160L, 160R, 167, 168, 170, 175L, 175R, 178,
179, 180, 187L, 191, 195, 204, 205, 206L, 209, 214, 215, 216/217, 219, 220L, 222, 223R, 227, 230, 231, 236/237, 239, 240, 242, 245L, 245R, 247, 251, 252L, 252R, 253, 254, 255, 264, 284/285, 288R, 289, 290L, 293L, 293R, 295, 298, 300L, 307, 310/311, 313, 318, 327, 334, 335, 336
Richard Nowitz 2, 9, 10/11, 12/13, 14/15, 16/17, 18, 21, 25, 48, 59, 60, 61, 64/65, 66, 71, 74, 78, 80, 84, 86, 88, 90, 91, 96, 99, 100, 106, 111, 113, 114, 115, 118/119, 122/123, 124, 125, 128/129, 130, 131, 138, 144/145, 148/149, 155, 156L, 157, 158L, 159, 161L, 161R, 163, 164L, 164R, 165, 166, 171, 173, 176L, 176R, 182, 183, 187R, 193, 196/197, 200/201, 202/203, 208, 210, 212, 213, 226, 232, 233, 238, 243, 244, 248/249, 256, 257, 258, 259, 260, 262, 263, 265, 266, 268/269, 276/277, 278, 286, 287, 290R, 296/297, 299, 300R, 301, 304, 308, 314/315, 316R, 319L, 319R, 325, 326, 329, 330, 337L, 337R, 340
P. Lavon Institute for Labor Research 41
Photri 146, 162, 192
Vivienne Silver 116
Silverprint Archives 39
Tony Stone Worldwide 64/65, 317L
Topham Picturepoint 51, 52, 53, 58, 147
Vautier-De-Nanxe 76

Maps Berndtson & Berndtson
Visual Consultant V. Barl

Index

Hisham's Palace 331
Histadrut (trade union organisation) 41, 45, 59–60, 131
Hitler, Adolf 41
Hizbullah 53
Holocaust 42, 43, 46, 47, 279
Holon 267
Hor Hahar 305
Horace Richter Gallery, Jaffa 254
Horns of Hittim 34, 205, 219
Horoscope Path, Jaffa 253
hot baths, springs 194, 204
House of St Veronica 161–2
Hula Nature Reserve 120–21
Hula Swamp 47, 120–21, 214
Hula Valley 214
Hurvah Synagogue, Jerusalem 154
Hussein, King of Jordan 49, 169, 315
Husseini, Faisal 86
Husseini, Haj Amin 42

I

IBM Building, Tel Aviv 266
immigration, immigrants 42, 46–7, 52, 57–9, 72–3, 74–5
Independence Hall, Tel Aviv 258
Independence Park, Tel Aviv 264
Independence, Declaration of 45, 258
industry 47, 60
Institute for Arid Zone Research, Sde Boker 307
Intifada 52, 86, 324
Irgun 42, 43
irrigation 308
Islam, Muslim rule 33–4, 149, 167, 205
Islamic Museum 169
Islamic University, Hebron 339
Israel Academy of Arts and Sciences, Jerusalem 181
Israel Defence Force Museum, Tel Aviv 258
Israel Defence Forces 41, 57, 90–1, 214, 313, 315
Israel Experience, Jaffa 254
Israel Museum 27, 105, 111, 115, 185, 288
Israel Philharmonic Orchestra 265
Israeli Arabs 77
Italian Hospital, Jerusalem 178
Italian Synagogue, Jerusalem 179
Iyun Nature Reserve 214

J

Jabotinsky, Vladimir 42
Jabotinsky, Ze'ev 220
Jacob's Well 327
Jaffa 251–4
Jaffa Gate, Jerusalem 150, 175
Jama El-Baher Mosque, Jaffa 253
Jeremiah's Grotto, Jerusalem 184
Jericho 27, 331–2
Jerusalem 29, 147–87
Jerusalem Great Synagogue 180
Jerusalem: New City 173–87

Jerusalem: Old City 147
Jesus 32, 149, 206, 208, 243, 273, 289 (also see Christianity, pages 32–3, 82–3, 199, 203, 206–7, 243)
Jewish Agency 42, 60
Jewish festivals 97–8
Jewish National Fund (JNF) 61, 119
Jewish Quarter Museum, Jerusalem 154
Jewish Quarter, Jerusalem 153–5
Jezreel Valley 199
Jordan Rift 202–4
Jordan River 215
Joshua's Tomb, Hebron 340
Judaica 109–11
Judaism 28
Judea 335–41
Judean Desert 287, 335
Judean Hills 335
Julius Caesar 219

K

Kababir, Haifa 230
Kabara Marshes 244
Kabbalah 33
Kadesh Barnea fortress 309
Karmiel 212
Katzrin 194
Ketef HaHermon 195
Ketura 306
Kfar Blum 214
Kfar Giladi 214
Kfar Hassidim 211
Khan el-Afranj, Acco 221–2
Khan el-Umdan, Acco 222
Khan Theater, Jerusalem 181
Khutzot HaYotzer (Arts and Crafts Lane), Jerusalem 176
kibbutzim 124–7
Kibbutz Bet Alpha 201
Kibbutz Bet Oren 246
Kibbutz Eilot 318
Kibbutz Kfar Etzion 341
Kibbutz Kinneret 206, 208
Kibbutz Ramat Rachel 185
Kibbutz Sdot Yam 244
Kidron River 337
Kidron Valley 157, 158
Kikar Namir, Tel Aviv 252
King David 29, 147, 148, 157, 340
King David Hotel 43, 180
King David's Tomb 159
King George V Street, Jerusalem 179
King Solomon's Mines 306
kippot 70
Kiryat Arba, Hebron 341
Kiryat Gat 271
Kiryat Shmona 214–15
Kishon River 235
Knesset 45, 46, 59, 185
Kotel Ha-Ma'aravi (see Western Wall, pages 32, 114, 147, 155)
Kubbet es-Sakhra 168

L

L. A. Mayer Museum of Islamic Art, Jerusalem 181
Ladder of Tyre 223
Ladino 36, 101, 106
language 101, 107
Law of Return 46
Lawrence, T. E. 117, 313
League of Nations 35
Lebanese War 51
Lehi 42, 43
Likud Party 51, 52, 68, 69
Lion's Gate (St Stephen's), Jerusalem 150, 160
literature 101–2
Lloyd George, David 41
Lot's Wife 293
Luna Gal 206
Lutheran Church of the Redeemer 163

M

Maccabees 30
Machtesh Gadol (crater) 304
Machtesh Ramon 309
Machtesh Katan (crater) 304
Maine Katz Museum, Haifa 231
Malkah Valley 186
Mameluke tower 283
Mamelukes 33, 167, 343
Mamshit 304
Mandelbaum Gate, Jerusalem 183
Mann Auditorium, Tel Aviv 265
Mapai Party 45
Mapam Party 46
Mar Elias 339
Mar Saba Monastery 337
Maritime Museum, Nasholim 246
markets 170, 254, 260–1
Napoleon 253
Marx, Karl 38
Mary's Tomb 166
Masada 33, 291–2
Mea Shearim, Jerusalem 70, 182
Meir, Golda 50
Memorial to the Negev Brigade of the Palmach 302
Menorah 109–10
Meron 210
Metzoke Dragot 289
Midgal 281
Military Cemetery 187
Milk Grotto Church, Bethlehem 336
minerals 60
Mitzpe Ramon 309
Mitzpe Shalem 289
Modiin 273
Mohammed 34, 147
Monastery of the Cross, Jerusalem 185
Montefiore, Sir Moses 38, 176
Montfort Fortress 211, 222
Monument to the Road Builders 274
Moon Valley Highway 317
Moses 28, 29
moshavim 127

A
B
C
D
E
F
G

I
J
a
b
c
d
e
f
g
h
i
j

l

The Insight Approach

The book you are holding is part of the world's largest range of guidebooks. Its purpose is to help you have the most valuable travel experience possible, and we try to achieve this by providing not only information about countries, regions and cities but also genuine insight into their history, culture, institutions and people.

Since the first Insight Guide – to Bali – was published in 1970, the series has been dedicated to the proposition that, with insight into a country's people and culture, visitors can both enhance their own experience and be accepted more easily by their hosts. Now, in a world where ethnic hostilities and nationalist conflicts are all too common, such attempts to increase understanding between peoples are more important than ever.

Insight Guides:
Essentials for understanding

Because a nation's past holds the key to its present, each Insight Guide kicks off with lively history chapters. These are followed by magazine-style essays on culture and daily life. This essential background information gives readers the necessary context for using the main Places section, with its comprehensive run-down on things worth seeing and doing. Finally, a listings section contains all the information you'll need on travel, hotels, restaurants and opening times.

As far as possible, we rely on local writers and specialists to ensure that the information is authoritative. The pictures, for which Insight Guides have become so celebrated, are just as important. Our photojournalistic approach aims not only to illustrate a destination but also to communicate visually and directly to readers life as it is lived by the locals.

Compact Guides
The "great little guides"

As invaluable as such background information is, it isn't always fun to carry an Insight Guide through a crowded souk or up a church tower. Could we, readers asked, distil the key reference material into a slim volume for on-the-spot use?

Our response was to design Compact Guides as an entirely new series, with original text carefully cross-referenced to detailed maps and more than 200 photographs. In essence, they're miniature encyclopedias, concise and comprehensive, displaying reliable and up-to-date information in an accessible way.

Pocket Guides:
A local host in book form
However wide-ranging the information in a book, human beings still value the personal touch. Our editors are often asked the same questions. Where do *you* go to eat? What do *you* think is the best beach? What would you recommend if I have only three days? We invited our local correspondents to act as "substitute hosts" by revealing their preferred walks and trips, listing the restaurants they go to and structuring a visit into a series of timed itineraries.

The result is our Pocket Guides, complete with full-size fold-out maps. These 100-plus titles help readers plan a trip precisely, particularly if their time is short.

Exploring with Insight:
A valuable travel experience
In conjunction with co-publishers all over the world, we print in up to 10 languages, from German to Chinese, from Danish to Russian. But our aim remains simple: to enhance your travel experience by combining our expertise in guidebook publishing with the on-the-spot knowledge of our correspondents.